D1001113

The Renaissance Bible

The New Historicism: Studies in Cultural Poetics
Stephen Greenblatt, General Editor

The Renaissance Bible

Scholarship, Sacrifice, and Subjectivity

DEBORA KULLER SHUGER

University of California Press

BERKELEY   LOS ANGELES   LONDON

University of California Press
Berkeley and Los Angeles, California

University of California Press, Ltd.
London, England

© 1994 by
The Regents of the University of California

Library of Congress Cataloging-in-Publication Data

Shuger, Debora K., 1953–
　The Renaissance Bible : scholarship, sacrifice, and subjectivity / Debora Kuller
Shuger.
　　p.　cm. — (The New historicism ; 29)
　Includes bibliographical references and index.
　ISBN 0–520–08480–2 (alk. paper)
　1. Bible—Criticism, interpretation, etc. —History—Modern period. 1500–
2. European literature—Renaissance, 1450–1600. 3. European literature—17th
century. 4. Christianity and literature. 5. Bible in literature.　I. Title. II. Series.
BS500.S46　1994
220′.094′09024—dc20　　　　　　　　　　　　　　　　　93–5892
　　　　　　　　　　　　　　　　　　　　　　　　　　　　　　CIP

Printed in the United States of America
9 8 7 6 5 4 3 2 1

The paper used in this publication meets the minimum requirements of American
National Standard for Information Sciences—Permanence of Paper for Printed
Library Materials, ANSI Z39.48-1984.

WIDENER UNIVERSITY
WOLFGRAM
LIBRARY
CHESTER, PA.
DISCARDED
WIDENER UNIVERSITY

To Scott and Dale

When, therefore, the objectors of whom we are speaking, say that the Bible ought to be tried by the same rules as other books, we can perhaps go a great way with them, provided we understand what they mean. It always, I believe, *will* be tried by the same standard as other books; that is to say, the habits of mind which we cultivate in regard to one, we shall cultivate in regard to the other. . . . We have had occasion to consider that view of it, so prevalent in our day, which tries to separate the idea from the event, to exhibit the one as common to all ages, the other as its mere accidental temporary clothing. I have endeavoured to shew how inadequate this doctrine is.

Frederick Denison Maurice,
The Kingdom of Christ (1842)

Contents

Figures

Acknowledgments

This book owes its being to the splendid collections and staff of the UCLA, Folger, Huntington, and Yale libraries, but particularly to the UCLA librarian who let me check out the 1698 edition of the *Critici sacri*, saving me endless, miserable hours trapped in Special Collections. I am also profoundly grateful to various friends, colleagues, and foundations for their unflagging assistance, both intellectual and financial. Without the generous support of the Guggenheim Foundation, the University of California President's Fellowship, and the Huntington Library Mellon Foundation, I could never have completed this book in a timely fashion. I am equally indebted to another kind of fellowship: my deepest thanks to William Bouwsma, the Reverend Howard Happ, Lorraine Helms, Peter Kaufmann, Anthony Low, David Riggs, Michael Schoenfeldt, and Robert Watson for their valuable corrections and invaluable encouragement. I am likewise grateful for the incisive and helpful comments of the readers for the University of California Press—Jeffrey Knapp and Regina Schwartz. Many thanks to Doris Kretschmer, Rose Anne White, and Dan Gunter for their ever-attentive supervision of the editorial process. Finally, I would like to thank the editor of Bucknell University Press, Julien Yoseloff, for permission to reprint material from my article in *Reconfiguring the Renaissance* in chapter 5 of this book.

One little book incurs so many debts: to a trusty computer, to teachers and mentors, to the patient souls who microfilmed every English book printed before 1700, to parents and grandparents who underwrote a long and costly education, and above all to a family that survived yet another book with good humor and loyal enthusiasm.

For the sake of uniformity, I have modernized the *u/v* and *i/j* orthography in both the Latin and early modern English quotations throughout the text.

Introduction

Modern society, at least in the West, emerges out of the differentiation between church and state. In the late twentieth century, Americans presuppose this separation along with the consequent confinement of religion to private beliefs. Writing this book has been a lengthy struggle with this rupture; I am a Christian and an academic and have no idea how to put these two together, how to formulate a language that would be both reverent and professional. I mention this not as a confession (although, given the topic, I felt obliged to put my cards on the table) but to register the difference between our social and discursive categories and those operative in the Renaissance, where Hooker could still maintain that the established church included the entire population of England and hence that church and nation were simply two aspects of the same entity. He does not say that they are identical—Western ecclesiology since Augustine is based on the separation of temporal from sacred order—but in practice social and religious existence formed a continuum at least up to the English Civil Wars and much later in many communities. "In sixteenth-century England," as Richard Helgerson succinctly observes, "there was very little to which religion was irrelevant."[1] Baptism, marriage, burial—the threshold rites of ordinary life—took place in church and were documented in the parish register. The first three Books of Common Prayer have, in fact, no rite for adult baptism, since (at least in theory) *everyone* was baptized in infancy.[2] The state mandated Lenten fasts and the burning of heretics; churchmen probated wills and ran universities. In England, virtually all advanced degrees were in theology, and more than half the books published during the reign of Elizabeth dealt with religious subjects.[3] During this period, as "never before or after . . . science, philosophy, and theology [were] seen as almost one and the same occupation."[4] Throughout the era, politics and religion remained impenetrably entangled.

1

All this is *trita et obvia* but at the same time curiously invisible in modern Renaissance scholarship, which, for complex political, ideological, and institutional reasons, brackets off religious materials from cultural analysis and vice versa. Books on the English Reformation do not usually engage questions of gender, sexuality, class, power, and selfhood; conversely, studies of Tudor and Stuart culture rarely consider sermons, sacraments, bishops, or prayer books. This peculiar division of mental labor derives, at least in part, from Burkhardt's monumental study of fourteenth- and fifteenth-century Italy, which conceptualized the Renaissance as an episode within secular culture—as the secularization of Western culture. Correspondingly, scholarship on sixteenth- and seventeenth-century religious history developed along confessional lines—Lutherans studying Luther, Catholics researching the Counter-Reformation, and so forth—and hence tended to focus on theological controversy rather than the sociocultural imbrications of religion.[5]

One result of this disciplinary segregation is that there exists no broadly conceived scholarship on the Bible between the decline of medieval allegory and the rise of Higher Criticism. There are some splendid books on Milton's biblical learning, a couple of monographs on Renaissance anticipations of modern exegesis, and little else. Yet, in A. G. Dickens's words, "concerning the immense influence of the vernacular Bible upon both the religious and the secular history of the English people and their colonial offspring, one cannot write save in the danger of perpetrating cant and cliché."[6] This book may achieve, it would seem, the rare distinction of being simultaneously arcane and commonplace. I have tried, however, to avoid both overspecialization—a pitfall endemic to modern biblical scholarship with its articles on such tantalizing subjects as baptismal regeneration in Bullinger's commentary on Galatians—and the obvious. I will not recount the story of the King James Bible or the controversy over vowel points or the hexameral background to *Paradise Lost*—not because these are not important topics but because they have been excellently discussed elsewhere. This book is instead an *essay* in the literal sense of the term, a tentative and partial exploration of the cultural work done by the Renaissance Bible—or rather by Renaissance biblical discourses: the heterogeneous mass of scriptural commentaries, treatises, plays, meditations, and poems filling the columns of the *Short Title Catalogue* and the early Bodleian inventories.[7]

The Bible remained the central cultural text in England, as in the rest of Europe, through the seventeenth century, although less exclusively so than in the Middle Ages. By this I do not mean simply that most people had read (or heard) it, but that it continued to generate knowledge and narrative. One might usefully think of the aggregate of biblical discourses circulating in the Renaissance as similar in function to Greco-Roman myth, where by "myth" I mean the sum total of scholia, tragedies, poems, histories, essays, and rituals that interpret and perform the stories of gods and heroes. In both cases, earlier religious materials (the Bible itself or the archaic myths of the prehistoric Mediterranean civilizations) were reshaped according to self-conscious exegetic and mythopoeic/literary procedures; often, as in Calvin's New Testament scholarship or Plutarch's essay on the Egyptian gods, learned commentary and mythic symbolization occurred together. In such gentile *midrashim*, the ancient stories served as a primary locus for synthetic, speculative, and symbolic production.

The Bible operated as a synthetic field, the site where the disciplines converge. To claim, however, that the Bible remained an active arena of discursive exchange reverses the accepted picture of early modern cultural transactions. Renaissance scholarship, speaking very generally now, operates in terms of three basic categories: Classical antiquity, the secular culture of the Renaissance, and Christianity. Traditional scholarship focused on the unidirectional influence of the first category on the second; in Foucault, Greenblatt, and other contemporary thinkers, one notes a growing interest in the passage of sacred forms and practices—monastic discipline, confession, exorcism, the cult of the Virgin Queen, Wolsey's hat—into the social and literary structures of secular culture. If the first model tends to marginalize religion, the second conceptualizes the sacred as that which is drained, is emptied out, in order to provide modern culture with sufficient intellectual and symbolic capital to start up its own economy.

The reverse or correlative circulation—from antiquity and secular culture to "religion"[8]—has received far less recognition or theoretical formulation, even though a vast quantity of specialized research has mapped the Classical prototypes for Renaissance altarpieces, the Christian appropriations of ancient philosophy, and the volatile interchanges between civic republicanism and radical millenarianism. It is, moreover, perfectly obvious that the canonical texts of English literature from Spenser to Milton rework Classical and secular materials as Protestant romance, devotional lyric, and biblical epic. But this double vector from Classical and secular discourses to sacred representation rarely figures into more broadly conceived studies of Renaissance culture and hence into the conceptualization of the Renaissance.[9] Nor has attention been paid to the centripetal pull of biblical inquiry on the disciplines—on philology, law, history, and related fields—and the sorts of knowledge resulting from these syntheses.

Renaissance biblical scholarship, however, is less a specialized discipline with its own internally generated topoi and methods than a disciplinary matrix where philological, historical, legal, antiquarian, and rhetorical procedures combine and recombine in response to fluctuations within the larger intellectual culture. It does not so much resemble a midwestern highway—a ribbon stretched across quiet fields connecting no place in particular to somewhere or other—as it does the four-level interchange in Los Angeles, where all roads meet, intersect, and divide; where lanes converge and split down unforeseen left- and right-hand exits; an arcing structural marvel littered with accidents and overloaded with interminable traffic.[10] The syncretic and interdisciplinary methods of such scholarship bear a lurking affinity to those characteristic of contemporary cultural studies; in the same way that Marxist economics, Lacanian psychoanalysis, structuralist anthropology, and Saussurean linguistics converge in a work like Goux's *Symbolic Economies*, so Grotius's *De satisfactione Christi* knits together Classical jurisprudence, universal history, colonial apologetics, and international law. In both cases, disciplinary fusion results in discursive synergy; synthetic procedures are themselves mothers of invention.

Hence, such discourses serve as modes of inquiry as well as exchange. This function has particular significance for the Renaissance in that, prior to the emergence of the social sciences as the secular disciplines of human nature and culture, speculation on such topics was frequently negotiated in terms of biblical commentary and narrative. By the sixteenth century, certain fields, especially law and political theory, had already broken off to form separate disciplines, albeit still shot through with biblical proof-texts and polemic. But the Bible remained the primary locus for a good deal of what we might classify as cultural, psychological, or anthropological reflection.

At times such theorization occurred in a fairly straightforward fashion; thus, the earliest arguments for liberalizing the canons on divorce show up in Erasmus's commentary on I Corinthians and Bucer's on Matthew. But more often, speculations that would later be analyzed in a more technical vocabulary remained enfolded within the symbolic forms of biblical narrative.[11] Theology, Aristotle remarked, stands between myth and philosophy—a speculative myth, as it were. Thus, as the Greek tragic poets use the old stories of Troy and Thebes to fashion their analyses of guilt, ethical conflict, and desire, so Milton articulates his reflections on gender, history, sin, and freedom by rewriting the first two chapters of Genesis. Such narratives, in Eric Voegelin's words, create "in the form of the myth, a highly theorized body of knowledge concerning the position of man in his world."[12] In the Renaissance, discussions of Christ's agony in the garden unfold into meditations on the conflictual and decentered structures of subjectivity, comparative anthropology unexpectedly surfaces in theological speculation on the Atonement, and passion narratives explore the psychological and historical dialectics of male violence and victimage—matters to which we shall return.

Specialized technical and philosophic vocabularies, when they develop, tend to take over the discursive spaces previously occupied by myth. But not infrequently (although not invariably) such encroachment radicalizes myth, freeing it, so to speak, from traditional and communal responsibilities. In Greece, the pre-Socratics and tragic poets were contemporaries. While the pre-Socratics bear little resemblance to Protestant scholastics, one suspects that the elaboration of dogma likewise allowed biblical myth to become an instrument for the symbolization of "transcendental border-problems," the tensions and mysteries massed along the outer walls of explicit ideological systems.[13] The devil, who disappeared from theology in the high Middle Ages, presided over the fantastic mythology of the witch craze. Less ominously, Christ's sacrifice, which occupied only a very minor place in Reformation controversy, became a resonant and volatile symbol for psychological and social exploration. The last four chapters of this study examine various translations of the Crucifixion into the language of border-problems—of sacrifice, selfhood, cruelty, sexuality.

Such mythic transformations were possible because in Renaissance practice the biblical narratives retained a certain (if limited) flexibility: not necessarily a theological flexibility but a sort of extradogmatic surplus of undetermined meaning—or rather meaning capable of being determined in various ways. Thus, Milton uses Christ's temptation in the wilderness to brood over the outcome and implications of the Civil War; similarly, scholarly Protestant exegetes analyze the Crucifixion in the context of first-century cultural praxis, while Grotius treats this sacrifice in terms of Roman law and archaic ritual, and Calvinist writers explore the same event as a paradigmatic narrative of psychological and social conflict. Such specific "determinations" of biblical narrative cannot and should not be reduced to theological positioning (although they have theological implications); they take shape at the intersection between the biblical text and other cultural materials, including English history, colonial policy, humanist jurisprudence, and late-medieval Christology. Precisely because Renaissance biblical narratives exerted a synthetic, centripetal pull on a disparate range of discourses and disciplines, they need to be read as *cultural* documents in the broadest sense.

Such claims, of course, do not apply to all Renaissance rewritings of the Bible. Lily Bess Campbell's painstaking *Divine Poetry and Drama in Sixteenth-Century England*, for instance, leaves the unmistakable impression that much biblical "literature" kept to the safety of paraphrase. In general, however, such hermeneutic timidity seems to have had a stronger grip on the vernacular than on neo-Latin texts. It occurred to me as I was sketching this introduction that most of the material I finally decided to discuss had been written in Latin, often by Continental rather than English authors. All advanced biblical scholarship and many of the finest biblical poems and dramas written during the Renaissance belonged to an international, Latinate culture, although, since works like Calvin's commentaries were quickly translated into English, originally neo-Latin texts did not always remain the exclusive property of an elite readership.[14] One therefore cannot get an accurate picture of the cultural workings of the Bible—of the polymorphic paper mountain of biblical discourses—in the English Renaissance by examining only insular, vernacular material. The intellectual culture of the English Renaissance, as well as a good deal of its literature, theology, and devotion, was part of a European discursive economy whose organization differed according to the textual commodities in question: the romantic epic imported from Italy, neo-Senecan drama from France, scholarship and theology from the Protestant civilizations of northern Europe. I point this out to clarify why I have drawn extensively on neo-Latin Dutch and French materials (although less on Italian and Spanish) while at the same time focusing on English culture. To deal with the Bible in Roman Catholic societies would require another book; to ignore the textual commerce linking England to Continental humanism and Protestantism would have produced a useless one.[15]

I had originally planned to range fairly broadly throughout the Bible, each chapter starting from a specific biblical passage and the various discourses accreting around it. For the first chapter, I thought I would focus on Matthew 26–27, which covers the Last Supper through the Crucifixion, looking initially at scholarly exegesis and then whatever else seemed important and interesting. This material, however, outgrew its preliminary framework, so that Matthew 26–27 and related passages ended up filling three chapters. Chapter 1 uses the passage from Matthew to survey advanced biblical scholarship between the decline of allegorical exegesis and the beginnings of Higher Criticism, particularly the crucial developments during the late sixteenth and early seventeenth centuries that transformed humanistic exegesis from a philological into a historical discipline. I have tried to avoid plotting the history of Renaissance biblical scholarship as a preface to the Enlightenment, instead focusing on the specific character of its historical method—the study of legal and customary codes, the fascination with the material culture of antiquity, and the unfamiliar coupling of essentialist and historicist interpretation that renders the past simultaneously exemplary and alien.

The second chapter deals with one of the most original and striking pieces of humanist biblical scholarship: Hugo Grotius's 1617 *De satisfactione Christi*, a defense of the orthodox theology of the Atonement whose final section unexpectedly invents comparative anthropology in order to explain the logic of sacrifice, including Christ's sacrifice. The chapter attempts to trace the genealogy of this method through international law, universal history, Spanish scholasticism, and New World ethnography—a case study of the synthetic and speculative operations of biblical scholarship in the early seventeenth-century intellectual economy.

But Grotius's essay also suggests that the problematic nature of sacrifice—at once the astonishing revelation of divine love and savage ritual—lay at the center of a cluster of theological and ethical controversies fissuring the intellectual landscape of the late Renaissance. This possibility shifted the focus of the book from the Bible as a whole to the Crucifixion and other biblical stories of sacrifice. Chapter 3 pursues this line of investigation from a rather different angle. The advanced biblical scholarship I examine in the first two chapters conspicuously ignores theological exegesis. In order to see whether the same sorts of issues that dominate scholarly discussions of the Atonement trickled down into more popular homiletic texts, I decided to look at Calvin's treatment of the Passion in his *Harmony of the Evangelists* and any English materials that seemed dependent on it. These Calvinist passion narratives turned out to be utterly unlike the scholarly commentaries—and also unlike patristic and medieval passion narratives. They are curious and problematic texts, particularly in their ambivalent fascination with revenge, torture, and the dialectics of male violence and victimization. The Calvinist passion narratives seem to encode some sort of cultural disturbance involving manhood, violence, and urban decadence. But they also present the Crucifixion as an allegory of subjectivity. By forcing the reader to identify with all the dramatis personae, good and evil, involved in the Crucifixion, these texts attempt to produce a specific version of Christian selfhood—a divided selfhood gripped by intense, contradictory emotions and an ineradicable tension between its natural inclinations and religious obligations. Although I did not realize it until I reached the last chapter of this book, it now seems to me that before the Enlightenment the dominant models of subjectivity in the Christian West originate as passion narratives.

Chapters 4 and 5 abandon Matthew's Gospel in order to examine biblical accounts of female sacrifice, focusing on two women—Jephthah's daughter and Mary Magdalene—whom Renaissance texts explicitly liken to the dying Christ. Chapter 4 concerns sacrifice and tragedy. It begins by examining sixteenth-century lexicons for evidence of the philological connections between sacrifice, tragedy, *katharsis*, scapegoats, and the Crucifixion. The bulk of the chapter, however, concerns the seminal instance of the transformation of sacrificial narrative into tragedy: George Buchanan's *Jephthah*—the first biblical play based on Attic models and one of the half-dozen or so greatest and most influential Renaissance tragedies, although now virtually unknown. (The modern division of academic labor cannot cope with a neo-Latin play written by a Scotsman living in France.) Like Grotius's *De satisfactione*, *Jephthah* struggles with the moral and theological implications of sacrifice. Moreover, in *Jephthah* the sacrificial victim is not only a type of Christ but a girl, which raises another and more current cluster of questions about female sacrifice, fathers and daughters, the erotics of violence (particularly violence against women), and so forth. These questions are hard to answer well; they often elicit the sort of sociological literalism that reads the representation of female suffering as a commentary on the actual plight of women. No one, however, maintains that passion narratives reflect the victimization of men in Christian societies. The notion that hermeneutics should be gender-specific seems to me untenable; the notion that a biblical tragedy should be read like a Victorian novel, unhistorical. In both this and the following chapter, therefore, I attempt to find a way to interpret stories about female sacrifice and sexuality that respects the otherness of Renaissance symbolic forms and makes them comprehensible.

The final chapter looks at an exceedingly popular group of texts—a mix of poems and sermons—that depict Mary Magdalene's lonely vigil at the tomb of Christ. The texts insist on the erotic character of Mary's longing for her beloved Lord. However, they present Mary Magdalene not as either a hysteric or a seductress but as an exemplary figure of Christian inwardness. The chapter investigates the premodern constructions of bodily, religious, and intellectual desire in order to explain how, in the Renaissance, female eroticism could provide the decorous symbol for a second dominant model of ideal subjectivity—a model vastly different from that found in the Calvinist passion narratives, although, like it, crystallized in a speculative myth about the death of Christ.

The decision to concentrate on sacrificial narratives seems plausible enough since the Crucifixion occupies the theological center of Western Christianity.[16] But I am not particularly concerned with theology per se, and, in any case, official Protestant teaching on the Atonement tends to be unremarkable. The Renaissance retellings of the Passion fascinated me because (outside of dogmatic formulations) they seemed to draw into themselves a wildly problematic and complex range of cultural issues. They are haunted by questions of selfhood, violence, gender, and history and provide the symbolic forms for such speculations. In the same way that the story of Antigone held a peculiar significance for the nineteenth century—the luminous symbol for its preoccupation with the conflict between the individual conscience and the state—so these biblical narratives of sacrifice encode the Renaissance's confrontation with the alien and its constructions of the self. In the Renaissance, the paradox of sacrifice—its double character as loving self-oblation and barbaric ritual—epitomized the pervasive ambiguities attached to the humanist interpretation of the past as simultaneously authoritative and alien, the same paradox infiltrating Renaissance attempts to locate New World cultures in relation to Christianity. Such confrontations with the alien sacrificial cultures of antiquity, Israel, and the Americas motivated both the new social sciences of the age and the new rationalist critique of Christian orthodoxy. In the theological and devotional writings of the period, however, stories of Christ's sacrifice supplied the primary language for the profoundly divergent Reformed and Catholic models of Christian selfhood. Yet in both, the torment, terror, grief, anguish, and longing that suffuse the biblical accounts of the Crucifixion shape, although in different ways, the early modern constructions of ideal subjectivity.

Yet by classifying Renaissance interpretations and representations of sacrifice, I do not mean to suggest that these should be viewed as connected moments in an intellectual history. Because sacrifice—the sacrifice of Christ—is the mythic center of a civilization rather than a specific topos like *carpe diem* or the problem of future contingents, the various dramatic, homiletic, exegetic, and systematic rewritings of this story do not share an intertextual genealogy but instead are diffusely embedded throughout their cultural field. Central discourses, paradoxically, tend toward dispersal and fragmentation (ideological conditions permitting); in contemporary feminisms, the debate over the Equal Rights Amendment has few methodological or conceptual affinities with French feminist theory, and both seem fairly marginal to the novels of Alice Walker. The level of generalization at which these differences no longer matter is not a very interesting one. Hence, chapter 1, which treats scholarly exegesis, has little to say about sacrifice per se for the simple reason that the philological commentaries on the Crucifixion do not address this topic; yet this chapter pertains to the subsequent discussions of sacrificial narratives not only because the methods of scholarly exegesis made possible the recognition of sacrifice as a *historical* phenomenon (the focus of chapter 2) but also because the contrast between the scholarly commentaries and the Calvinist passion narratives discussed in the third chapter clarifies the implications of each. The historical import of a particular discourse emerges against the range of *available* discourses that could have been chosen and were not. To determine what sorts of cultural work take place at the site of sacrifice, one has to take up one by one the disparate filaments that get knotted together with these biblical narratives. What threads are interwoven— or discarded—here and what patterns do they form? What are, quite literally, the implications of sacrifice? The chapters that follow do not tell a story (and most assuredly do not point a moral); they are rather tentative and fragmentary attempts to map the early modern discourses criss-crossing the redemptive bodies of dead virgins.

1 After Allegory
New Testament Scholarship in the Renaissance

Tenuis mea scientia versatur circa Grammaticam & Historiam.
Dogmata fidei aliis tractanda relinquo. In Historia nulla haeresis,
multo minus in Grammatica.

Drusius, *De Hasidaeis*

Early modern biblical scholarship has never attracted much attention. Some information is available on the origins of humanist exegesis; the growing interest during the late Middle Ages in the literal sense of the Hebrew Old Testament has been well documented, as has Valla's application of philological techniques to the Vulgate New Testament, continued and broadened by Erasmus in the early sixteenth century.[1] But the history of biblical interpretation between Erasmus's *Novum Instrumentum* of 1516 and the first stirrings of Higher Criticism in the late seventeenth century has received only fitful regard, especially among Anglo-American scholars.[2] The *index authorum* for the Gospel volume of the *Critici sacri*, the great Restoration compendium of Renaissance biblical scholarship, is a roll call of forgotten names—Drusius, Zegerus, Gualtperius, Cappel, Vatabulus—intermingled with those remembered only in the histories of classical philology—Scaliger, Stephanus, Casaubon.[3] The greatest Renaissance exegete, Hugo Grotius, has been handed over to the safekeeping of legal historians, despite Hugh Trevor-Roper's observation that as a biblical scholar, poet, and theologian he was the "immediate tutelary spirit, the father-figure" of the intellectual avant-garde in seventeenth-century England.[4]

The lack of modern interest in Renaissance biblical scholarship is not due to a paucity of material; the *Critici sacri* alone weighs in at approximately one hundred pounds, divided into nine double-column folio volumes, and it includes neither Jesuit scholarship nor the less strictly philological Protestant commentaries of Luther, Calvin, Beza, Bucer, or Melanchthon. There is no paucity of material but only considerable uncertainty concerning its significance. Patristic and medieval biblical scholarship has received detailed and intelligent study because its cultural import has generally seemed unproblematic, given the near identity of theology and intellectual culture during the centuries between Origen and Ockham. For the three centuries following Ockham's death during the Black Plague, this identity no longer obtains; whether viewed as the Renaissance or the early modern period, these centuries have, at least since Burkhardt, narrated the long *Gotterdammerung* that preceded Nietzsche's succinct obituary. Given such a governing narrative, biblical exegesis seems either a lingering anachronism or yet another instance of secularization, its history thus being either too marginal or too familiar to occasion much interest.[5] The Renaissance Bible has therefore little historical importance unless one can demonstrate its larger significance for the interpretation of early modern culture. The primary aim of this book is to show, however partially, what this significance might be.

Except in primitive societies, however, culture is not a homogeneous domain. In this chapter I discuss mainly elite culture, what in the Renaissance was called the *respublica litterarum*, the international and interdisciplinary community of academics, diplomats, poets, lawyers, civil servants, and churchmen engaged in producing and consuming advanced humanist scholarship. The chapter thus addresses the implications of Renaissance biblical scholarship for (quite literally) intellectual history.

However, in recent years intellectual history has become a suspect discipline. As traditionally practiced, it seems vulnerable to the charge of constructing the past as an atemporal conversation between canonical texts: a scholar decided on a list of "important" works and then imagined each as a response to its predecessor. The recent emphasis on "local knowledge" seeks to avoid such pseudohistorical constructs by ignoring the afterlife of texts altogether. Modern historicisms, influenced by the cult of the newspaper as well as Foucault, tend to conceive of history as a discontinuous sequence of current events—politics, scandal, patronage, and plague—a dotted line, as it were, where each chronological point both succeeds and secedes from its immediate predecessor.

But the tendency to oppose cultural studies to intellectual history poses a false dilemma. As Milton noted, old books "are not absolutely dead things." They impinge directly on subsequent eras because social entities organize themselves around specific texts and exegetic practices. Calvinists, Roman Catholics, legal humanists, and Aristotelians define themselves, at least in part, by their commitment and approach to certain books. They are, in Brian Stock's phrase, "textual communities."[6]

In the Renaissance, biblical scholarship took place within a textual community. Although there were virtually endless "readings" of the Bible in the Renaissance—cabbalist, hermetic, Socinian, Lutheran, rabbinic, Miltonic—the practitioners of biblical *scholarship* for the most part formed a self-conscious community, bound by personal and professional ties.[7] While I am interested primarily in the nature of Renaissance exegetic practice, in order to locate this "intellectual tradition" as the activity of a historically determinate community I want to begin with a brief narrative—one that will have the additional advantages of sketching England's position in this hermeneutic circle and of providing some basic biographical scaffolding for the ensuing discussion of exegetical method.

The *Respublica Litterarum Sacrarum*

We may start on June 18, 1612, when Isaac Casaubon and his wife drove from London to Tottenham to visit the local vicar, William Bedwell.[8] Casaubon (1559–1614), one of the greatest Classical philologists of the era, had come to England in 1610 and in 1612 was just beginning his major work of biblical scholarship—the refutation of Baronius's *Annales*. Bedwell (1562?–1632) was the founder of Arabic studies in England. A graduate of Trinity College, Cambridge, in 1604 he had been selected to assist the Westminster company, led by Lancelot Andrewes, in the new translation of the Bible. In 1607 Andrewes presented him to the vicarage of Tottenham and continued to assist him in his research, whose fruits included a seven-volume lexicon of Hebrew, Syriac, Chaldee, and Arabic words, which, left in manuscript at his death, became the basis for Castell's *Lexicon Heptaglotton*, published as part of Walton's magisterial *Polyglot* (1654–1657).

Andrewes, a close friend of Casaubon since the latter's arrival in England, was himself a student of Arabic; Casaubon remarks that the bishop owned one of the two copies of Raphelengius's Arabic dictionary available in England at the time. Apparently both Andrewes and Casaubon urged Bedwell to travel to Leiden in order to consult the rare Arabic manuscripts left to the university by Scaliger, Andrewes offering to defray expenses.

So in the same year, Bedwell arrived at Leiden with letters from both Andrewes and Casaubon to the university librarian, Daniel Heinsius (1580–1655), a biblical scholar as well as poet and classical philologist. Heinsius had been Scaliger's student at Leiden, as had Grotius (1583–1645), probably the greatest of the Renaissance exegetes as well as a distinguished jurist, dramatist, historian, and philologist. The biblical scholarship of both Heinsius and Grotius was deeply influenced by Scaliger's teaching.[9] Scaliger introduced Heinsius and Grotius to Casaubon; in 1603–1604 they collaborated on an edition of Theocritus; Grotius and Casaubon remained friends until the latter's death. When Bedwell arrived, Heinsius was living in the former home of the Arabic scholar Franciscus Raphelengius (d. 1597)—a professor of Hebrew at Leiden and official printer to the university. But before his conversion to Calvinism, Raphelengius had been part of the cadre of Catholic scholars, including Benito Montano and Andreas Masius, who brought out the eight-volume Antwerp *Polyglot* in 1571; he thus supplies a link between the humanist Catholic scholarship of the mid-sixteenth century and the largely Protestant *respublica litterarum* of the post-Tridentine period.

Casaubon had urged Heinsius to come to England, in 1613 sending an invitation via the chaplain to Frederick V, Abraham Scultetus, himself a respected biblical scholar.[10] Heinsius, however, decided against crossing the Channel, but around the same time he began corresponding with several English scholars, among them Andrewes, Ussher, and Prideaux; from 1614 on he also maintained a close friendship with John Selden, who was a biblical scholar and Arabist as well as a jurist, member of Parliament, and student of English antiquities. Heinsius had Selden's *De diis Syris* reprinted in Leiden in 1636 and helped distribute several of Selden's other works on the Continent.[11] In any case, Heinsius was apparently most helpful to Bedwell, who returned to England in 1613.

Casaubon, however, had not been the first Continental scholar to visit Tottenham. We have record of at least two earlier visits. In 1610 the young Frenchman Louis Cappel, having just finished his theological studies at Sedan, commenced a *peregrinatio academica* to Paris, Leiden, and Oxford. While he was in England he went to see Bedwell, who apparently stimulated the beginning scholar's interest in Semitic languages. Cappel returned to France in 1613 and was appointed professor of Hebrew at Saumur, the Protestant academy founded by Mornay in 1593. In 1624 he published his *Arcanum punctationis*, arguing for the recent origin of Hebrew vowel-points; in 1629 the *Spicilegium*, a philological-historical commentary on the New Testament (reprinted in the *Critici sacri*). In 1634 he completed the manuscript of the *Critica sacra*, a detailed and original study of the text of the Scriptures sufficiently disturbing to Protestant orthodoxy as to be unprintable. Cappel circulated it unsuccessfully for sixteen years until finally in 1650 it came out in Paris—a Catholic city.

A year before Cappel's visit, Bedwell had entertained another young scholar, Thomas Erpenius (1584–1624), who had entered Leiden in 1602 where Scaliger encouraged him to study Arabic. At that time, however,

Leiden had no professor in the field. Instead, Erpenius finished his studies in 1608 and, still uncertain about his future plans, left for England with a letter from Scaliger. As in the case of Cappel, Bedwell's influence seems to have been crucial, and Erpenius departed from England to Paris to study Arabic with a Coptic émigré. There he met Casaubon, then librarian to the French king, who lent him rare Arabic manuscripts and encouraged his studies. In 1612 Casaubon wrote Grotius and Heinsius, recommending Erpenius for the chair in Arabic at Leiden, where he remained until his death.

Erpenius also taught Arabic to Sixtinus Amama (1593–1629), the professor of Oriental languages at the University of Franeker, which, founded ten years after Leiden, quickly became a second important Dutch center of humanistic scholarship. In 1613 Amama had gone to England to teach Hebrew and study Oriental languages with Prideaux, at that time rector of Exeter College, Oxford. The following year he went to Leiden, where he studied under Erpenius and met Heinsius. But Amama is better known as the student of Johannes Drusius (1550–1616), the first great Dutch Hebraist; Drusius died in his arms, and over the next two decades Amama published his teacher's massive commentaries and biblical essays in ten volumes.

Drusius was born to a prominent Protestant family in Flanders, but in 1567 the Inquisition forced him to escape to London, where his father had already fled. There he studied Hebrew with another exile, the French Hebraist Cevallerius. When Cevallerius became regius professor at Cambridge, Drusius and other young French exiles followed him. At Cambridge Drusius became a close friend of Thomas Cartwright, remaining at the university after Cevallerius returned to France, studying Greek and privately giving instruction in rabbinics to two English students, one of whom was Edward Lively (1545?–1605), later regius professor of Hebrew at Cambridge. In 1572 Drusius planned to return to France, but, prevented by the Saint Bartholomew massacre, he instead accepted Lawrence Humphry's offer to teach Hebrew, Chaldee, and Syriac at Oxford, where he remained until 1576. In 1577 he went to Louvain to study law but shortly thereafter was appointed professor of Hebrew at Leiden, where he taught until 1585, when the university's increasingly rigid Calvinism led him to accept a professorship at Franeker.

And here the circle begins to close, for Drusius's student, Lively, was a fellow of Trinity and taught Hebrew at Cambridge from 1575 until the year before his death in 1605. But Bedwell and Andrewes, both protégés of Chaderton at that time, were also at Cambridge during the last quarter of the sixteenth century. Bedwell had become a scholar of Trinity in 1584; Andrewes entered Pembroke in 1575 and remained at Cambridge until 1589.[12] Given their interest in Oriental languages, it seems probable that Bedwell and Andrewes were Lively's students.[13] The three names appear in conjunction at least once: on the original list of the committee appointed in 1604 to translate Genesis through 2 Kings for the Authorized Version. A year later, Andrewes had left Cambridge for the See of Chichester and Lively was dead, but for a moment these three English citizens of the *respublica litterarum* converge around a stack of old Bibles.[14]

As this partial circuit of biblical scholars in the late sixteenth and early seventeenth centuries suggests, the *respublica litterarum sacrarum* possessed a social existence; it is not an a posteriori label imposed on diverse materials but a close-knit textual community whose axis ran from Geneva, Sweden, and the Palatinate in central Europe through France and the Low Countries to England in the west.[15]

The fact that English scholarship belonged to this international and interconfessional milieu is significant. Although England produced no major biblical or Classical scholars, with the exception of Ussher and Selden, until the mid-seventeenth century, English erudite culture in the Renaissance was no more insular than it had been in the Middle Ages and cannot be understood except in the context of European scholarship. Beginning with Erasmus's first visit to England in 1499, important Continental biblical scholars traveled and taught there on a regular basis: Paulus Fagius, a Hebrew scholar and student of Reuchlin; Immanuel Tremellius, translator of the major Protestant Latin Bible; Cameron, the teacher of Cappel and Amyraut; Bucer, Drusius, Scaliger, Amama, Casaubon, Cappel, Erpenius, Grotius. The two great seventeenth-century compendia of Renaissance biblical scholarship both come from England: the *Critici sacri* of 1660, compiled by a group of high-church divines led by John Pearson (later bishop of Chester), which prints in full the works of the major Renaissance exegetes; and Matthew Poole's *Synopsis criticorum* (1669), an exegetical catena summarizing a vast number of Catholic as well as Protestant commentaries—somewhat surprisingly, since Poole was a nonconformist Presbyterian.

The presence of Continental biblical scholars and scholarship in England is not simply an academic matter. The leading figures in the *respublica litterarum* stood close to the centers of power; this was, after all, the era in which colonial administrators consulted professors of theology before moving against native insurgency, and Leiden had to request permission from the king of France to hire Scaliger in 1593.[16] When Casaubon came to England at Archbishop Bancroft's invitation, James, who valued learning in clerics as much as good legs in courtiers, requested his company on a weekly basis. James also encouraged and underwrote Ussher's research; Buckingham bought Erpinius's library for the Irish primate. Drusius was a correspondent of King James. Grotius likewise corresponded with the king and his bishops, attempting to enlist their support for the Remonstrants and his own eirenic projects. Knowledge may always be politicized, but only in the Renaissance was biblical erudition a recognized instrument of international affairs. One cannot imagine distinguished modern philologists assuming, simply in virtue of their scholarly attainments, such proximity to power.

One should not, however, confuse Renaissance biblical scholarship with its political uses. With a few exceptions, these works were not commissioned to serve specific government agenda, nor did the *respublica litterarum sacrarum* as a whole align with any one ideological faction. Renaissance princes and statesmen shared an interest in sacred erudition because, as Anthony Grafton observes, these "swollen and prodigious volumes, running to hundreds of pages and studded with interminable quotations in Greek and Hebrew," constituted "the staple of Europe's intellectual life."[17] If biblical scholars formed a small, tightly linked textual community, it was not therefore a culturally marginal or isolated one.

Rewriting the Vulgate

The Renaissance republic of sacred letters traced its own ancestry to the revolutionary biblical scholarship of the late fifteenth and early sixteenth centuries. The chronological parameters of the *Critici sacri* reflect this historical self-consciousness; the anthology, whose selections span the two centuries separating Valla from Grotius, implicitly defines a single philosophical "moment," distinct from both the allegorical methods of medieval exegesis and the deconstructive textual criticism pioneered by Spinoza and Richard Simon. Yet, on closer examination, this moment forks and fissures along several trajectories. If biblical commentaries written between 1450 and 1650 share certain features, they also betray considerable divergences. The biblical scholarship characteristic of the late Renaissance republic of letters differs in crucial respects from the philological criticism of Valla and Erasmus and, more pointedly, from the methods employed by humanistically trained Protestant theologians. A history of Renaissance exegesis must attend to both the continuities and ruptures.

Beryl Smalley's rediscovery of medieval biblical humanism makes Renaissance exegesis seem somewhat less unprecedented than was once thought.[18] But Renaissance exegetes, who generally did not know about this earlier humanism, defined their own project by contrasting it to medieval practice. For our purposes this sixteenth-century periodization provides the relevant starting point.

We can begin by looking at Matthew 26:13, which the Vulgate renders "*Amen dico vobis, ubicunque praedicatum fuerit hoc evangelium in toto mundo, dicetur quod haec fecit in memoriam eius.*" The interlinear gloss on this verse explains simply that *mundus* (world) means the church and *eius*, which can be either masculine or feminine, refers to Mary Magdalene; the citations added in the margins of the *Biblia Sacra*—a multivolume Vulgate including the Gloss, postils of Nicholas of Lyra, and patristic commentaries—go on to note that the ointment Mary pours on Christ's feet signifies "*bona fama*" and that Christ's prophecy about Mary has been fulfilled.[19] The allegorization is light here, just a passing tropological extension, giving the moral and connecting Mary's act to the subsequent history of the church. But a comparison between these notes and Valla's comment on the same passage sets in clear relief the break between medieval and early humanist exegesis. In his *Collatio Novi Testamenti* (written between 1442 and 1457 but not published until 1505, after Erasmus stumbled on the manuscript),[20] Valla gives the Vulgate reading and then observes, "*Eius* in Greek is feminine. To what, then, does it refer? Certainly to the pronoun *haec*. Therefore it should read *in memoriam suam. Quod*, however, is a relative [pronoun]."[21] Valla does not discuss the meaning of Mary's anointing but its grammar, correcting the Vulgate on the basis of the original Greek and the rules of Classical Latin.

This sort of critique points in two directions, both characteristic of early sixteenth-century biblical scholarship. On the one hand, Valla treats the New Testament as a *text*—a series of words governed by formal lexical and syntactic rules—not as a *document* supplying information about the world. The *Collatio* is really a critique of the Vulgate rather than a biblical commentary. It exposes the barbarisms, grammatical errors, and false idioms of the received translation.[22] For example, Valla's note on Matthew 26:10 criticizes the Vulgate's unidiomatic *quid molesti estis*, remarking that "the Greek words are more properly and correctly (*eleganter*) translated according to the practice of educated persons as *Quid negotium exhibetis mulieri?* (that is, 'why do you accuse this woman?') as we have explained in *De elegantia linguae Latinae*" (6:862).

Valla's notes tend to identify "good" Latin with Classical Latin, a position that entails a fundamentally ahistorical and nonreferential approach to language—the sort of Renaissance Atticism that would later shrink into

Ciceronianism. For Valla, non-Classical Latin was both aesthetically and conceptually incorrect. Thus, in the *Elegantiae* he argues that Boethius's definition of the Trinity is meaningless because Boethius uses the term *persona* in an unclassical sense; Valla's entry under *caritas* simply ignores the Christian definition, explaining it as costliness (from *carus*).[23] This linguistic purism occurs less frequently in the *Collatio* but lurks behind various notes as a background assumption. The note on Matthew 2:4 thus attacks the Vulgate's *principes sacerdotum* (chief priests)—a literal translation of the Greek—since the proper Latin term would be *pontifex* or *praesul* (6:55); it does not consider the possibility that the Jewish chief priests differed from Roman *pontifices*. Valla's apparently historicizing claim that meaning is determined by usage always has, in fact, a neoclassical twist, since he identifies "usage" with the literary Latin of the late republican and early imperial periods.[24] This Atticizing approach reached its climax in Castellio's Bible of 1551, which translates both testaments into excellent neo-Latin prose,[25] but by the later sixteenth century it had been replaced by a radically different understanding of language and philological method. This new hermeneutic, as we shall see, also derived from Valla's pioneering scholarship, but from his historical argument in the *Donation of Constantine* rather than from his biblical exegesis.

On the other hand, Valla's emendation of the Vulgate on the basis of the Greek heralded more permanent changes insofar as it privileged learning over logic (or fasting, for that matter) in the attempt to render luminous the *magnalia Dei*. Valla was virtually the first Western scholar since the end of antiquity to study the Greek manuscripts of the New Testament (medieval exegetes were more likely to know Hebrew than Greek), and all subsequent biblical scholarship in the Renaissance presupposes his intuition that learning dead languages is the beginning of wisdom. Even in the decade after Dort and the revenge of scholasticism, the Dutch Hebraist Amama could convince the Friesian Synod to make Greek and Hebrew requirements for all aspiring ministers.[26] Moreover, the notion that one approaches the eternal Word by studying *biblical* Greek implicitly severed humanist scholarship from neoclassical aesthetics. Valla did not correct the Greek of the New Testament, as barbarous with respect to Classical Greek as the Vulgate is to Ciceronian Latin. It was as a Greek scholar rather than a Latin formalist that Valla inaugurated Renaissance biblical exegesis.

Erasmus's *Annotationes*, first published in 1516 and successively revised until the fifth edition of 1535, borrows liberally from Valla (Erasmus's entries often begin by restating, without attribution, Valla's observations on the same passage). Like Valla, Erasmus was attempting to produce an accurate Latin version of the New Testament in place of the solecisms and mistranslations of the Vulgate. But Erasmus was less of a neoclassicist than his predecessor; the *Annotationes* bears the same relation to Valla's commentaries as the former's *De copia* does to Valla's *Elegantiae*. Where Valla generally treats the correct Classical usage of single words, focusing on questions of vocabulary and syntax, Erasmus tends to explore nuance and idiom, handling longer discursive units as well as individual words and emphasizing expressivity over correctness.

In Erasmus, a basically rhetorical understanding of language takes the place of medieval allegoresis.[27] When Christ tells his already sleeping disciples to "sleep and rest" (Matt. 26:45), Erasmus thus remarks that although Origen, Chrysostom, Hilary, and Jerome explain the passage allegorically, "with all due respect to others' opinions, it is possible that Christ is being somewhat ironic" (6:867). Verbal nuance functions rhetorically; it specifies the tonal shades of social interactions and relationships. For example, although the beginning of Erasmus's note on Matthew 26:13 follows Valla closely, it then continues: "furthermore μνημόσυνον does not simply signify *memory* but a *token of affection* or a *memorial* (*monumentum*) *that one leaves behind with a friend to remind him of the giver.* Hence it might not badly be translated *as a memorial of her* (*in monumentum ipsius*)" (6:864). Erasmus's sense of the nuance of the Greek, of the precise social register of meaning, is apparent in his distinction between a simple remembering and the symbolic "remembrance" denoting and sustaining intimacy (one thinks of Donne's "bracelet of bright hair"). At Matthew 5:47 he explains that *salutaveritis* ("if you salute" in the Authorized Version) signifies "not simply 'to greet' someone but 'to greet them with a kiss and embrace,' which was formerly customary for friends to do, not only among the Jews but also among the Greeks and Romans" (6:136–37). As before, Erasmus regards the meaning of a word as inseparable from its rhetorical occasions; language points to social praxis, not theological subtleties.[28]

But the *Annotationes* is also theological, particularly in the later editions, which supplement the basically philological notes of the 1516 text with patristic, polemical, and ethical commentary.[29] The notes on the fifth chapter of Matthew, for example, attack the characteristic enemies of the Erasmian *philosophia Christi*: monks, warmongering bishops, scholastic ignorance, false allegorization. In large part, the freshness of the *Annotationes* stems from Erasmus's application of rhetorical and philological method to theological questions. Erasmus's philological notes often have an explicit theological bearing. The most controversial entries in the *Anno-*

tationes—those on the Johannine comma, the correct translation of *logos*, and the subordination of Christ to God in the Pauline Epistles—all use philological argument to clarify and problematize doctrine.

Similarly, Erasmus's attempts to identify the original audience and occasion behind biblical utterances and his focus on the intention (*voluntas*) of the speaker as opposed to literal sense of his statement (*scriptum*) rely on essentially rhetorical procedures. In Erasmus's commentaries, these procedures serve, as they do in Classical rhetoric, to distinguish the universally valid *thesis* implicit in a passage from the historical contingencies informing it (what in rhetoric is called the *hypothesis*). In a long note on 1 Corinthians 7:39, for example, Erasmus argues that Saint Paul did not forbid remarriage after divorce in all cases: he was addressing a Jewish audience concerning the Jewish practice of allowing divorce for relatively minor marital disputes where reconciliation was still possible (7:1031–34). Had he taken account of more serious conjugal disasters, Erasmus concludes, "perhaps the Apostle would have responded differently, according to the circumstances of the case, and relaxed somewhat from the rigor of his earlier advice; he would, I think, have interpreted his own writings more humanely (*civilius*) for us than we ourselves interpret them" (7:1032–33). This passage analyzes the historical context in order to differentiate culturally specific injunctions from the theological "sense" of Paul's teaching on marriage, the same "sense" informing all of Scripture: namely, "Christian charity" or "equity" (7:1025, 1034). Erasmus, that is, distinguishes the historical from the universal in order to bracket the former as no longer pertinent; the whole point of his rhetorical method is to isolate the unchanging, general principles that should govern a Christian understanding of divorce from the parasitic tangles of historical detritus that medieval literalism often mistook for the main trunk.[30]

Erasmus's philological and rhetorical procedures were, of course, seminal; as an exegete, he was a forerunner both of liberal theologians like Castellio, Hooker, and Milton and of such humanistically trained Reformers as Calvin, Zwingli, and Beza—although the Erasmian *philosophia Christi* is more concerned with mores than dogma. But the main lines of late Renaissance biblical *scholarship*, while clearly indebted to Erasmus, advanced in a different direction.

Dogmatic Humanism

In his generally excellent book on early humanist biblical scholarship, Jerry Bentley concludes, "Problems of doctrine and discipline, not philology or criticism, engaged the attention of most students of the New Testament, whether Protestant or Catholic, in the middle and later years of the sixteenth century. Meanwhile, sixteenth-century scholars broke little new philological ground after Erasmus."[31] This negative assessment helps explain why so little work has been done on post-Erasmian biblical scholarship. However, even for the mid-sixteenth century it is not altogether true, and by 1600 biblical scholars were cultivating terra incognita. Sixteenth-century humanists slowly assembled an exegetic infrastructure, publishing Hebrew grammars and the basic texts of ancient lexicography, translating rabbinic commentaries, editing the early Church Fathers, and inaugurating the study of inscriptions, coinage, and chronology. Contemporary biblical commentaries assimilated this material and were transformed by it, although in two rather different ways.

One type of assimilation produced what might be called *dogmatic humanism*: the deployment of the new philology in the service of doctrine. Thus, Beza, although commonly considered the first Protestant scholastic, relies heavily on humanist scholarship, particularly that of Scaliger, Drusius, and Erasmus, in his New Testament commentary. Baronius, the conservative papal apologist, also has a remarkable range of (at least secondhand) erudition, citing numerous Classical and rabbinic authors in the first book of the *Annales,* which deals with the life of Christ. But both tend to use their erudition to defend theological positions. Beza, for instance, argues that New Testament Greek employs the present tense for the proximate future—a nicely grammatical point—to teach that justifying faith apprehends the unseen as if it were present; similarly, Baronius cites the Talmud as evidence that Jews buried criminals together with the instruments of their punishment, thus providing a historical basis for the Roman church's claim to possess the crown of thorns and similar relics of the Crucifixion.[32]

This assimilation of advanced scholarship to theological controversy rests on the premise that the Scriptures are *specula ecclesiae* or types of church history. For Baronius, New Testament narrative provides both the origin and model of ecclesiastical practice and dogma: transsubstantiation, fasting, reliquaries, pilgrimages. For Beza, as for Calvin, the biblical accounts of the elect persecuted by institutionalized power and superstition foreshadow the struggles of the early Reformed churches. Dogmatic humanism minimized temporal distinctions because the past is type and (rhetorical) figure of the present.[33] T. H. L. Parker thus remarks of Calvin's New Testament commentaries:

> We almost forget which century we are in; we hardly know whether the participants are *they* or *we*. We are talking about the Judaizers in

Galatia—no, we are not, they are the Romanists in France and Switzer-
land—indeed, we are not talking about the Judaizers at all, we are join-
ing in the controversy, we are taking sides. . . . Or St John is speaking:
but as we listen, his Greek strangely becomes the sort of Latin or French
with which we are familiar and we find to our surprise that he knows
about our modern problems and says the definitive thing about them.[34]

Calvin was a trilingual humanist, as was Beza; they were students of the
historical sense of Scripture—but their history is a hall of mirrors. This is
not allegory; the letter contains no hidden spiritual sense; yet Calvin replaces the language of medieval allegoresis with rhetorical terms like
synecdoche and *complexus* "to cover an extended meaning virtually identical in content to that covered by allegory or trope. . . . None of the [Re-
formed] exegetes—Luther, Oecolampadius, Melanchthon, and Calvin—
wanted to lose the flexibility of reference available to the allegorical
method: The text must be allowed to speak to the church."[35]

Vetustissimus Mos

This interpretation of history differentiates dogmatic humanism from the
biblical scholarship characteristic of the *respublica litterarum*. This second strand of exegetical humanism—what Laplanche calls *"l'érudition
philologico-antiquaire"*[36]—while deeply indebted to the humanist philology of Valla and Erasmus, slowly shifted its focus from textual to historical criticism. That is, unlike dogmatic humanism, it presupposed the
fundamental alteriority of the past. Its intuition of a rupture between antiquity and modern civilization probably derived from sixteenth-century
French legal historiography, which both investigated the multiple historical layers redacted in the Justinian *Code* and exposed the estrangement of
contemporary society from the world presupposed by Roman law.[37] Cujas,
one of the seminal figures in this new jurisprudence, taught Scaliger as
well as Franciscus Junius (along with Tremellius, translator of the great
Protestant Latin Bible). Grotius and Heinsius were pupils of both at Leiden.
   Beginning probably in the 1580s—Scaliger's *De emendatione temporum* came out in 1583, Casaubon's New Testament scholia in 1587—a new
sensitivity to historical discontinuity developed, replacing the seamless
fabric of typological time with the stratified divisions of a cultural archaeology that disclosed the break between the early ecclesiastical traditions of
Baronius and the underlying Semitic culture of the New Testament.
Scaliger's chronological treatise *De emendatione temporum* differs from
its predecessors by refusing to organize history as typological or numero-
logical recurrence.[38] Such scholarly exegesis operates from a synchronic

perspective rather than the typological one of both medieval and Reformation historiography. The biblical text becomes a historical document that both implies and elucidates late antique culture.

This avant-garde scholarship, it should be noted, was not disinterested. To take just one example, Scaliger's polymathic historical output was, as H. J. de Jonge has noted, "an immense effort to shew [sic] that . . . the critical use of the historical sources removed the foundations of Catholic tradition."[39] Nor was it secularized. No biblical scholar during this period seems particularly skeptical of either the mystical or the miraculous, both of which continued to occupy historical space. Hence, in his reply to Baronius, Casaubon carefully explicates the nature of Christ's splendid robe (*vestis candida*) in Luke 23:11, citing Valerius Maximus, Hirtius, Jerome, Suetonius, Josephus, Clement, Plutarch, and Theophrastus to show that in antiquity it could have been either a royal or a priestly garment. This learned discussion concludes: "Who does not see that divine providence mysteriously contrived that Christ, who is the true king and true priest, should thus be garbed in a splendid robe by his mockers!"[40] Neither Grotius nor any of the other *critici sacri* questions the earthquake at the Crucifixion—nor do they defend it; it remains a fact rather than a problem. Hence, it will not do simply to describe biblical scholarship in the late Renaissance as historicist; its philological antiquarianism differs in essence from the skeptical and secularizing tendencies central to Higher Criticism.

The Sociology of Language

The developments in biblical scholarship between the mid-fifteenth and mid-seventeenth centuries were first of all changes in philological *method*.

In his 1519 edition of the *Annotationes*, Erasmus occasioned considerable controversy by translating the *logos* of John 1:1 as *sermo* rather than *verbum*. The justifications he gives for this revision are of particular interest. After pointing out that *logos* can have a variety of meanings—*verbum, oratio, sermo, ratio, modum,* and so forth—he defends the superiority of his reading to the Vulgate *verbum* as theologically more precise, since "whatever the Father speaks, he speaks through the Son" (6:4); but *sermo*, which refers to an extended discourse, better captures this speaking than does *verbum*, which means just a single word. The bulk of the note, however, defends the orthodoxy of *sermo* by providing extensive evidence that the Latin Fathers regularly employed it as a translation for *logos*. For Erasmus, as for most early humanists, the crucial historical break came around the year A.D. 600, dividing the learned and holy Fathers from the baleful Schoolmen; the difference between the Semitic milieu of the

Gospels and the Hellenistic culture of the patristic era weighs far less heavily on his historical consciousness. Hence, Erasmus simply does not pose the question of what *logos* might have meant to John or his original readership. Nor does he really consider the question in historical terms at all. He cites the Fathers in order to rebut charges of heretical innovation, but his principal argument for translating *logos* as *sermo* is that it better expresses the orthodox understanding of the Trinity and (implicitly) Erasmus's own rhetorical understanding of the relation between human and divine discourse.[41] Erasmus is not primarily a historical critic but a rhetorically trained philologist, engaged in a debate with medieval tradition rather than attempting to tease out the praxes of late antiquity from the traces glancingly imprinted in the biblical text.

Three-quarters of a century later, Johannes Drusius—among the earliest of the new biblical scholars—comments on the same passage:

> *In the beginning was the word* [*verbum*] Or *Sermo* . . . whence . . . the Targums generally refer to the messiah as the *sermo DOMINI*. In the Koran also Christ is called the word of God as a proper name. In a letter to Rabbi Isahac, the leader of the synagogue, Rabbi Samuel Israelita writes, "They say in the Koran that *Eise* (i.e., Jesus Christ), is the Word of God. And among these Saracens, the Word of God is the proper name of Jesus Christ, since no one else is called by this name except Jesus, whom in Arabic they call *Eise*." (6:26)

It is not quite clear what Drusius is getting at here. Are the citations from the Koran and the rabbis supposed to demonstrate that Moslems and Jews recognize Christ as the Word of God, or is Drusius attempting to show that John's terminology needs to be contextualized in terms not of Trinitarian theology but of Semitic idiom? The note is methodologically confusing, but its choice of quotations points to a crucial reorientation of exegesis from patristics to orientalism.

Drusius's recognition that the Johannine description of Christ as *logos* bore some relation to the phraseology of the Targums is clarified and expanded in subsequent commentaries. Cameron (1579–1625) and Grotius thus note that the Chaldee Paraphrase (the Palestinian Targum) consistently renders Hebrew expressions like "God did" or "God said" as "God did or said something through his word (*per verbum suum*)." Cameron concludes, "In the Jewish church (as the Chaldee Paraphrase clearly shows) that by which God does and ordains all things is termed . . . λόγος. . . . Hence I think Christ was called Λόγος because God is said to have made all things by Him, both in the works of the first and the second creation" (6:31–32). More clearly than Drusius, Cameron and Grotius grasp the significance of the Aramaic idiom (the language that Jesus spoke) for understanding the theology implicit in New Testament phrasing. It is of little importance whether either was correct in assuming a Semitic substrate for biblical Greek—a view held by Scaliger, Heinsius, and other important seventeenth-century scholars. The significance of their observation is methodological: it treats semiotics as a branch of cultural history rather than of either lexicography or theology. The earlier humanist claim that meaning is a function of usage underlies such scholarship, but it has now been stripped of the classicizing premise that restricts legitimate usage to certain specified periods and hence tends toward a formalist rather than historical approach to language. This sense of the historical embeddedness of discourse deepens in Grotius's final comment on this passage: "John here rejects the theories (*figmentum*) of the Gnostics, who said that Mind was born only after many ages from a prior principle, and that Mind then bore the Only-Begotten, who bore the Word" (6:38). With this, Grotius moves from a consideration of the New Testament's cultural idiom to its ideological context. Words have a politics as well as a history.

This historicized approach to language had a polemical edge, since, as Casaubon observes, Counter-Reformation theology rests on the fallacy of attributing more recent meanings to biblical terms.[42] But it also enabled a new sensitivity to the complex relations between semantics and social practice. In a fairly lengthy discussion, Casaubon thus shows that the Old Testament has no word specifically designating a cross or crucifixion, although it implies that criminals were sometimes strung up on a tree after having been stoned or executed; following the Roman conquest of Palestine, the term for this sort of postmortem shaming came to be used for crucifixion. Therefore, Casaubon argues, since the term that means "crucifixion" in late Hebrew previously had a more general reference and since in biblical Hebrew there is no word for crucifixion per se, it is highly probable that this punishment was unknown to the ancient Jews—despite the contrary claims not only of Baronius but of the more scholarly Carolus Sigonius and Justus Lipsius.[43] Casaubon is not arguing that every *res* must have it own *verbum*, which is clearly false, but that usage follows praxis, that philology recapitulates sociology, that the very instability of language—the historical drift of the signifier—enables reference, enables one to distinguish historical strata according to the type of linguistic artifacts deposited there.

Like Casaubon, other late Renaissance exegetes tend to view individual words less in terms of either theology or lexical meaning—the fixed relation between signifier and signified—than as elements in a culturally specific discursive system, whether the Hebraic penal code or ritual practice. Whereas, for example, Beza reads "testament" according to Protestant covenant theology, Grotius interprets the testament as a treaty (*foedus*) and analyzes its relevance to the Gospel narratives by establishing the ancient role of blood sacrifice in ratifying such agreements (6:33–34). Meaning here derives from cultural practice. Similarly, commenting on Mary's anointing of Christ (Matt. 26:8), Drusius connects the apostles' protest against such extravagant waste (*perditio*) with a rabbinic observation that even the rulers of the Jews were not allowed expensive burial rites because "this is wasteful (*perditio*) and the work of gentiles" (6:878); that is, by linking the apostles' reaction to Jewish burial customs, Drusius implies that the events represented in the New Testament operate within a cultural system and are intelligible only in terms of it.

Frequently the commentators explicate biblical terminology with reference to Hebraic legal codes, treating law as the articulation of cultural categories. Thus, in a passage that gives the post-Freudian reader pause, Daniel Heinsius shows that the Pharisees' claim that Christ was a "deceiver" (Matt. 27:63) explains why they resolved to kill him, for according to Jewish law, "*Filio necessitatem aut ministerium caedendi patris aut devovendi nunquam imponi, nisi sit seductor*"—that is, a son is obliged to kill or curse his father only if the father is a "seducer" (*seductor* [or *planos* in the Greek], meaning, however, simply one who leads astray).[44] One can compare Heinsius's explanation with the more strictly philological note characteristic of mid-sixteenth-century exegesis; thus, in 1572 the Lutheran scholar Joachim Camerarius glosses the same passage by observing that "Horace uses the term 'planus' for a mountebank and vagabond who deceives men with idle nonsense."[45] Camerarius approaches semantics from the standpoint of Classical usage, whereas in the previous examples ordinary language is treated as in some sense "technical," as belonging to a specific and systematic body of rules. Just as one cannot understand a rook in chess without knowing the rules of the game, so even apparently general terms like "deceiver" or "testament" have a precise significance inseparable from the codes and customs operative in a given society.

Renaissance biblical scholarship likewise sifts textual cruxes for evidence of rule-governed praxis. A particularly interesting sequence of notes considers the problem of miscitation. The beginning of Matthew 27:9 reads: "Then was fulfilled that which was spoken by Jeremy the prophet," a line that always presented difficulties since the ensuing passage does not appear in Jeremiah but instead closely resembles Zechariah 11:12–13. Earlier sixteenth-century exegetes like Erasmus and Sebastian Munster generally view the transposition as an early scribal error or as a mistake on Matthew's part.[46] But Erasmus also offers an alternative explanation, based on Origen and Jerome, which found wide acceptance among subsequent Roman Catholic exegetes: the citation derives from a lost apocrypha of Jeremiah. Interestingly, Erasmus is far less uneasy than Jerome about the possibility that "an oracle explicating the mystery of the Passion" could have a noncanonical source (6:930); he elsewhere notes in passing that

> clearly not a few books of the Old Testament have been lost, the titles of which still remain in the canonical books: the books of the Wars of the Lord, cited in Numbers 21, and the book of the Just (*librum Justorum*) cited in Joshua 10 and 2 Kings 1. . . . [Such books] must have had great authority, since canonical Scripture so often rests on that authority. But whether they belonged to the Hebrew canon I leave to others to discover. (6:132)

This explanation, repeated in the commentaries of Clarius and Zegerus, moves toward a historical understanding of the Hebrew sacred texts before the Synod of Jamnia fixed the Old Testament canon in its final form at the end of the first century A.D. These scholars, all of whom were Roman Catholic (since Protestant orthodoxy was committed to a rigidly literalist view of biblical inspiration),[47] begin to treat the misquotation not in terms of faulty recension but as evidence for the corpus and circulation of texts in ancient Jewish society. The locus of the problem shifts from the individual, whether scribe or apostle, to the cultural and textual conditions presupposed by Matthew's citation.

Grotius's note on the same passage goes far beyond patristic conjecture in analyzing the rules governing ancient textual production and canon formation. He begins by positing the existence of *oral* traditions: "It should be considered certain that among the Jews many of the prophecies (*oracula*) of the ancient prophets were preserved in memory rather than writing, although subsequently those who received [such prophecies] from their parents privately wrote them down." Inasmuch as Grotius was not a Roman Catholic but an Erastian Erasmian (or something like that), this is not a jury-rigged apologia for Roman traditions. The note begins with a discussion of intertextuality, observing that later prophets frequently wove their own works out of the words of their predecessors: "Thus many passages in Ezekiel have been taken verbatim from Jeremiah . . . and many portions of the Apocalypse of John can be found in Ezekiel and Daniel." Moreover, since Zechariah drew extensively from the text of Jeremiah, so much so that "the Jews were accustomed to say that *the spirit of Jeremiah was in Zechariah*," it is not improbable that he also quoted Jeremiah's *unwritten* sayings. The fact that such sayings are "noncanonical" does not mean they are not true but simply that they lack the sanction of "public authority" (6:948–49).

However briefly and awkwardly, Grotius is here attempting to account for the crux in Matthew by adducing culturally specific rules for textual transmission. He thus considers not only the generic intertextuality of prophetic discourse (a notion seemingly incompatible with direct divine inspiration) but also the interplay between textuality and orality in biblical culture, whereby the sayings of one prophet could be incorporated into the text of a later one and yet simultaneously survive within an oral tradition still attached to the name of the earlier figure. Elsewhere, dealing with a similar problem of miscitation, he comments on how passages in *written* texts detach themselves and begin to circulate orally as *sententiae* or proverbs and as such later find their way into subsequent texts (6:904). Hence, folk sayings are not necessarily earlier than texts; rather than an irreversible shift from oral to literate culture, Grotius hypothesizes a reciprocal exchange between scribal and popular traditions.[48]

De natura rerum

While the largest number of entries in Renaissance biblical commentaries discuss philological matters, antiquities form the second most popular category; miniature essays on such topics as Mary's alabaster box, the nature of hyssop, whether Jews reclined during meals, Pilate's atrium, and the location of Golgotha fill the great folio columns. Minor exegetes like Gualtperius and Zegerus deal with little else. Such notes, which usually involve quotations in multiple alphabets, fonts, and languages (English even shows up once: "DAD" printed in gothic capitals as a literal translation of the opening words of the Lord's Prayer), initially seem both unfamiliar (why would anyone research such stuff?) and tedious. Insofar as post-Enlightenment historiography concerned itself with the great shaping forces of civilization—whether kings, *Geist*, or class struggle—it could have little sympathy for the Renaissance's scholarly fascination with the material culture of antiquity: the detailed explanations of clothing, pots and pans, burial customs, coinage, table manners, and other such ephemera. The Renaissance borrows this methodology from Classical philology: ancient literary criticism, especially practical criticism, involves supplying

lengthy explanations for place-names, unfamiliar artifacts, and ancient customs; it is correspondingly far weaker on modern topics like character
analysis and thematic structure. Both ancient literary criticism and Renaissance scholarship have received virtually no attention primarily because
they traffic in little objects rather than large ideas. But this archaeology of
knowledge, so oddly parallel to contemporary cultural materialisms, shapes
Renaissance historical method and is fundamental for its interpretation.[49]
It suggests a view of history as synchronic structure rather than causal
process, a refusal to privilege agency over artifacts as historical signifiers, a
sensitivity to social behavior rather than the infamous/autonomous individual. That is, the material focus of Renaissance exegesis is not mere antiquarianism; rather, it assumes (again using modern terminology) that
thick description provides a basis for cultural interpretation.

One can see this relationship between the specification of artifacts and
historical analysis in the notes on biblical clothing. For instance, medieval
exegetes generally treated the passage (Mark 14:51) about the young man
wearing only a linen cloth (*sindon*) who appears suddenly at the moment
of Jesus' capture, is seized by the soldiers, and escapes naked—a noto-
riously opaque verse[50]—as an allegory about fleeing the entanglements
of the world and *nudus sequens nudum Christum*, often identifying
the nameless youth with Saint John: partly because he was probably still
young, partly because he loved Christ most and thus remained after all the
other disciples had fled.[51] Neither medieval nor earlier Renaissance exegetes mention the *sindon*. Then beginning with Reformed commentators
like Calvin and Beza, one finds notes that ignore the traditional association
of the youth with John and the allegory based on it, instead asserting that
the *sindon* is, in Beza's words, "*une chemise*"; the anonymous young man,
awakened by the tumult, has dashed outdoors in his undergarments, and
the fact that the soldiers apprehend this half-dressed bystander demonstrates their barbarity—which is the point of the episode.[52] The passage
does not seem to have been particularly controversial, however, until 1588,
when Baronius published the first volume of his *Annales*, in which he defends the traditional identification of the youth with John based on a
rather extended argument to the effect that Jesus and his disciples ate
wearing *cenatoria*, or Roman dining robes; Jesus put this robe over his
clothes for the sake of decency, but the other disciples wore it without any
undergarments. When John heard that his master had been captured, he
was so stricken by grief that he forgot to change into his regular clothes
and ran out wearing only this dining robe, which Mark calls a *sindon*.[53] To
this Casaubon responds with considerable erudition and sarcasm that an-

cient peoples did not strip for dinner, and hence there is no reason to connect the unnamed youth with the Evangelist; furthermore, the *sindon* was not a *cenatoria* but "probably should be understood as nightclothes or pajamas (*cubitoria*), as Petronius calls them, which the youth took along when he hastened out of bed."[54] Later commentators like Grotius and Hammond follow Casaubon's reading, adding that the youth was probably unknown to Jesus, just a nearby villager drawn out by curiosity.[55]

What is at stake in this debate is the construction of narrative background and simultaneously of social milieu: Baronius and the Fathers almost always identify the minor figures in the Gospels with familiar names; narrative background is shallow and well-lit, occupied mostly by Christ's family and friends. In Protestant exegesis, events recede into a shadowy hinterground peopled by hostile or anonymous figures. The young man who shows up during the nightmarish scene at Gethsemane is a curious villager, a nameless intruder into salvation history, a figure from ordinary Jewish society who accidentally wanders into the sacred text. These opposed constructions unfold as readings of *sindon*, since the nature of that garment provides the sole clue concerning the identity and purposes of the mysterious youth.

Casaubon's interpretation of the *sindon* seems to have been widely accepted, but in 1663 the English Hebraist John Lightfoot (1602–1675) suggested a new reading, arguing that the youth was probably an Essene; the details in the text—that on a chilly night (the same night Saint Peter tried to warm himself in front of the fire at the High Priest's house) he was wearing only a simple cloth, that he had no cloak or undergarments—are particularized cultural signifiers, intelligible only via Talmudic research into the social context of late Judaism. According to the rabbis, a *sindon* is a tallis, worn by the ascetic Essenes without undergarments in order to "macerate their bodies, and afflict them with hunger and cold even above the severe rule of other Sects."[56] Lightfoot does not suggest a relation between the Essenes and the followers of Jesus; rather, he is interested in the *sindon* as a clue to the social structures of first-century Palestine. The artifact functions as a historical trace, allowing one to reconstruct the chiaroscuro and alien landscape of Christian origins, where the self-enclosed sacral realm of medieval *Heilsgeschichte* has been replaced by an unfamiliar world with its own alien sects and objects.

The gradual evolution of both antiquarianism and philology into the study of the underlying rules, both written and unwritten, governing social behavior (including textual production) differentiates biblical historicism from its Classical counterpart. Classical history, from Thucydides to Gibbon, is largely political and biographical, dealing with generals, emperors, demagogues, and statesmen. A few Renaissance works attempt to adapt the Bible to this generic model. Thus, the 1554 edition of Castellio's Bible (which, incidentally, translates *ecclesia* as *respublica*) reshapes the biblical text along the lines of ancient history by inserting long passages from Josephus's *Jewish Wars* between the Old and New Testaments in order to supply a continuous political narrative.[57] But in general, biblical scholarship in the Renaissance focuses on culture rather than politics. Since the events of the New Testament are only marginally related to the vicissitudes of imperial power, exegesis turned instead to the exploration of social praxis and the fabric of ordinary existence, studying clothing, table manners, dishware, marital and burial customs, penal codes, kinship structures, and ritual practice. Hence, it seems possible to extend Auerbach's seminal description of biblical mimesis from literature to scholarship. In the commentaries of the late Renaissance *critici sacri* the "random everyday depths of popular life" enter the domain of historical representation.[58] The half-lit recesses of biblical narrative, first discovered by these Renaissance exegetes, become sites for the *serious* representation of cultural forms. In these commentaries, "the two realms of the sublime and the everyday are not only actually unseparated but basically inseparable."[59] The *magnalia Christi* occur not merely against a realistic backdrop but within a social milieu where *locus* and *platea* form a single whole; the events of sacred history occupy the same space as ordinary workings of local politics and unfold according to the cultural logics of Roman provincial government and intertestamental Judaism. Exegesis becomes less an explication of things (*res*) mentioned in the text than an inquiry into the codes and customary practices (*mos*) implicit in both the composition and content of scriptural narrative. Perhaps unsurprisingly, Grotius, the best practitioner of this sort of cultural history, was also the greatest jurist of his age, since humanist jurisprudence from its inception dealt with the cultural entanglements of law and the historical mechanisms of its transmission.

The Last Supper

The rise of cultural analysis resulted from the fusion of this legal historiography with the wealth of information pouring in from newly rediscovered Jewish texts: Josephus, Philo, the Targums (Aramaic paraphrases of the Old Testament produced between 250 B.C. and A.D. 300), the Midrash (rabbinic commentaries on the Old Testament), the Mishnah (a collection of rabbinic laws composed around A.D. 200), the Talmud (commentaries on the Mishnah incorporating a variety of sources dating from before A.D. 200 to as late as the mid-sixth century).[60] Access to these texts marks the critical rupture between Renaissance biblical scholarship and patristic exegesis. After the mid-sixteenth century the Church Fathers, still principal authorities for Erasmus, were gradually replaced by Hebraic texts as sources for the philological and cultural interpretation of the New Testament. As early as 1535 Sebastian Munster (1489–1552)—student of Reuchlin and teacher of Calvin—remarked on the inadequacy of patristic scholarship. He explains to Henry VIII:

> In our era we are assisted by the multitude of books, which we know were unavailable in earlier ages. For St. Jerome himself had no help in interpreting the Old Testament except a naked Bible and an uneducated (and untrustworthy) teacher: no Aramaic translation or Targum, no commentaries, not even a Hebrew grammar—without which many places of Scripture cannot possibly be accurately explained, no matter what some people say. (6:ii)

The majority of Renaissance exegetes were professors of Hebrew or Oriental philology; the evolution of biblical scholarship took place outside the theological faculty, which remained heir to the scholastic tradition even (or especially) in Protestant countries.

The works of some medieval Hebraists, particularly Nicholas of Lyra and Paulus Burgensis, remained in print throughout the Renaissance. But Renaissance Hebrew scholarship began with Reuchlin's *De rudimentis linguae Hebraicae* of 1506, the first printed Hebrew grammar and dictionary.[61] During the early sixteenth century, Christian Hebraists, including Reuchlin, often inclined toward cabbalistic esoterica rather than scholarship, but some of Reuchlin's students began the work of editing and translating Hebrew texts and the lexical tools needed to understand them. In 1508 Fagius published the first Aramaic dictionary, in 1546 an edition of the *Targum Onkelos*. In 1517 the first rabbinic Bible appeared, complete with the Hebrew text, commentary, and Targums; the next year Petrus Galatinus printed his *De arcanis*, which opens with a survey of the Talmud.[62] Sebastian Munster, like Fagius a student of Reuchlin, brought out an Aramaic grammar in 1527 and a literal translation of the Hebrew Bible in 1535. With the founding of the trilingual colleges in the early sixteenth century—Corpus Christi, Louvain, Alcala, the Collège de France, Wittenberg—Hebrew became an integral part of humanistic philology.[63]

By the middle of the sixteenth century, France had replaced Germany as the center of Hebraic studies, and at the same time such research loosened its connections with cabbalistic mysticism. In addition, biblical philology began to include the other Semitic languages. Thus, the newly discovered Syriac Bible came out in 1555, followed by a Syriac grammar in 1556; between 1613 and 1616 Thomas Erpinius published the first Arabic grammar and New Testament. By that time the Wars of Religion and the Jesuits had driven the two greatest Hebraists of the period, Scaliger and Casaubon, from Paris, leaving the Dutch universities and the French Calvinist academy at Saumur the dominant forces in Semitic studies during the seventeenth century; the great Orientalists of this period—Erpinius, Cappel, Drusius, L'Empereur, Amama, de Dieu—were all professors at Saumur, Leiden, or Franeker. Significantly, starting with Coccejus's *Sanhedrin* (1629), Dutch scholars begin translating the Mishnah and Talmudic tracts, which had previously been accessible only to a small cadre of specialists. Earlier translations from the Oriental languages had concentrated on the text of the Old Testament and the Targums; the growing interest in the Mishnah and Talmud, which treat Jewish laws and customs, derived from and informed the new scholarship on biblical culture and social praxis that dominated exegesis in the late Renaissance.[64]

The discovery of Jewish antiquities transformed biblical scholarship from a philological to a historical discipline. The *apparatus* to the Antwerp *Polyglot* of 1572, written by the Erasmian Catholic and secret Familist Arius Montanus (and placed on the *Index* in 1607), includes essays on Hebrew idioms, measures, coinage, architecture, clothing, and political geography, along with a translation of the Targums and Masius's Syriac grammar and dictionary.[65] In 1585 another Erasmian, Carolus Sigonius, published his influential work on Jewish political institutions, *De republica Hebraeorum*. This type of exegesis dominated seventeenth-century biblical scholarship; the inset essays in the *Critici sacri* include Cappel on the nature of the Corban, Drusius on Jewish sects (*De Hasidaeis*), Edward Brerewood on the weights and values of ancient coins, Montanus on Jewish antiquities, and so forth.

English biblical scholarship, which reached maturity in the mid-seventeenth century, belongs to the same tradition. Henry Hammond, one of the first English biblical scholars of international stature, has an elegant and characteristic note on Jesus' reply to Nicodemus (John 3):

> And when *Nicodemus* a learned Jew, and a Master among them, seems to be ignorant, and wonders how this can be, and asks this gross question . . . how one that is of *age can be born again*, *Christ* wonders at

him . . . intimating that this is the very doctrine of Proselytism, which
no knowing Jew can be ignorant of, to wit, that he is to be wash'd and
circumcised, and being so, is by the Jews counted as one *recens natus*,
new born, brought forth by another mother, so that he who was kin to
him before, is now no longer kin to him.[66]

Hammond locates this apparently cryptic exchange in the customs and
rituals of first-century Judaism, treating the mystery of new birth as an
idiom, a borrowing from the rabbinic theology of conversion, familiar to
both Christ and Nicodemus. One may compare this reading with Erasmus's note, which cites Chrysostom and Cyril to the effect that "born
again" in Greek may also mean "born from above" (6:62) and hence signifies baptismal regeneration. In Hammond interpretation does not point
forward—to the church—but reinserts the text in its discursive milieu.

We may look at one example of such scholarship in some detail. With a
certain scholarly exultation, Scaliger recounts the Talmudic prescriptions
concerning the Passover seder in his *De emendatione temporum* of 1583.
"*Ecce* [behold], they reclined during the seder as a sign of security," he begins—a small point but one that had confused earlier commentators since
the Old Testament mandates that the Passover be eaten *standing*.[67] Scaliger
goes on to describe how the seder involved a double ablution (thus explaining why in John's Gospel Jesus apparently washes the disciples' feet
after rather than before the meal), because two meals were eaten in the
paschal ceremony, each preceded by an ablution. In the first, he continues,
they ate the sacrificial lamb; in the second, which was called the *caena
dimissoria* and which corresponds to the *secunda mensa* of the Gentiles,
they gave thanks to God, passed a ceremonial cup around the table, dipped
the bitter herbs, and broke the unleavened bread.

> This was the true rite of celebrating the Passover at the time of the
> Messiah, as the ancient canons of the Talmud clearly demonstrate. . . .
> If Christ, as certain enemies of good letters pretend, did not bind him-
> self to the rites of the Jews, why did all these things, which can be
> found in the Jewish ritual codes, take place here? Why are they virtu-
> ally identical?[68]

Earlier biblical exegesis either had not recognized that the Last Supper was
a seder or had not considered the fact significant, instead treating the gospel
narratives in terms of the origin of the Eucharist. But just a year after the
publication of *De emendatione*, Beza incorporates Scaliger's discoveries,

along with similar observations by Tremellius, into his New Testament commentaries; he rehearses the double meal, the distribution of the cup and pieces of broken matzoh, the custom of reclining. One grasps how novel this information appeared from Beza's final remark that because of the research of Scaliger and Tremellius, the Last Supper "is *finally* intelligible."[69]

Subsequent exegesis of this passage refined Scaliger's original observations; for example, Hammond suggests the cultural provenance of the words of institution in his remark that the paschal lamb "was wont to be called . . . *the body of the Passover,* or . . . *the body of the Paschal Lamb.* So in the *Talmud.*"[70] But the process of refinement also led to a more complex account of late biblical society than that implicit in Scaliger's comparison of paschal and eucharistic ritual. To see this, one needs to look at a second and more problematic aspect of the Gospel accounts of the Last Supper. The synoptic Gospels clearly depict Jesus as eating the Passover the evening before the Crucifixion. John, however, does not include the narrative of the Last Supper and seems to imply that the Crucifixion took place before the Passover meal; for example, John 18:28 reports that the leaders of the Jews led Jesus to Pilate, but "they themselves went not into the judgment hall, lest they should be defiled; but that they might eat the passover."

The Western fathers (and Roman Catholic exegetes like Baronius and à Lapide) followed the synoptic narrative and explained John's references to the passover as pertaining to the whole seven days of unleavened bread.[71] This explanation, however, has its difficulties, as Casaubon observes, since elsewhere "the Passover" always refers exclusively to the festal meal held on the first night; furthermore, Jewish apologists pointed out that if the Last Supper were a passover meal, Jesus could not have been captured, tried, and killed that day, since Jews do not work on high feasts.[72]

In the fifteenth century, Paulus Burgensis, a Spanish bishop of Jewish descent and to my knowledge the first exegete since Saint Jerome to apply Hebrew scholarship to New Testament questions, proposed a solution based on Hebrew calendrical tracts. The argument is fairly technical but in essence states that according to Jewish law, if a feast day falls on the day before the Sabbath it will be transferred to coincide with the Sabbath, since otherwise, given that Jews cannot work on either high feasts or the Sabbath, salads and corpses would have to be left standing for two days in the subtropical heat, with unfortunate consequences. In the year Jesus died, the passover, which should have begun Thursday night (15 Nisan), had for the above reason been postponed to the subsequent evening. Jesus, however, chose to eat it on Thursday, the day prescribed by the Old Testament, although the other Jews celebrated it the following night. Hence, both the synoptics and John are correct since they are referring to different events. The majority of Protestant scholars—Munster, Bucer, Lively, Beza, Scaliger, Casaubon, Cameron—accepted the Spanish bishop's analysis,[73] but in the 1630s Johannes Cloppenburg, a professor at Franeker, raised a further problem: how could Jesus have gotten a ritually sacrificed lamb on Thursday if such lambs were not slaughtered in the Temple until the following day, when the rest of the Jews celebrated the passover?[74]

Modern scholars are not likely to find these discussions of much interest, although the problem of dating the Last Supper fascinated Renaissance exegetes, who treated the issue in extraordinary detail, partly because it was theologically insignificant and hence allowed speculative latitude.[75] But the discussions are themselves suggestive—in their use of rabbinic law to reconstruct Jewish customs and rituals but also in their feeling for the *actuality* of bodies: Casaubon's vegetables (*olera*) wilting in the Judean sun and the "bodies of the dead [which] cannot last in the autumnal heat of these warmer regions,"[76] or Cloppenberg's lambs still alive and bleating on Thursday night. At one point, when Scaliger wants to confute the post-Talmudic Jewish claim that the paschal lamb was killed and eaten between the time the sun touched the horizon and its disappearance from sight, he queries "how in such a brief time, virtually no time at all, can a lamb be killed, flayed, eviscerated, dressed, roasted, [and] served?"[77] These discussions of calendrical matters are lit by a new historical imagination: a realization of the solidity of historical existence, of bodies located in chronological rather than sacral time, bodies that putrefy after two days.

Grotius rejects the solution given by Paulus Burgensis, in part because it failed to explain Christ's reason for anticipating the date mandated by the Sanhedrin for that year. Instead, he argues that Jesus ate the Passover a day early but ate it without the sacrificial lamb, which would not yet have been ritually slaughtered. Grotius defends this unusual reading by noting that in the first century there would have been *two* Passover ceremonies. The Passover ritual described in the Old Testament could be celebrated only at Jerusalem, since the lambs had to be killed in the Temple; "but because in times of war the people could not come together, and after the Babylonian exile and other *diasporas* it became increasingly impossible for the Jews, now scattered far afield, to come to Jerusalem, in place of the sacrificial passover they substituted a memorial passover" (6:894). Christ knew he was going to die before he could eat the sacrificial passover, but mindful of his Father's law (*observantissimus legis Paternae*), he wanted to celebrate this sacred feast and thus, following the custom of the Jews of the Diaspora, held a memorial passover (6:894–95).

This explanation is notable because it differentiates ancient from post-exilic Judaism, whereas previous commentators generally regarded Judaism more as a fixed doctrinal system than a historical entity. Moreover, Protestant theology periodized biblical history according to the different covenants and empires established by God; Grotius divides sacred time into political segments.[78] The passage points to a new sensitivity to cultural discontinuity and change, which it analyzes in terms of legal and ritual practice rather than divine revelation. At least at one point, this approach allows Grotius to anticipate the nineteenth-century concept of the development of dogma. Again the Babylonian Exile is the turning point. Before that time, Grotius notes, Judaism contained no explicit teaching concerning life after death, although a few may have held this belief; but after the Exile

> when the splendor of the Jewish empire had been taken away, when the people, groaning under external threats and punishment, suffering, and oppressed by the fear of death, began to lapse from Judaism, Daniel first used the word "resurrection"—ambiguously but in a way that seemed to veil something of great import. Ezekiel followed Daniel. . . . And the Chaldee Paraphrase, which is believed to have been written before Christ, makes open mention of a judgment after death, both in the story of Abel and elsewhere. (6:185–86)

Yet, Grotius continues, in the first century belief in an afterlife remained a matter of doubt and anxiety, denied by the Sadducees, who adhered to the explicit teachings of Moses and the Prophets, but affirmed by the Pharisees, who had only the "authority of tradition" to support their view; thus, "amid the quarrels of different schools, many souls wavered to and fro." Christ's teachings and resurrection resolve this eschatological crisis, but the terms he uses—"the kingdom of God," "paradise," "gehenna"— come not from the Old Testament but "have been lifted from popular speech." Grotius's account of doctrinal development, like his account of liturgical evolution, attempts to get "behind" the explicit witness of the sacred texts, which know nothing of memorial passovers or the gradual elaboration of soteriology, to investigate the oral traditions and customary praxis of late biblical Judaism, reconstructing a specific cultural moment from the silences and indirections scattered in the Bible, the rabbis, and the Fathers.

Law and Narrative

As the preceding examples indicate, Grotius basically understands culture as a body of rules. That is, he analyzes Christ's words and actions by grounding them in the customary and legal codes governing social praxis at the time: Christ eats the passover without the sacrificial lamb because there existed a *mos* allowing him to do so. This concern for the juridical context of narrative, as noted above, characterizes late Renaissance exegesis, directing its research into the Mishnah and Talmud—the central texts of Jewish law.

Selden, for example, includes a striking chapter in his *De jure naturali* (1640) on the legal background for Christ's cleansing of the Temple. Selden argues that, according to Hebraic legal codes, if a private citizen came upon another Jew publicly violating the Law, he could punish him, even by death, on the spot.[79] Such self-appointed defenders of God's majesty were legally recognized as "zealots." In whipping the merchants and moneychangers out of the Temple, Christ acted according to the *jus Zelotarum*; the existence of such a law, acknowledged both by Christ and the Sanhedrin, explains why the latter did not arrest Jesus, who of course lacked any official jurisdiction, for disturbing the peace. The same religious zeal, in fact, motivated the stoning of Saint Stephen and the fury of Caiaphas's officers against Christ.[80] What interests Selden is not the timeless moral exemplarity of Christ's actions but how both Christ and his persecutors behaved according to shared cultural assumptions and, consequently, how Jewish legal codes structure the biblical narrative. In 1640 Selden's observations may also have had a political resonance; given that Selden was a common lawyer and member of the Society of Antiquaries, one is inclined to detect a parliamentarian undertone in his remark that

> it is nothing new for wicked men to conceal their misdeeds under the pretext of some sort of ancestral law, as those wicked men did under pretext of the law of zealotry. But as long as pious and virtuous men used it, who although private citizens were nevertheless warranted by public authority and the customs handed down from their ancestors, it was well done.[81]

This Machiavellian moment hints at the connections between the seventeenth-century obsession with customary law and the new biblical scholarship. In fact, the links between legal historiography and biblical exegesis in the Renaissance are pervasive and methodological. The resistance of legal historians to royal and papal absolutism encouraged them to analyze political bodies in terms of their laws, traditions, and customs rather than their rulers. Both on the Continent and in Britain, the constitutional crises of the late Renaissance lay behind the new interest in ancient constitutions, whether feudal or biblical, directing scholarly attention to the evolution, supersession, and authority of customary law and to the way such codes govern and interpret social praxis.

Kinship and Calendars

The common-law mind tended to view immemorial custom as normative for subsequent practice. This politicized antiquarianism also marks important strands of Renaissance biblical interpretation; witness Andrewes's *A Summary View of the Government both of the Old and New Testament*, which outlines the sacerdotal organization of the Aaronic priesthood as a validating paradigm for Anglican episcopal orders. But Andrewes was a theologian rather than a historical philologist. The later *critici sacri* of Pearson's magisterial compilation, and preeminently Grotius, do not excavate the structures of biblical culture in order to live in them again; they describe the alteriority of antiquity. Their subject matter thus resembles that studied by cultural anthropology: not the normative precedents that interested the common lawyers, nor fairly universal practices like marriage or promise keeping, nor simply odd customs—the sort of thing that fascinated Montaigne—but underlying and culturally specific rules, like kinship laws and temporal categories, which they see as governing both social behavior and narrative form. Grotius, to be sure, invokes such rules to explain textual cruxes, but he grasps the philological occasion as an opportunity to sketch the latent structures of an ancient society; that is, he analyzes texts as part of a cultural economy. Thus, in order to explain the biblical phrase "from the sixth hour" (Matt. 27:45), he provides a brief explanation of the Hebraic system of temporal divisions:

> For this manner of speaking (*mos loquendi*) arose from the customary practice of the Temple, where sacrifices and prayers generally took place at the third, sixth, and ninth hours. . . . Especially on festal days, these times were signified by blowing a trumpet . . . so that these hours might be celebrated by the people, as being of greater importance. (6:958)

One glimpses here momentarily the connection between ritual and chronology, the cultural embeddedness of temporal systems. The detail about the trumpet (*tuba*), which is not required by anything in the biblical text, deepens the sense of historical actuality: the explanation of the rule governing temporal divisions gives way to a brief image of the shofar sounding over ancient Jerusalem as the priests pray and sacrifice in the Temple.

A longer and more complicated passage analyzes the Hebraic rules concerning endogamous and exogamous marriage, which, as Mieke Bal has shown, are a crucial subtext of biblical narrative.[82] Grotius is here dealing with the problem that Matthew derives Christ's genealogy from Joseph, to whom he had no biological connection, rather than from Mary (Matt. 1:16). The Gloss had suggested that Mary and Joseph might have belonged to the same tribe.[83] Grotius rejects this suggestion, showing that in general Jewish marriages were exogamous, but then he goes on to argue that *if* a woman had no brothers she was obliged by the Law to marry her nearest relative (*agnatus proximus*) so that the family's ancestral goods would not pass to strangers. This relative was called a redeemer (*vindicans*), one who married according to the law of inheritance (*hereditario iure ducens*). The law, Grotius notes, is given in Numbers 36:8, but he demonstrates its continued force by analyzing patterns of endogamy and exogamy elsewhere in the Old Testament and Apocrypha, concluding that it remained in effect during the Babylonian Exile, when inheritance of property was no longer a meaningful consideration for the dispossessed tribes, because the emergent hope of a Davidic messiah depended on preserving genealogical continuity.[84] Hence, if Mary were an only child, as the biblical narratives suggest, she would have married not only within her tribe but within the same family; she is related to Joseph and belongs to the same messianic bloodline (6:39–41).

As is often the case, a summary cannot convey the range of historical and philological erudition involved in such an argument. Grotius moves through biblical, Talmudic, and Classical authorities—including Donatus, Demosthenes, Isaeus, Josephus, Origen, Epiphanius, Theodoretus, Chrysostom, the Theodosian Code, Philo, and the Talmudic writers—in order to build his case for the endogamous marriage of only daughters, reconstructing from the scraps and fragments of available evidence the kinship structures of ancient Judaism and their bases in social and religious ideologies. The passage is simultaneously special pleading and investigation of the internal cultural logic structuring social/textual events. It is as if, for Grotius, the textual crux functions as an oddly shaped mound does in archaeology: as the surface manifestation of a buried culture. Hence, exegesis becomes an occasion for anthropology. This sort of inquiry stands in sharp, if implicit, tension to the Reformation program for restoring modern society on the basis of Holy Scripture. Grotius's notes defamiliarize and denaturalize biblical culture—without, however, questioning the sacred authority of the biblical text.

The Mediterranean World in the Age of Christ

A further aspect of Grotius's genealogical investigation deserves mention. At one point, he introduces a Classical witness for the practice of endogamous marriage with the comment that ancient Athenian law derives from the laws of Moses and therefore can be used as evidence for Hebraic culture (6:40). This belief in a fundamental connection between Hebraic and Classical civilizations seems to have been widely shared by late Renaissance scholars, who, however, do *not* cite either Orpheus or the Hermetic corpus—the traditional texts of the ancient theology—which Casaubon had discredited in 1614.[85] But Casaubon himself also hypothesized that Greek derives from Hebrew, and Scaliger's edition of Varro argues at length for the Near Eastern origin of Latin words.[86] Heinsius at one point even conjectured that Homer had read the Old Testament,[87] while both Selden and Grotius defended the tradition that Pythagoras studied among the Jews.

These cultural etiologies, which are rarely worked out in any detail, provided a rationale for the prior methodological intuition, encapsulated in Scaliger's advice to biblical exegetes: "*Lisez les bons auteurs, la Metamorphose d'Ovide, le Thalmud, illa sunt necessaria ad Biblia.*"[88] From Erasmus through the seventeenth century, almost all biblical scholars drew extensively on Classical texts to illustrate biblical customs and usages, generally without theorizing the grounds validating such comparisons.[89] Yet since theological commentators, particularly among Protestants, pointedly did not employ Classical citations, their use among scholarly exegetes (keeping in mind the imprecision of these labels) cannot have been merely reflexive.

Scaliger again appears as a seminal figure. Mark Pattison remarks of the *De emendatione temporum*:

> We are so accustomed to take this point of view of Universal History that we do not readily imagine the effort required to rise to it at a time when the primitive classical ages were imperfectly known, when nothing at all was known of the extra-classical world (Syria, Egypt, etc.), and when between the classical and biblical world an impassable barrier was considered to exist, and it was a cherished principle of Protestant exegesis not to bring any secular knowledge to the interpretation of Holy

Scripture. Scaliger was the first to perceive that the history of the ancient world, so far as it could be known at all, could only be known as a whole.[90]

Scaliger's sense of the interpenetrations of Classical and biblical culture developed along two lines of inquiry.

All the New Testament commentaries recognize that Palestine had been partially hellenized beginning in the third century B.C. and was, during Jesus' lifetime, a Roman province, operating under Roman legal and penal codes—an awareness that can occasionally be found in medieval authors; thus, the twelfth-century *Glossa Ordinaria* (which Erasmus cites without acknowledgment) explains the flagellation of Christ by noting that according to Roman law those sentenced to be crucified were first whipped.[91] Renaissance exegesis complicates and extends this investigation, focusing particularly on the interpenetration of Roman and Hebraic legal and penal institutions. Lipsius's *De cruce* (1593) is a book-length treatment of the death of Christ, analyzing the different types of crucifixion used by the Romans, their legal bases, and the various tortures prefacing their performance.[92] Such research supplements the study of Talmudic law, both functioning to explicate the codes shaping social behavior and, consequently, narrative organization. Thus, Casaubon explains the apparent oddity that, although lacking the right to impose capital punishment, the Sanhedrin nevertheless passed a sentence of death against Christ, by observing that "among the Romans, *inquisitores*, from whom the praetor demanded cognizance of the crime, could establish whether someone were indictable or not; however, the praetor retained the right of pronouncing the final sentence."[93] Similarly, Grotius gives Classical precedents for the way Pilate's soldiers humiliate Christ by dressing him up as a king: Livy and Philo narrate similar events (6:954–55). The recognition that for ancient peoples this sort of mockery had a ritualized, customary aspect replaces the traditional interpretation of the scene as an outburst of savage blasphemy and the *furor impietatis*.[94]

This interest in political symbolism shades over into considerations of political power. Thus, many of the notes dealing with Christ's trial and execution attempt to sort out the competing spheres of imperial and local authority—the structures of power in colonized societies. The nature of the *custodia* sent to apprehend Christ and guard his tomb, for example, occasions a debate on the relations between Roman and Jewish militia: Drusius claiming that the *custodia* formed part of the Temple guard (6:943) against Scaliger, who thinks that "they were Roman soldiers, garrisoned, according to Josephus, in the tower of Antonia" (6:943). Grotius, again citing

Josephus, supplies additional detail, arguing that the guard accompanying Judas to Gethsemane, although perhaps led by Temple officials, was probably composed of Roman soldiers, who were regularly sent from the imperial garrison on high feasts, since the authorities felt that the crowds flocking to Jerusalem required additional police protection. Hence, Jesus calls them "sinners" (Matt. 26:45), the customary Jewish term for those living outside the Law (6:909–10).

Alongside this fairly straightforward clarification of the Roman juridical background to the New Testament, Renaissance exegesis began to explore the murkier terrain of cross-cultural relations. Especially after 1580, biblical scholarship increasingly treated New Testament society as part of ancient Mediterranean civilization, pointing out shared customs, rituals, and codes, sometimes hypothesizing a process of cultural transmission although more often simply remarking on the similarity. Hammond thus notes that the Jewish customs of carrying palm branches and singing were likewise "usual among the Grecians in any time of sacred festivity."[95] In 1572 Pierre Pithou, a French medievalist and friend of Scaliger, published and annotated a late antique manuscript on the parallels between Mosaic law and the Twelve Tables.[96] Other late-Renaissance biblical scholars likewise remarked on the homology between Greco-Roman and Hebraic social conventions: the lustral ceremonies, the twofold ritual meal, the custom of reclining rather than sitting to eat.[97] Almost invariably, the annotated similarities pertain to customs *no longer* practiced in the sixteenth and seventeenth centuries. Rather, such comparisons presuppose what Grotius calls the *"jus vetustissimum apud omnes prope gentes"* (6:216), a sociocultural substrate common to all archaic societies, constituting them as anthropological other rather than the subject of mimetic retrieval; one returns to the source only to discover the estrangement of the past. The Jewish practice of meticulously removing every trace of leavened bread from their houses before the Passover reminds Scaliger of "the scrupulosity of women celebrating the rites of the Bona Dea, who would destroy even a mouse-nest rather than allow a male mouse in such a place."[98] Ancient societies share strange taboos, sometimes savage ones—as when Grotius observes that the notion of a "new testament in Christ's blood" (Matt. 26:28) derives from the widespread ancient custom of ratifying treaties with animal or human sacrifice.

Yet if the perception of the cultural unity of the ancient Mediterranean world exposed the primitive origins of Western civilization, it also revealed the universality of the moral law (*jus naturale*); much of Grotius's *De veritate* is spent showing that Classical poets and philosophers acknowledged the fundamental tenets of Christianity: the existence of God, the immortality of the soul, and similar axioms. Grotius was, in fact, a friend of Edward Herbert and encouraged him to publish his own *De veritate*.[99] Grotius thus seems simultaneously an ancient theologian and an anthropologist—a paradox that the next chapter will attempt to unravel.

The Mirror of History

In his essay on modern biblical scholarship in *The Cambridge History of the Bible*, Alan Richardson remarks that "a new type of exegesis" appeared during the nineteenth century, "namely one which is based upon sound historical scholarship. . . . [It was] no longer possible to treat the words of the Bible as timeless truths addressed to the world at large . . . since their real meaning cannot be understood apart from their historical context."[100] This is not, however, true. Renaissance biblical scholarship is no less historical than the Higher Criticism of the nineteenth century. Their historicisms differ in that after the Renaissance biblical research focused on questions of authorship—on the extratextual site of cultural production rather than the cultural milieu implicit in the text. For example, *Harper's Bible Dictionary*—a fairly standard modern reference work—defines historical criticism as concerned with the "time and place of composition [of a biblical book], the circumstances in which it was produced or written, its author or authors . . . how it came to be written, and the audience(s) to which it was addressed"—all basically questions concerning the author or authors.

Renaissance biblical scholarship does not often deal with such issues—to my surprise, since I began this chapter planning to record the emergence of the subject out of the ashes of medieval allegorical exegesis. This project failed because Renaissance biblical scholarship evinces almost no interest in the intentions, motives, or inner life of either the biblical writers or the texts' sacred personae. Subjectivity dissolves into language and culture—that is, into philological and historical analysis.[101] One almost never finds phrases signaling authorial intention, like "Matthew here attempts to show" or "Luke includes this episode because"—the familiar currency of modern biblical exegesis. Renaissance scholars generally consider the author only as an "authority"—as a passive witness to the events depicted in his narrative and hence the guarantor of its veracity. The author thus pertains to a prefatory note, having no further relevance to the shape of the narrative, which is analyzed as a linguistic and cultural performance.

This lack of interest in the author as a category of explanation corresponds to a lack of interest in either the moral or psychological character of the narrative personae. The notes in the *Critici sacri* deal with alabaster pots, linen undergarments, ritual codes, chronologies, flagella, kinship laws, and lexical glosses; they rarely treat personal agency, and then not directly. Christ's final cry of desolation, "My God, my God, why hast thou forsaken me?"—where one would expect commentators at least to touch upon his sorrow and agony—raises only questions of dialect: is Christ speaking Aramaic or Hebrew?[102] This disappearance of the subject intensifies in Protestant commentaries since they omit the pious fictions concerning Christ's family and friends with which medieval and Roman Catholic exegetes filled the dark background of New Testament narratives. The little intimacies characteristic of Cornelius à Lapide's *Great Commentary*—how "Simon and his friends" feasted Christ, while "Martha ministered at this supper . . . because she was a neighbour"[103]—do not occur in Protestant scholarship. In granting analytic priority to the cultural codes marking the text over both characterization and authorial intention, Renaissance biblical commentaries resemble the new historicisms of the late twentieth century, which may help explain the elective affinity these approaches seem to have for early modern studies.

Yet if the philological antiquarianism of biblical exegesis during the Renaissance seems a distant precursor of modern cultural studies, it is also, at least in one respect, crucially different. We can approach this difference by looking in some detail at Grotius's note on the tearing of the veil concealing the Holy of Holies at the moment of Christ's death (Matt. 27:51). After a somewhat technical discussion of the architecture of the Temple, Grotius remarks that one needs to understand the symbolism of the veil itself in order to understand the significance of its tearing. When the author of Hebrews says that the Holy of Holies

> is a figure of true things (*verorum figura*), namely of the highest heavens, he said nothing new but mentions what would have been known to all Jews, as I shall show by explicit testimonies. Josephus says . . . "the third section of the building . . . was like the heaven set apart for God." . . . Philo, in his life of Moses, [writes] that "the innermost part of the Temple symbolizes the intelligible realm." . . . The objects outside this penetralia not obscurely shadowed forth the visible world. For the red of the veil [signified] fire; the linen, earth; the hyacinth, air; the purple, the sea; the seven lamps, the planets. . . . Therefore it seems fairly clear that the innermost part symbolized the intelligible world. . . . Philo, almost certainly drawing on ancient traditions, says that the *propitiatorium* was a symbol of divine mercy. He thought the Cherubim designated God's creative and kingly powers. . . . Given all this, I think

the significance of the tearing of the veil is not unclear. For it signifies the access opened through the death of Christ—first to Christ himself, and then by his goodness to the saints of the Old and New Covenants—to that invisible heaven which Holy Scriptures call the heaven of heavens, the dwelling place of the Divine Majesty. . . . For the Romans and other gentiles, however, this miracle would not obscurely signify the atrocity of the crime committed against Christ. In a comedy, Philippides, here speaking about Demetrius, who dared to compare himself to the gods, thus says: "the veil was torn because of his impiety." (6:962–63)

The logic of this passage is curious; it begins by trying to establish what the veil would have signified to the Jews of the first century and also attempting to picture it—to give some sense of its historical reality as an object. But it then seamlessly moves into theology, as though cultural symbolism provided access to the eternal wisdom of God—as though there were no veil between the visible and intelligible worlds. The passage ends with a discussion of how the Roman inhabitants of Judea might have understood the miracle, whose historicity Grotius never questions.

The juxtaposition of cultural hermeneutics and theological essentialism here is jarring, since in the modern academy these are ideologically incompatible.[104] Yet Grotius does not even seem to distinguish them as separate discourses; the colorless scholarly Latin of the passage flows across apparent discursive boundaries without the slightest hesitation.[105] Reality is a stylistic effect, and in Grotius the same style serves for miracles and old curtains. The passage pulls one behind the Enlightenment, prior to the moment when the Western intelligentsia turned against their Fathers, shutting up theology from the rest of the *respublica litterarum* behind bars of irony. The deicidal urges characteristic of modern culture are not emergent here; this passage provides singularly little evidence for encroaching skepticism and secularization; it does not belong to post-Enlightenment narratives.[106]

The rhetoric of biblical scholarship does not demystify; it demythologizes sacred history. The implications of this particular discursive rendering of the world are perhaps clearest at its origin: Valla's *Donation of Constantine*, one of the earliest and most brilliant works of cultural analysis. What Valla does, in effect, is identify rhetorical probability with cultural rules and customs. The donation lacks probability because it does not "fit" the cultural logic of the late Roman Empire; it does not square with codes regulating social praxis during that period. The strictly philological aspect of Valla's argument—his demonstration that this forgery was written in medieval Latin—forms only a part of the *Donation*, which also examines how power was customarily transferred under the Empire, what ancient peoples wore on ceremonial occasions, how old coins reflect political history, how the whole texture of late antique culture—its rituals, political organization, dress, laws—bears on historical interpretation. In place of the forged donation's mythic background of virgin-eating dragons and miraculous cures, Valla sets the social fabric of fourth-century Rome, a fabric conspicuously lacking in dragons but stocked with leather neck bands, crescent-shaped shoe ornaments, silk diadems, and horse-cloths.[107] The rhetorical construction of history is thick description, the rendering of cultural artifacts and customs rather than saints and monsters.

Valla's identification of rhetorical probability with the conformity between an event and its cultural milieu—his sense of historical verisimilitude—clarifies the *resonance* of the biblical commentaries, which seem triumphant rather than anxious about their discovery of the historical embeddedness of scriptural narrative. The demonstration that biblical events belong to a specific culture and are governed by its codes renders them alien, but it also makes them seem real, attaches them to the historical world of late antique bedclothes and Roman provincial government rather than the mythic domain of hagiography, fables, and *piae fraudes*.

Both Valla's revolutionary essay and Renaissance biblical scholarship, it seems to me, should be viewed as an episode in the conceptual management of diversity, as a way of categorizing and analyzing the unfamiliar—rather, that is, than as a stage in the gradual secularization of Western culture. The commentaries examined in this chapter differ from earlier texts precisely in their handling of the mass of alien and exotic details unearthed by humanist scholarship. The Renaissance inherited two traditional methods of managing diversity. The first and more familiar erases history, subordinating diversity to repetitive pattern, whether exemplary or typological. Augustine's two cities, Protestant ecclesiology, and the moralized history of humanist pedagogy all construct the past as proleptic repetition rather than linear sequence.[108]

The second method derives from Aristotle's biological works (including the *Problems*), which record the almost limitless variety of habitats, social organizations, sexual preferences, morphological structures, and domestic arrangements found in nature. Aristotle's approach is singularly amoral;

he is not interested in animal behavior as evidence of a normative *jus naturale* or as a model for human society. He simply lists, column after column, the variety and strangeness of things found in nature:

> Some animals at first live in water, and by and by change their shape and live out of water. . . . Furthermore, some animals are stationary, and some move about. . . . Other creatures adhere at one time to an object and detach themselves from it at other times. . . . Again, many animals move by walking as well as by swimming. . . . Some are gregarious, some are solitary. . . . Again, of these social creatures some submit to a ruler, other are subject to no rule. . . . And again, both of gregarious and of solitary animals, some are attached to a fixed home and others are nomadic. . . .
>
> Crabs copulate at the front parts of one another, throwing their overlapping opercula to meet one another. . . . Insects copulate at the hinder end, and the smaller individuals mount the larger; and the smaller individual is the male. The female pushes from underneath her sexual organ into the body of the male above. . . .
>
> Partridges build a nest in two compartments; the male broods on the one and the female on the other. After hatching, each of the parent birds rears its brood. But the male, when he first takes his young out of the nest, treads them.[109]

In the pseudo-Aristotelian corpus, the fascination with heteroclite multiplicity overwhelms Aristotle's taxonomic method; scientific classification dissolves into rehearsing wonders. A randomly selected passage from *On Marvellous Things Heard* thus records:

> 68. They say that the frogs in Cyrene are altogether dumb, and that in Macedonia, in the country of the Emathiotae, the swine have solid hoofs.
> 69. They say that in Cappadocia there are fertile mules, and in Crete black poplars which yield fruit.
> 70. They say also that in Seriphos the frogs do not croak; but if they are transferred to another place they croak.
> 71. Among the Indians, in what is called the Horn, it is stated that there are little fishes, which wander about on the dry land, and run away again into the river.[110]

Wonder, as Bacon noted, is broken knowledge. The listing of curiosities constructs nature as an assemblage of alien and amoral oddities, unstructured by hierarchical order or the cosmological analogies in which "even the least thing in the whole world . . . serveth to minister rules, canons, and laws, for men."[111] Nature here is the principle of heterogeneity rather than plenitude.

This is also the method of Montaigne's "On Cannibals" and "Of Custom"; Montaigne simply transposes the rhetoric of Aristotelian biology to the human sciences, fashioning a litany of the variety and strangeness of things found in culture—a textual *Wunderkammer*.[112] The methodology in both cases is aggregative and paratactic, an encyclopedic "heaping" of unrelated exotic details. This pack-rat accumulation of curiosities and broken pieces of knowledge characterizes empirical and humanistic studies (in contrast to scholastic philosophy) through the sixteenth century. It is endemic to the topical organization recommended in Renaissance rhetorics; Erasmus, for example, proposes this as a model entry: "remarkable longevity, vigorous old age, old head on young shoulders, remarkable happiness, remarkable memory, sudden change of fortune, sudden death, self-inflicted death, horrible death, monstrous births, remarkable eloquence, remarkable wealth, famous men of humble birth, . . . and so on."[113]

Late Renaissance exegesis treats its materials neither as timeless exempla nor isolated curiosities. The difference is evident in Drusius's little essay, written sometime before 1616, on the pre-Christian Hasidim ("Assideans" in the Authorized Version) mentioned in 1 and 2 Maccabees—a strange and unfamiliar item, if not as luridly foreign as cannibals. Rather than either marveling at or moralizing these mysterious Hasids,[114] the essay attempts to untangle their relation to the New Testament Pharisees and to the Essenes ("Hessaei" or "Hesseni") described by Philo and Josephus, in order to elucidate how the various sects and factions are genetically or politically interrelated. He locates the strange name within the ideological configurations of intertestamental Judaism (5:339–52).

Drusius treats the Hasids in terms of their placement within a cultural *syntax*—a system of written and unwritten laws that order items in relation to one another and regulate their interaction. This example, clearly similar to those already discussed, registers a new mode of managing diversity, in which law—or a sort of legal structuralism—replaces heteroclite order and typological pattern. Especially after the middle of the sixteenth century, the philological antiquarianism of earlier Renaissance exegesis modulates into a study of the codes governing social praxis. The commentaries increasingly read unfamiliar detail as participating in a system of rules organizing behavior and discourse in a particular society. To explain something is to discover the culturally specific customs or laws implicit in its alien morphology. The odd details of the text become vestiges of a cultural logic, which in turn renders them intelligible.

In the second half of his essay, Drusius rejects the possibility that the Essenes are simply the Old Testament Nazerites under a different name. Instead, he hypothesizes that they originated in the second century B.C. when the Sadducee high priest Hyrcanus began a fierce persecution of the Pharisees, driving some of them into the woods and deserts where they formed separate communities, which then split off from those Pharisees who chose to temporize rather than flee (5:339–52). Like most late Renaissance exegetes, Drusius views the laws governing praxis as themselves historicized, thus giving cultural forms both a diachronic and synchronic extension. The organization of biblical society is not immutable, not fixed by Mosaic law. Instead, philological inquiry opens out onto the development and structures of late biblical Judaism; the strange bits of nomenclature with their perplexing variants—Hasids, Hessens, Chasids, Assidians, Hessaes—belong to an unfamiliar yet intelligible historical narrative.

As in Valla's *Donation*, the historical estrangement of the text itself endows the events it relates with the solidity and actuality of history. In the mid-seventeenth century, the Dutch Hebraist Coccejus thus defends his rabbinic studies on the grounds that the Talmud supplies "confirmation of the account in the Gospels, where there is abundant mention of Jewish custom, law and traditions."[115] Cultural analysis manages its diverse and strange materials by granting them the plausibility of free-standing form and perspectival space. Yet, as has long been recognized, the mutual entailments of authenticity and estrangement generate the central problematic of Renaissance humanism. The "legal structuralism" of late Renaissance exegesis links this hermeneutic—this mode of handling diversity—to the legal crisis that dominates the *respublica litterarum* in the sixteenth and seventeenth centuries.[116]

Law occupies the troubled center of the Renaissance episteme because the past traditionally bears the character of law; it is binding precedent. This understanding of history suffuses the ideological struggles of the Renaissance and consequently its scholarship. Antiquarian erudition is political knowledge and the narrative legitimation of power. The whole point of Coke's ancient constitution or Baronius's *Annales* depends on the legal, normative force of historical antecedents—the *vetustissimus mos*. But legal historiography, by treating law as a cultural code, operated precisely to remove its deontological authority; the past can be analyzed in terms of law, but it is not a law *for us*. Law thus presents the same ambiguity as

Grotius's veil: it is simultaneously a manifestation of divine reason and a cultural artifact.

Law is the characteristic discipline of the late Renaissance, in much the same way that logic is the characteristic discipline of the Middle Ages: it leaves its mark on other fields of inquiry. Law was of course a specialized field but it was also part of the erudite *encyclios paideia*; Donald Kelley thus notes that during the Renaissance "the study of law, mainly civil law, provided a major source—perhaps the major source—of secular, higher education for European society as a whole."[117] A considerable number of Renaissance exegetes had legal training. Grotius and Selden were prominent jurists; Scaliger and Junius studied with Cujas; Beza, Drusius, Heinsius, and Calvin had brushes with the law—generally, then as now, under parental duress. By the late seventeenth century the undergraduate arts curriculum at Oxford frequently required Justinian's *Institutes* as part of the moral and political knowledge essential for "an accomplished gentleman."[118]

More important, the *duplex sensus* of law, its character as both a normative and empirical science, structures the production of knowledge. The characteristic fields of sixteenth- and early seventeenth-century scholarship locate themselves around this legal dialectic: Coke's ancient constitution, Hooker's laws of ecclesiastical polity, Hotman's study of feudal tenures, the research undertaken by the Society of Antiquaries, the emergent disciplines of international law and medieval customary law, the revival of Thomist and neo-Stoic theories of the *jus naturale*, and Daille's study of the Church Fathers. Even outside history and legal studies, one observes the same tendency to view precedent as simultaneously normative and alien. The tension in humanist poetic between the Classical subtext and its rewriting—between the mimetic imperative and the sensitivity to historical distance—is the literary manifestation of the historico-legal problematic that shapes Renaissance inquiry.[119] The *Poetices libri septem* of the elder Scaliger, with its unresolved mixture of antiquarian erudition and prescriptive legislation, is an utterly typical product. The Renaissance is also the early modern period; rebirth and rupture exist simultaneously.

As these examples indicate, the pursuit of cultural and textual law leads back to the ancient and medieval sources of Renaissance civilization. Contemporary rewritings of the Renaissance have emphasized the role of imperialism in the production of knowledge. However, colonialist discourse in this period lacks a "clear and exclusive Europe/exotic dichotomy"; it tends rather to assimilate the New World peoples to the traditional bricolage of the *Wunderkammer* or invariant categories of human nature.[120] While the museum, with its systematic organization of knowledge, may have been, as Steven Mullaney suggests, the successor of the *Wunder-kammer*'s heterogeneous exotica, one did not evolve from the other.[121] Most museums (until recently) housed the creations of dead, white, Indo-European males, not the *Wunderkammer*'s tribal artifacts. The systematic study of culture during the sixteenth and seventeenth centuries does not reflect on tribal peoples: it analyzes its own progenitors and founding texts. The other, the object of cultural investigation, is also one's ances-tor.[122] Humanist scholarship, struggling to "blaze a path through pseude-pigrapha and textual errors back to the early, incorrupt church" and Classical civilization,[123] is a search for one's real parents, a philological romance. But its own methodology, designed to retrieve the exemplary past from the ravages of time, unearthed alien cultures fixed in time. Yet although unfamiliar, the rediscovered visage remained the face (and law) of the father, remained the matrix of early modern identity. The estrange-ment of the past did not destroy the longing for it.

Erasmus's *Ciceronianus*, which insists on the *essential* rupture between Classical and Renaissance civilization, closes with the curious confession of Erasmus's love for Horace based on a "secret affinity of minds" that obliterates historical distance: "the very thing that delights the reader es-pecially [is] to discover from the language [of the ancient authors] the feel-ings, the characteristics, the judgment, and the ability of the writer as well as if one had known him for years."[124] The sharp sense of separation from the past intensifies the pleasures of intimacy—like finding an old friend in a strange city.

The *duplicity* of the ancestral past during the Renaissance—its double status as mirror and other—constituted it as the site of ideological crisis and therefore also of knowledge. The Renaissance disciplines struggled with the ancestor who is at once normative and unfamiliar, exemplar and foreigner, origin and alien. The *respublica litterarum* was shaped by the tension between the exemplarity and alteriority of its own origins, not the post-Romantic tension between culture and nature—although maybe "tension" is the wrong word, since it implies an achieved polarization, whereas the distinctive characteristic of the Renaissance episteme lies in its imperfect differentiation of essentialist and historicist method, in the failure to polarize the deontological and empirical senses of law: Grotius's veil again.

We need to grasp this failure not as confusion but as enabling a specific *form* of knowledge, a form most fully realized at the intersection of legal, historical, and biblical studies—the point of maximal exemplarity and maximal estrangement . . . the bloody sacrifice of Christ.

2 The Key to All Mythologies

The real religion of nature is not to be found in the optimistic platitudes of Deism but in the dark and bloody superstitions of the heathen.

Christopher Dawson, *The Spirit of the Oxford Movement*

We may begin with two rather lengthy accounts of human sacrifice:

Early peoples grasped instinctively that the more valuable the object they offered to God, the more easily they might obtain forgiveness, especially if the payment were somehow equivalent to the purchase. They therefore began to sacrifice men rather than animals for sin offerings. Caesar explains the rationale in his discussion of the Gauls: "They thought the immortal gods could not be placated unless the life of a man were given for the life of men." The Canaanites (i.e., the Phoenicians) seem to have been the first to practice this; the Bible mentions that they were accustomed to placate Moloch by sacrificing their children. . . . Some of these had been Tyrians, among whom it was anciently customary to sacrifice a free-born boy to Saturn. . . . Carthage, a colony of Tyre, also received this ritual from its founders. . . . Lactantius, citing Pescennius Festus, reports that the Carthaginians immolated two hundred noble children to propitiate the god, whom they believed angry at them. . . . Similarly, the ancient Egyptians sacrificed people, particularly those of exceptional beauty, a practice they maintained up to the time of Amosis, who substituted wax images. . . . In Cyprus likewise a man was slain until the age of King Diphilus, who replaced this with animal sacrifice. Rhodes, Chios, Tenedos, and Salamis had similar rites. . . . The Persians buried men alive. The Albanians in particular were known for sacrificing those believed to possess a special holiness. According to Pausanius, the Ionians sacrificed a maiden and a youth to placate Diana's wrath. We read similar things about the Blemyi, Massagetes, Thracians, Neuri, and the Scythians in general. Thus much may suffice for Asia and Africa, although one might add that explorers found the same rite both in India . . . and in America. In the Canary Islands such practices only recently ceased.

Turning now to Europe: Ister and Apollodorus relate that the Cretans used to sacrifice boys to Saturn and the Spartans to sacrifice men to Mars. The Greeks generally practiced the same custom . . . instances of which can be found up to the times of the Persian Wars. Two Greeks—a male and a female—and likewise two Gauls were annually slain in Rome; Jupiter Latiaris and Diana Aricina were both worshipped with a human victim. Pliny reports that this sort of sacrifice was very common throughout Italy and Sicily at one time . . . and lasted in Gaul up to the principate of Tiberius; thus Cicero notes that the Gauls placated their gods by human victims. . . . The Thracians worshipped Zamolxin in the same fashion—likewise the German cult of Mercury and their other gods. . . . Tacitus and Pliny observe that the same sort of rites were celebrated in Britain. Procopius writes that in the Shetland Islands the same practice continued up to his own day—that is, to the time of Justinian. One finds particular mention of the inhabitants of Marseilles, who, during times of pestilence, used to feed a pauper at public expense and then, having dressed him in sacred branches and priestly garments, they led him through the city accompanied by curses that all the evils of the city might devolve upon him; finally they sacrificed him to the gods. . . . This widespread custom of expiating sins by slaying men or beasts throws considerable light on the nature of expiatory sacrifice and the terminology proper to this subject. . . . Whence now it is easy to understand what is signified when Christ is called a sacrifice for sins or expiatory victim.[1]

It seems instructive to compare this quotation to the second passage:

Human scapegoats . . . were well known in classical antiquity, and even in mediaeval Europe the custom seems not to have been wholly extinct. . . . In the temple of the Moon the Albanians of the Eastern Caucasus kept a number of sacred slaves. . . . When one of these men exhibited more than usual symptoms of inspiration or insanity . . . the high priest had him bound with a sacred chain and maintained him in luxury for a year. At the end of the year he was anointed with unguents and led forth to be sacrificed. . . . Then the body was carried to a certain spot where all the people stood upon it as a purificatory ceremony. This last circumstance clearly indicates that the sins of the people were transferred to the victim, just as the Jewish priest transferred the sins of the people to the scapegoat by laying his hands on the animal's head. . . . We have here an undoubted example of a man-god slain to take away the sins and misfortunes of the people.

The ancient Greeks were also familiar with the use of a human scapegoat. . . . Whenever Marseilles, one of the busiest and most brilliant of Greek colonies, was ravaged by a plague, a man of the poorer classes used to offer himself as a scapegoat. For a whole year he was maintained at the public expense, being fed on choice and pure food. At the expiry of the year he was dressed in sacred garments, decked with holy branches, and led through the whole city, while prayers were uttered that all the evils of the people might fall on his head. He was then cast out of the city or stoned to death by the people outside of the walls. The Athenians regularly maintained a number of degraded and useless beings at the public expense; and when any calamity . . . befell the city, they sacrificed two of these outcasts as scapegoats. One of the victims was sacrificed for the men and the other for the women. . . . The city of Abdera in Thrace was publicly purified once a year, and one of the burghers, set apart for the purpose, was stoned to death as a scapegoat or vicarious sacrifice for the life of all the others.[2]

One notes some stylistic differences between the two passages; the prose of the second excerpt is more luxuriant and richer in cultural detail. But the overall similarity seems evident. Both contain the same lists of ancient or primitive sacrificial rituals, the same marshaling of ethnographic evidence to support a general theory about the expiatory-apotropaic function of sacrifice, the same implication that Christianity properly belongs among the ancient religions of human sacrifice. The second passage comes from Frazer's *Golden Bough*, first published in 1880. But the first was written over two and a half centuries earlier; it appears in the final chapter of Hugo Grotius's *De satisfactione Christi*, published in 1617, a work that Jaroslav Pelikan calls "one of the most important theories in the whole history . . . of the atonement," although, like every other commentator on this text, he does not mention the contents of this last chapter.[3] The quotation from Frazer presents little problem; the role of this sort of comparative anthropology in the late nineteenth century seems relatively obvious. But what is it doing barely a year before the Synod of Dort? Granted that, as Foucault observes, during the Renaissance "resemblance played a constructive role in the knowledge of Western culture," how does one get from the magical and hermetic analogies cited by Foucault (or Tillyard, for that matter) to the ethnographic parallels of comparative religion? Why does Grotius locate the Crucifixion in the context of primitive scapegoat rituals and human sacrifice?

Grotius's treatise is now virtually unknown, although it was translated into English at least twice—once in the late seventeenth century and again in 1889—and its theory of the Atonement influenced Restoration Anglicanism, Methodism, and New England Calvinism.[4] But the afterlife of *De satisfactione* is not our present concern. Rather, this strange piece of theology interests me for three reasons: it clarifies the relation between Renaissance jurisprudence and historiography sketched in the previous chapter; it exemplifies the pivotal role of biblical scholarship in the transition from medieval to modern habits of thought—in particular, the paradoxical birth of "modern" theoretical and comparativist methods out of Grotius's attempt to defend Christian orthodoxy *against* "modern" ethical rationalism; and, finally, it discloses the centrality of sacrifice in the legal, theological, and political controversies of the late Renaissance.

The full title of Grotius's work is *Defensio fidei catholicae de satisfactione Christi adversus Faustum Socinum*. It is, as the title suggests, a defense of the orthodox theology of the Atonement against the heretical *De Jesu Christo servatore* of Faustus Socinus, a sixteenth-century anti-Trinitarian and Erasmian rationalist of the same stripe as Castellio and Servetus. Grotius, then thirty-four years old and a pensionary of Rotterdam, undertook the piece in the year before Dort to repel accusations that the Remonstrants—the Arminian party to which Grotius belonged—were fundamentally Socinians. Hence, in order to understand Grotius's arguments, it is necessary to untangle a bit of this theological background, especially Socinus's quarrel with the Anselmian analysis of the Atonement, an analysis that had passed, with some modifications, into Reformed orthodoxy.

Economics, Politics, and the Law

Drawing on analogies borrowed from Roman private law and probably also feudal custom, Anselm's massively influential eleventh-century *Cur Deus Homo* describes how man failed to pay God the honor owed him and thus "robs God of his own and dishonors him"; man therefore stands obliged both to pay back the original debt and provide a recompense satisfactory to the injured party or creditor.[5] Since man can do neither, God would justly punish him with eternal death, but in his mercy instead appoints the innocent man-god to pay "for sinners what he owed not for himself" by giving something (namely, his life) "to the honor of God, which he did not owe as a debtor."[6]

Socinus's critique of this account is a classic statement of theological rationalism, strongly ethical and hostile to any quasi-mystical notions of substitution, participation, or vicarious punishment. He begins by arguing that since God is lord and owner of all things (*omnium Dominus*), he could simply have remitted the debt at his pleasure, without requiring Christ's death; a creditor may always forgive what is owed to him. Furthermore, penal satisfaction must be personal since, unlike debts, corporal punishments cannot be transferred; conversely, it would have been unjust for God to have imputed all human sins to Christ since imputation "is not a mere matter of the Divine will . . . [but] involves the rights of individuals, and demands a sufficient cause, in fact desert (*meritum*)."[7] Christ therefore did not die for our sins, nor did his death procure divine forgiveness. Rather, the Crucifixion demonstrates God's power and love, while Christ's patient and faithful suffering on the cross provides a good *exemplum*, designed to inspire people to act virtuously and hence deserve forgiveness. Faith, according to Socinus, justifies because it makes us just.

The first part of Grotius's essay is fairly straightforward. It undertakes to neutralize Socinus's objections by replacing the Anselmian argument Socinus had savaged with a more defensible and morally coherent account of the Atonement in terms of Roman public law (which includes criminal law) and Aristotelian political theory. Anselm had also borrowed arguments from Roman law, but only from Roman private law, which deals with matters of debt and payment. Grotius rejects the private law analogy and therefore Anselm's whole notion of sin as a debt owed to God as creditor or rightful owner (*dominus*). Instead, Grotius maintains that God should be viewed as a ruler (*rector*) and therefore as one obliged to punish criminals in order to preserve the common good of the state by instilling respect for the law.

Grotius's argument differs from *all* prior theories of the Atonement in that it does not regard the universe as the private property of God; he is not a *dominus*, not the lord and owner. Instead, God stands in a "political" relation to the world, which he, like Aristotle's ideal king, rules for the common good of its citizens, not as his own domain. This distinction between public and private law—or, put another way, between politics and economics—exactly parallels the early modern differentiation of public power from property and office from fief.[8] Anselm's theory presupposes the feudal assimilation of government to property; conversely, Grotius's sharp distinction between *rector* and *dominus* reflects the early modern transformation of kingdoms into nation-states.

If God is viewed as *rector* rather than *dominus*, then in dealing with human sins he is not, contra Anselm, the injured party; as Grotius notes, a plaintiff may neither punish nor forgive crimes. Here again one notes the theological replication of the emergent separation between political and economic spheres—between crimes against the state, which demand punishment, and injuries to private individuals, which require compensation. God does not punish in order to revenge an injury against himself or to exact payment of a debt but "*ad boni ordinis conservationem*" (317). And precisely because God acts as *rector* rather than a private individual, he may not simply permit crime to remain unpunished.

> Laws of property and debt are based on a relation of a thing to a person; criminal law, however, on the relation of one thing to another, namely the adequation of the punishment to the offense in a way agreeable to public order and the common good. Hence it is simply untrue . . . that the state commits no injustice if it pardons an offender. . . . Part of the justice of a ruler is to preserve even positive laws and ones he has promulgated . . . as the jurists have proven. (317)

Because criminal law is impersonal, the *rector* cannot arbitrarily suspend it but must govern according to the law in the interest of the commonwealth—an argument familiar from countless humanist tracts on political theory.

However, Grotius continues, he may moderate the penalty prescribed by law or impose additional conditions, since "the act of enforcing or relaxing the law is not an act of unrestricted property rights (*absolutum dominium*) but an *actus imperii*, which properly pertains to the protection of good order" (317). What God possesses is not *dominium* but *imperium*—the central concept in Roman public law.[9] Hence, in the Atonement, God exercises his *imperium* by relaxing the universal sentence of death the law imposed on humankind for the sin of Adam and substituting the Crucifixion as a minatory exemplum—again, a notion derived from Roman law.[10]

This is the governmental theory of the Atonement, which implies, one notes, an account of law and sovereignty virtually identical to that given by Hooker in the last book of *The Laws of Ecclesiastical Polity*.[11] Yet if Grotius's sacred polity "reflects" its temporal counterpart, it is not therefore a symbolic projection of the social order—not, that is, a Durkheimian myth. Grotius's argument relies on theoretical modeling, not totemic tropes. The terminology and principles of political jurisprudence provide both a language of analysis and an ethical framework, in terms of which the Atonement appears morally coherent insofar as it can be shown to conform to Roman law.

For example, Socinus argued that remission (*remissio*) excludes, by definition, any notion of payment (*solutio*); hence, if God promises remission of sins, he cannot also require Christ's death as the price of this forgiveness. Grotius responds by analyzing the legal modes of canceling an obligation or penalty described in the *Corpus juris civilis*: *liberatio, novatio, satisfactio, acceptilatio,* and *solutio* (319–20). Socinus, he points out, incorrectly treats the Atonement as an instance of *acceptilatio* or the formal discharge from a debt, a procedure that applies only to private law. Rather,

the Atonement should be understood in terms of the legal mechanisms involved in a case where a person, instead of paying what is owed (*solutio*),
offers an alternative recompense or has someone else offer it on his behalf
(*satisfactio*).[12] If the ruler (or creditor, in cases of debt) agrees to accept this
partial compensation, he is properly said to remit or relax (*remissio* has
both senses) the punishment. Hence, according to the principles of Roman
law, remission does not exclude some sort of antecedent payment, so that
God does not act unjustly in requiring the death of Christ as an exemplary
satisfaction offered in place of the eternal death all persons deserve as punishment for their sins.

In light of recent scholarship on Roman law during the Renaissance,
this is an odd argument and requires explanation. Modern historians have
viewed the emergence of legal historiography in the early sixteenth century as the seminal episode in the formation of a modern historicist consciousness. The currently accepted narrative of this episode describes how
medieval secular jurisprudence, which reached its fullest development in
the fourteenth-century commentaries of Bartolus of Saxoferrato, invested
the *Corpus juris civilis* with a universally valid *auctoritas*. Beginning in the
late fifteenth century, however, humanist scholars like Valla, Bude, and
Alciato gradually realized that Roman law belonged to a prior civilization,
that its principles were contingent, grounded in a specific culture, and
hence no longer applicable to modern society.[13] This historicization of
Roman law was already underway by the first half of the sixteenth century and reached maturity in the midcentury works of Cujas and Hotman.
The development of comparative jurisprudence and international law in
the writings of Bodin and Grotius, according to this interpretation, rises
on the ruins of Bartolism.

Therefore, it is surprising to find Grotius in 1617 still presupposing the
normative authority of Roman law, which he considers uniquely equitable
(*aequitatis plenissima*; 330, 314). This is matter out of place, not perhaps
as strikingly so as the comparative study of ancient sacrificial rituals, but
still unexpected terrain. It may be the case that Renaissance theology per-
sisted in employing a basically medieval approach to law; patristic and
medieval theologians frequently used legal analogies. Were Grotius not
already by 1617 one of the more distinguished jurists in Europe, his re-
liance on Roman law could be explained as a pious anachronism and hence
evidence of the inability of religious thought to assimilate the new sciences of the early modern era. But perhaps there is other game afoot. In
such perplexities, it seems necessary to reexamine the uses of Roman law

during the Renaissance—and simultaneously the modern narrativization of the Renaissance in terms of the birth and triumph of historicism.

And so on into the first of several scholarly labyrinths.

Roman Law in the Renaissance

A historicist approach to Roman law unquestionably did develop at the University of Bourges during the sixteenth century. But it developed contemporaneously with the reception of Roman law, which in 1495 became the common law of the Holy Roman Empire and which (except in England and, to a lesser extent, France) remained the official legal code during the Renaissance throughout Europe. Furthermore, the medieval attitude toward Roman law (known as the *mos italicus* or Bartolism) continued to be the dominant approach to practical jurisprudence. The new humanist legal studies (the *mos gallicus*) had some influence on legal practice; they led to greater purity of style, better texts, and sounder erudition. But they did not fundamentally alter the analytic and ahistorical methods of the Civilians.[14] The University of Orleans, where Grotius did his legal training, remained a Bartolist institution. As late as the early seventeenth century, Leiden was still publishing new works in the tradition of the *mos italicus*.[15] This approach was only gradually and partially replaced in the middle of the seventeenth century, not by humanist jurisprudence per se but by the codification of national customs and the rise of natural law theory.[16] All of this has led one distinguished legal historian to conclude that "the persistence of the ideas and methods of the glossators and post-glossators throughout Europe in the sixteenth and early seventeenth centuries, at a time when the ideas and methods of the Renaissance were spreading and leaving their mark on modern society, is one of the most remarkable aspects of European history."[17]

With respect to Roman law, one cannot disentangle this dialectic into a professional split between humanists and lawyers. A deep respect for Roman law—not only as a historical document but as an equitable and functional legal code—surfaces in unexpected quarters. The magisterial Reformers stressed the authority of the *Corpus juris civilis*, partly as an alternative to canon law (which Luther publicly burned), partly as a counterpoise to the turbulent energies stirred up by the Reformation. In the aftermath of the Peasants' Revolt, Luther affirmed that the Romans "had an excellent legal and judicial system, one based on reason. . . . Our German state must and shall base itself on Roman, imperial law, which is also our wisdom and law, given to us by God."[18] Melanchthon made the same points, although at greater length and in humanistic Latin. Between 1525 and 1550 he delivered a series of orations describing Roman law as essentially just and rational.[19] In 1537 he devoted a lecture to the praise of Bartolus. But Melanchthon had originally been a legal humanist. He moved from a historicist jurisprudence to the belief that Roman law should be considered the authoritative code of the Empire—evidence that in the sixteenth century one could travel the road from Bologna to Bourges in both directions.[20]

Calvin, who was both a lawyer and a humanist, shared this extraordinary reverence for Roman law. "If," he wrote, "we believe that the spirit of God is the sole source of truth, and neither reject nor condemn that truth where ever it appears . . . will we deny that the truth radiates out in the ancient juriconsults who established civil order and discipline with such equity?" Like James I, Calvin considered Roman law the common law of Europe; in Geneva he generally replaced the old canon law with Justinian's *Corpus*.[21]

Even more curiously, legal humanists themselves, including those trained at Bourges, continued to attribute a practical and contemporary importance to Roman law. This is obviously not true of all legal humanists: Cujas considered the *Corpus juris civilis* exclusively as a historical document; at least in the *Anti-Tribonianus*, Hotman is vociferously anti-Romanist. Moreover, legal humanists generally had little appreciation for medieval commentaries on Roman law. But Cujas and the postglossators did not occupy the only available ideological positions. It seems clear that other legal humanists valued Roman law as a living jurisprudence—not because it was the law of the Empire but because it was intrinsically rational; or, in Dumoulin's elegant chiasmus, *non ratione imperii sed rationis imperio*.[22]

The *mos gallicus* has, in fact, two sides: one, the historicist, has already been mentioned; but beginning with Duaren, a professor at Bourges, and Connanus, a student of Alciato, a second rival to the *mos italicus* emerged. This new approach to Roman law, which deeply influenced subsequent legal practice and theoretical developments, involved the systematic reorganization of Roman law along Ramist lines. It was an attempt to articulate the inner structures and connections implicit in the *Corpus*, to reorganize Justinian's hodgepodge compilation into a coherent exposition unfolding from first principles into their increasingly particularized ramifications. It was therefore, to use the terminology of nineteenth-century German legal historians, "synthetic," interested in the relation of the parts to the whole rather than the separate intricacies of each specific title—the vermiculate analytic method of medieval legal scholasticism.

Donellus, a student of Duaren at Bourges and later professor of law at Leiden, was the most important of the systematizers.[23] In his *Commentarii de jure civili*, published between 1589 and 1591, Donellus undertook the unprecedented task of totally restructuring the contents of Roman law to form "a perfect, universal system." But such a project, one fundamentally opposed to Cujas's antiquarian concern for the ancient sources of the *Corpus*, makes sense only because Donellus still considered Roman law a living jurisprudence, not a historical document. "I do not," he writes in his preface to the *Commentarii*, "at all repudiate the civil law composed by the order of Justinian. On the contrary, I strive with all my might for its retention."[24] The preface as a whole is a sweeping defense of (in his words) the intrinsic justice, beauty, and majesty of Roman law.[25]

It seems hard to agree with Julian Franklin, one of the few modern scholars to mention this systematic school, that it was principally significant insofar as it (unintentionally) assisted in discrediting Roman law.[26] Rather, Donellus's immensely influential work revitalized the authority of the *Corpus*. By treating it as an abstract and generalized system rather than a collection of particular rules, he made Roman law into a legal theory and hence available for further theoretical appropriation—understanding "theory" here in Jonathan Culler's sense as those "works that succeed in challenging and reorienting thinking in fields other than those to which they ostensibly belong."[27] Grotius's application of Roman law to theology in *De satisfactione* employs just such theorizing.

Nor was *De satisfactione* an anomalous instance. Rather, it participated in a general tendency in the late Renaissance to use Roman law as the theoretical basis for the development of new disciplines. For example, both in France and the Empire, the initial codification of customary law was often carried out by civil lawyers along Romanist lines. Thus, Dumoulin's study of the French constitution, as Myron Gilmore remarks, applied "Roman law without historical sense to contemporary and general theory," a method frequently known as neo-Bartolism.[28] A similar transposition appeared in international law and comparative political science—the two major new disciplines of the late sixteenth century. One can thus view the developments in late Renaissance legal and political philosophy as theoretical extensions of Roman law now regarded as an abstract and unitary system—and hence argue that legal humanism served as the matrix not only of historicism but also of theory.

Thus, in *Europa und das römische Recht*, still the best study of the topic, Paul Koschaker points out that the actual substance of international law in the works of Gentili, Grotius, and their successors is in fact Roman law.[29] This application of Roman law to international relations assumes the inherent rationality of the former. Alberico Gentili's *De jure belli* (1598), one of the most important pre-Grotian studies of international law, observes that the general acceptance of Roman civil law demonstrates that it possesses natural reason and therefore can provide a framework for the development of a *jus inter gentes*.[30] Grotius makes the same point in *The Jurisprudence of Holland* (c. 1619–1621), describing Roman law as "full of wisdom and equity."[31] But this application also involves a more specific and complex kind of borrowing. The middle sections of *De jure belli ac pacis* include, as one of Grotius's biographers observes, an entire "body of municipal law, private and public—the rights and obligations of persons—and have nothing to do with international law as we understand it."[32] This municipal (and largely Roman) law enters Grotius's text because his analysis of international law rests on treating states as quasi persons and thus applying to national conflicts the rules pertaining to civil and criminal law. The procedure here is clearly similar to that operative in *De satisfactione*; by transposing Roman law to fields other than those to which it ostensibly belongs, both theology and international law employ theoretical modeling, in much the same way that transposing psychoanalysis or Marxism to literary interpretation presently constitutes critical theory.

Roman law also structured the new science of politics.[33] The generalization of Roman law as the basis of a universal and comparative system of jurisprudence underlies the method of the neo-Bartolists: Dumoulin, Hotman, and, above all, Bodin. They form a deliberate countermovement to the historicist and antiquarian tendencies of Cujas and his followers, a movement designed to refute charges that Roman law had become irrelevant in postclassical society.[34] At the same time, they did not regard the *Corpus* as an authoritative text, as did the medieval Civilians; rather, like Donellus, they viewed Roman law as containing principles of abiding validity that could be distilled and employed as the framework for a comprehensive jurisprudence grounded in the comparative study of all known systems of law. Hence, in neo-Bartolism the terms and concepts of Roman law became detached from their specific contexts in the *Corpus* and began to operate as generalized philosophic terminology—as theory. In the *Methodus*, for example, Bodin borrows Roman legal categories like *merum imperium* to structure his analysis of sovereignty, arguing "from the Roman constitution to a general philosophy of the state,"[35] just as Grotius argues from the Roman constitution to a civic theology of the Atonement.

It seems fairly obvious by now that Grotius's use of Roman law as the basis for theological argument need not be viewed as a residual reflex of prehistoricist method. The appropriation of Roman law as a theoretical instrument—what Donald Kelley calls the "transcendent impulse" in Renaissance legal humanism[36]—presided over the morphology of both politics and theology in the late Renaissance, providing not only a terminology for the analysis of social praxis—the conceptualization of debt, credit, power, punishment, and obligation—but also a generally accepted statement of the moral rules governing such practices. That is, Roman law functioned as both a descriptive and a normative science; it was open to theorization precisely because it was felt to embody rational principles of justice and fairness.

Hence, the contradiction that Anthony Grafton notes between the historicist tendencies of Renaissance humanism and its commitment to the universal, exemplary significance of antiquity should not (at least not with respect to legal humanism) be construed as a conflict between progressive and traditional hermeneutics.[37] The transformation of Roman law from a textual *auctoritas* to an instrument of theoretical analysis is as properly a Renaissance phenomenon as the recognition of the law's contingent contexts. And both are potentially forms of demythologization.

Law and Theology

To some extent, by the sixteenth century this extension of Roman legal principles to new areas of inquiry was scarcely a novel development. As Harold J. Berman has shown in his splendid *Law and Revolution*, Roman law enabled the rationalization (in the Weberian sense) of social relations that emerged quite suddenly in the eleventh century.[38] In theology the appropriation of Roman law occurred even earlier. Beginning with Tertullian and Ambrose, the Western Church drew key theological concepts from Roman law in order to describe the transaction involved in Christ's sacrifice; Tertullian, Ambrose, Anselm, and Thomas all treated the Atonement as a species of *satisfactio*.[39] However, at least in theology, the extent of this rationalization ought not be exaggerated. Before Grotius, the borrowings from Roman law were usually unsystematic, closer to nonce analogies than theorization. As Amos Funkenstein has noted, "Within the Aristotelian and Scholastic tradition, it was forbidden to transplant methods and models from one area of knowledge to another, because it would lead to a category-mistake."[40] Furthermore, figurative and narrative (that is, mythic) explanation survived as a theological hermeneutic through the Reformation. According to a sober and learned seventeenth-century Anglican bishop, the Atonement relates how Christ "stepped betweene the blow and us, and latched it in his owne body and soule, even the dint of the fiercenesse of the wrath of God."[41] In Calvin's version of the story, the Crucifixion "was an astonishing display of the wrath of God that he did not spare even his only begotten Son, and was not appeased in any other way than by that price of expiation."[42]

But Calvin also betrays a certain discomfort with his own narrative, remarking in the *Institutes* that, properly speaking, since God gave his only begotten Son in order to redeem humanity, he must have "embraced us with his free favor" prior to being appeased by Christ's expiatory death. God would not have willed the Crucifixion had his wrath not already been mollified. Calvin justifies his own mythic representation, however, as a rhetorical strategy:

> Expressions of this sort have been accommodated to our capacity. . . .
> For example, suppose someone is told . . . that he was estranged from
> God through sin, is an heir of wrath, subject to the curse of eternal
> death, excluded from all hope of salvation, beyond every blessing of
> God, the slave of Satan . . . and that at this point Christ interceded as
> his advocate . . . that he purged with his blood those evils which had
> rendered sinners hateful to God. . . . Will the man not then be even
> more moved by all these things which so vividly portray the greatness
> of the calamity from which he has been rescued?[43]

Calvin's admission that this language, which he chooses to retain, is only an accommodation, that it cannot articulate the actual motives and principles operative in the Atonement, is as close as one comes in Protestant orthodoxy to finding a recognition of the rational insufficiency of traditional theological discourse. Grotius's use of Roman law, in turn, marks a significant departure from earlier Protestant versions of the Atonement because it self-consciously demythologizes theological explanation. The juridic rationalization of Christian doctrine found in the opening chapters of Grotius's *De satisfactione* takes the place of wrathful fathers appeased by filial submission, knights rescuing prisoners from the powers of darkness, and feudal lords with an overdeveloped sense of personal honor. It is an attempt to analyze Christ's death in terms of coherent and widely accepted normative principles, an attempt to replace myth with theory.

The Subject of Substitution

De satisfactione appears to have a three-part structure, each section circling closer and closer to the problem of sacrifice. The first part, chapters 1 through 3, deals primarily with the governmental theory of the Atonement: God, acting as *rector*, relaxes the penalty due to sin but wills the death of Christ as an exemplary deterrent. But this fairly clear-cut application of jurisprudence to theology is followed by a more problematic section on substitution—that is, the ethical and legal grounds for punishing an innocent person for someone else's crime. Socinus found the whole business of vicarious punishment morally revolting, to which Grotius responds that "it belongs to the essence of punishment that it be inflicted on account of sin; but it is not likewise essential that it be inflicted on the one who sinned" (313). His arguments for this rather startling proposition fall into two main classes. He first maintains that when a "mystical conjunction" exists between persons, one may bear the punishments due to the other; hence, children may be punished for the sins of their parents, and the people for those of their prince (312).

> On account of the deed of Cham, Canaan was accursed (Gen. 9:25). On account of the deed of Saul, his sons and grandsons were hung with God's approval (2 Sam. 21:8, 14). On account of the deed of David, seventy thousand perished, and David exclaims "I have sinned and committed iniquity; but these lambs, what have they done?" (2 Sam. 24:15, 17). . . . In the Greek cities it was customary to kill the children of tyrants along with the tyrants themselves. . . . It can be seen from these examples that the conjunction of persons alone, without any consent, sufficed for punishment. (312–14)

The second argument rests on legal precedent: namely, that the Greeks and Roman generally allowed substitution. In Roman law, sureties could be mulcted for debtors and thieves (313); all ancient peoples justified the killing of hostages; both Greeks and Romans required the life of the surety (*vas*) if he failed to produce the guilty party in court (314); and the Roman legions practiced decimation, where soldiers could be executed not only for their own wrongdoing but for a crime committed by their fellow soldiers as well (315). Hence, Grotius concludes, neither God, nature, nor the *consensus gentium* consider substitute punishment unjust (315).

There is, however, as Grotius admits, a problem with this argument: the *Corpus juris civilis* explicitly forbids the substitution of *corporal* punishments, the only case directly relevant to the Crucifixion.[44] According to

Justinian's text, although a surety could be forced to pay another's debts or restore the value of stolen property, he could not be physically punished for someone else's crime (313). Likewise, Roman law also denied that children could inherit their parents' punishments (314).

Grotius attempts to mitigate the force of these counterexamples by relocating the moral basis of substitution in the individual's willingness to be sacrificed for another rather than in the mystical unity of the group. He thus points out that all ancient law, including Roman law, allowed the substitution of corporal punishments if the victim consented, even if the consent were only implicit; the Romans, for example, had no problem with killing hostages.[45] But the biblical examples of substitution do not involve the victim's consent; rather, as Grotius himself observes, they presuppose only the notion of a mystical conjunction between the members of a family or community.

More difficulties arise from the fact that Christian jurisprudence also prohibits one person from assuming another's corporal punishment. Grotius does not specify his legal sources here, apparently considering the prohibition too well known to require documentation. He simply remarks that, unlike ancient peoples, Christians cannot legally or morally volunteer to lay down their lives for another (314–15).[46] If the biblical examples tend to pull Grotius's rationalized account of legal, consensual substitution back toward murkier notions of mystical bodies, this prohibition only deepens the rift between substitution and moral rationality by eliminating even consensual substitution from Christian (and therefore culturally accepted) practice. The arguments in these chapters seem finally to expose what they were intended to eliminate: the incommensurability between the logic of substitution and normative legal principles.

Taken in isolation and at this historical distance, Grotius's arguments for penal substitution seem merely dubious. The text does not inform the reader whether its claims are simply an ad hoc response to Socinus (the typical Renaissance rhetorical strategy of attacking with whatever ammunition comes to hand and hoping something hits the target) or whether they have a historical context, whether they belong to a broader discussion, which might illuminate their implications and point. Like most Renaissance writers, Grotius rarely notes his debts to contemporary authors. The chapters on substitution in *De satisfactione* mention a variety of Classical sources, principally Plutarch's "On the Delays of the Divine Vengeance," which gives Grotius's arguments for the mystical ties of kin and community that justify punishing one member of a family or state for the crimes committed by another. But since an ancient source is still not a context, these borrowings do not explain very much.

The search for context takes us back to Roman law—and, interestingly, to England. Grotius's most important predecessor in the field of international relations was the Oxford regius professor of civil law Alberico Gentili, an Italian Protestant, whose major work, *De jure belli*, appeared in three parts between 1588 and 1589 and then in a single-volume revised version in 1598. Grotius knew Gentili's work prior to writing *De satisfactione* since he cites him in *De jure praedae*, composed around 1604. And *De jure belli* contains a defense of penal substitution. Almost all of Grotius's arguments, including the references to Plutarch, appear in Gentili, who is, of course, not discussing the Atonement but the rules of warfare. Gentili maintains that Roman law and the laws of nature allow children to be punished for the sins of their parents because the family forms a mystical body in which the child is a part of the parent. Likewise, a nation may be punished for wrongs committed centuries earlier since states "are in a certain sense immortal."[47] Furthermore, Gentili claims, it is permissible to kill hostages, even if they are innocent, which, he notes, "seems even to me cruel" but is nevertheless "both just and expedient. . . . Every great principle has some element of injustice, in which the loss of the individual is compensated by the public advantage."[48]

In 1604 Gentili took up the problem of penal substitution again in a commentary on the *lex Julia maiestatis* (title 48.4 of the *Digest*), which deals with the penalties for treason. Chapter 7 of this work covers the permissibility of punishing children for their father's crimes, chapter 9 the legal and moral grounds for transferring penalties from the responsible party to someone else. The arguments, although more technical, follow those found in *De jure belli*. In particular, Gentili emphasizes that substitution presupposes a *"conjunctio"* between the offender and the victim, since "one person cannot be held for another . . . if he is wholly other." But children, who are "inseparable parts of their parents"—as well as spouses, kin, friends, and fellow citizens—participate in a corporate identity that, in turn, sanctions punishing one member of the *conjunctio* for the offenses committed by another member.[49] In crimes involving treason, civil revolt, and warfare, corporal as well as monetary penalties become transferable.[50]

Gentili was not the only Renaissance thinker concerned with the legality of vicarious punishment; the killing of hostages and the heritability of delict seem to have been standard topics in international law. What distinguishes Gentili is that he was apparently the *only* Renaissance jurist to sanction penal substitution. The great Spanish theological jurists Domingo de Soto and Francisco de Vitoria, whose works Grotius also knew, state unequivocally that neither hostages nor the children of an enemy can be killed, even if the welfare of the state depends on it.[51] Gentili himself makes it perfectly clear that most Classical authorities disallowed substitution. The 1589 version of the third book of *De jure belli* presents the issue *in utramque partem*, citing the opinions of Arrian, Cicero, Josephus, and Seneca *against* any form of vicarious punishment.[52] And in *De jure belli ac pacis* (1625), Grotius himself argues emphatically that "it is impossible that an innocent person should suffer for another's crime."[53]

But Grotius then has to reconcile this theorem with the Old Testament passages where God threatens to punish children for the sins of their fathers; *De jure belli ac pacis* sidesteps the apparent contradiction by conceding that God "has full sovereign dominion over both our lives and possessions, as being his gift, which he may take away from any one without giving any reason and whenever he pleases. . . . But such acts of God should not be imitated by men."[54] That is, by 1625 the project of *De satisfactione* has collapsed: divine justice is not the same as human justice; God is no longer viewed as the *rector* of the universe, entrusted with enforcing or mitigating intelligible laws, but as its *dominus*, the owner of human property which He may dispose of at his pleasure. One catches a glimpse here of one of the issues threading through Renaissance discourses of substitution and sacrifice. They grapple with Protestant voluntarism, with the problematic fissure between the dictates of right reason and divine will. Sacrificial narrative, as will become evident when we turn to Buchanan's *Jephthah*, broods on the heteronomous God of Scotus and Calvin.

The problem of divine heteronomy belongs to a later chapter. At this point, what has become clear is that the analysis of substitution in *De satisfactione* incorporates contemporary debates in international law. As in its opening chapters on the *rector* and relaxation of punishment, this juridic context profoundly affects traditional theological language by locating the structures of redemption in a discursive field composed of decimations, the obligations of hostages and sureties, treason laws, and related social facts. It thus represents penal substitution not as a unique and mysterious divine act but as a rather common ancient practice—but not necessarily a morally defensible practice. Most theologians and jurists considered it unjust. The arguments that Grotius takes from Gentili thus provide a rather fragile and contested peg on which to hang one's theology.

Moreover, the fact that penal substitution was not generally practiced or permitted in the Renaissance alters the logical function of Roman law in

De satisfactione. Inasmuch as Roman law allows substitution under certain conditions, it ceases to function as a universally valid theoretical structure. Instead, Grotius seems to imply that both ancient history and Roman law serve less as normative paradigms than as evidence for an archaic code: the Atonement becomes *historically* intelligible insofar as one grasps that the New Testament presupposes a cultural milieu where penal substitution was in fact normal legal practice. Ancient customs and codes thus explicate theology because they supply documentary evidence for the moral logic of premodern societies and *not* because they state universally valid principles. Grotius's argument, that is, hinges on the *duplex sensus* of law.

In the chapters on substitution one thus finds for the first time the listing of alien customs that reappears in the final discussion of blood sacrifice:

> I am particularly astonished by the fact that Socinus says that the laws and customs of all peoples and ages proves that the corporal punishments owing to one person cannot be paid by another. For, according to Marcellinus, the ancient Persians held that if one person committed a crime his whole kin were to be put to death. The Macedonians condemned the blood-relatives of traitors, as Curtius relates. Dionysius of Halicarnassus and Cicero report that in the Greek cities it was customary to kill the children of tyrants together with the tyrants themselves. These practices, indeed, ought not be approved, but they nevertheless demonstrate that [Socinus's claim] concerning the consensus of all peoples is not everywhere true. . . . Plutarch writes that the Thessalians once killed 250 hostages. According to Livy, the Romans, although not in any immediate danger, slew three hundred Volscians and hurled the Tarentines from the Tarpeian rock. (314)

The argument is rather ambiguous; it apparently sets out to show that penal substitution is not impermissible since it was allowed by the ancient *consensus gentium*. But the acts described in this passage are horrific rather than exemplary, and Grotius's explicit disapproval of them blocks the inference from practice to principle. The ancient laws do not constitute a normative theoretical framework but instead give access to earlier notions of persons and ideologies. They imply a historicization of theory, in which the legal structures underlying substitution suggest a model for the Atonement, but now a historical model, a theory of *archaic* jurisprudence.

The intuition of the archaic reciprocally implies the consciousness of modernity. "Archaic" does not simply mean old, since some beliefs and practices—democracy, the nuclear family—existed both in the past and currently; rather, the archaic is the not-modern: hurling hostages off of rocks, wiping out the family of the condemned, and so on. This distinction between modern culture and archaic civilizations rarely occurs during the Renaissance, which tended to venerate the remote past as the *fons et origo* of its own culture. But the distinction can be felt in Grotius. The legal and historical instances of substitution he records trace the outlines of an earlier era possessing fundamentally different laws and moral intuitions.[55]

Different in what sense? Grotius does not shrink from penal substitution on humanitarian grounds; he does not object to its cruelty. Instead, he observes that modern Western societies no longer practice penal substitution because they do not accept that a person has the right to control his or her own body (*jus sibi in corpus suum* [315]):

> Because [the ancients] believed that a person had no less power over his own life than over other things (as the oft rehearsed right to commit suicide, found among Greek, Romans, and other peoples, teaches) . . . it plainly follows that they believed they could validly offer their lives as ransom no less than other things. (314)[56]

Substitution and suicide—assertions of one's *dominium* over the body—mark the break between archaic and modern cultures. The sacrifice of Christ is inimitable because it is now illegal.[57] This seems peculiar. If the claim to have power over one's body defines the archaic, it also looks at first glance like the kind of assertion typically associated with post-Lockean theories of individual rights. Locke, like Grotius, understands selfhood as a "forensick term," specifying "in what circumstances societies or civil combinations of men have in *fact* agreed to inflict evil upon individuals, in order to prevent evils to the whole body from any irregular member."[58] But the sort of *jus* over one's own body that Grotius ascribes to archaic societies has very little to do with possessive individualism. Locke's forensic personality resides in the private recesses of individual memory; for him, punishment presupposes continuity of consciousness over time—Locke's definition of personal identity—since punishment is just only when the accused can remember his offense.[59] For Grotius, however, the liability to punishment in sacrificial cultures derives not from self-awareness but from the subordination of the individual to the group; substitution depends on "a certain *conjunctio* between the one who sinned and the one punished" (313). Hence, according to Grotius, the archaic *jus* granting the individual a right to punish his or her body, even by death, does not presuppose private ownership of one's body, but the opposite. Grotius's sacrificial victim belongs to the suprapersonal compactness of the *conjunctio*.

Grotius's Spanish sources make the correlative point. De Soto argues against substitution on the ground that while "a part (*membrum*) does not have an existence distinct from that of the whole . . . a person, although he may be part of a republic, is nevertheless a subject (*suppositum*) existing for himself."[60] Hence, Molina and Vitoria both maintain that everyone has the right to prevent an innocent person from being killed, even if he does not wish to be saved.[61] Sacrifice, even voluntary sacrifice, becomes impermissible because it violates the inalienable right of the individual: the right to exist as an autonomous subject rather than merely part of a communal body.[62] Conversely, as Grotius acknowledges, substitution entails corporate identity—a collective selfhood that, in Renaissance jurisprudence as in late Roman law, normally survives only in economic transactions, so that one may ransom another's debts but not his life (313). The joint stock company replaces the mystical *conjunctio*.

But Grotius's argument requires corporate identity as the ethical ground for penal substitution. He thus searches outside the law for Classical precedent, reinterpreting the story of Damon and Pythias, for instance, not as an exemplum of true friendship—the standard Renaissance reading—but as evidence for the ancient practice of executing sureties if they failed to produce the accused in court (314). For Grotius, the story witnesses to the archaic solidarity of the group—the *conjunctio*—in which one member can substitute for another. To the extent that persons are regarded as parts of a whole, they may offer their lives for that whole, whereas insofar as a person is viewed as an autonomous moral subject *coram Deo*, he has an obligation to preserve his life, to stand sentry where God has placed him, as Spenser would say. Expelled from the mystical bodies of the family and state, one no longer possesses the right to be a victim. Hence, Grotius's own treatises on international law make individual self-preservation the foundational imperative of rational ethics—and this postulate, adopted by Selden, Hobbes, and Pufendorf, becomes the basis of seventeenth-century moral philosophy.[63] The modern individual, as we shall see in more detail later, is thus defined in terms of alienation from sacrifice.

The Price of Redemption

The final section of *De satisfactione*, which begins midway in chapter 7, initially seems tacked on. Having concluded his discussion of exemplary punishment and substitution, Grotius comments that he will produce "some other evidence" to confirm his argument that Christ's death brought about the remission of sins (323). But the subsequent discussion in fact veers in a different direction from the previous arguments, since it takes up the question of how the Crucifixion pertains to God rather than the prior issue of its exemplary role with respect to human beings (326). And this shifts the focus from substitution to sacrifice.

The shift starts with the observation that to redeem means to liberate someone from some difficulty by paying a price (*pretium*); hence, Matthew 20:28 states that "the Son of Man came to give his soul as the price of redemption (*redemptionis pretium*) for many."[64] We would seem to have returned to the economic analogies Grotius had previously disallowed, but *pretium* is not the correlate of *debitum*; that is, it is not exactly paying something owed but includes any act or object that satisfies (*satisfacere*) another and thus moves him to grant something (327–28). In this sense, the concept of *pretium* belongs less to the domain of the economic per se than to a social organization prior to the differentiation of economic and personal transactions; this passage thus differs from the opening section of *De satisfactione*, which had assumed the early modern (and Roman) differentiation of public and private spheres. The *redemptionis pretium* is close to tribute or homage—or sacrifice. Grotius illustrates the term by observing that "Castor was freed from perpetual death at a price, namely the alternating death of his brother" (327). The transactions detailed here belong to an apparently primitive economics of blood-price.[65] As in the previous section on substitution, Grotius's analysis begins to slip from theory toward the description of archaic cultural practices.

This slippage becomes evident in what follows. Grotius proceeds to explain that the Greek equivalent for *pretium* is *lutron* (λύτρον) and that *lutron* in Latin becomes *lustrum*, a purificatory sacrifice. Hence, the Decii, who devoted themselves to death to save their country, are said to have purified (*lustrare*) the Roman army; likewise, an ancient scholiast reports that "the Gauls had a custom of purifying (*lustrare*) their city by a human victim. In the same sense, Caesar speaks of placating (*placare*) the gods" (328). One after another, etymologies disclose sacrifice. Thus, Grotius points out that the word "punishment" (*supplicium*) originally had a ritual sense and only later came to mean a legal penalty (*poena*) (334). Similarly "'to slay' (*mactare*) means both to sacrifice and also, having enlarged its meaning from sacrifice to other things, simply 'to kill'" (338).[66] The etymologies pave a descent to a moment prior to the cultural-linguistic split between crime, tort, and pollution, a moment when economic and penal discourses still betray their sacrificial origins.

The discussion of sacrifice, which takes up the final chapter of *De satisfactione*, begins by sketching a rational account of the theory underlying sacrificial practices correspondent to the governmental theory set out in the first four chapters: under certain conditions, God relaxes the penalty due to sinners, transferring the punishment to an expiatory victim whose death serves as an example and warning; conversely, by offering a sacrifice to God, the penitent simultaneously honors God and punishes himself by depriving himself of one of his possessions (332–33). This interpretation, however, is quickly discarded, since it does not account for the examples Grotius cites. For instance, "Deuteronomy 21 establishes that if a murderer cannot be found, the people make expiation by killing an animal. . . . The earth cannot otherwise be cleansed (*expiari*) from the blood that has been shed, except by the blood of the one who shed it" (332). This is a pollution ritual, not an act of penance; as Grotius notes, the ancients considered guilt a sort of uncleanliness (334). By the middle of the chapter, mystical and magical notions of sacrifice have replaced the initial political-penitential account. Hence, at one point Grotius remarks that in Scripture "remission does not occur without effusion of blood; rather expiation takes place in blood (*expiatio fiat in sanguine*)" (336). The bulk of chapter 10, in fact, does not investigate the rational basis of sacrifice but demonstrates, with characteristic erudition, both the universality of ritual sacrifice and its logic of blood. Grotius offers extensive philological evidence for his claim that ancient religious language—both Greco-Roman and biblical— is largely composed of terms relating to sacrificial purification, evincing a historicist sensitivity to the ritual origins of biblical phrasing. For instance, Grotius notes that the expression in Hebrews 7:27 that Christ "offered up himself" (*sursum tulisse*) derives from the practice of dragging the sacrificial victim *up* to the altar (299). The arguments consistently replace transcendent with cultural signification. This emphasis on blood, one should note, rarely surfaces in other Renaissance accounts of the Atonement, even intransigent Tridentine defenses of the sacrificial character of the mass. De Soto, for instance, stresses the reverential submission to power implied in the act of sacrifice, while Baronius connects Christ's oblation with Melchizedek's offering of wheat and wine.

But Grotius focuses on blood. The passage on human sacrifice quoted at the beginning of this chapter occurs as part of a comparative analysis of ancient expiatory rites, introduced, Grotius remarks, because human sacrifice best illustrates the mechanisms of substitution, scapegoating, and placation involved in all sacrifice and hence clarifies "what it means when Christ is called a sacrifice for sins or expiatory victim" (336). I know of nothing equivalent to this anthropological explanation anywhere in Renaissance literature. It drastically problematizes Grotius's argument, since it throws in stark relief the primitive character of sacrificial substitution and thus seems to raise serious difficulties about the moral basis of Christianity—a strange thing to do in an explicit defense of the orthodox theology of the Atonement.

Jurists and Indians

D. P. Walker once remarked that "it is rare for Renaissance Platonists to mention pagan prototypes of the crucifixion, even when these lie close to hand."[67] Reformation Protestants typically claim that the absence of sacrifice distinguishes Christianity from other religions. Suckling (better known as a Cavalier poet) comments that by rejecting the notion that God could "be pleased with the blood of beasts, or delighted with the steam of fat . . . Christians have gone beyond all others except the Mahometans; besides whom there has been no Nation that had not sacrifice, and was not guilty of this pious cruelty"; or, as Hooker puts it, Christians "have properly now no sacrifice."[68]

The voyages of discovery produced an early form of comparative ethnography, which does remark and analyze the similarities between pagan religion and Christianity. Nevertheless, these texts do not seem to be anthropological in anything remotely like the modern sense of the word; they are more often defenses against anthropology, designed to empty apparent similarities of any theological significance. Protestant writers note the likeness of pagan and Roman Catholic ceremonies in order to show that Roman Catholics are in fact pagans.[69] Other "early anthropologists," to use Margaret Hodgen's somewhat misleading label, argue that pagan religion is either a demonic parody of the true faith or a distorted vestige of an original divine revelation—both views entailing the belatedness and inferiority of the Gentiles.[70] All three explanatory models resist any tendency to blur the cultural boundaries between self and other, Christian and non-Christian.

Grotius's argument departs radically from these conventional Renaissance accounts of primitive religion. He simply handles his examples differently, using them as ethnographic data capable of generalization. Cross-cultural similarities in religious praxis and terminology thus provide the empirical foundations for a theory of sacrifice applicable to both Christianity and paganism. The method is therefore both essentialist and historicist. Its premises can be gathered from Grotius's remark prefacing his discussion of pagan sacrificial practices:

> I should like to explain the nature of ritual expiation a bit more fully by looking at the common opinion of early peoples (*communis Gentium notitia*), or rather the primitive tradition (*vetustissima traditio*) diffused throughout all lands. Without question sacrifices existed prior to the law of Moses under what is called the state of natural law (*sub statu legis naturalis*). (334)

Elsewhere Grotius invokes a similar connection between *Scriptura, natura*, and the *consensus gentium* (315) and between the *gentes* and *natura* (335). But the implied identification of the customs shared by all primitive communities with the law of nature allows the inference from cultural similarities to general (that is, natural) laws, from the fact of sacrifice to a theory of sacrifice. Hence, if a practice can be shown to have been common to all peoples from earliest times, it may be regarded as an expression of natural law, understood as both a descriptive and normative principle. The inquiry into ancient sacrificial practices allows Grotius to hypothesize a theoretical paradigm (a natural law), which he then uses to isolate and interpret the basic structures of Christian theology.

The premises of Grotius's argument are scarcely novel. The connection he posits between the *consensus gentium* and natural law can be found in Cicero's assertion that "in every matter the consent of nations is to be considered the law of nature," as well as in Hooker's famous declaration that "the general and perpetual voice of men is as the sentence of God himself. For that which all men have at all times learned, Nature herself must needs have taught; and God being the author of Nature, her voice is but his instrument."[71] Hooker, however, lists divine worship and the golden rule as examples of this *jus naturale et gentium*—the standard examples from Scholastic natural law theology—not human sacrifice.

But with the identification of the *jus gentium* and *jus naturale* we return for the third time to the fields of Roman law. This identification, ultimately derived from Aristotle and the Stoics, is a postulate of Roman law. Thus, the opening chapter of the *Digest* cites Gaius, a second-century jurist, to the effect that "the law established by natural reason among all men is observed equally everywhere and is called the *lex gentium*, obligatory on all nations."[72] However, mainly because the principal terms have several different meanings,[73] the historical development of the relation between the *jus naturale* and the *jus gentium* can be exasperatingly confused. For our purposes, it will be sufficient to sketch the Renaissance debate.[74]

This debate took place in three domains: universal history, international law (or, more properly, the theological and juridic antecedents of international law), and colonial policy.[75] All three bear on *De satisfactione*—Grotius was interested in all three areas—although, surprisingly, the last seems of special significance.

In the dedication to the *Methodus*, Bodin states that "in history the best part of universal law lies hidden," an echo of Vives's observation that "*jus manet in historia.*"[76] Bodin's program, which involved the comparative study of all known legal and political institutions in order to elicit the principles of universal law, established a new field of historical research on the basis of the traditional identification of the law of nature with the *jus gentium*. His massive investigations into Greek, Roman, Egyptian, Hebrew, European, and Turkish constitutions are organized by the search for underlying normative principles—an attempt to reshape humanist antiquarianism into political science similar to Grotius's endeavor to elicit the structures of religion and international law from the *consensus gentium*.[77] But, although one suspects that Bodin's comparative historiography stands behind the cross-cultural method of *De satisfactione*, the two works in fact are rather different. Bodin basically treats his historical material as rhetorical *exempla* rather than evidence; he thus recommends that one should divide human activities according to topics, noting under each "whatever memorable fact is met in reading histories," and then, having decided "what in the details is honorable, base, or indifferent," mark the margins accordingly—a sort of politicized commonplace book.[78] Principles are to be applied to the material rather than derived from it. Nor does Bodin ever assume that the *consensus gentium* of antiquity implies a normative standard; rather, like Hobbes he holds that "the golden and silver ages" were periods of barbaric violence from which people were only gradually reclaimed "to the refinement of customs and the law-abiding society which we see about us." From this evolutionary view, it follows that nothing could be more impious than that "men should be sacrificed most cruelly both at funerals and in religious rites. But this used to be done among almost all peoples."[79]

The resemblance between Bodin and Grotius thus seems rather superficial, which suggests that the new comparative historiography is the wrong place to look for the methodological antecedents of *De satisfactione*. For these we need instead to return to sixteenth-century jurisprudence.

Most Renaissance jurists defended the existence of some sort of intrinsic connection between the *consensus gentium* and natural law.[80] Gentili unmistakably considers them identical: "the law of nations . . . is the law of nature."[81] His explanation shows that he clearly grasps the comparative ethnographic basis of the *jus gentium*; the Roman jurists, he comments, discovered the laws of nations precisely because Roman expansionism brought the Empire into contact with numerous diverse cultures, which could then be compared and their common features isolated.[82] But Gentili's identification of the *jus naturale* and *jus gentium* seems unusually unambiguous. The Spanish writers on international law—Molina, Vitoria, Suarez, De Soto—tend to regard the *jus gentium* as being, like civil law, a positive law established by human consent, although, again like civil law, one derived from natural law.[83] For example, in the third book of his massive *De justitia et jure*, De Soto addresses the question "whether the *jus gentium* is identical to the *jus naturale*." He argues in the negative since, although some principles of the law of nations are also laws of nature, others—for instance, slavery and contracts—depend on human enactment and are not necessarily binding.[84] In general, both Grotius and the Spanish jurists tend toward a rationalist interpretation of natural law, the view, in Hooker's words, that "the Laws of well-doing are the dictates of right Reason" rather than of universal custom.[85]

But on one crucial topic the Spanish jurists do not abandon the ancient identification of custom and natural law, of *mos* and *jus*. The ninth book of *De justitia* thus opens with the claim that "at all times and among all persons there always existed some sort of sacrifice; but what all persons have taught, they learned from the instruction of nature."[86] Since sacrifice belongs to the *jus gentium*, it must also belong to the *jus naturale*, precisely the position De Soto previously rejected. The ambivalence here about the relation between these two *jura* seems to parallel the conceptual uncertainties of *De satisfactione*, which defends the "naturalness" of sacrifice while exposing its primitive and violent mechanisms. In both one notes the same confusion about the exact relation of the *consensus gentium* to the laws of nature, the same tension between descriptive and normative readings of culture. We are back to the duplicity of law and the legal crisis of the late Renaissance. Nor does it seem coincidental that these tensions gather around the subject of sacrifice (in fact, in both instances, around Christ's sacrifice). The possibility arises that sacrifice itself is located on the site of this crisis, lying athwart, as it were, the fault line where nascent rationalism and the ancestral past touch precariously.

Another Spanish monk may help elucidate this possibility. There is, I think, only one Renaissance text that seriously takes up the question of human sacrifice along the lines of Grotius's work: Bartholome de Las Casas's *In Defense of the Indians*, the first extensive work of comparative ethnology, as Anthony Pagden notes, "to be written in a European language."[87] This fact suggests the surprising conclusion that the problem of human sacrifice emerges during the Renaissance in the context of colonial policy, in particular, the Spanish conquest and enslavement of the South American peoples.[88] Las Casas's five-hundred-page Latin *Defense* was originally presented to the judges assembled at Valladolid in 1550 to determine the lawfulness of the Spanish conquest—a five-day oratorical marathon.[89] Sepulveda, who spoke for the conquistadores, claimed that since the Indians violated natural law by practicing cannibalism and human sacrifice, the Spanish had a moral obligation to intervene and prevent such atrocities. Las Casas, who spent his life fighting the Spanish destruction of Indian civilizations, responded with a remarkable apologia for human sacrifice.

What he says is that "by natural law, men are obliged to honor God . . . and to offer the best things in sacrifice," since "there is no better way to worship God than by sacrifice." Furthermore, although the specific items offered in sacrifice fall under the determination of positive law, "the same natural reason" shows "that men should be sacrificed to God," because "nature teaches that it is just to offer God . . . those things that are precious and excellent. . . . [But] nothing in nature is greater or more valuable than the life of man or man himself." Christian doctrine forbids such sacrifice, but nature does not; human sacrifice is therefore an error, but a probable error and not an atrocity.[90] Likewise, the *jus gentium*, which Las Casas considers part of natural law, permits human sacrifice, since it is a virtually universal practice, and, according to Aristotle, "that must necessarily be judged to be good or better which is so judged by all, or the majority of persons of good judgment."[91] The Gauls, Romans, Carthaginians, Scythians, Greeks, Galatians, and ancient Spaniards all worshiped with human victims—as in Grotius, the New World peoples merge into *gentes* of the ancestral past.[92]

Moreover, Las Casas continues, the fact that one sacrifices an innocent victim against his or her will does not entail that such sacrifice is unjust; the individual is only "a part of the whole state . . . and therefore, in order to preserve that common welfare, he is obliged by the natural law to do and suffer all he can, even by sacrificing his life."[93] Individuals exist only as part of a community and may lawfully be killed to ensure its safety.

This final argument again brings up the issue of penal substitution discussed by Gentili and the Spanish theologians. Among the latter, the prohibitions against sacrifice and substitution follow from the same sixteenth-century version of the "right to life" argument. For Molina, Vitoria, and De Soto, the good of the individual can never be finally subordinated to the common good. Like Sepulveda, both Molina and Vitoria explicitly relate this claim to colonial policy: the Spanish may suppress Indian cults (and culture) because all people have the right forcibly to prevent innocent persons from being killed, even if the victim consents. Because a person is ultimately a *suppositum* rather than a *membrum*, an individual rather than a part, one cannot use him as food or a sacrificial offering, just as one cannot kill the children of an enemy or innocent hostages.[94] Human sacrifice thus comes to signify, as Stephen Greenblatt suggests, the "absolute difference" between Christian civilization "and the culture of the other."[95] Indians, children, hostages—and Christ—occupy the intersection of theology and jurisprudence as the subjects of sacrificial discourse, which is at the same time a discourse about subjects, about the emergence of the autonomous subject from his archaic subjection to the *mystica conjunctio.* They are liminal figures, occupying the contested border between sacrificial communities and atomistic selfhood, where the Renaissance play of intersubstitutable similitudes polarizes into the episteme of identity and difference, where the *consensus gentium,* with its repetitive homologies, discloses the rupture between archaic and modern culture, between sacrificial victims and ethical subjects.[96]

But why then would liberal Christian humanists like Grotius and Las Casas—the one the founder of international law, the other the foremost critic of Spanish colonial policy—make the case *for* human sacrifice? Perhaps one can approach this seeming paradox by noting that they both offer a critique of what may be loosely called "Eurocentrism"—the valorization of modern Western ideologies over both earlier and foreign cultures. This critique is overt in Las Casas's defense of Indian culture against Spanish imperialism, but it also motivates, although more obliquely, Grotius's objections to Socinus. The characteristic emphases of Socinianism—reasonability, individualism, and moral seriousness—mark it as the precursor of Western rationalism. The arguments of *Jesu Christo servatore* are variations on the theme of the superiority of modern ethical rationality to apparently immoral, primitive, and illogical concepts like sacrifice and substitution; they announce the "transition from an ethics of solidarity to one of civility"—that is, from the sacrificial exchanges of the *conjunctio* to the moral autonomy of the civil *suppositum.*[97] Conversely, Grotius defends the traditional understanding of the sacrificial character of the Atonement by arguing for the rationality of exotic and ancestral *gentes*—Las Casas's position. The apologia for Christian orthodoxy is thus an exploration of alien rationalities, one that problematizes the whole concept of reason by blurring the distinction between the rational and the primitive. For Grotius, the moral and spiritual intelligibility of Christianity depends on grasping vicarious blood sacrifice as a precept of natural law (336). He identifies natural law with the archaic *consensus gentium* in order to denaturalize the hegemonic claims of modern rationalism.

Hence, Las Casas and Grotius both invert the traditional function of natural law arguments. From the Stoics through the Renaissance, philosophers appealed to natural law and the *consensus gentium* in order to supply an ontological foundation for the values central to their own culture: piety, patriarchy, and property. Grotius and Las Casas transform this appeal by focusing on praxis rather than values or beliefs—a fusion of natural law theories and the new ethnography.[98] It is the ritual itself that points toward the fundamental structures of religion. Cultural transmission thus takes place along the axis of the signifier rather than the signified. This is the ancient theology in reverse: instead of arbitrary forms concealing a universal essence, one now finds universal forms transferred to an arbitrary essence. Grotius and Las Casas would seem to anticipate structuralist anthropology rather than deism.

However, Grotius almost certainly had not read *In Defense of the Indians*, since it survived in a single manuscript not printed until this century.[99] After the conference at Valladolid, Las Casas published a summary of the proceedings in Spanish, which Grotius could conceivably have known—he was thoroughly familiar with the Spanish controversies over colonial policy—but I have no evidence for this. *De satisfactione* and the *Defense* should be viewed as independent reinterpretations of natural law theory, whose similarities point to a diffuse common context linking sacrifice to the problematic configuration of the boundaries between modern European civilization and alien territories, where the defense of sacrifice voices a profoundly ambivalent response to the aggressive rationalism and rationalized aggression of the late Renaissance.

Estrangement and Exemplarity

The juxtaposition of *In Defense of the Indians* and *De satisfactione* also throws into relief the utter and disturbing singularity of the latter. Las Casas never attempts to give a theoretical account of sacrificial logic. The *Defense* is a scholasticized deliberative oration on behalf of the Indians rather than a comparativist study, however brief and tentative, of the deep structures of archaic religions. In addition, it never associates human sacrifice with the Crucifixion.[100] Las Casas, in fact, maintains a consistent distinction between revealed truth and the dictates of natural reason. He thus asserts the legitimacy of the other without suggesting its perilous connections to the self. In Grotius, however, blood sacrifice penetrates the realms of grace. He is less interested in the probable rationality of premodern peoples than in the presence of an archaic and savage mythos at the center of Christian doctrine. What chapter 10 argues is that the essential rites and narratives of Christianity embody the logic of blood sacrifice and originate *within* an archaic episteme. It uses ethnographic data to penetrate behind the civilized veneer of Western ideology to its violent and unfamiliar hinterground, where the alien becomes the mirror of the self. Grotius resembles Frazer in precisely those respects in which he differs from Las Casas.

What is missing in Grotius's argument is typology. Traditional Christian theology, both Roman and Reformed, always considers Old Testament sacrifices as types of the Crucifixion, muffling the strangeness of these ancient rituals by treating them as signs rather than as actual practices. *De satisfactione* mentions typology only once and even there views the link between type and antetype less as a relation between figure and fulfillment than as one between two similar expiatory rites, the earlier differing from the later only in being less efficacious (333).[101] Grotius is interested in parallels rather than prolepsis, in observing the residue of archaic religion within Christianity rather than searching for intimations of Christian truth. The movement of the passage on human sacrifice enacts this progressive realization of one's own uncomfortable proximity to all that seems barbaric and foreign. Beginning with Moloch, the bloodthirsty Canaanite deity, Grotius lists Near Eastern, African, and New World rituals—all remote and clearly primitive examples. But then he turns to Europe: first preclassical culture (Crete and Sparta), but next Greece in general and the Rome of Cicero, Livy, and Pliny. He then concludes with the most recent and proximate instances: the Gauls, the Germans, and finally the Britons, who continued to practice human sacrifice into the sixth century A.D. (335–36). The passage moves from foreigners to ancestors and conflates them, both obliterating the distinction between exotic and Western cultures and establishing that Christianity belongs to a period when human sacrifice was still widely practiced. The Crucifixion occurred *within* a sacrificial episteme and presupposes the validity of blood expiation. Christianity is an archaic religion.[102]

Grotius's resistance to Socinian rationalism is finally much more ambivalent than the anti-imperialism of Las Casas. Grotius, after all, set out
to provide a rational and morally coherent theory of the Atonement. It is
as though the attempt to demythologize Christianity led rather accidentally and disturbingly to the discovery of its mythic substrate. By the end
of chapter 10, one begins to suspect that Socinus was not wholly wrong in
viewing sacrifice as primitive and repugnant. Grotius's own late commentaries on Hebrews and the Catholic Epistles give a Socinian reading of
Christ's sacrifice.[103]

Yet one needs to be careful here. *De satisfactione* is not *The Golden
Bough*. If Grotius assimilates Christianity to the blood religions of antiquity, that likeness does not have the same implications it came to possess
in the nineteenth century. Simply put, the difference lies in the fact that
Grotius thinks that sacrifice works. He seems to believe in both the efficacy
of Levitical ceremonies and the reality of pagan portents as signs of divine
anger requiring expiation. Blood sacrifice works because God ordained it:
"Those who survived the Flood and were now dispersed over the whole
earth transmitted the sacrificial rituals they had received from God (*a Deo
traditi*) to their posterity" (334). All peoples practice sacrifice because the
sons of Noah taught this sacred custom to their own descendants. But this
is the traditional Renaissance explanation for cultural diffusion—the
Noah's Ark theory, as it were—common to ancient theologians and humanist philologists alike.[104] In Grotius the movement back toward the anthropological other is always-already a movement toward the site of an
original revelation; historicism is always-already essentialist.

Put another way, for Grotius there can be no significant rupture between sacrificial and postsacrificial cultures. The archaic past remains normative and continuous with both its sacred origins and modern Christian
societies, a cultural unity guaranteed by the eternal unity of God and the
monogenetic unity of Noah's offspring. This continuity helps explain
the tone of *De satisfactione*, which reports its ethnographic discoveries
without a whisper of the ironic condescension that characterizes post-
Enlightenment anthropology. Grotius does not watch antiquity from the
panopticon; he observes from a position still within its ideological confines.
If Gentili could defend penal substitution as a live political option, why
need sacrifice appear remote and alien to Grotius? De Soto also held that
natural law mandated sacrifice and that Christianity must have its own
sacrificial ritual (the mass) if it were not to be inferior to paganism.[105] Perhaps it is the late twentieth-century reader, not Grotius, who finds sacrifice
problematic and alien.

Yet this will not do either. If one compares Grotius's attitude toward human sacrifice with that held by Christians living in cultures where such sacrifice still occurred or had only recently ceased—the Church Fathers, for example—the difficulties become apparent. Patristic writers considered such sacrifice perverse, cruel, and repulsive, a vivid witness to the demonic barbarity of paganism. Lactantius may serve as an example:

> Among the people of Taurus, an inhuman and savage nation, there was a law that a stranger should be sacrificed to Diana. . . . Indeed, even now the Latin Jupiter is worshiped with human blood. However, we should not be astonished at the barbarians whose religion matches their morals. . . . I find no words to tell of the children who were sacrificed to the same Saturn. . . . Men were so barbarous and so inhuman that they labeled as sacrifice that foul and detestable crime against the human race which is parricide, when . . . they blotted out tender and innocent lives at an age which is especially dear to parents.[106]

Augustine and Chrysostom find even Old Testament sacrifices morally offensive; they justify them by explaining that the carnal perversity of the Israelites forced God reluctantly to institute blood rituals.[107] Grotius, however, does not find sacrifice appalling; he finds it interesting.

Grotius can treat sacrifice with a certain objectivity and analytic detachment precisely because he no longer inhabits a sacrificial culture. The immense gulf separating him from the dripping altars and cries of burning children only half drowned out by cymbals and drums creates a perspective from which distinctions fade into the distance. Thus, at the end of chapter 10 Grotius observes:

> Plutarch also says that the Gauls and Scythians believed that the gods delighted in the blood of slain humans and that this was the most perfect sacrifice. Sacrifice therefore consists in slaying. Nor does Scripture speak differently in this matter. Having been commanded to offer his son, Abraham prepared to kill him. (338)

From a distance, Abraham resembles the Scythians. The comparison itself marks Grotius's estrangement from both profane and biblical antiquity. No earlier Christian writer would have thought to remark that parallel.

For Grotius, the ancient world is both remote and at hand—*et procul et prope*. The authorial voice slips in and out of the cultural domain it attempts to analyze, as though one were to look at the same scene first through one end of a pair of binoculars, then through the other. This simultaneous register of proximity and distance characterizes the representational strategies of Renaissance historical consciousness but also seems peculiarly related to sacrifice. In *Marvelous Possessions*, Greenblatt describes how Cortez's soldiers shrank in horror at their first encounter with the Aztec rites of human sacrifice, which they nevertheless represented as distorted but recognizable analogues of eucharistic sacrifice, with "temple, high altar, cult of holy blood, statues before which offerings are made, 'symbols like crosses.'" Their narratives thus establish "absolute difference . . . at the site of the most intimate and uncanny parallel."[108] Grotius betrays the same paradox almost in reverse. The parallel sacrificial rituals that establish the cultural unity of humankind disclose the absolute difference between Renaissance civilization and the archaic cultures where Abraham, the Scythians, and Christ offered human blood to appease an angry God. In either version of the paradox, the sacrifice of Christ peers from behind both the uncanny parallels and the sense of absolute difference. The more or less concealed presence of *this* sacrifice configures the representations of sacrificial cultures in terms of what Greenblatt terms "the oscillation between brother and other," allowing the unstable perception of both maximal exemplarity and maximal estrangement that alternately fixes and denies the boundary between the self and the alien. The conceptualization of primitive cultures takes place under the sign of the Cross.[109]

These anamorphic ambiguities contribute to the generic uncertainty of Grotius's text, which begins by using Roman law to theorize Christian doctrine, then seems to historicize its own theoretical frame, and ends up halfway between anthropology and ancient theology. Foucault's description of the seemingly antithetical "stances" characteristic of Renaissance intellectuals might have been written about Grotius: their learning "was made up of an unstable mixture . . . where fidelity to the Ancients, a taste for the supernatural, and an already awakened awareness of that sovereign rationality in which we recognize ourselves, confronted one another in equal freedom."[110] This combination of humanism, Christianity, and rationalism may have been, in Foucault's words, "structurally weak," but it also enabled (as the last chapter suggested) a specific form of knowledge, a specific self-consciousness—a demystified critical intelligence that accepts mystical bodies, inherited guilt, ritual pollution, portents, and scapegoats. The perception of one's own estrangement from the past dissolves into a deep sense of historical continuity; a subversive and reflexive historicism intertwines with belief in the transcendent origins of cultural praxis.

This consciousness of one's simultaneous detachment from and participation in the ancestral past is reflected in the mirror of sacrifice, precisely because sacrifice remains the supremely valuable act, the luminous gesture of self-abnegation and *caritas* constituting the heroic—whether Christ's self-oblation or the Decii's suicidal patriotism. Yet the legal prohibition of sacrifice, voluntary and involuntary, also marks the exclusion of modern societies from their ancestral killing fields. And this prohibition registers the differentiation of the individual from the mystical solidarity of the patriarchal family and tribal community.

·   ·   ·

Sometime between 1601 and 1610, Grotius composed a poem on one of the most famous episodes in the Dutch struggle for independence from Spain. In 1574 the Spanish army had blockaded Leiden, attempting to starve the city into submission. As the death toll from plague and famine rose, the burgomaster, Pieter A. van der Werff, offered himself to the desperate and mutinous citizens as an edible sacrifice. As Grotius describes it, van der Werff pleads with the crowd:

> Put your teeth into my body . . . and put an end to your hunger. I offer you . . . my throat and my limbs, which cry for their death. . . . Thus strengthened go on defending our city walls for a few more days, until the Prince [William of Orange] will come relieving us.[111]

The defiant gesture of revolutionary republicanism seems poised to recapitulate a pre-Freudian version of primal parricide—the only known instance of politically correct cannibalism. It is a moment of national heroism, heavy with symbolic resonance; van der Werff takes on the lineaments of both Stoic patriot and eucharistic victim. Yet Grotius's burgomaster is not Dante's Cato. There is something odd about his speech; it seems too graphic, too explicitly cannibalist, making it impossible for the reader to dissociate the *idea* of sacrifice from its corporeal enactment. The heroic gesture verges on the barbaric and repulsive.

And the sacrifice never occurred, since the citizens of Leiden decided not to eat their mayor. Instead, they held out until the siege was raised a few days later. All that remains of sacrificial climax is van der Werff's speech (or, rather, Grotius's version of that speech). The flesh has become word. At the same time, the fact that the citizens rejected their mayor's offer shifts the moral center of the episode. The pivotal act turns out not to have been the sacrificial oblation but the heroic refusal of the starving Dutch to revert to savagery, to allow an individual to die for the common good. The temptation of cannibalism was in fact a topos of Renaissance Dutch literature, whose travel narratives and patriotic history represent this temptation as a choice between "degeneration into a Hobbesian state of animal chaos" and the twin moral bases of the Dutch republic: the "humanist ideal of community and the Calvinist precept of obedience to the divine will."[112] Van der Werff's self-denying gesture retains the heroic pathos radiating from its Christian and Roman prototypes, but, as in *De satisfactione*, it also casts bizarre and violent shadows. In the end, the sacrificial economy has no place in Grotius's new mercantile republic.

3 The Death of Christ

But ever sicke, crost, grevid and livinge-dyinge,
Thinke of the subject in this sorrowe lyinge.
> Breton, "The Countesse
> of Penbrook's Passion"

Voyez la tragedie, abbaissez vos courages,
Vous n'estes spectateurs, vous estes personnages.
> D'Aubigne, *Les tragiques*

Calvinist piety in England produced only a handful of passion narratives during the period stretching from the mid-sixteenth century through the Civil Wars. The figure of the crucified Jesus slips to the margins of English Protestantism, which favored dogmatic theology and devotional introspection over retelling the story of Christ's suffering and death—the pervasive focus of late medieval and Tridentine Catholicism[1]—a disappearance that results, at least in part, from Calvinism's indifference to the church calendar. Of the dozen or so passion narratives published in England between 1550 and 1650 (including texts by English authors and English translations of Continental works), several adhere closely to traditional patristic and medieval motifs.[2] There is, however, another fairly distinctive and unusual group of texts, all of which share a marked debt to Calvin's reading of the Passion in his *Harmony of the Evangelists*, first published in 1558 and translated into English by Eusebius Pagit in 1584. The present chapter concerns this latter group. Along with Calvin's *Harmony*, it includes Joseph Hall's "Passion Sermon" (1609) and his posthumously published *Contemplations upon the History of the New Testament* (1662), a 1619 translation of Daniel Heinsius's "Upon the Passion of Christ," several sermons by obscure English clergymen, and Thomas Nashe's *Christs Teares over Jerusalem* (1593).[3]

The paucity of extant Calvinist passions does not indicate their cultural insignificance. Calvin's immense prestige during the sixteenth and seventeenth centuries makes it unlikely that one of his major New Testament commentaries would languish unnoticed. More important, the account of Christ's inner struggle given in the Calvinist passions, having detached itself (as it were) from its biblical locus, becomes the exemplary subtext for

Calvinist representations of Christian selfhood. As I will attempt to show, Calvinist anthropology thus mirrors (and may derive from) its Christology. The two discourses proffer duplicate versions of the same paradigm, although the structure and meaning of this paradigm is registered with peculiar clarity in the compact rendering of the biblical myth. But if the various Reformed discourses of experiential inwardness—spiritual autobiography, pilgrims' progresses, devotional lyric—duplicate the passion narratives, they also suppress them; they suppress the appalling sacrificial subtext of the Calvinist subject.

For in the process of disappearing, something happens to the traditional story of Christ's death; it warps under specific historical pressures to the point that it no longer functions as a dominant cultural myth. If, following Durkheim's influential thesis, the function of dominant myths is to provide normative values and ontological solace—to relieve anxiety by grounding social experience in sacred order—then disintegrating myths, what we may call "end myths," can be characterized by their failure to effect this.[4] The end myth does not validate traditional symbols but discloses their inadequacy to provide moral coherence, stable boundaries between right and wrong, strategies for escaping dread. Rather than proffering an idealized objectification of society, it tends to appropriate the symbols of social order for the articulation of the psyche; myth becomes a language for registering the recesses and complexities of inner experience.[5] The end myth thus approaches tragedy. Euripides, whose introspective character studies dramatize crumbling cultural values and ambiguous intimations about both social and cosmic intelligibility, is the great ancient poet of end myths. One notes a similar tendency in the Renaissance for traditional stories to acquire simultaneously tragic form and psychological complexity: the transformation of *Mankind* to *Doctor Faustus*, of *Leir* to *Lear*.[6]

Anyone familiar with *Christs Teares* will immediately grasp why such representations of Christ's suffering do not work as Durkheimian myths. Like Nashe's jeremiad, all the Calvinist passions are troubling, dark, bordering on the grotesque. Although they lack Grotius's anthropological curiosity about ancient blood rituals, they share the same uneasy fascination with the violence of the sacred.[7] They are suffused with lurid and perverse detail, with images of sadism, torture, eroticism, vengeance, and parricide, with the suggestions of menace and retribution of the sort that William Empson long ago remarked in Herbert's "Sacrifice."[8] The agony of Christ becomes a locus for the articulation of strange desires and moral uncertainties, disclosing rather than resolving cultural paradoxes.

The Calvinist passion narratives share three central characteristics. The causal trajectory from the Crucifixion to the fall of Jerusalem partially or wholly replaces the biblical plot, which moves from the Crucifixion to the Resurrection. These are stories of crime and punishment, not redemptive sacrifice. They also tend to employ a double, interlaced structure; the trial scenes are dominated by the political violence of the priests and soldiers, the Agony in the Garden and the Crucifixion by the domestic violence of the Father toward his Son. Finally, they rely on a rhetoric of identification. A sermon, for example, will relate the sufferings of the elect to Christ's dereliction or conflate the brutality of the soldiers with the inquisitorial cruelty of Roman Catholic persecutions. This is, of course, classic Protestant typology in which biblical events prefigure the tribulations and triumphs of the elect, but, at least in these texts, this proleptic strategy seems more complex and significant than is often realized.

Political Violence

I look down towards his feet, but that's a fable.
                    Othello

In the sixteenth century, cruelty, the forgotten deadly sin, became the essence of evil, and its symbol was the torturer.[9] Huldrich Zwingli defines it as the opposite of "humanitie," that which makes people "beastes [rather] then men."[10] A fascination with cruelty is unmistakable in the art of the period. The late Renaissance paintings at the Getty Museum in Los Angeles constitute a pictorial torture chamber: saints burned, shot, grilled, decapitated, and boiled. The Calvinist passion narratives, while less absorbed by the techniques of cruelty, fix compulsively on its psychology. The representation of cruelty remains constant throughout these texts. The priests, people, and soldiers who participate in the Crucifixion seem gripped by an irrational malice—a motiveless malice compounded of psychotic wrath and a demonic hatred of God. Calvin's *Harmony* reiterates this analysis in almost a litany of *furor*: Christ's enemies are consumed by "amazing rage," "astonishing madness," "treacherous cruelty," "malicious hatred," "unreasonable cruelty," "insatiable cruelty," and "amazing madness."[11] The same terminology pervades all the Calvinist passion narratives. Heinsius describes the soldiers as "Canibals . . . transported with furie and madnesse"; Hall's apostrophe to Caiaphas begins, "O monster, whether of malice or unjustice"; a 1584 passion sermon by one Dr. Chamberlaine collapses into the plosive repetitions of "beastly traiterous

Beast . . . Barbarian . . . shamefull and beastly."[12] Because Heinsius identifies Christ with the Old Testament Jehovah, the Crucifixion approaches parricide: "O cruell and abominable people! . . . how forgetfull wert thou of him that begate thee? You have slaine him that *brought you out of the land of Egypt*."[13] Climaxing in the flagellation, the scenes of insane malice and bestial cruelty converge in the figure of the torturer—the symbol of evil as a sadistic and "most eager malice . . . [that] might enjoy thy torment."[14]

These narratives do not endow Christ's enemies with anything we might consider a *realistic* psychology. Rather the reverse—especially since they emphasize that the Jews *knew* Christ was "both God, a King, and a Prophet" and crucified him anyway (or maybe for that reason).[15] They disregard the possibility that Christ's persecutors acted on political or ideological grounds, that they had any intelligible motive, any justification.[16] This is not just faulty characterization. As Elaine Scarry has noted, a motive is "one way of deflecting the natural reflex of sympathy away from the actual sufferer."[17] A reason is a justification; it implies that there are two sides to the story, that the victim may share the responsibility for his own suffering. Calvinist passion narratives do not legitimate the torturer. Rather, evil is essentially opaque; it discloses itself in the inexplicable desire to cause pain to another creature, in a cruelty whose symbols are the demonic others of the Renaissance imagination: parricide, barbarian, cannibal, Jew, beast, madman.[18]

The representation of Christ's friends and disciples in these narratives does not relieve their grim portrayal of human depravity. The Blessed Virgin is rarely mentioned; Peter and the rest of the disciples appear as exemplars of cowardice and ingratitude. In the end, Christ is "left alone by his Disciples, and forsaken by all his familiars and acquaintance. . . . All those, I say . . . basely hide their heads, and withdraw themselves cleane away."[19] His betrayal by his friends hurts Christ more perhaps than the soldiers' lashes. All the characters just take turns wounding Christ.

The presence of both the reader and the author *in* the text, however, complicates the unambiguous contrast between the suffering Christ and his tormentors in two ways.[20] First, the texts make it clear that if the torturer is the demonic other, he is also the reader. The reader must *identify* with the torturer. The notion that since Christ died for our sins we are all responsible for the Crucifixion originates early in Christian thought,[21] but the Calvinist passion narratives intensify this complicity by merging the position of the reader with that of the torturer. Our sins become not simply the antecedent cause of Christ's sacrifice; rather, we find ourselves sucked into the scene as participants in the act of cruelty. Hall puts it explicitly enough:

> Thou hatest the Jews, spittest at the name of Judas, railest on Pilate, condemnest the cruel butchers of Christ; yet thou canst blaspheme and swear him quite over, curse, swagger, lie, oppress, boil with lust, scoff, riot, and livest like a debauched man; yea like an human beast; yea, like an unclean devil. Cry Hosanna as long as thou wilt, thou art a Pilate, a Jew, a Judas, an executioner of the Lord of life. . . . Every of our sins is a thorn and nail and spear to him.[22]

In Heinsius, the suffering figure on the cross addresses his persecutors; we, however, are instructed to "suppose him speaking unto us with these words: O my people what have I done unto thee, and wherein have I wearied thee?"[23] The passage continues, weaving a prosopopoeia out of the Reproaches from the traditional Good Friday liturgy, in which Christ's pathetic accusations of indifference and ingratitude apply equally to the citizens of Jerusalem and to "us"—both author and reader. The reader/author, that is, enters the typological stage in the role of Christ's tormentor—or worse, since (in Donne's words) "They kill'd once an inglorious man, but I / Crucifie him daily, being now glorified." All sins resolve into reenactments of the Passion's sadistic violence; even to pamper the flesh is "to seeke to crucifie [Christ] againe."[24] This typology thus locates the barbarian, parricide, and cannibal within the self as well as "out there," the rhetoric of identification entailing a logic of introjection. The text creates the guilty self.

The reader/author is also a torturer in a different sense. In the Calvinist passion narratives torture is essentially evil—the essence of evil—but it is also seductive. The overt ethic of these texts rests on the antithesis between violence and a sort of harmless passivity: "We walke after the spirit, when we embrace love, follow peace and holines, shew long-suffering, gentlenes, meeknes, temperance."[25] But an attraction toward violence escapes the authorial voice in strange places. Heinsius concludes a pathetic description of the Crucifixion with an account of how the "love [Christ] bare unto man, was even then no lesse entire than ever it was. For even then I say, hee saved the theefe at the crosse, and prayed for his enemies." This encomium on Christ's merciful compassion, however, immediately leads Heinsius to an outburst of furious anti-Semitism: "What shall I now say unto you sinfull *Jewes*, by whose barbarous fury, and fatall blindnesse the Son of God was crucified? . . . O hatefull and hated Nation! O cruell and abominable people!"[26] In Hall's version of this execration, hatred includes a nasty, vindictive pleasure in another's misfortune: "And have ye not now felt, O nation worthy of plagues, have ye not now felt what blood it was whose guilt ye affected? Sixteen hundred years are now past since you wished yourselves thus wretched: have ye not been, ever since, the hate and scorn of the world?"[27] The violence is not only anti-Semitic, although it is primarily so; less often the curse is directed against Roman Catholics. In either case, the malice of the torturer seems to infect the author/reader. An almost Dantesque metamorphosis occurs in Hall's *Passion Sermon*, where, after summarizing the Roman view that the sufferings of the saints possess an expiatory power, Hall cries out, "Blasphemy, worthy the tearing of garments!"[28] But the biblical passage Hall is preaching on recounts how *Caiaphas*, the high priest, tears his garments in response to Jesus' blasphemy and then condemns him to death. It is a moment of uncanny identification between the Jewish priest and the Christian one.

The same attraction toward violence surfaces in fantasies of retribution and vengeance, when, in Calvin's words, God "will rise with a drawn sword against those whose sins he appeared for a time not to observe."[29] Over the historical figure of the suffering Jesus the texts superimpose the apocalyptic Christ, returning to torment his tormentors: "Ye, that now see him with contempt, shall behold him with horror."[30] Even though Jesus "was exposed to contempt, and almost annihilated . . . at the proper time he will at length come with royal majesty, that they may tremble before the Judge, whom they now refuse to acknowledge as the Author of salvation."[31]

A second fantasy of retribution, more pervasive and central than that of *Christus Judex*, evokes the fall of Jerusalem, where God "justly revenged" Christ's murder "by dreadful and unusual methods."[32] The narrative voice in these scenes betrays its exultant cruelty, gloating maliciously over the destruction of the Jews. Hall tauntingly addresses them:

> Little did the desperate Jews know the weight of that blood which they
> were so forward to wish upon themselves and their children. . . . It is
> pity they should not be miserable. . . . Did ye not live, many of you,
> to see your city buried in ashes, and drowned in blood? to see your-
> selves no nation? Was there ever people under heaven that was made
> so famous a spectacle of misery and desolation? Have ye yet enough of
> that blood which ye called for upon yourselves and your children?[33]

I want to return to the fall of Jerusalem at a later point. It is significant here as the primary site where malice seeps from the representation of evil, infiltrating the desires of the author and reader, who imaginatively identify with these visions of past and future retribution. Priest, soldier, reader, and author share an undifferentiated, miasmic cruelty. Indeed, the will to torment leaves a double mark on the author/reader: as evidence of guilt and as sacred thirst for revenge on the guilty. The author/reader both bears the responsibility for torturing Christ and enjoys the prospect of torturing his torturers. In stanza 53 of "The Countesse of Penbrook's Passion," Nicholas Breton confesses that "my deed was cawser of his death"; stanza 57 reads:

> Shall I not curse those hatefull hellish fiends,
> That led the worlde to worke such wickednes? . . .
> Cut of the head, firste hands upon him layde,
> And helpe to hange the dog that hime betrayed?

Corpus Christi

The graphic representations of Christ's sufferings characteristic of late medieval drama, painting, and preaching all probably derive from a single text, the *Meditations on the Life of Jesus Christ* by the pseudo-Bonaventure, a thirteenth-century Franciscan.[34] Sixteenth-century Calvinist piety recoiled from this visual and affective piety; Calvin himself never portrayed Christ's physical pain. But the pathetic iconography of the *Meditations* reenters Calvinist representations of the Crucifixion in the next century; both Hall and Heinsius, as well as several English preachers, dwell with an almost Ignatian vividness on the horrific agony of Christ's tortured body—the only body registered in these texts.

The Calvinist depiction of this body differs markedly from that found in contemporary Roman Catholic devotional texts. In the latter, the dominant colors are red and white—"the crimson of blood or the royal purple, accompanied by the pure whiteness of innocence and the delicate texture of Christ's skin."[35] The Calvinist Christ, however, is black and blue. Instead of the Counter-Reformation's sentimental "ecstasies of sweet pain,"[36] the Calvinist narratives depict the grotesque physicality of the tortured body:

> Ye see his face blue and black with buffeting, his eyes swoln, his cheeks beslavered with spittle, his skin torn with scourges, his whole body bathed in blood. . . . so wofully disfigured, that the blessed mother that bore thee could not now have known thee; so bloody were thy temples, so swoln and discoloured was thy face, so was the skin of thy whole body streaked with red and blue stripes . . . so did the streams of thy blood cover and deform all thy parts.[37]

This is the victim of cruelty: bruised, mangled beyond recognition, utterly powerless to resist his tormentors or even "to wipe away either his bloud or his Teares, that trickled downe all about his precious bodie."[38] He is impotent and grotesque. Heinsius describes Christ after the flagellation as "beaten with fists, bruised with staves; his face beslimed with spittle, his cheekes swelled out with blowes."[39] A sermon preached before James in 1607 recounts how Pilate "stript him not so much of his clothes as of his skinne by cruell . . . scourging with thornes, scourging with ropes, scourging with chaines" until "by reason of his divers-coloured blowes, and spittings, and stripes, and wounds, and goare, he seemeth as it were in a Leprosie."[40] The texts all record the destruction of manhood, the reduction of a person to a leprous, pulpy, abject body, naked and powerless.

They seem to lay particular stress on bodily fluids: the spit that "beslimes" Christ's face, but also the blood dripping from the crown of thorns and the "sweating of bloud in thicke dropes" during the Agony in the Garden—"nasty mixtures of sweat and blood and spittings on."[41] The power of the torturer both to turn the body inside out and to defile it with his own excrement symbolizes the acute degradation of the victim. The bleeding pores resemble Rabelais's carnival orifices in reverse; instead of incorporating the world, they mark the victim's loss of privacy, his inability to exert control over the peripheries of his own body.[42] In Heinsius, Christ cannot even move his arms to wipe away the blood and saliva—the symbols of shame. All the Calvinist passion narratives, in fact, dwell repeatedly on the shamefulness of Christ's sufferings.[43] It is almost as though the central contrast between gentleness and malice slips over into a still more fundamental contrast between humiliation and power—a distinction grounded less in moral qualities than in the simple physical distinction between the agent and object of social violence. Christ died "bleeding, pained, cursed, shamed, forsaken, despised and mocked."[44]

The passion narratives ascribe both a metonymic and metaphoric function to Christ's torments. Particularly in Calvin, Christ's suffering and humiliation work something like a projective charm, where what happens to Christ will not happen to me. A highly literal version of substitution allows each of Christ's torments to "undo" a piece of our deserved punishment. Thus, "our filthiness deserves that God should hold it in abhorrence, and that all the angels should *spit* upon us; but Christ, in order to present us pure and unspotted in presence of the Father, resolved to be *spat upon*, and to be dishonoured by every kind of reproaches."[45] But more often a logic of identification replaces this logic of substitution. On this second reading, Christ's agony is *like* the sufferings of the elect. "True it is,"

Heinsius thus notes, that like Christ "the Saints on earth are frequently perplexed with variety of exquisite torments."[46] The persecution of the early Reformed communities made men like Calvin resist the common-place association of social marginality and spiritual illegitimacy. He thus reports how "wicked men" mock the Protestants by pointing out their lack of power:

> "Where," they say, "is that immortal glory of which weak and credu-
> lous men are accustomed to boast? while the greater part of them are
> mean and despised, some are slenderly provided with food, others drag
> out a wretched life, amidst uninterrupted disease; others are driven
> about in flight, or in banishment; others pine away in prisons, and
> others are burnt and reduced to ashes?"[47]

The representation of the suffering Christ responds to this taunt, allowing the reader/author to objectify anxieties about the loss of power and to as-suage them by identifying with the innocent victim who is morally and spiritually superior to his tormenters. Under this interpretation, weakness is not shameful; it is the badge of the saints. Furthermore, one suspects, the construction of the self as the victim allows the displacement of the re-sponsibility for torture (the recognition that I crucified Christ) and the desire *to* torture (the hate and vengefulness that at times convulse the au-thorial voice) from the self onto the other. The author/reader's identifica-tion with Christ in agony enables him to disown his own cruelty by constituting himself as the victim of torture *rather than* the torturer.

But, although the Calvinist passion narratives ascribe both exchange and exemplary value to the suffering Christ, they still betray a certain dis-comfort with this figure of abject vulnerability. The passages describing the man of sorrows tend to intersperse two radically different images: the lover of Canticles and the youthful knight. Pictures of desirable and pow-erful manhood replace the shameful body in an anamorphic sequence— the bruised and deformed figure of Christ suddenly reconfigured as beautiful and virile. The images of the grotesque and erotic bodies are very closely juxtaposed. Christ is, Ailesbury announces, "fairer then the chil-dren of men, grace is powred into thy lips: *Intuere sane pannis sordidum, plagis lividum, illitum sputis, pallidum morte*"; Heinsius similarly ex-claims, "Behold the man, behold the man of sorrow. Behold him that was the *fayrest among men, being both white and ruddie. . . . His cheekes as a bed of spices, as sweet flowers. . . .* [He] lyeth now disfigured with wounds, weltring and panting in a crimson river of his owne bloud."[48] The juxtapo-sitions register the terrible contrast, but by mapping the erotic body onto the disfigured one, they also fuse the two images. One is made aware of the erotic resonance of the body in pain—that the victim is a beautiful young man. In an early theological dialogue, Erasmus thus observes that Christ's agonies render him desirable (amabilis).[49]

Like the identification of Christ with the lover of Canticles, the image of the crucified as a knight battling the forces of sin, death, and hell is traditional.[50] Particularly in Lutheran theology, this latter figure dominates representations of the Passion. In the Calvinist passion narratives it comes into view only briefly and abruptly—a half line that then dissolves back into the spit and shame of the historical scene. Its theological import is ambiguous; unlike Lutherans and Roman Catholics, Reformed theologians generally deny that Christ literally descended into hell, instead interpreting the Creed to mean that he suffered something close to the torments of the damned in his last moments on the cross.[51] The anachronistic figure of Christ as the "champion that scorns to be overcome," who "enter[s] the lists with . . . furious Antagonists," retains only a figurative existence.[52] It intimates a discomfort with Christ's powerlessness; but also—in the murky drama where each actor is both torturer and tortured; where the torturers (the Jews) will be tortured by their victim (the Christ of the Apocalypse); where the torturers (we sinners) *are* the victims (types of the suffering Christ)—the knight seems to convey a nostalgic longing for clean violence: the noble champion who triumphs over personified abstractions instead of the horrible sufferings of real bodies.

Subject Positions

The Calvinist passion narratives disclose the reciprocal metamorphoses of the torturer and the tortured. They are mythic stagings not only of violence but also of subjectivity. The rhetorical strategy characteristic of these works establishes multiple and shifting lines of identification between the reader and the personae of the Passion;[53] the reader associates himself with the suffering Christ, the apocalyptic Christ, the Jews, the enemies of the Jews, the barbaric soldiers. He longs for revenge and displaces that longing onto the monsters of cruelty (priests and soldiers), who thus become mirrors of the self; he perceives himself as a type of the innocently suffering Christ, but Christ himself turns out to possess a concealed violence—the violence of the judge and champion. The victim is the self but also both its substitute (Christ tortured instead of me) and finally its object (Christ tortured by me). At times, the voices of the torturer and his victim become indistinguishable. Thus, stanza six of Breton's "Countesse of Penbrook's Passion" reads,

> Put all the woes of all the worlde together,
> Sorrow and Death sitt downe in all ther pryde;
> Lett Miserye bringe all her muses hether,
> With all the horrors that the harte may hyde;
>> Then reade the state but of my rufull storye,
>> And saye my gref hath gotten sorrowe's glorye.

One cannot tell whether the speaker is the suffering Christ or a guilty soul agonized over his complicity in the Crucifixion; one, I think, automatically—and incorrectly—assumes the former throughout the first ten stanzas of Breton's poem. The rhetorical ambiguity intimates a psychological *coincidentia oppositorum* in which the tortured sufferer and the suffering torturer rehearse the same agony.[54]

These texts generate a rhetorical system of cross-identifications in order to produce an unstable, divided selfhood, fissured by its own ambivalent responses to violence.[55] The texts disclose (or produce) the reader's own cruelty and impotence, complicity and victimization. It is the selfhood of Shakespeare's tragic protagonists—Hamlet, Lear, Othello—who are themselves implicated in the evils they attempt to avenge and implicated by attempting to avenge them, who are both cruel and tormented by cruelty, both sinned against and sinning.[56]

It may be considering the matter too curiously to remark that the penultimate moment of all three of these tragedies presents an inverted and perverted pieta: a dead woman, whether mother, daughter, or wife, lamented by the man who both loved and killed her (and who is, therefore, both tortured and torturer).[57] Shakespeare's tragedies are not secular allegories of the Passion, but in *Lear* and *Othello* and in the Calvinist passion narratives the decentering of the subject involves the destruction of radiant figures of womanly compassion and love—destruction rather than death, since women do not literally die in the Calvinist passions; they disappear.[58] These works are prototypical narratives of the absent mother. In medieval accounts of the Passion the reader generally identifies with the Blessed Virgin; her anguished pity and grief model the normative response of the worshiper to this scene of horror. In the thirteenth-century *Stabat Mater*, the poet thus addresses Mary:

> Eia, Mater, fons amoris,
> me sentire vim doloris
>> fac, ut tecum lugeam.

> Fac me vere tecum flere,
> crucifixo condolere,

> donec ego vixero.
> iuxta crucem tecum stare,
> te libenter sociare
> in planctu desidero.[59]

The triple *tecum* (with thee) highlights the poet's identification with Mary and thus locates him, along with her, *outside* the dialectic of tortured and torturer. Mother and worshiper together watch and weep. By remaining outside this dialectic, the Virgin grounds the distinction between the sacred and demonic, between the faithful who mourn their dying Lord and the barbaric soldiers who kill him.

The only women in the Calvinist passion narratives are the "Daughters of Jerusalem" who sorrow for Jesus as he is led out of the city toward Golgotha (Luke 23:27–31). These, however, are not types of Christian pity but themselves guilty and to be destroyed. In Calvin's reading of the episode, Christ "warns them [the women] that there will be far greater reason for *weeping* on account of the dreadful judgment of God which hangs over them; as if he had said, that his death was not the end, but the beginning, of evils to Jerusalem and to the whole nation."[60] Ailesbury is more graphic; Christ tells the women to "still their plaint" until "the rage of slaughter [*sic*] Infants blood shall be more plentifull then Mothers teares, and a screeching voice shall be heard in *Hierusalem*."[61] The little encounter between Christ and the women does not validate the reader's compassion; rather, it makes explicit the link between the Crucifixion and Titus's sack of Jerusalem. It calls attention to the pervasive, reciprocal exchanges of victimization and violence that structure these Calvinist narratives and deconstruct the Calvinist subject.

The Decentered Subject

What kind of god art thou, that suff'rest more
Of mortal griefs than do thy worshippers?

Henry V

The connection between the rhetorical strategies and subject matter of these narratives is not fortuitous. The production of an unstable, internally riven selfhood occurs at the site of the Passion because that selfhood is a product of late medieval Christology. Patristic theology tends to envisage Christ's humanity as largely impersonal. Leo the Great, for example, affirms that when Christ cried out "O God, My God, look upon Me: why hast Thou forsaken Me," he was "speaking for those whom He was redeeming. . . . That cry . . . is a lesson, not a complaint. . . . it is on behalf of us, trembling and weak ones, that He asks why the flesh that is afraid to suffer has not been heard."[62] The body of Christ—the flesh vulnerable to pain—is not Christ's body but the church; as in Grotius, sacrifice presupposes a mystical conjunction between the victim and community. Orthodox Christology thus posits a hypostatic but not a hylomorphic union between Christ's human and divine natures.[63] But the Franciscan stress on the humanity of Christ insisted on his real, personal suffering—the evidence and consequence of his real human nature.[64] In the late Middle Ages, as Caroline Bynum has noted, the humanity of Christ reveals itself as pain.[65] Hence, implicitly or explicitly, the Passion impinges on questions of individuation and selfhood: whether the concept of humanness entails a self that is the subject of its own experiences and feels its own pains.

In 1499 Erasmus and Colet struggled with these issues during the former's visit to Oxford. Four years later, Erasmus published his account of their debate in a little treatise on Christ's Agony in the Garden called *Disputatiuncula de taedio, pavore, tristitia Jesu*, included in the *Lucubratiunculae* of 1503.[66] This essay bears on the present discussion, since it points to the discursive origins of the self-divided subject, the subject of the Calvinist passion narratives, in the self-divided consciousness of the suffering Christ.

As Erasmus describes the debate, Colet argues for the patristic side while Erasmus defends the "modern"—that is, late medieval—theologians (1265). According to Colet, who relies principally on Saint Jerome, Christ could not have been actually frightened or agonized over the prospect of his own death. To deny this would be to imagine him as less loving and less courageous then the martyrs of the primitive church, who faced the worst tortures with cheerful alacrity and an ardent *caritas* that extinguished all sense of pain; indeed, Christ would have been less courageous than even the pagan Stoics, who confronted death unterrified and unwhimpering. For love, Colet insists, entails self-forgetfulness; the lover shakes off all consciousness of self (*"nihil ad se spectare"*), instead passionately diffusing his whole being into his beloved object (*"totam semet aliis profundere"*) (1266). Christ's immense love for us thus destroyed all self-directed anxieties or sufferings. When he prays to his Father, "if it be possible, let this cup pass from me," Colet continues, he does not express a reluctance to die but begs "that his death, by which he desired to redeem the whole world, would not prove catastrophic for the Jews" (1266). He is not afraid for himself but for them—or if not for the Jews, then for the elect: "since the head and body are one, Christ transposes the weakness of his members into himself. . . . On their behalf (*pro his*) he begged his Father to take the cup of bitter death from him; that is, from his body—from Peter, from Paul, from the martyrs" (1268–69). The self is neither the object of Christ's agonized plea nor really its subject. For Colet, the Passion remains embedded in the hagiographic paradigm of torture, where the victim approaches his death with a cheerful tranquillity born of perfect *caritas*.

The Erasmian Christ, however, unlike Colet's spiritual athlete, resembles the terrible and piteous figure of late medieval art: "deformed, destitute, and abject" (1290). The *Disputatiuncula* centers on the claim that Christ truly "feared his own death" (1281), a claim Erasmus derives from anthropological rather than strictly christological premises. He thus begins with a definition of human nature. In a most un-Cartesian manner, he identifies this with the instinct of self-preservation: nature teaches people to flee from whatever might injure or destroy them. Hence, human nature is intrinsically personal or self-regarding, innocently and instinctively caring for the body and fearful of death and pain (1271). As true man, therefore, Christ experienced a natural fear of his own approaching sufferings; as a man endowed with an extraordinarily finely tuned body and soul, his sufferings possessed a unique bitterness (1271). He achieved an unexampled moral heroism because, despite this horrible anguish, he obeyed his Father's will, not because his love deadened all consciousness of torment (1268). For Erasmus, virtue is thus essentially conflictual, a struggle between nature—which he identifies with the maternal flesh—and the Father's sacrificial command (1272–75, 1288).

Erasmus, however, never denies Colet's assertion that Christ felt intense love for humankind and sorrowed over the impending fate of his people. The need to demonstrate how this *caritas* might coexist alongside self-regarding fears leads him to revise traditional Pauline anthropology, with its ontological dualism of flesh and spirit, in order to defend what he at one point calls the "chimerical" self—by which he does not mean that it is imaginary but that it is composed of heterogeneous and heteronomous parts.[67] Instead of Saint Paul's binary psyche, Erasmus posits the existence of three wills or a triple will ("*tres voluntates*," "*triplex nisus animi*")—the disparate impulses of spirit, nature, and flesh (1286–87). The flesh, the base appetites of fallen nature, plays no role in the perfect humanity of Christ, nor does it, Erasmus claims, disturb the sanctified souls of regenerate persons. Christ and his saints struggle not with carnal concupiscence but with nature, whose infirmities may result from primal sin but are not in themselves sinful. This second will tends neither toward the good qua good nor to evil qua evil; rather, it "inclines toward that which is friendly to nature and shrinks from whatever endangers its safety or tranquility" (1287). Such inclinations—hunger, exhaustion, aversion to pain—constitute the "most certain proof of [one's] humanity" and are therefore ineradicable. But since Erasmus equates the spiritual will with sacrificial obedience, this third will opposes the natural urge toward self-preservation; hence, conflict is neither temporary or evitable but, in Fulke Greville's words, the "wearisome condition of humanity / Borne under one Law, to another bound."[68] Moreover, Erasmus insists not only that these individual "parts" or wills pull the psyche asunder but that each will itself fissures internally, self-divided by contradictory desires and affects (1289). That is, the traditional hierarchically structured model of conflict between higher and lower faculties is here supplemented by a series of vertical rifts splitting each faculty into tense fragments. Even in his "rational part," Christ simultaneously experienced both incomparable joy and extreme agony; "He willed and did not will, feared and did not fear, suffered and rejoyced" (1289).

In this chimerical self, one impulse or sensation does not intensify at the expense of the others; it is a psychology not of limited resources but of self-generating capital, where, at least in Christ, all the contradictory and conflictual energies attain their own maximal intensity. Hence "the same object at the same time can generate in him both extreme terror and longing, desire and aversion, profound joy and profound agony" (1286; cf. 1279–80). His cheerful willingness to sacrifice himself in obedience to his Father's will does not mitigate either his physical or psychological torment, "but he perfectly felt each and every one of the thousand torments his body endured as if it had been the only one" (1284).[69] His fear, weakness, and pain exceed those of ordinary persons:

> Those who experience acute fear break out in a cold sweat. Christ sweat blood, not from his face alone but from his whole body and so abundantly that the drops flowed on to the ground. Extremely timid people grow pale and tremble. But Jesus was in agony. . . . Compare two similar crosses; compare two dissimilar crucifieds. The moment Saint Andrew glimpsed the cross from a distance, he rejoyced, he exulted, he congratulated himself, he poured forth words of happiness. . . . This is the disciple. But his master meanwhile sorrows, is oppressed by weariness, is sorrowful unto death, drips bloody sweat (1280).

Yet, Erasmus insists, Christ also and at the same time felt love, tranquillity, and joy. The hagiographic model of the "harmonic" self—a self, that is, unified by a single dominant affect—has been replaced by an "atonal" subjectivity: self-divided, decentered, dissonant. This version of the exemplary subject, one drastically more complex than either the martyr or the Stoic, bears a structural likeness to the readerly self produced by the narrative strategies of the Calvinist passions. Although the Erasmian Christ seems gentler and more loving than the reader implied in these subsequent texts, with his guilty complicity in the act of torture, both *disintegrate* into multiple, contradictory impulses, producing a psyche that is at once decentered and self-divided, incoherent and conflictual.

The Calvinist Automachia

Although in the works I have examined, Calvin nowhere refers to the *Disputatiuncula*, his portrayal of Christ closely resembles the Erasmian prototype. He thus stresses the distracted confusions and disorder of Christ's internal state during his agony, when "struck with fear and seized with anguish . . . amidst the violent shocks of temptation, he vacillated—as it were—from one wish to another."[70] His agony results not from selfless love (whether for the Jews or for the church) but from the "contest," the "test of virtue," in which "the weakness of the flesh, which was formerly concealed, shows itself, and the secret feelings are abundantly displayed." Calvin's ascription of "weakness" to Christ seems all the more remarkable in that he does not distinguish the flesh from nature; but his basic point is the same as Erasmus's: the prospect of death "strikes his [Christ's] mind with a terror to which he had not been accustomed."[71] The conflict Calvin depicts between Christ's "human passions" and obedience to the Father replicates the Erasmian struggle between the heteronomous imperatives of nature and spirit. Christ combats not infernal powers but himself. Calvin moreover depicts this struggle between human terror and obedience to the paternal will as a conflict between doubt and faith; thus, on the cross, "the inward sadness of his [Christ's] soul was so powerful and violent, that it forced him to break out into a *cry*. . . . [Yet] though the perception of the flesh would have led him to dread destruction, still in his heart faith remained firm, by which he beheld the presence of God, of whose absence he complains."[72]

Calvin's Erasmian Christology clarifies some of the more puzzling aspects of his epistemology, particularly his understanding of faith. For Calvin, faith "requires a full and fixed certainty, such as men are wont to have from things experienced and proved." This seems clear enough, although perhaps humanly impossible. But he confuses matters by adding, "We cannot imagine any certainty that is not tinged with doubt, or any assurance that is not assailed by some anxiety. . . . Believers are in perpetual conflict with their own unbelief."[73] Calvin's apparently contradictory assertions that the elect possess unshakable assurance of God's love and that they invariably doubt it depend on the Erasmian psychology of the chimerical self, but here applied to the common experience of Christians rather than to the mind of Christ. According to the *Institutes*,

> The godly heart feels in itself a division because it is partly imbued
> with sweetness from its recognition of the divine goodness, partly
> grieves in bitterness from an awareness of its calamity; partly rests
> upon the promise of the gospel, partly trembles at the evidence of its
> own iniquity; partly rejoices at the expectation of life, partly shudders
> at death.[74]

The antithetic "parts" (sweetness/bitterness, rests/trembles, rejoices/shudders) do not regress toward an experiential mean; rejoicing and shuddering, that is, do not produce an intermediate sensation of mild anxiety. Rather, as in Erasmus, the godly heart tastes the particular sweetness or bitterness of each sip, contains within itself intense and contradictory emotions. But Erasmus's account of the fissured and conflictual chimerical self was developed to explain why Christ seemed so much weaker and more troubled than the hagiographic hero. In Calvin, this account is generalized into a representation of the inner life of the elect—the new model saint. The Calvinist saint inherits the Erasmian Christ's decentered and complex subjectivity.

The struggle between doubt and assurance, Calvin notes, results from the Pauline "division of flesh and spirit."[75] Calvin's immensely influential Augustinian reading of Romans 7 points in the same direction as Erasmus's discussion of the war between spirit and nature. Both deny that this conflict belongs either to the unregenerate or to the early, painful stages of sanctification. Calvin differs from Augustine in the exact point he most closely approaches Erasmus: in the claim that Christ too endured this sort of Christian warfare. This claim becomes possible because, even though Calvin does not distinguish timid "nature" from the sinful "flesh," he maintains that "this conflict . . . is not in any man before he be sanctified by the Spirit of God." The godly alone suffer this self-division, where "they fight against their nature, and their nature fighteth against them," until "distracted with divers desires, [each] is now in a manner divided, (and of one made two men)."[76] As Montaigne remarked from quite a different perspective, "Even good authors are wrong to insist on fashioning a consistent and solid fabric out of us."[77] The self-divided reader produced by the Calvinist passion narratives is thus the rhetorical mirror of the

Protestant psyche, which, in turn, incorporates the decentered, chimerical selfhood of the late medieval Christ. Moreover, as terms like "conflict," "Christian warfare," and "struggle" indicate, the divisions are not static compartments but sites of violence.

In Calvin, awareness of the opposing surges of intense, contradictory emotions sweeping across this psyche gives rise to an urgent demand for self-control, moderation, and obedience to external authority in order to halt this inner turbulence. Calvin thus reasons that since even Christ had to struggle against his fear of death, "how carefully ought we to repress the violence of our feelings, which are always inconsiderate, and rash, and full of rebellion?"[78] In many of the Calvinist passion narratives, self-control and cognate virtues like moderation, patience, and submission virtually displace *caritas* as the ethical substance of the Crucifixion. But in the same passion narratives, self-control itself turns out to be a form of violence and hence unable to still the eddying repetitions of torture, in which the victim and aggressor exchange roles in a seemingly endless cycle.

There is an odd scene in Heinsius where he imagines the divine and human natures of Christ splitting apart in the Crucifixion, so that "it was the *flesh* that was the sacrifice; It was the *Deity* that was the Priest that sacrificed it."[79] This division of the self (insofar as this term can be applied to Christ) into the object and agent of sacrifice in turn provides the fundamental Calvinist metaphor for sanctified self-fashioning. Hall writes:

> Ye must either kill or die. Kill your sins or else they will be sure to kill your souls; apprehend, arraign, condemn them; fasten them to the tree of shame, and if they be not dead already, break their legs and arms. . . . What a torture must there needs be in this act of violence! what a distension of the body, whose weight is rack enough to itself! what straining of the joints! what nailing of hands and feet![80]

The opening sentence of this passage hints at a lurking apotropaic fantasy that by punishing the self one can ward off further punishments—a disciplinary logic characteristic of these texts. For Hall, the appropriate response to the Crucifixion is to repeat it, self-inflicted violence replacing penal suffering—the Freudian strategy of the superego here construed as an *imitatio Christi*. The revulsion from cruelty characteristic of these texts brushes uncomfortably against such ecstasies of aggression toward the self, where the Christian must introject the scene of torture, becoming both crucified and crucifier. But this sort of internalized violence pervades Calvinist anthropology, which regularly describes the conscience as the faculty of self-torment: the "internal executioner," the "*testis, iudex, tor-*

tor."[81] For the rigidly Calvinist John Owen, the essence of spiritual discipline is "Autothusias or self-slaughter, crucifying the old man."[82] Hence, the attempt to regulate violence merely transposes it, so that the imitation of Christ involves always-already the impersonation of his torturers. The Calvinist end myth narrates what Michael Schoenfeldt calls "the internal migration of authority that produces the modern subject."[83] But instead of Freud's steam-engine allegory, this subject enacts a passion play.

If, as previously noted, the Calvinist passion narratives fashion the self as the typological victim persecuted by monsters of cruelty—whether Roman soldiers or Roman Catholics—the self, or at least a part of the self, is also the guilty victim who must be crucified by the self; that is, the internal executioner, witness, judge, and torturer must "crucifie the flesh with the affections."[84] The elect, Calvin writes, are ambushed, attacked, and wounded by the enemies of the Gospel, but "the principal combat we must wage is against ourselves."[85] The self is both victim and enemy. Despite its official theology of penal substitution, Calvinism thus tends to view the Atonement as a mimetic opportunity. It becomes the exemplary and originary site of violence, one that does not satisfy the demand for punishment but instead intensifies it. The church has the duty, "by bringing men into the obedience of the Gospel, to offer them as it were in sacrifice unto God," Calvin explains, "and not as the papists have hitherto proudly bragged, by the offering up of Christ to reconcile men unto God."[86]

Domestic Violence

In Erasmus, Christ's agony results from his natural fear of death. The Calvinist passion narratives, however, almost never locate this decentering inner torment either in Christ's instinctive reluctance to die (which these narratives generally minimize) or in his physical suffering at the hands of the soldiers. The representation of agony belongs not to the scenes of political violence but to those of domestic violence—the confrontation of Father and Son. This latter violence is more terrible than the other, Hall explains, as "God's wrath [is] beyond the malice of men."[87] All the Calvinist passion narratives stress that Christ's most excruciating misery stems from his sense that he has been abandoned by his Father, who now menaces him with the full force of his paternal wrath. The texts thus report that when Christ "saw the wrath of God exhibited to him, as he stood at the tribunal of God charged with the sins of the whole world, he unavoidably shrunk with horror from the deep abyss of death"; it was "as if an offended God had thrown him into a whirlpool of afflictions."[88] These passages, which repeatedly emphasize that it is the *Father* (rather than "God" or "the Almighty," for example) who causes Christ's suffering, configure the Crucifixion as a desexualized version (if such a thing is possible) of the oedipal agon.[89] Their harshness is unrelenting; nothing in any of the Calvinist passion narratives is remotely comparable to the passage in the pseudo-Bonaventure's *Life of Christ*, where the Father speaks to his dead child: "Come my sweete and beloved Sonne, for thou hast consummate all things wonderfull well, nor will I that thou suffer any further torment: wherefore come unto me, come and I shall embrace thee with in mine armes, come and repose thee in thy Fathers bosome."[90] In the Calvinist texts, the wrathful Father threatens the child, who shrieks out in agony while submitting to this punitive, paternal will.

This scene is central to the Calvinist interpretation of the Passion. It effects a radical rereading of the credal claim that Christ descended into hell. Calvin and some English Calvinists rejected the traditional notion of Christ's triumphal harrowing of hell during the period between his death and the Resurrection, instead locating Christ's "descent" in his agony and desolation on the cross, where, according to the English Separatist Henry Jacob, "seeing the sorrowes and horrors of Gods firie wrath are equal to *Hell*: So wee affirme, Christ was in *Hell* even in this life, he suffered *Hell* for us, or rather *Hellish* sorrows."[91] The descent into hell here does not narrate Christ's victory over the demonic powers but figures his exquisite vulnerability to the Father's anger.

Mainstream English Calvinists use the same images. Thus, Hall speaks of Christ's "inward torments . . . in the sense and apprehension of thy Father's wrath," which "pressed thy soul, as it were, to the nethermost hell."[92] Chamberlaine likewise explains: "Behold the Passion of Christ. He cried, with aloude [*sic*] voice he cried: My God, my God, why hast thou forsaken me? No tongue can expresse, nor heart conceive the pangs, the paines, the punishment which he suffered. For the time the paines of the damned, the torments of hell fell upon him."[93] The fear, weakness, and inner agony of Christ disclose themselves in this scenario of domestic torture—of child abuse, if one excuses the anachronism. Christ's victory, on this reading, lies in his obedience to the Father even when he "turns his back upon him as a stranger; yea, he woundeth him as an enemy."[94] Although the traditional images of Christ's victory over the powers of death linger on the margins of these narratives, the theological revision here effects a pervasive generic shift from romance to tragedy: from the supernal knight-errant rescuing the souls of the patriarchs and prophets to the darker scene of psychological anguish, domestic conflict, and bloodshed.

This scene, like the other episodes in the Calvinist passion narratives, operates according to the rhetoric of identification. Christ's agony typifies the desolation of the sixteenth-century Reformed churches, of the persecuted elect, whose sufferings seem to intimate that they have been abandoned by God to their enemies. Christ endured these sufferings, Calvin comments, so that "they might not at the present day strike us with excessive alarm, as if they had been unusual."[95] The moral of this story is always the same: the pedagogy of pain, which teaches patient trust in a God who seems absent or hostile.[96] The world, Hall explains, is a passion play; "We [are] set upon the sandy pavement of our theatre, and are matched with all sorts of evils. . . . God and his angels sit upon the scaffolds of heaven, and behold us." The script requires us to "groan and bleed."[97]

But the descriptions of Christ's agony possess a more complex resonance than this pedagogic model would suggest, in part because they consistently remind the reader that the wrathful judge is Christ's *Father*. In this family romance, the Father invariably figures punitive anger; he is, according to Heinsius, "a devouring fire, an overflowing torrent of wrath, as violent as a rough storme of hayle, as impetuous as a tempestuous gust of wind."[98]

A more complex and contradictory series of images, however, characterizes the Son. The representation of the dying Christ braids together four strands, each dominated by a specific figuration of male identity. First there is sheer terror, the terror of a child "lamentably shriek[ing] out under his Father's wrath." Hall thus rewrites Christ's final speech from the cross: "What! *forsaken me!* Not only brought me to this shame, smitten me, unregarded me, but as it were forgotten, yea, forsaken me. What! even me, my Father! . . . me, thine only, dear, natural, eternal Son?"[99] Jacob likewise compares the dying Christ to a forsaken child, one whose appearance, "all tombled in blood, or mire, & most stincking filth," revolts his parent.[100] As in the scenes of physical torture, these passages detail the impotence, weakness, and humiliating dependency produced by pain: Christ lies "groveling and gasping"; "like a worme *hee* crawles upon the ground."[101]

Yet the passion narratives juxtapose these images of infantile misery with the traditional figure of the youthful knight triumphing over his enemies. "Our Saviour," Hall remarks, "stays not death's leisure, but willingly and courageously meets him in the way."[102] Heinsius describes how "God the Father together with his whole family & Court of Heaven, stood and behelde the pangs and passion of his beloved Sonne" as he "enter[s] the lists with these furious Antagonists."[103] In such a passage, the Father resembles a Renaissance nobleman watching his son prove himself on the field of battle. The Passion here enacts a chivalric rite of passage, not the tragic destruction of masculine strength. But these representations occur infrequently in the Calvinist passion narratives; as in an anamorphic painting, where one angle suddenly reveals an unexpected and otherwise invisible image, these texts allow a momentary glimpse of the radiant young knight amid the somber and bloody scenes of passive victimization.

In general, the school of suffering replaces the tournament; the obedient (although terrified) son supplants the victorious knight. The texts considered here stress the trial of obedience, where, to use Erasmus's terms, the Son must reject "mother nature"—the instinct of self-preservation—in order to drink from the Father's cup. Yet their emphasis on the Son's meek submission to this economy of sacrificial suffering, which quantifies moral value in terms of pain, only partially conceals traces of filial aggression *against* the Father. The hostility flickers out of the verbs: Christ "is wrestling with the wrath of his Father"; in the end, the "wrath of his Father . . . lie[s] gasping at his foot."[104] Heinsius at one point depicts Christ as a Promethean figure, standing "in the vanguard of the battell" to protect us "from the gunneshot of his Fathers indignation."[105] These parricidal metaphors occur frequently in Lutheran texts, but there they have a specific theological import;[106] in Calvinist works, which do not employ Luther's potentially antinomian dialectic of law versus love, the images of Christ battling with or trampling on the wrathful Father attach themselves uneasily to the circumambient narrative of paternal violence directed against the prostrate Son, as though the hurt child were now getting even with his father. They seem dramatic, not dogmatic, intimating psychological complications rather than theological explanations. Even in Calvin, who avoids any such allusion to filial hostility, Christ's self-control, which allows him to face the threatenings of the paternal judge without being crushed or losing his inner balance, seems itself almost a form of opposition. In Calvinist piety, as students of Herbert will recognize, self-control usually implies a covert resistance to "the Lord of Powre"; the attempt to withstand the torturer is itself a suspect assertion of inner autonomy.

The Calvinist passion narratives thus depict Christ's relation to his Father as an unstable compound of dependence, self-assertion, obedience, and subversion. (One thinks of the Prince of Denmark and his father.) The frightened child who cries out for his wrathful Father is also the divine hero conquering the forces of darkness. The Son who meekly obeys the Father at the same time attacks him, the demand for submission itself eliciting a repressed anger. Christ is simultaneously child, champion, dutiful son, and aggressor; these are the personae of the Calvinist chimerical self. For the intercalated representations of the dying Christ split into the same polarities of weakness and power, victimization and violence that characterize the implied reader of the torture scenes. Both rhetorically and dramatically, the passion narratives present violence (both acted and endured) as the site of self-division and subjective contradiction.

This crumbling of the psyche into opposing figures or roles produces the apparently contradictory impression that expected oppositions have been eroded. One gets the sense that things are fragmenting and coagulating at the same time. As the reader turns out to incarnate both the victim and the torturer, so Christ ends up, as most oedipal sons do, becoming *like* his Father. Although the crucifixion scenes are structured by the contrast between the harsh patriarch and the desolate child, the apocalyptic Christ depicted in the same passion narratives burns with a paternal wrath. Hall thus apostrophizes the soldiers who tormented Christ: "Was not that hand fit for a reed, whose iron scepter crushes you to death? was not that face fit to be spat upon, from the dreadful aspect whereof ye are ready to desire the mountains to cover you?"[107] The present tense of the main verbs suggests that Christ has *already* replaced his Father as the terrible judge of souls. One may contrast this to George Sandys's dedicatory epistle to his translation of Grotius's *Christus patiens*, in which Sandys observes that because of Christ's sacrifice, "That terrible Lord of Hosts is now This meek God of Peace."[108] It is precisely this transformation that does *not* occur in the Calvinist narratives. Instead, Christ carries on the ancient retributive economy: "Thou strikest; Christ Jesus smarteth, and will revenge. These are the ὑστερήματα, *afterings* of Christ's sufferings."[109] The fissuring of the self collapses distinctions between selves, because all the persons, whether implied or represented, in these narratives share a taste for violence and revenge. It is as though in this case the killing of the scapegoat does not resolve the crisis of differentiation, as Girard would have it, but produces it; at the site of sacrifice, torturer and tortured, Father and Son, victim and aggressor converge and exchange roles.

One can isolate three sequential "moments" in the representational syntax of these texts: the inner fragmentation of the central figures, the erosion of difference between figures, and finally an overarching narrative structure based on repetition rather than transformation. As the first implies the second, so the second "moment" implies the third: since violence infiltrates all the textual positions, crime and punishment continue to alternate in an interminable cycle. The Lord of Hosts does not become the

God of Peace. A 1614 passion sermon preached at Canterbury Cathedral by one Thomas Wilson is explicit on this point; one ought not imagine, he states,

> as though there were two Gods, one of the olde Testament, and another of the new: and that the God of the new Testament, of the twaine was the milder, whereas there is but one onely God, and the same always like to himselfe. God is ever but one . . . as extreamely hating and punishing sin now under the Gospell, as he was wont to doe under the Law; nay, more extreamly.

The conclusion of this paragraph introduces the crucial instance of the new dispensation: "All the olde Testament cannot yeeld an example of such severitie in punishing sinne as here is threatened touching the destruction of Jerusalem and downefall of the Jewes. No sorrow was like their sorrow."[110]

The final sentence, of course, with its christological allusion, configures the destruction of the Jews as a restaging of the Crucifixion, violence begetting violence according to a logic whereby the torturer becomes the victim and vice versa. In the Calvinist narratives, the Passion culminates in the fall of Jerusalem "by dreadful and unusual methods"—and not in the Resurrection.[111] The Passion, in fact, causes the fall of Jerusalem, since "from the punishment which immediately followed, it was manifest that the life of Christ was dear to God the Father, at the time when all imagined that he had been wholly forsaken and cast off."[112] The Father, that is, reveals his love for his Son by destroying the Jews. Calvin additionally observes that the Father ignored Christ's final prayers for mercy on his tormentors; despite his "compassion," Christ acquiesces "in the righteous judgment of God, which he knew to be ordained for reprobate and obstinate men."[113] All the Calvinist passion narratives note that Christ's horrible death had, in Hall's words, "slender fruit."[114] This death is not the final convulsive spasm of violence ending the retributive economy but the "irreparable crime" that can be punished only by being repeated: in the destruction of the Jews and in the obligatory self-crucifixion imposed on all guilty parties—that is, on everyone.[115]

Violence, Subjectivity, and Manhood

The rhetoric of identification in Calvinist passion narratives requires the reader to introject both the normative cultural personae (the knight and the obedient child) and the more disturbing and problematic figures of the torturer and the agonized Christ, to recognize them as voices of the self. The lines of identification are not grounded in a single antetype but crisscrossed and entangled so that the self finally occupies all narrative positions. The reader, like Christ, endures persecution, but the reader also resembles the Jews, whose penalty for killing Christ is to be—like Christ—killed; the reader participates in the Crucifixion and hence must also be crucified. The persecutors thirst for blood; the Father strikes his Son and then revenges his death on the Jews; the Son returns as a wrathful judge; the reader eagerly anticipates the destruction of Christ's enemies. Christ is bruised, humiliated, shamed—like the elect and like the Jews. The kaleidoscopic regress produced by these cross-identifications is the narrative counterpart to the self-divided, decentered psyche, a psyche mirrored in the similarly kaleidoscopic sequence of images used to portray the chimerical Christ.

This complex and conflictual Christian subjectivity differs profoundly from prior conceptualizations of ideal selfhood. As Erasmus points out, the dominant cultural models of the self from late antiquity through the Middle Ages are the Catholic martyr and Stoic sage, both of whom embody what might be called a "monothelite" ideal—an undeviating singleness of will and purpose, a limpid simplicity of intention.[116] Erasmus, however, seems openly uncomfortable with the hagiographic model of personality, finding it unreal and inhuman. Calvin also largely abandoned this model. As William J. Bouwsma notes, the ruthless self-examination Calvinism demanded splits the self "into observer and observed, audience and actor, neither capable of natural and spontaneous behavior. . . . He was driven back to theatricality even by his effort to escape it."[117] In both Erasmus and Calvin, the chimerical self, with its conflicting wills and internal divisions, replaces the integral subjectivities of martyr and sage, although, interestingly, all three cultural types are produced by violence. The chimerical self, one should stress, is not a late version of the psychomachia—the interior battleground between the virtues and vices; as the *Disputatiuncula* makes clear, the chimerical self originates in Christology, not ethics. Like the martyr and the sage, it therefore lays claim to an ideal cultural value. The struggling and suffering Christ replaces the tranquil martyr as the prototype (and antetype) of the sanctified personality.

Erasmus's Christ still belongs to the late medieval representations of the Man of Sorrows, whose terror and anguish do not lessen his inextinguishable love; in fact, they render him more lovely, since they reveal the extent of his sacrifice. The Calvinist Christ seems more troubling. The images of impotent victim, frightened child, vengeful judge, and rebellious son—images of abjection and violence—possess a tragic darkness. The implied reader is likewise a disturbing presence, both guilty and victimized, a torturer and tortured. One hesitates to call the Calvinist Christ an ideal figure; he is rather a persona of the end myth, in which the characters who traditionally embodied objective cultural values become instead symbols of inner conflict and contradiction.

The cultural import of this end myth can be approached by noting the structure and circulation of its images. Whether portraying inner, psychological divisions or relations between separate figures, these images tend to occur in twos, organized by the binary alternatives of impotence and power. With respect to Christ, the two principal image pairs articulate, first, the duality of Christ himself as the hurt, forsaken child and as the conqueror triumphing over both personified (death, sin) and historical (the Jews) enemies and, second, the opposition between the hideously tormented Christ and his torturers. The inner split between victim and knight replicates the objective contrast between victim and tormentor insofar as the antithesis of weakness and power structures both. This double set of opposing images encodes an ambivalence about violence. On the one hand, violence manifests itself as cruelty, as the demonic. But its victim seems curiously repellent; in the Calvinist passion narratives, the suffering Christ is grotesque, frightened, weak, unable even to wipe off the blood and spit running down his face, groveling wormlike on the ground in his terrified desolation. The narratives betray a revulsion from this pathetic passivity; the figure of the victim keeps slipping toward contrasting images of strength and self-assertion: the knight, the apocalyptic avenger, the child trampling on the Father. The victim, that is, slips toward the torturer—and the torturer toward the victim, since those who crucified Christ will be destroyed in the fall of Jerusalem. The brief images of Christ as eroticized ephebe that surface during the torture scenes further complicate the presentation of violence with hints of a sadistic interest in the mangled body of the beautiful youth, as though the revulsion from the pathetic enclosed an attraction toward the pathic.

A similar metamorphic circulation of violence involves the reader, who belongs among the innocently suffering elect and who gloats over the sufferings of Christ's enemies but who also, finally, is one of the torturers and complicit in the Crucifixion. The passion narratives by Breton and Nashe describe Christ as a mother pelican feeding her young with her own blood—a traditional emblem of self-giving love—but they focus on the baby birds, the fledglings who tear out the bowels and womb (the terms are Nashe's) of their parent like Lear's "pelican daughters."[118] The image of maternal sacrifice, rewritten as filial ingratitude, emblematizes the guilty awareness of one's own cruelty. It sketches in miniature the shift from the pathos of the late medieval passions to the problematic violence of the Calvinist narratives. The sacrificial pelican, like the martyr, recedes, displaced by vicious little birds and the perhaps equally discomforting images of the hurt and humiliated child. The narratives offer only two positions: one is either a victim or violent. And these positions turn out to be interchangeable. Moreover, attempts at self-control fail to halt the oscillations of violence and victimization, since the effort to repress one's own impulses toward cruelty itself requires violence and hence merely internalizes the dialectic of the torturer and tortured rather than resolving it; the reader avenges his complicity in the Crucifixion by becoming the victim of his own violence.

What is this story about? Thomas Wilson's *Art of Rhetoric* translates *fortitudo*, the virtue involved in inflicting and enduring pain, as manhood.[119] Renaissance usage generally overlaps notions of violence and masculinity. Their entanglement in the passion narratives seems fairly evident, inasmuch as the problematics of violence are rendered through sequential images of male figures: knight, child, judge, soldier, priest, father, son, and so forth. The texts represent violence primarily in terms of masculine identity rather than social conflict, references to economic or political motives being minimal. The self-divisions and cross-identifications that take place under the sign of the scapegoat—the site of social and supernatural violence—present a deeply disturbed vision of Christian manhood.

Thus, in the Calvinist passion narratives, violence releases neither the triumphant energies of the spirit (the martyr) nor, generally, the heroic splendor of the undaunted will (the warrior). Instead, one gets the frightened Christ, whose body is exquisitely tender "as beeing shaped of Virginsubstance without commixture of the male nature."[120] Erasmus similarly suggests that Christ's "female" temperament might provide a physiological explanation for his terror, people with "cold, scanty blood . . . [and] thinned spirits"—characteristics of female bodies—being more likely to show fear than those of hotter constitutions (1274). Questions about Christ's "femaleness" occur in a more overtly anxious form in Calvin, who several times feels impelled to deny that Christ had an "effeminate mind"—a curious protest.[121] It is clear in each case that "female" or "effeminate" does not connote "swishy" but belongs to a complex of notions relating to cowardice and the inability to withstand pain. In this sense, Christ's agony raises obvious questions about his manhood.

It is not just his "female" terror. Almost all the images of Christ carry suggestions of male inadequacy. The sole exception occurs in the depiction of Christ as a young knight battling evil personifications while the Father looks on approvingly—an allegorical picture of safe violence. But this image only throws into relief the troubling representations of the passive and terrified Christ, of the wrathful Father unmanning his Son, and the various other scenes of brutality, weakness, and unallegorical suffering. The agonized Christ seems a peculiarly Renaissance nightmare of emasculation, of the loss of power, autonomy, strength, and status. Conversely, the figures who possess the power to hurt are frighteningly sadistic. The texts portray male strength almost exclusively as the capacity to inflict pain on human bodies in a crescendo of violence stretching from the flagellation to the destruction of Jerusalem. "If it be man's work I'll do't," says the Captain in *King Lear*. And then he strangles the Christlike Cordelia.[122]

The narratives likewise assail the manhood of the reader, demanding that he confess his guilt, apologize, and submit—forcing him into the position of a bad child—and at the same time encouraging fantasies of revenge, the pleasures of anticipating other people's pain. The excruciatingly contradictory images of male abjection and cruelty structuring the narrative function rhetorically as emblems of masculine selfhood. The texts insist that the reader perceive these figures as psychological projections of his own malice and impotence.

The catastrophic representations of male identity in the Calvinist passion narratives do not seem to be anomalous. Rather, one may view them as mythic versions of a larger crisis of manhood that leaves its traces throughout the characteristic discourses of the period. Perhaps *crisis* is the wrong word for something more like a convulsive shudder running through a culture, a conceptual disturbance that never achieves direct articulation but is obliquely apprehended through the distortions effected in a society's symbolic forms. One notes the tendency for Renaissance versions of the morality play and the prodigal son story—both male *Bildungsfabeln*—to take tragic form. A diffuse anxiety about manhood also hangs over the plots of Shakespeare's major tragedies, especially *Hamlet*, *Coriolanus*, *Othello*, *Lear*, and *Macbeth*.[123] The first three climax in the protagonist's catastrophic attempt violently to assert his own masculinity: a son proving himself to his oedipal father, another son entangled in the fantasies of a domineering mother, a husband destroying his castrating wife. *Lear* is, of course, about fathers and children, about the terrible vulnerability of old men. Fears of being unmanned, cowardly, cuckolded, and soft suffuse the plays. Renaissance erotic literature likewise tells of male insufficiency. Astrophel ends up alone on a deserted road at night cursing ridiculously into the empty air.[124] The romantic aspirations of Petrarch, Wyatt, and Troilus also miscarry badly. Even the single extant sixteenth-century English pornographic poem, Nashe's *Choice of Valentines*, does not record the triumph of the patriarchal phallus but a humiliating episode where the man first cannot perform and then finishes so quickly that his partner is left to solace herself with an artificial surrogate.

The Christian Petrarchist

And in any case lette us take heede howe daungerous a thynge it is to make Christe Jesus weepe.

> John Stockwood, *"A very fruitful and necessary sermon of the destruction of Jerusalem"*

The agonies of Christian manhood intimated in the Calvinist passion narratives just discussed surface unmistakably in the strangest of the Renaissance retellings of Christ's final suffering: Thomas Nashe's *Christs Teares over Jerusalem*, written during the plague of 1593 right after Nashe had finished *The Unfortunate Traveler*. Students of Nashe have found the work puzzling: Charles Nicholl considers it evidence of an incipient nervous breakdown; Jonathan Crewe raises the possibility that the whole thing may be a blasphemous parody.[125] I cannot dismiss either opinion out of hand, but neither do I think they explain very much. Although the first part of *Christs Teares* relates an episode immediately prior to the Crucifixion, it is, in fact, a passion narrative—a meditation on Christ's suffering and death—thematically and structurally very close to the Calvinist passions. Any historically plausible interpretation of this piece has to take into account its relation to these orthodox compositions.

The work has three sections. The first develops an extended prosopopoeia in which Christ struggles with his own impending death and the subsequent fall of the city that rejected him; the second describes the siege of Jerusalem in grisly detail, including the infamous episode in which a famished mother eats her son; the third anatomizes London's sins, threatening her with the fate of Jerusalem if she does not repent. Nashe's focus on the causal link between the Passion and the destruction of Jerusalem (and London) immediately connects this work to the Calvinist narratives, but I want to bracket that link for the time being and focus on the first section.

Nashe's Christ suffers the unbearable sorrows of unreciprocated affection. He is passionately in love with Jerusalem; he longs to "engraspe" her walls "in myne amorous enfoldment."[126] He woos her, promising to "bee to thee all in all, thy riches, thy strength, thine honour, thy Patron, thy provider" (32). Standing beside the Temple, he bursts out, "O let mee embrace thee while thou yet standest," and he bends to cover its "Alablaster out-side"—so like Desdemona's "monumental alabaster"[127]—with "scalding sighes & dimming kisses" (51). There are echoes here of the ancient allegorical reading of Canticles as the story of Christ's rapturous love for his church. But this Christ is not the comely youth of Canticles: his "eyebals" have shrunken to "pinnes-heads with weeping"; "black and cindry (like Smithes-water) are those excrements that source downe my cheekes, and farre more sluttish then the uglie oous of the channell" (36). He claims to have beaten his hands against his breast so often while praying for his beloved that they have been reduced to a withered, bony pulp (37). These descriptions resemble the flagellation scenes in the Calvinist passion narratives; it is the same vision of the deformed, battered, abject Christ, although now tormented by erotic melancholy rather than whips and nails.

The allegorical romance begins to remind one of unpleasant high-school episodes. The pitifully ugly young man prostrates himself before an amazed female, begging,

> Relieve my languor. . . . Glance but halfe a kind looke at mee, though thou canst not resolve to love me; by halfe a looke my love may steale into thine eyes unlookt for. . . . I have kneel'd, wept bitterly, lift up myne handes, hunge upon her, and vowed never to let her goe, til shee consented to retire herselfe into my tuition, & aunswerd pleasingly to my petition. (55–56)

She, not surprisingly, disdainfully refuses these groveling entreaties. The personified city resembles Wyatt's mistresses: cold, deceitful, and contemptuous of gentle men. Nashe captures both her scornful malice and Christ's unmasculine tenderness in a strange image where she bites his breasts rather than sucking them (53)—a pelican lady. Christ tries to hold her, but when she sees Satan, "she will touch him, he stretcheth not out his hande to her, but she breaketh violently from mee, to runne ravishtlie into his rugged armes" (22). The crucial word in this sentence is, of course, "rugged."[128] Nashe's Petrarchan Lady, like Spenser's Lucifera—both incarnations of the evil city—turns out to be a "gorgious strumpet" (16) whose beauty conceals her inner syphilitic contamination (51).

In despair, Christ pleads with his Father for her, but "(enrag'd) hee hath bid me out of his sight, chyd me, rebukt me" (57). This is the wrathful Father of the Calvinist passion narratives. Disgusted with his puling Son, who will not stop pining after a woman who despises him, the Father thrusts Christ away, ordering him to "let mee alone, that I may wreake myne anger on her and consume her" (57).

Christ's love turns to violence as well. Like Wyatt's embittered Petrarchist, this tender, passive male avenges his spurned affection by attacking (verbally and physically) the beloved. Nashe astonishingly compares him to the hero of Marlowe's *Tamburlaine*, published only three years before *Christs Teares*. Emulating Tamburlaine, Christ first offers "the Jewes the White-flagge of forgivenesse and remission, and the Red-flag of shedding his Blood for them, [and] when these two might not take effect . . . the Black-flagge of confusion and desolation" (20). Christ struggles one final time to make Jerusalem relent, but in the end he turns away with the futile warning, "Save thy selfe as well as thou mayst, for I have forsaken thee; to *desolation* have I resigned thee" (59). Christ cannot save his beloved; rather, he causes her destruction, since the city falls as punishment for the Crucifixion. He knows this. He is aware that, although he became man "to the end that Hell (not *Jerusalem*) might perish," nevertheless his coming to Jerusalem has "opend & enwidened Hell mouth, to swallow thee and devoure thee" (29).

Christs Teares thus relates the *failure* of redemption. Christ himself recognizes the failure: "I must be slaughtered for thee, & yet worke no salvation for thee" (35).[129] His speeches alternate between threatening Jerusalem if she does not respond and pleading with his Father or with no one in particular that somehow his death might finally prove redemptive:

> Not a nayle that takes hold of me, but I wil (expresly) enjoyne it to take hold of her deflectings and errors. Death, (as ever thou hopest at my hands to have thy Commission enlarged,) when thou killest me, kill her iniquities also. . . . Forgyve them, Lord, they forget what they doe. (53–54)

But, of course, the cycle of violence does not break off, and the second part of *Christs Teares* recounts the ghastly end of the city.

Christ does not gloat over her destruction. As he contemplates her "divastation," he feels "some essentiall parte of my life seemeth to forsake me and droppe from mee" (51). One's sense of Christ's sacrificial agony— of how much his love costs—increases as he moves toward his murderous resolution, as if his love only fully manifests itself in his anguish over killing what he cherishes; one thinks of Othello's explanation: "This sorrow's heavenly, / It strikes where it doth love."[130] In Nashe, as in Shakespeare, the intermingling of cruelty and *caritas* gives these scenes a deep and unusual pathos. In the end both Christ and Jerusalem stand confronting each other frozen in a tableau of endless sorrow, where "for ever I must mourne what thou for ever must suffer" (45).

Christs Teares reproduces the dialectic of the torturer and the tortured characteristic of the Calvinist passion narratives, only making more explicit their connection between the myth of the agonized avenger and issues of manhood by braiding the Petrarchan narrative of male erotic failure into the Calvinist story of political and paternal torture. These motifs, as the uncanny echoes of Christ's *liebestod* in *Othello* suggest, are not confined to a specifically religious discourse but pervade the characteristic products of the Renaissance imagination: tragedy and Petrarchan lyric as well as the eroticized violence of late Renaissance religious art.

In a general way, one can account for the disturbing configurations of manhood in the passion narratives by locating them in what Jean Delumeau has termed the Renaissance culture of sin and fear. Although Delumeau does not deal with masculinity per se, he views the morbidly authoritarian and sadistic piety suffusing Renaissance Christianity as the result of violence, particularly religious violence,[131] and, as we have seen, violence and manhood during this period belong to a single conceptual field. Hence, the endless ugly violence recorded in the passion narratives can be read as a projection of the religious strife tearing apart the social fabric of the sixteenth century. Marlowe's *Massacre at Paris* thus links the catastrophic aftermath of the Reformation to the crisis of manhood with its dialectic of torturer and tortured; the play's Protestants are either helpless victims of prelatical malice or, in Coligny's case, no less cruel than their Romanist adversaries. As in the passion narratives, both villains and heroes deconstruct into interchangeable victims and avengers.

Delumeau, however, focuses primarily on the Roman Catholic societies of the European continent. In the Calvinist milieus of England, Holland, and Geneva one may hypothesize a more specific cultural context for the troubled conceptualization of manhood, a context that has less to do with particular events than with changes in a culture's symbolic resources, its stock of available images for interpreting and representing social ideals. In northern Europe during the sixteenth century, Erasmian humanism and Protestantism conjointly discredited the two principal medieval types of Christian manhood: the monk and the knight. It is not difficult to hypothesize that the total or partial loss of the ancient ideal images of masculine identity—of idealized social roles based on the renunciation or mystification of violence—produced, for a time, a sort of shuddering uncertainty about "man's work," about man's violence.

Students of English literature, who know their monks from Chaucer, tend to overlook this ideal type of silent, chaste, and obedient manhood, while the recent fascination with Western phallocentric individualism makes it difficult to recognize how prominently the celibate, unarmed, cenobitic male figures among the culture heroes of premodern European civilization. But before the sixteenth century, the gentle, compassionate virgin is a figure of ideal masculinity. The lowly and merciful Christ of the medieval passions derives from this vision of maternal manhood. In the Calvinist equivalents, however, Christ typifies not saintly monks but the persecuted elect. He is an exemplar less of supernatural charity than of victimage, a type less of ideal masculinity than of the historical dialectic implicating the Reformation in the interminable violence lacerating the Christian social order. The traditional, monastic constructions of male identity, symbolized by the gentle Jesus, disappear from Protestant culture along with the monks themselves, replaced by more ambivalent and contradictory representations that betray the loss of a compelling vision of Christian manhood.

Erasmian humanism, the humanism of the young Calvin, distrusted contemplative celibacy, but it detested the aristocratic warrior culture of medieval Christendom. Although Calvinism proved more successful in abolishing monks than humanism was in eradicating knights, the Erasmian demystification of warfare tended to desecrate the chivalric ideal of manhood—the dominant cultural image of secular *virtu*—in much the same way that the Reformation erased the monastic vision of male excellence. Norbert Elias's description of the civilizing process is illuminating here because it links this critique of the warrior aristocracy with the increasing "regulation of the whole instinctual and affective life," with the emphases on self-restraint and self-control characteristic of humanist pedagogy as well as Calvinist ethics.[132] Thus, Delumeau argues that humanism's hostility to the culture of violence encouraged an "excessively constraining education," one designed to quash all expressions of aggressiveness and sexuality, producing a pandemic of obsessional neurosis in which

> the repression of aggressiveness, compounding that of sexuality, exalted the passive virtues of obedience and humility beyond all reasonable limits. As a result, there was a simultaneous turning against both one's self—the bad conscience and sickly scruples—and other sinners. . . . The simultaneous presence of self-denied hatred and love accentuated by the very denial . . . consume the subject in a ceaseless inner struggle.[133]

Although retrospective psychiatry presents its own theoretical problems, the description captures the ambivalence pervading the Calvinist passion narratives.

It is not, therefore, altogether surprising that the problematic manhood of these texts recurs, although in a less acute form, in the sixteenth-century humanist (and Protestant) romance. The harsh punitive father who condemns his son to death reappears in the final book of Sidney's *Arcadia*, a work permeated by contradictory and ambivalent constructions of both chivalric violence and Christian passivity. The endless jousts, tourneys, combats, battles, and general mayhem of the *New Arcadia* cast ironic shadows over the old warrior ethos. While Pyrocles and Musidorus initially defeat some villains and restore social harmony, the final flashback episodes of the *Arcadia*, in Richard McCoy's words, depict "chaotic conflict, heroic inadequacy, and vulnerable subordination to fortune."[134] But if knightly prowess fails to make the world safe for timocracy, neither can the passive virtues of patient suffering and meek resignation—virtues exemplified by Sidney's heroines—provide an acceptable basis for male self-fashioning. As McCoy notes, "Sexual distinctions are maintained with schematic precision, for the heroes' virility precludes subjection 'to each unworthy misery.'"[135] Here, as in the passion narratives, there is no unproblematic manhood: the wise, disinterested judge turns out to be rigidly legalistic and authoritarian; the idealistic young knights are compromised by their self-destructive, immature romanticism.

In Sidney, Basilius's resurrection prevents romance from darkening into tragedy. In the passion narratives, the end point of the story shifts from the Resurrection to the fall of Jerusalem, replacing triumphant closure with the cyclic repetitions of violence. These portray a more drastic version of failed manhood, of failed Christian manhood, in which there is (except in the occasional *Christus Victor* scenes) no clean violence, no compassionate strength, no gentle fathers or virile sons. Instead, the Calvinist passion narratives, including *Christs Teares*, stage a scapegoat ritual in which the grotesque and terrible figures of oppressor and oppressed first polarize and then merge into a single figure. They construct a new male subjectivity, one formed not by identifying with ideal types—the rhetorical mode of the medieval passions—but by internalizing the whole *drama*, by restaging the Crucifixion in the theatrical subject. The end myth produces and mirrors a conflictual, decentered, and chimerical manhood.

The *Civitas Mulierum*

Jerusalem is both Lady and City. At the same time that the Calvinist passion narratives register anxieties concerning the (male) subject, they also intimate forebodings about society, particularly urban society. The texts, that is, construct myths of social (dis)order in which the Passion leads to the fall, thus inverting the divine comedy of Christian history. The imbrication of sacrificial agony and civic tragedy emerges most distinctly in Nashe. While all the Calvinist passion narratives link the Crucifixion to the fall of Jerusalem, in *Christs Teares* the relation between Christ and the city occupies the thematic center, governing the text's triple interlocked structure.

Beginning in the first section, the agonized Christ seems strangely akin to the devastated capital. Thus, Nashe appropriates the conventional iconographic symbols of Christ to describe the ruined city; she becomes, for example, a "Pellican in the Wildernesse, that . . . hath her bowels unnaturally torne out by her young ones" (57–58). The desolate city, destroyed by "those whom thou most expectest love of" (58), begins to resemble the forsaken Christ. In the second part, which describes the siege of Jerusalem, the parallels between Savior and city thicken and complicate. The scene in which Miriam, the starving mother, cannibalizes her only son is explicitly presented as a mimesis of the Crucifixion. Miriam reflects:

> God will have pitty of thee [her child], and (perhaps) pittie *Jerusalem* for thee. He surely wil melt in remorse, and wither uppe the hand of hys wrath, when in his eares it shall be clamored, how the *desolation* hee hath layde on *Jerusalem* hath compelled a tender-starved Mother to kill and eate her onely sonne. And yet his owne only chyld, *Christ Jesus*, (as deere to him as thou to mee, my sonne) he sent into the World to be crucified. (73–74)

Here the eucharistic sacrifice prefigures the cannibal feast, but if Christ resembles the slain child, he also impersonates the murderous mother, who kills what she loves. Miriam's anguish over her son sounds very like Christ's ominous sorrowing; she tells the boy, "I am thy Mother and must desire for thee: I love thee more then thou canst thy selfe. . . . At one stroke (even as these words were in speaking) she beheaded him" (74–75). Like the Father, Miriam kills her son; like Christ, she destroys her beloved; like Jerusalem, who bites Christ's breasts instead of sucking them, she sinks her teeth into the child's "two round teat-like cheeks" (76). The bizarre comparison of infant cheeks to breasts seems deliberately to hearken back to the earlier image of a woman devouring the feminized male. These intratextual cross-identifications construct the mother—and hence the city—as a narrative counterpart to the reader who replays the Crucifixion within himself. The fall of Jerusalem, imaged in Miriam's descent into savagery, not only results from the Passion but reenacts it, and, as Nashe warns in the third section of *Christs Teares*, London will stage it once again if it (or she) does not repent (80). As in the other Calvinist passion narratives, a logic of repetition displaces the theology of sacrificial substitution, but now at the level of civic history.[136]

The narrative progression in Nashe from Christ to Jerusalem to London, together with the implication common to all the Calvinist passions that the fall of Jerusalem recapitulates and avenges Christ's torment, suggest that these texts encode some sort of anxiety about cities. An unarticulated association of ideas draws the city into the representational matrix of the Crucifixion, into the mythic center of Renaissance culture. The texts' dark fascination with urban catastrophe lends support to Bouwsma's claim that the shift from an agrarian to an urban society lies behind the pervasive and unfocused anxieties darkening the interior landscape of the Renaissance. The dirt and greed of the early modern city, its encouragement of social mobility, predatory individualism, and material accumulation— all these eroded the symbolic and social orders of medieval cosmology, eroded the traditional "conceptual boundaries which were reflected in the structures of life as well as thought."[137]

Bouwsma's thesis is too broad to explain the cultural logic connecting Jerusalem to cities in general or civic tragedy to the Crucifixion. What elicits the anxiety of urbanization, and why does it become attached to the passion narrative? One can approach these questions by comparing *Christs Teares* with two slightly later accounts of sacked cities: Thomas Deloney's *Canaans Calamitie* (1618) and the anonymous play *A Larum for London*.[138] Like Nashe's lurid homily, Deloney's poem deals with the siege of Jerusalem. *A Larum for London*, printed in 1602 but probably first performed between 1594 and 1600, depicts Antwerp's capitulation to the Hapsburg army—an event symbolically linked to the Crucifixion and its aftermath first because Protestant ideology viewed Spanish soldiers as latter-day incarnations of Christ's tormentors but also because Jerusalem and Antwerp—and London—shared a certain family resemblance. Thus, for Nashe, London mirrors Jerusalem, but it is also the new Antwerp, since "after the destruction of *Antwerpe*," pride "embarkedst for *England*," for "riche *London*" (81). The texts occupy the same discursive ambit because Jerusalem, Antwerp, and London are successive local embodiments of a single conceptual schema.

Hence, the same iconographic pattern informs all three works, and it is this pattern, drawn from both biblical and Classical sources, that explicates the relation between urbanization and the passion narratives. In Deloney and the *Larum*, as in Nashe, sexual politics allegorizes urban catastrophe. The doomed city is thus imagined as a delicate, proud, and splendid lady.

The Spanish captain in the *Larum* justifies the surprise attack on Antwerp to one of his confederates:

> What patient eye can looke upon yond Turrets,
> And see the beauty of that flower of *Europe*,
> And in't [sic] be ravisht with the sight of her?
> O she is amorous as the wanton ayre,
> And must be Courted: from het [sic] nostrils comes
> A breath, as sweete as the Arabian spice.
> Her garments are imbrodered with pure golde;
> And every part so rich and sumptuous,
> As Indias not to be compar'd to her;
> She must be Courted, mary her selfe invites,
> And beckons us unto her sportfull bed.[139]

The gorgeous lady who seems to invite erotic conquest is the *prosperous* city, the paragon of urban capitalism (as Antwerp was in the early sixteenth century). Nashe and Deloney similarly stress the "daintinesse and delicasie" of Jerusalem before the sack: her "sweet daintie gardens," "pleasant bowers," "pompe and pride," "delight and pleasure."[140] The proud, Petrarchan she-city, an urban "bower of earthly blisse," images a civilization "glutted with to much wealth and plentie."[141]

The excesses of capitalism, not surprisingly, precipitate its decline and fall. The prosperous citizens of Antwerp become "us'd to soft effeminate silkes, / And their nice mindes set all on dalliance; / Which makes them fat for slaughter, fit for spoile."[142] The sack becomes a rape, where the Spanish soldiers or Tamburlaine-like Christ defiles the proud lady. Nashe thus has Christ mentally undress Jerusalem: "The resplendent eye-outbraving buildings of your Temple (like a Drum) shal be ungirt & unbraced: the soule of it, which is the (fore-named) *Sanctum sanctorum*, cleane shall be strypt and unclothed" (49). Death also violates the secret recesses of the urban female body; Nashe describes to London matrons how toads will "engender them young" in "the jelly of your decayed eyes" and "in theyr hollowe Caves . . . shelly Snayles shall keepe house" (139). In these works, rape is, in any case, the allegorical equivalent of murder, since the soldiers "court" Jerusalem and Antwerp by killing their inhabitants. The Spanish captain's eagerness to "attempt" the city in the "heate of vallour" similarly conflates sexual and military violence.[143]

As the siege (or "rape") proceeds, the fancy, delicate she-city succumbs to male savagery. The *Larum* thus depicts the Spaniards who conquer Antwerp as negative images of its soft burghers: cruel, virile, ruthless, strong.

Alva, the Spanish general, commands his soldiers to "spare neither wid-dow, matron, nor young maide, / Gray-bearded Fathers, nor the babe that suckes."[144] In *Christs Teares*, the rebels who take over Jerusalem in its final days use the Temple as a slaughter house, until finally its silver portals seem "slimie flood-gates for thicke jellied gore to sluce out by" (66). As the famine engulfs Jerusalem, civilization collapses into a Hobbesian night-mare in which

> the Father stole from the Sonne, and oftentimes tore the meate out of his mouth; the Sonne could scarce refraine from byting out his Fathers throateboule, when he saw him swallow downe a bitte that he dyde for. The Mother lurcht from them both; her young weaned Children (fam-isht for want of nourishment) fastned theyr sharpe edged gums on her fingers, and would not let them goe till shee pluckt the morsell out of her owne mawe to put into theyrs. (70)

Deloney describes how the effeminate Jews, who before had eaten "sugred Junkets" in gold and silver dishes, end up "gnawing the stones" and "lick[ing] . . . vomit."[145] These cities, softened by luxury, sink into bestial degradation. In the end, they become military outposts of the Roman or Spanish empire, prizes for strong men.

These urban apocalypses imply a conceptual link between economic prosperity and the decomposition of manhood into effeminacy or brutal-ity. Like the Calvinist passion narratives, they are structured by the gen-dered antithesis of weakness and power. The passion narratives seem almost obsessively fascinated by the fall of Jerusalem precisely because the early modern city—at once cruel and soft—threatened the cultural sym-bolization of male identity. Their representation of the Crucifixion gives symbolic form to the anxieties of the urban male, anxieties more directly voiced in the related stories of soft, effeminate cities destroyed by ruthless warriors. The crisis of manhood takes place in cities because this secular, bourgeois environment had little use for the traditional ideal types of mas-culinity: the monk and the knight again. The final section of *Christs Teares*, a lively satire on London's crafty, decadent, and emasculated urban personae, associates the city with two interrelated vices: the decline of Christian virtues, particularly faith and charity; and the corruption of young aristocrats, tricked by urban parasites to fritter away their ancestral property. Charity, faith, and inherited land—the socio-iconographic at-tributes of the monk and the knight—decay in this civic landscape popu-lated by usurers and merchants, courtiers and courtesans. Divine violence impends over the epicene city. Nashe presents London with the alternatives of submitting to the penal law of the Father, already operative in the plague infesting the city, or being wiped out at his command by more virile and rugged men. One way or another, the cruel, delicate lady must yield—the lady who at once personifies her soft male citizens and darkly mirrors Nashe's impotent and murderous Christ.

Christ's agony provides the primary symbol for early modern speculation on selfhood and society. The tortured and torturing males who supply the dramatis personae of the Crucifixion—the brutal soldiers, abject lover, frightened child, submissive son, wrathful father, apocalyptic avenger, agonized murderer, grotesque victim, politic priests—also haunt the interior landscape of the Puritan automachia and the (actual or anticipated) historical denouement of the secular city. The story that had embodied a civilization's ideals also serves to encode its discontents. Biblical interpretation thus germinates, in the form of myth, the two obsessive themes of the postmedieval West: psychological fragmentation and socioeconomic decadence, themes heavy with gendered anxieties about violence and weakness.

4   Iphigenia in Israel

Anna Karenina has escaped from my control.
Tolstoy

Et nos servasti [. . .] sanguine fuso.
Inscription in the Mithraeum
of Santa Prisca, Rome

Donne's fourth Holy Sonnet ends with the curious, if unambiguous, couplet: "Or wash thee in Christs blood, which hath this might / That being red, it dyes red soules to white."[1] This seems an unlikely sort of washing, but since the previous line equates "red" with "blushing"—that is, penitence—the distich evidently means something along the lines of "Christ's atonement is able to redeem and sanctify penitent souls." The peculiar notion that washing a red object in red blood could make it turn white apparently depends on the trivial pun whereby "wash" means both "to launder" and "to remove spiritual pollution." But, in fact, the trope is both deeper and simpler. In New Testament Greek, "wash" and related terms generally do not refer to cleaning something with soap and water. As in Donne's couplet, they signify sacrificial purification—that is, cleaning something with blood. Hebrews 9:22 thus reads "and almost all things are by the law purged [*mundantur* in the Vulgate] with blood"; similarly, 1 John 1:7 describes how "the blood of Jesus Christ his Son cleanseth (*emundat*) us from all sin." The literal sense of cleaning in both passages is ritual rather than hygienic. And in both passages the original Greek word for this sort of bloodbath is *katharsis*.[2]

Since the modern discussion of *katharsis*, which centers on Aristotle's *Poetics*, defines it either as "purgation" in a medical sense or "purification" in a moral one, the notion of *katharsis* as blood sacrifice seems startling.[3] I noticed it only because the word occurs repeatedly in the last section of *De satisfactione*, where Grotius undertakes to show that sacrificial concepts and terms underlie all ancient religious discourse. Grotius, who regularly cites his Greek authorities in the original, giving a Latin equivalent in brackets, translates it (or a cognate) nine times as *expiare/expiatio* (to make atonement, to purge by sacrifice), nine again as *mundare/emundare* (to purify, to purge by sacrifice), and once each as *piamen* (expiatory/propitiatory sacrifice) and *averrunca* (a charm to ward off evil).[4] While the Aristotelian *katharsis* of pity and fear cannot refer to blood sacrifice[5]—and no Renaissance commentary on Aristotle suggests that it does—the fact that the Aristotelian term for the telos of tragedy and an ordinary Greek term for ritual sacrifice, including the sacrifice of Christ, are identical would have been obvious to any Renaissance Graecist.[6]

De satisfactione also suggests a further connection between tragedy and sacrifice. The specific legal and quasi-legal issues Grotius treats in connection with the Atonement include exemplary punishment, expiation, inherited guilt, mystical pollutions, penal substitution, innocent victims, and purification. But this could also be a list of the principal themes in both ancient and Renaissance tragedy. Given Walter Burkert's convincing hypothesis that Greek tragedy evolved from ritual sacrifice, as well as the traditional derivation of Renaissance drama from the sacrificial liturgy of Holy Week, such philological and thematic parallels provide additional evidence for the ritual origins of tragedy. However, it by no means follows that this origin has any bearing on the subsequent development of the genre, particularly its postclassical development.[7] To determine whether these origins remain present, even if vestigially, in the Renaissance, one needs to trace Burkert's investigation in reverse. The remainder of this chapter attempts to locate the discursive sites where *katharsis*, tragedy, and sacrifice (including Christ's sacrifice) intersect. It begins with the connections that early modern philology posits between these terms and then takes up the staging of sacrifice in the earliest postclassical biblical drama to have been influenced by Attic tragedy.[8]

The Name of the Goat

To the best of my knowledge, no Renaissance *ars poetica* associates the tragic *katharsis* with sacrifice. However, a good deal of indirect evidence does suggest that the imbrications of tragedy and sacrifice would have been, if not evident, at least available in this period. The thematic connection could have been observed even by the Greekless reader. With the partial exceptions of *Medea* and *Electra*, all translations of Greek tragedy (including both Latin and vernacular) printed before 1560 concern human sacrifice, especially female sacrifice: Euripides' *Hecuba* (1506), *Iphigenia in Aulis* (1506), *Alcestis* (1554), and *Phoenissae* (1560) and Sophocles' *Antigone* (1533).[9] The texts selected for translation would have left the distinct impression that tragedy was, in its origin and essence, a staging of sacrifice. As Goethe later remarked, tragedy seems to be *"eine Art Menchenopfer."*[10]

Renaissance philology corroborates and complicates this impression. The earliest humanist Greek lexicon, Guillaume Bude's *Commentarii linguae Graecae* (1529), and its magisterial successor, Stephanus's *Thesaurus Graecae linguae* (1572), provide particularly valuable information, since they would have been the primary reference works available to a Renaissance literary scholar trying to determine the meaning of the mysterious Aristotelian *katharsis*. For a modern reader, their definitions seem startlingly beside the point. Neither Bude nor Stephanus associates *katharsis* with a specifically aesthetic discourse; neither cites the *Poetics*. While both lexica recognize that *katharsis* may refer to any sort of cleaning and that it has a specific medical sense, they unmistakably consider its ritual context primary. Bude defines it as a *purgatio* (cleansing, religious purification) and *lustratio* (purification by sacrifice).[11] Stephanus gives a similar account; he begins by defining *katharsis* as *purgatio* or *expiatio* (atonement, purgation by sacrifice) and then (in the same entry) translates *katharsion* as *piamen, lustratio, piaculum*—basically equivalent terms for propitiatory or purificatory sacrifice. In its principal significations, the term belongs to the sacrificial vocabulary of ancient Greek religion.[12]

Renaissance commentaries on the ninth chapter of Hebrews give a similar reading of *katharsis*. Discussing the passage "almost all things . . . are purged (*katharizo*) with blood," Matthew Poole remarks that "although certain legal cleansings (*mundationes*) took place without blood, nevertheless there were no ceremonies instituted for the remission of sins that did not require the effusion of blood."[13] Quite clearly, Poole connects purging and cleaning not with removing dirt by water but with expiating sin by blood. Calvin's *Commentaries on the Epistle to the Hebrews* makes this point explicitly. Noting that "purgation under the Old Testament . . . was done by means of blood," Calvin then remarks that the apostle says "*almost* all things . . . are purged with blood" because

> doubtless they often washed themselves and other unclean things with water. But even water itself derived its power to cleanse from the sacrifices; so that the Apostle at length truly declares that without blood there was no remission. . . . And as without Christ there is no purity nor salvation, so nothing without blood can be either pure or saving.[14]

Cleanliness, finally, is next to godliness.

But *katharsis* also has a relation to *human* sacrifice—the subject of tragedy and the Crucifixion. Bude's and Stephanus's entries under *katharma* (a cognate of *katharsis*) begin by defining it as basically equivalent to *ka-*

tharsis; it is a *purgamentum*, a *piaculum*. But each entry then specifies the term along similar lines:

> In this sense, sinful men were called *katharmata* as being sacrificial vic-
> tims (*piaculares*); that is, men consecrated for the sacrificial purification
> (*lustratio*) and expiation of their fatherland. The Romans also called
> them the Holy Ones (*Sacri*), those whose death atoned for all the sins
> of the city or people and who were sacrificed (*mactare*) in order to avert
> the wrath of the Gods.[15]

To be sacred is to be sacrificed, an etymological connection preserved both in Latin (*sacer/sacrificare*) and Greek (*hieron/hiereion*).

As before, the biblical commentaries register the same reading. In his *Apologia confessionis* (1537), for instance, Melanchthon identifies Christ with the *'asham* (expiatory victim) of Isaiah 53:10 and then notes: "The word *'asham* is better understood in the context of pagan customs. . . . The Latins called *piaculum* the victim which in the great calamities was offered up *to placate the wrath of God.* . . . The Greeks called it *katharmata.*"[16] The chain of signifiers thus links the *katharmata* to apotropaic human sac-rifice, to expiating the sins of one's land and people, to Christ. The *kathar-mata* are scapegoats.

This identification presents itself in Stephanus's entry under *phar-makos* (scapegoat). He explains that "sacrificial purification (*lustratio*) took place by means of blood, as history attests. . . . The Athenians call masters of this art 'pharmakous,' or expiators of cities. . . . But the *phar-makos* . . . is also called *to katharma.*"[17] Like the *katharma*, the scapegoat also signifies Christ, a reading of Leviticus 16 that remained standard from the patristic era through the Renaissance; as Poole summarizes, "This goat sent into the wilderness foreshadows the salvation Christ offers to the gentiles."[18] Poole additionally links the scapegoat to another aspect of Greek sacrificial practice, noting that the scapegoat corresponds to the pagan *apheton zoon*, an animal allowed to roam freely without a master (*libre sine custode*) prior to being ritually slaughtered.[19] The significance of the *apheton* for sacrificial tragedy in the Renaissance will become clear in what follows.

In the meantime, one further meaning of *katharsis* emphasized in the Renaissance lexica deserves mention. Among the principal senses of the term, both Bude and Stephanus list menstruation, since women are cleansed (*purgantur*) by the menstrual flow.[20] This definition, in turn, yokes the ritual and medical/Aristotelian senses of *katharsis*, both being types of purificatory bleeding, a restoration of humoral or moral balance through the shedding of blood.[21] The complex semantic field of *katharsis* thus suggests, however obliquely, a connection between ritual death and female bodies.

Renaissance definitions of *katharsis* and its cognates locate these terms in ritual sacrifice but do not, except at one point, relate them to tragedy. The exception appears under the explanation of *katharsion*, which according to Bude and Stephanus refers to a piglet sacrificed to purify (*lustrare*) a theater audience and which, Stephanus adds, could also be called a *katharma*.[22] While this definition throws little light on the relation between drama and sacrifice, it does indicate that sacrifices took place at the site of tragedy and thus may serve as a bridge to the second part of this philological investigation: the Renaissance definition of tragedy.[23]

Like the *pharmakos/katharma*, tragedy concerns slaughtered goats. Burkert's argument that "tragedy" derives from the *trugos* or goat sacrificed to Dionysus during ancient religious festivals corresponds to the etymology preserved in all Renaissance discussions of tragedy.[24] Stephanus thus explains that "when the altars had been lit and the goat brought forth, the song that the sacred chorus offered to Father Dionysius was called a *tragodia*."[25] In his *Poeticarum institutionum libri tres*, Gerhard Vossius—an early seventeenth-century Dutch scholar and close friend of Grotius—offers a fairly detailed account of the sacrificial origins of poetry in early Greek harvest festivals, describing how the dithyrambic hymns sung by ecstatic worshipers in honor of Dionysus gave birth to tragedy proper.[26] For the Renaissance, as for the late Romantics, tragedy evolves from the frenzied, Dionysian song chanted around the sacrificial victim.

In their entries under *tragodia*, Bude and Stephanus also cite the sixth book of Polybius's *Histories*, the crucial book on the Roman constitution.[27] Toward the end of this book, Polybius turns to the question of Roman religion; it is to this section that Bude and Stephanus refer. The passage requires close consideration inasmuch as it is the Renaissance's principal ancient authority for the religious connotations of the "tragic" and its relation to sacrifice.

Polybius observes that while a wise man (*sophos andros*) does not need holy fictions to be virtuous, the common people do. Religion therefore "maintains the cohesion of the Roman State" because, by filling its rituals with theatrical marvels (*ektragodein*), it inspires the fickle and lawless multitude with terror and wonder (*tragodia*), which produce civic virtue.[28] Having offered this demystified analysis of state religion, Polybius concludes with a story exemplifying how the moral fiber produced by such rituals led to Roman imperial hegemony. It is a story about sacrificing sureties. After Hannibal captured the Roman garrison at Cannae, he sent ten hostages back to Rome to negotiate ransom, making them swear to return. The Romans, however, refused to ransom the garrison; nor did they "allow their pity for their kinsmen . . . to prevail" but also sent back the sureties, "who returned of their own free will, as bound by their oath."[29] Such greatness of soul (*megalopsychia*), in turn, terrified Hannibal and, Polybius implies, caused his ultimate defeat. While Polybius does not explicitly state that the "tragic" staging of religion creates sacrificial patriotism, the implication seems unmistakable, if only because it itself restates the tacit link between tragedy and patriotic sacrifices common to much Greek tragedy, particularly Euripidean tragedy, whose heroes and heroines die (whether ironically or not) for the greater glory of Hellas.

This passage probably stands behind a good deal of what strikes the modern reader of Renaissance texts as "Machiavellian." It also bears centrally on Renaissance interpretations of tragedy. Both Bude and Stephanus cite Polybius, defining *ektragodein/tragodein* as "to fill with wonder (*admiratio*)" or, more specifically, "the wonder and terror of religion infused into the people by augurs and priests"—a definition that may have contributed to the emergence of wonder as a primary tragic emotion in the sixteenth century.[30] The triple relation Polybius implies between the tragic, religion, and patriotic sacrifice—a relation already implicit in the definition of the *katharmata*—both assimilates tragedy to religion and associates both with the problematic of sacrificial substitution discussed in chapter 2. The religious character of tragedy, which seems obvious to modern readers, was not, one should remember, part of the Renaissance's basically political and/or erotic understanding of tragic suffering. Plays that brood over the ways of God to men, like *Doctor Faustus* and *King Lear*, are fairly rare. But the Polybian equation seems implicit in the genesis of Renaissance *biblical* tragedy.

The philological evidence available in sixteenth-century lexica, poetics, and biblical commentaries indicates that *katharsis, tragodia*, and cognate terms overlap to construct a semiotic field composed of multiple links between tragedy and sacrifice, one that draws into its ambit not only patriotic expiation, female blood, and the scapegoat but also the Crucifixion. The "tragic" nature of Christ's sacrifice was *not* a theological topos. Prior to the Renaissance, the Crucifixion was virtually never described as a tragedy. The considerable erudition devoted to identifying the sources for Herrick's extraordinary Good Friday poem, "Tragicus Rex," has located numerous patristic and medieval references to the Passion as a drama, a spectacle, a play, or a pageant, but not (except in Herrick) as a tragedy; even during the Renaissance, such references rarely occur.[31] Likewise, prior to Quintianus Stoa's *Theoandrothanatos*, first published in 1508, the word *tragedy* seems not to have been applied to passion plays. As Stoa's ostentatiously Greek title suggests, the conceptualization of the Atonement as a tragedy is bound up with the recovery of Attic drama and the beginnings of Greek philology in Western Europe. It remains to be seen what significance this entanglement might possess for the development of Renaissance tragedy, its possible connection to the inverted *pietas* in the final scenes of Shakespearean tragedy—to the passions of tragic women. Does the development of Greek tragedy out of ancient ritual repeat itself in the Renaissance, linking this rebirth of tragedy to the Grotian moment when sacrifice begins to slip toward the archaic?

Among Schoolchildren:
Sixteenth-century Biblical Tragedy

Why, Sir, I should not have said of Buchanan, had he been an *Englishman,* what I will now say of him as a *Scotchman,*—that he was the only man of genius his country ever produced.

Samuel Johnson

To pursue this line of questioning, the rest of this chapter will consider one of the earliest and most influential neoclassical tragedies, itself the first Renaissance biblical drama modeled on Greek tragedy: George Buchanan's *Jephthes sive votum tragoedia*, composed sometime between 1540 and 1547 and published in 1554.[32] Buchanan (1506–1582) is probably better known as the Calvinist regicidal-republican tutor to James I, but these commitments belong to the last two decades of his life and thus do not concern us here. When he was writing *Jephthah*, Buchanan, still an Erasmian Catholic although probably inclining toward Protestantism, was teaching at the College de Guyenne in Bordeaux; Montaigne, who was enrolled in the college at the time, later recalled having a leading role in a performance of the play.[33] A brilliant neo-Latin poet and translator of Greek tragedy, Buchanan belonged to the small circle of midcentury French humanists; he was a friend of Dorat, Lazare de Baif, Muret, du Bellay, Ronsard, and Turnebe. Stephanus and the younger Scaliger describe him as the foremost Latin poet of the century.[34] Buchanan's friendship with the elder Scaliger, author of *Poetices libri septem* and preeminent sixteenth-century authority on Aristotle's *Poetics*, has particular significance, because it strengthens the likelihood that Buchanan would have known the *Poetics*, before Robertello's 1548 edition still a fairly esoteric text, making *Jephthah* perhaps the first Renaissance drama written by a poet cognizant of the relation between *katharsis* and tragedy.[35]

Jephthah is a neo-Latin school play, written for the annual dramatic performance put on by the boys at the College de Guyenne. Despite its pedagogical origins, it became stunningly successful after its first publication in 1554. Eighteen more Latin editions followed in the sixteenth century, and twenty-eight in the seventeenth. The play was translated into French seven times before 1614 (not counting multiple editions of individual translations), as well as into Italian, German, Hungarian, and Polish.[36] Although not translated into English during the Renaissance, the original Latin text went through three London printings before 1600 and two more in the seventeenth century as part of Buchanan's *Opera omnia*. In *The Scholemaster* (1570), Roger Ascham praises *Jephthah* as one of only two modern tragedies "able to abide the true touch of Aristotle's precepts and Euripides' examples."[37] Similarly, after traducing the indecorums of native English drama, Sidney proposes as an alternative "the tragedies of Buchanan [which] do justly bring forth a divine admiration."[38] In *Children of Oedipus*, Martin Mueller makes a convincing case for *Jephthah*'s influence on *Samson Agonistes*, the sole English biblical tragedy *à la grecque*.[39] *Jephthah* remained influential through the eighteenth century, supplying the basis for Handel's oratorio of the same name.[40]

The play itself transposes Euripides' *Iphigenia in Aulis* into the story of Jephthah and his daughter (Judges 11:30–40), which tells how the Israelite chieftain Jephthah vowed before a battle with the Ammonites that if he were victorious he would sacrifice the first "thing" he met on his return home; to his horror, his daughter, an only child, greets him. He confesses his vow, to which she responds, "My father, if thou hast opened thy mouth unto the Lord, do to me according to that which hath proceeded out of thy mouth," asking only two months' reprieve to bewail her virginity. This granted, the daughter then returns to fulfill her father's vow. The chapter ends by noting that it became an annual "custom in Israel" for young women to lament Jephthah's daughter. Like *Iphigenia*, *Jephthah* thus narrates the scene of sacrifice; it also raises the question—the same question that will reappear in the following chapter—of the significance of neoclassical *imitatio* for the representation of biblical stories: the literary significance, that is, of Christian humanism. Additionally, since both *Jephthah* and the texts considered in the next chapter focus on female suffering, we need to look at Buchanan's play in terms of the triple relation among neoclassical mimesis, biblical narrative, and the representation of women.

The obvious question the text initially raises is, why dramatize this story at all? Lynda Boose has made a plausible case that "within the patriarchal narrative is something more specific than just a general erasure of women. What is specifically absent is the *daughter*."[41] If Buchanan had wanted to write a tragedy about child sacrifice, why not use the story of Abraham and Isaac, as his friend Beza would do in his *Abraham sacrifiant* (1550), a play likewise influenced by Euripides' *Iphigenia*? Why focus on the daughter's sacrifice? Buchanan's play, in fact, alters the biblical narrative to give prominence to female roles. His two principal deviations from the scriptural account (along with the debate between Jephthah and a priest) emphasize the woman's part. He adds a mother, loosely based on Euripides' Clytemnestra but without her deadly resentment, a difference apparent from the fact that Buchanan names her "Storge," the Greek term for the natural affection between parents and children, and a word, as I have elsewhere attempted to demonstrate, that beginning in the sixteenth century frequently replaced both *agape* and *eros* as the term for the love binding God to humanity and rulers to people, as well as parents to children; in Renaissance usage, the term implies that the affectionate family provides the most adequate symbol for both supernatural and political society.[42]

Buchanan also enhances the role of Jephthah's daughter, whom he calls "Iphis"—an obvious allusion to Iphigenia, but moreover a neuter Greek word that means strength. It is also, oddly, the name of the lesbian transsexual in Ovid's *Metamorphosis* (a connection Heinsius notes in his hostile analysis of the play at the end of *On Plot in Tragedy*).[43] Such changes only further problematize the significance of gender in a Latin play for boys—a play, that is, neither written for a female audience nor capable of being read by the vast majority of Renaissance women. Moreover, the question of why Buchanan represents the *daughter's* sacrifice raises the equally pressing question of why he represents the daughter's *sacrifice*. Sixteenth-century parents were not in the habit of ritually slaughtering their children, and in any case infanticide was generally a crime attributed to *mothers* during this period. What sort of cultural negotiations attach themselves to this narrative that would render it of interest to an audience where daughters are not present and to a society where human sacrifice is not an issue?[44]

The following discussion attempts to answer these questions by examining the text itself, but some preliminary information concerning the exegetical and literary afterlife of the biblical episode elucidates the historical context of Buchanan's reading. The story of Jephthah quite suddenly became important in the sixteenth century. Wilbur Sypherd's *Jephthah and His Daughter* documents the pan-European proliferation of Jephthah poems, plays, ballads, oratorios, and operas from the Renaissance through the nineteenth century, most later than Buchanan's version and hence worth mentioning only as evidence of the pervasive cultural investment in this story. More directly relevant to Buchanan are the biblical commentaries, beginning with Augustine's remark that the Jephthah episode differs from the sacrifice of Isaac because in the former the Bible passes no judgment on either the vow or the sacrifice, instead leaving the moral to be discerned by the reader.[45] The ethical opacity of the biblical text opens a space for interpretive maneuvering—for using narrative to discern meaning rather than merely enforce it.

The exegetical tradition on this passage, in fact, evinces a good deal of interpretive maneuvering, some of it highly suggestive. Prior to Nicholas de Lyra's *Postilla*, medieval commentators generally held both that Jephthah is a type of Christ who (in Chrysostom's words) "sanctified His Church by the blood of martyrs during the time of persecution" *and* that Jephthah's sacrifice was an abomination, displeasing to God and morally wrong.[46] From de Lyra through the Renaissance, the interpretation changes drastically. Drawing on Jewish sources, Lyra and subsequent exegetes, particularly Protestant ones, argue that Jephthah did *not* kill his daughter but consecrated her virginity to God; that is, he offered her up as a sort of proto-nun.[47] The overt motive for this shift is to get rid of the embarrassing fact that the Epistle to the Hebrews mentions Jephthah among the Old Testament heroes of faith—a tribute seemingly incompatible with infanticide—but one also suspects deeper discomforts with blood sacrifice motivating this attempt to restrict paternal power to the sexuality of the daughter. The important early seventeenth-century biblical scholar Louis Cappel offers the sole Protestant critique of this sanitized reading. But Cappel himself was almost certainly influenced by Buchanan's play—an interesting instance of the bilateral relation between literature and exegesis. As a reading of the play as well as the biblical text, Cappel's interpretation will prove useful for corroborating the apparent implications of Buchanan's *Jephthah*.

Alien Transcendence

To keep that oath were more impiety
Than Jephthah's, when he sacrific'd his daughter.

3 Henry VI

Jephthah is about the moral heteronomy of God: whether, according to the judgments of human reason, God delights in evil. The play begins with an angelic prologue announcing Israel's victory over the Ammonites that concludes with the ominous decree:

> Further, lest Jephthah, he too, should aspire
> To measure his own prowess by the event
> Of battle, and presume on his success,
> Full soon domestic sorrow shall bedim
> His shining victory. Triumph and woe shall meet,
> And woe shall triumph.[48]

This sounds like standard Renaissance penal pedagogy, but nothing in the character of Jephthah warrants the angel's charge of incipient arrogance. When the messenger enters to describe Jephthah's triumph, he portrays him as a warrior of unwavering piety and justice who attempts to negotiate a bloodless settlement and, that failing, trusts in God to deliver his army. The devout faith in God's fatherly love that suffuses Jephthah's first speech is, in the wake of the angelic prologue, bitterly ironic:

> Monarch of all the world, my voice to thee
> I lift in adoration—lift to thee,
> For thou alone art God, and thou alone
> Bendest to kneeling worshipper an ear
> Attentive to his prayer. Omnipotent!
> What mortal tongue may speak thee as thou art,
> Or frame fit words to name thy character?
> A stern avenger art thou, yet thy heart
> Melts with a father's pity; to thy foes
> A God of terror and severity.
> But to all those that love thee thou art good
> and gentle.[49]

Jephthah is not arrogant but pious and grateful—and then stricken by God.[50]

Buchanan intensifies the tragic ironies here by having Jephthah offer his vow *after* the victory. As he returns home, Jephthah prays,

> O most High!
> Remembering thy covenant of old—
> Gentle and gracious as thou ever art—
> Deign to accept my vow.[51]

He then goes on to promise to sacrifice "whatsoever" first meets him at his return home. The vow is presented not as a self-interested bargain with

God but "the gift . . . [of] a grateful heart."[52] Moreover, since the angel relates both the vow and its terrible consequences *before* the audience hears
Jephthah promise that "whatsoever first / Shall come to meet me from my
threshold forth / To thee shall be devoted," a dark possibility emerges that
the same power that punishes Jephthah's vow has also, in some sense,
staged it.[53] Consequently, as Donald Stone observes, "the situation in
which man is wholly responsible for his punishment becomes one in
which disaster derives from those forces outside man who are responsible
for ordering the universe."[54] The specter of predestination to evil—the
grim corollary of Calvinism and, for Ricoeur, the theological essence of
Greek tragedy—reverberates through these scenes.[55]

The realization of the vow's murderous entailment devastates the
pieties of Jephthah and the play's chorus of Jewish maidens. They lapse
into classical pessimism.[56] Until the final scene, no character prays to or
addresses God as a loving father. Instead, they lament the malicious indifference of what the text now calls fortune or fate:

> For so the Power Supreme enacts
> That change shall ever follow change
> Swiftly through life's allotted range;
> And 'tis immutably decreed
> That sorrows shall to joys succeed. . . .
> A gleam of joy shine on our hearts,
> 'Tis but a gleam and soon departs.[57]

Classical pessimism is perhaps too limiting a description. What is at stake
here is whether the Christian God wishes to destroy human happiness—a
good question to ask a religion whose central symbol is an instrument of
torture and whose praxis celebrates fasting, celibacy, and martyrdom. It is
the persistent question of Renaissance sacrifice dramas, raised in the final
choruses of Greville's *Mustapha* as well as Dekker's *Virgin-Martyr* (although with opposite answers).[58] In Dekker's play, the principal argument
the pagan maidens make against Christianity is that it compels its adher-
ents to abjure "those blessings which our gods gives [sic] freely, / And
showr'd upon us with a prodigall hand, / As to be noble borne, youth,
beauty, wealth."[59] Instead, they tell the saintly Dorothea,

> by our example
> Bequeathing misery to such as love it,
> Learne to be happy, the Christian yokes too heavy
> For such a dainty necke.[60]

In this play, the joys of heaven make ample recompense for all worldly losses—a solution absent both in the Islamic world of Greville's tragedy and Buchanan's Jewish setting, where characters contemplate the possibility that religion is a masochistic fiction or that the gods themselves demand human suffering "and why, I know not," Buchanan's Storge confesses, "if it be not mirth / And sport to her [Fortune] to thwart our purposes."[61]

Jephthah is the earliest exemplar of what Walter Benjamin calls the *Trauerspiel* or baroque drama "of suffering and despair in which a full vision of transcendence is systematically withheld," in which characters grope in a twilight world emptied of providential order.[62] By the middle of the play, the chorus has already entered this *selva oscura*:

> But, as the dim and scanty light,
> That half dispels the lingering night
> From underneath the leafy boughs
> Of the deep forest, dimly shows
> In interlaced perplexing maze
> The windings of a thousand ways
> That wind and part so endlessly
> The traveller knows not which to try,
> And wanders in the forest dim
> All paths become alike to him:
> So in life's journey still we stray,
> Uncertain where to choose our way.[63]

In Utramque Partem

Take heed, lest, by gendering errors and discords . . . [you] turn into a sacrifice to Satan the very same law of God which has been given for hindering sacrifices to Satan.

Gregory the Great, *The Book of Pastoral Rule*

In order to specify the theological and ethical crisis at stake in the play, Buchanan expands Euripides' stichomythic exchanges into two full-length debates, first between Jephthah and a priest, then between Jephthah and Storge, both interlocutors attempting to dissuade Jephthah from carrying out his vow.[64] Although their arguments overlap, the priest primarily considers human sacrifice as an irrational perversity; Storge, as a violation of natural law.

The debate between Jephthah and the priest begins with the father in agony, staggering under his conviction that God requires him to commit what he can regard only as a loathsome crime, begging to sink into hell "if only I may there abide unnamed / A parricide, the slayer of my child."[65] The priest, however, cannot fathom Jephthah's sense of entrapment; instead, he invokes the capacity of the ethical subject to fashion his own destiny.

> The choice is thine
> To be, or not be, miserable. No power
> Compels the dreadful sacrifice; 'tis left
> In thine own choosing.[66]

The priest's defense of human freedom against the mystified notion of an inviolable vow rests on his identification of the divine will with the dictates of right reason. He thus counters Jephthah's primitive and legalistic sense of the word as vow with a more philosophic conception of the word as *logos* or unchanging rational order.

> Be thy vow
> Whate'er thy folly framed it . . .
> . . . . The voice divine
> Sounds one clear note, one ever with itself,
> And self-accordant—all is purest truth.[67]

Identifying the divine with natural law, the priest argues that the love all creatures feel for their offspring demonstrates that this "voice divine" forbids fathers to kill their children. In fact, God takes no delight in "gory sacrifice . . . [or] the blood of bulls" but instead requires only the offering of "a heart polluted by no villainy, / A mind by simple truth informed and ruled, / A conscience that is sullied by no stain."[68] The priest thus opposes sacrifice to the related standards of ethical rationalism, moral autonomy, and religious inwardness. These are, of course, also the central virtues of Protestant humanism, which, like the priest, attempts to avert the sacrificial ending of this story.

But an odd word that occurs in the chorus immediately preceding this debate gives a further resonance to its theological positioning. The chorus laments that Iphis shall be killed by *"patrio . . . mactatu,"* a "fatherly slaughtering."[69] The word *mactatu* is highly unusual, occurring only once in the extant corpus of Latin literature. It appears in the first book of *De rerum natura* as part of Lucretius's own account of the sacrifice of Iphigenia, whose moral immediately follows in the famous line: *"tantum religio potuit suadere malorum."*[70] The Lucretian invective against religion as the source of human misery—epitomized in its legitimation of murder disguised as sacrifice—carries over into the priest's arguments. He thus informs Jephthah that his conviction that God demands the promised sacrifice is his own "mocking dream," for "too rashly we impute / To Heaven itself crimes . . . / And hideous things beyond all utterance." As in Lucretius, the sacrificial gods turn out to be fabrications, the projection of human cruelty onto the divine: "We feign the Eternal Deity to delight / In gory offerings."[71] The priest's humanist rationalism, that is, opens out onto a Lucretian critique of sacrificial religion—and therefore, implicitly, of biblical religion.

Jephthah responds to the priest by lashing out at the comfortable and casuistical deceptions invented by intellectuals, who, despite their seeming wisdom, are typically "negligent / In their observance of the ancient rites" and devoid of "reverent regard / [for] religion's mysteries."[72] For Jephthah, the priest's sophistic rationalism conceals the terrible otherness of the divine will and its ineluctable demands. Jephthah bitterly recognizes that the sacrifice is a "crime" that will bring "nought . . . but sorrows ever new / And still succeeding sorrows."[73] He will not morally justify the sacrifice of his daughter, yet he refuses to abjure his conviction that God requires performance of vows. Unlike the priest, Jephthah has no rational defense of his position; instead, entangled in the contradictory imperatives of paternal love and archaic legalism, he can only struggle to articulate his tragic recognition that the God of Israel is in fact the inscrutable *Deus absconditus*, the alien God.

After the priest departs, a more poignant debate ensues between Jephthah and his angry, terrified wife. The wife, as her name indicates, represents *storge*, the divinely implanted law of nature that commands parents to love and protect their children. The debate between mother and father thus dramatizes the Erasmian conflict between the maternal instinct of self-preservation and the sacrificial law of the father. Storge claims it as the mother's duty, "armed with a right as strong as nature's law, / . . . [to] snatch her girl from a stern father's hand / Who dooms her to destruction."[74] Moreover, her opposition to this sacrificial law leads her to reiterate the priest's Lucretian suspicions that the "air of sad religion veils . . . / the horror under Duty's guise."[75]

In addition, she emphasizes what was already implicit in the priest's argument: that the sacrifice of Iphis erodes the distinction between Israel and the pagans Jephthah has just conquered. As the latter "with rites abhorred have laid / Upon thine altars fire profane / And victims impiously slain," so now in Israel "the altar smokes / With the warm blood of human sacrifice, / As in the lands that worship idols grim."[76] The sacrificial law of the father undoes the stable opposition between the people of God and the barbaric enemy and therefore also collapses that between Israel's God and the idols. As in Grotius, sacrifice establishes uncanny parallels at the site of absolute difference.

Although Storge personifies the claims of the family, the priest, chorus, and Jephthah himself likewise acknowledge its moral and emotional primacy. Jephthah passionately loves his daughter—and also his wife.[77] The priest begins his arguments with a defense of *storge* as the common source of natural, human, and divine law and therefore also the analogical bond that guarantees the moral intelligibility of the universe.

> Parental love—is there a stronger power
> Implanted in our breast?. . . .
>   Eternal Providence
> This strong affection deeply hath infixed
> In mortal bosoms. . . .
>   And deeper still
> To engrave upon our minds the hallowed name,
> It is his will to be, and to be called,
> Our Father; sanctioning the primal bond
> Of love parental.[78]

Because all the characters, and not only the mother, regard the family as the paradigmatic ground of ethical relations, the opposition between *storge* and sacrifice does not precisely correspond to the usual Vergilian conflict between the private and public, where the man must choose between domestic happiness and sacred duty.[79] By shifting the focus of the conflict from eros to *storge*, Buchanan allows the claims of the private sphere a moral validity independent of personal gratification. Conversely, Jephthah's insistence that God demands child sacrifice does not merely assert the rights of the *polis* over those of the *oikos* but calls into question the intelligibility and goodness of God. Hence, like the priest's rationalism, the mother's *storge* exposes the tragic heteronomy of ethical consciousness and divine will. The fact that the characters refer to Jephthah's deed as a "parricide"—the primal taboo—merely underscores this drastic rupture between moral and supernatural law.

The claims of moral rationalism and of the family are linked as the two primary manifestations of what, loosely speaking, we may call the bourgeois ethos; that is, although both obviously existed earlier, in the sixteenth century a rational ethics set itself over and against customary authority while at the same time the nuclear family engulfed the more diffused social groupings of the Middle Ages; More's *Utopia* exemplifies both shifts. Moreover, they seem internally related, since (as *Jephthah* suggests) the early modern patriarchal family supplied the rationally apprehensible model for all social and supernatural obligations. Hence, the debates in *Jephthah* can be viewed as arraying the defining commitments of bourgeois society against an earlier cultural system based on the quasi-magical word-as-vow and, more important, on sacrifice. The sacrificial economy opposes any rational ethic precisely because (in Hegel's words) it epitomizes the abandonment "of man's inmost to an alien transcendence."[80] Or, put in the legal terms discussed in chapter 2, sacrifice brings into sharp focus the conflict between the notion of a person as part of a *mystica conjunctio* and as a *suppositum* within the bourgeois family. The ethical significance of this connection between the *conjunctio* and sacrifice is starkly articulated in Isidore's seventh-century commentary on the Jephthah story. Jephthah, Isidore observes, is a type of Christ, "who fulfilled all the sacraments of human salvation and offered God his own flesh—his daughter, as it were—for the redemption of Israel."[81] Here the daughter simply disappears into the flesh of her father; she possesses no independent existence, and therefore her sacrifice poses no moral dilemma.

During her debate with Jephthah, Storge contests this view of the daughter as the sacrificial flesh (or property) of the father. She asks her husband, "Canst thou promise that which is not thine?" He responds in apparent surprise, "Is not my daughter mine?" Her answer is "Thine wholly, no! / Thine is she even so as mine she is, / No otherwise."[82] Who owns the daughter: the nurturing mother or the sacrificial father? "Reason," Storge suggests, "would urge the mother's stronger claim," since she tends the child and guards it from harm.[83] In fact, the ambiguous relation between fathers and their families has come up earlier in the play, in the ominous dream Storge relates before her husband's return. She thought she saw, she tells the chorus, a pack of starving wolves descend on a defenseless flock, when

> Alert, and instantly, a faithful dog,
> Intrepid guardian of the trembling fold,
> Rushed forth and drove the wolves away—and then,
> Returning to the timid flock that still
> Panted in wildest terror, suddenly,
> From where I held it in my folded arms,
> A trembling lamb he snatched, and with his fangs
> Remorselessly its quivering flesh he tore.[84]

In the dream, the father is the watchdog, the protector of his family but yet descendant of the wolf and still capable of reverting to his ancestral nature. Moreover, even as dog, the father is not part of the flock; he guards the family but does not really belong to the domestic units composed of ewes and their lambs. Storge's dream raises the question of the father's place in the family—a question implicated in the play's theological agon since the father is the agent of sacrifice, in which God is disclosed as the secret threat to the domestic enclosure and hence to ethical consciousness.[85]

But Storge's picture of the father as wolfish alien misrepresents Buchanan's Jephthah. The play insists on the abiding mutual affection between father and daughter. Iphis herself admits that "no man than he was tenderer, / Nor ever child by parent held more dear."[86] Their intimacy comes to the fore in the dreadful scene where she rushes toward her returning father, exclaiming, "O next to God to be revered by me! / Suffer me now to feel my father's arms / Enfold me to his bosom," and again when she later pleads with him to spare her "if e'er, with little arms enclasped around, / I hung upon thy neck, and thou wast glad / To feel the pendent burden."[87] Jephthah's deep love for his daughter is everywhere apparent; Buchanan, in fact, departs from Euripides by making the father in the end decide *not* to kill his daughter (a decision she overrides) but to die himself in her place.[88] Heinsius criticizes the play primarily because he finds the domestic tenderness of its diction—the affectionate diminutives, the colloquial intimacies of father and child—indecorously "low" for tragedy.[89]

But this affectionate father-daughter relationship poses its own problems. Modern feminist scholarship reads the narrative of the sacrificial daughter as encoding the father's incestuous desire for his nubile daughter and unacknowledged jealousy of the man who will take her from him. In Mieke Bal's analysis of Judges, for example, Jephthah "blame[s] his daughter, not, of course, for celebrating his victory but for being prepared to marry the real victor, for being ready to leave him."[90] In the important essay "The Father's House and the Daughter in It," Lynda Boose generalizes this paradigm, suggesting that the father generally turns away from his adolescent daughter as a defense against "conscious recognition" of his incestuous propensities and that "the daughter's movement to cross that threshold and move out of the father's house" into the arms of another man "threatens the father . . . with loss."[91] In other words, daughter sacrifice is a doubly sexualized signifier, enacting both the father's avoidance of the desirable object and the loss he sustains by her marriage. So one could speculate that when Jephthah turns away from Iphis after she "crosses the threshold" to meet him, he ceases to be a loving father in response to her new sexual maturity and that her death—and his grief over that death—represent the father's ambivalence about "giving away" his daughter to a rival.

Renaissance commentaries on the Jephthah episode tend, on the whole, to bear out this reading, since their substitution of celibacy for death implies some sort of equivalence between sacrificial and sexual narratives. As de Lyra notes, virginity *is* a form of civil death; hence, canon law treats castration under suicide.[92] Buchanan, by contrast, suppresses virtually every reference to Iphis's sexuality until the final scene. He totally omits the biblical passage where the daughter asks her father to spare her life for two months so that she can bewail her virginity, and he mutes any reference to her as a prospective wife; Storge mentions it once, Jephthah never. Buchanan, in fact, seems deliberately to exclude an erotic subtext by adding an episode immediately after Iphis comes to greet Jephthah. Hurt by his cold and bizarre response, in the next scene she worries that her father has heard false rumors of her unchastity, that somehow, as Boose puts it, her crossing "over the threshold of the father's house unaccompanied by a male . . . signifies random sexual availability."[93] But Jephthah has not been upset by lewd gossip; the whole matter of the daughter's chastity is brought up only to be rejected as profoundly irrelevant. Throughout these scenes Iphis remains a child—still daddy's girl (and mommy's too), who is loved and valued but not, until the end, sexualized.[94] *Jephthah*, as we shall see, profoundly engages the relationship of daughters and fathers, but it does not advert to the erotic possibilities latent in this domestic scenario; the tragedy is not about these.

We have yet to look at Iphis, since she does not have an important role in the first half of the tragedy. Up to this point, Mueller's summary perceptively states the implications of the play: "deferral [of salvation] had virtually become denial: nothing mitigates the appalling vision of a God who for reasons of his own rejects rulers who are pious, prudent, and humane. . . . Buchanan asserts the inevitability of sacrificial violence and stresses its indifference to reason and justice."[95] What is at stake in the play is whether or not the biblical God is, in human terms, morally perverse. But to stop here, as Mueller does, leaves out the final scenes—leaves out the daughter.

The Sacrificial Virgin

O Jephthah, judge of Israel, what a treasure hadst thou!

Hamlet

Iphis enters with her mother at the beginning of the second debate. She speaks only after Storge has finished, initially pleading with her father to spare her; however, upset by her parents' quarrel, she assents to the sacrifice as soon as she grasps that her father is not angry, that he is "unwillingly, by strong compulsion, driven / To do this deed."[96] But her filial obedience swiftly gives way to further motives. Unlike Jephthah's tormented submission to a command he can neither justify nor comprehend, her response modulates toward a joyful affirmation of sacrificial duty; hence, she will, Iphis declares, "of free accord / And with a grateful heart, requite to Heaven / The slaughter of so many thousand foes."[97] "Requite," in the original, is *piemus*—expiate; she recognizes the sacrificial logic that transforms her from a victim into a patriotic *katharma*, outstripping her father, whose relation to transcendent structures, like his relation to domestic ones, remains problematic. The supernatural and the domestic, the arenas figured by Iphis and Storge, are female spaces, ones in which the father seems an awkward, marginal presence.[98]

But again the conventional contrast between private/female and public/male has only a limited explanatory value here. *Piemus*, one notes, is plural—the royal "we"; this is the first time Iphis has referred to herself this way, as a *public* persona. In subsequent speeches, her civic role as deliverer and defender of her people repeatedly recurs: the following chorus asserts her "honour" (*laus*) and "fame" (*gloria*), declaring that her "name shall spread to many a land" and distant peoples "shall in their lays remembrance yield / Of her who for her country died / . . . A maiden, yet as warrior brave."[99] The chorus thus calls her a "virile virgin" (*virgo virilis*), as if by dying she had attained heroic manhood. The messenger who reports her death likewise terms her a "noble heroine" (*nobilis virago*) and tells how her courage "had drawn / The eyes of the whole multitude, who gazed / Awe-struck and wondering"—not typical praise for a Renaissance woman but strongly reminiscent of the Polybian associations of patriotic sacrifice and tragic wonder.[100] Iphis herself acknowledges her public, "patriarchal" status, invoking the shades of her "dead forefathers" (*morte defuncti patres*) to receive her spirit and justifying her resolution by declaring,

> Nor ever, while day follows day to mark
> The lapse of time, shall it be said of me,
> I am unworthy of my name and race:
> And I am Jephthah's daughter.[101]

Nor does she die only for her "fatherland." Throughout these last scenes, her understanding of her own death changes rapidly. Iphis first seems to

view her sacrifice as an act of filial obedience, then as submission to the
fates (*fata*) in order to save her country, and finally as a voluntary self-
oblation to a being she addresses as "the eternal Father of all things"
(*aeterne rerum genitor*).[102] She moves from domestic and patriotic motives to a new insight into the supernatural justice of expiatory sacrifice
and the *mystica conjunctio*, to what Kierkegaard calls the "acceptance of
inherited guilt . . . [as the] essential act of piety."[103] As in Shakespeare's
Lucrece, it is the female victim who grasps the sacrificial law of the father,
while, curiously, the men surrounding her persist in trying to assign punishment in terms of individual responsibility.

Iphis's breakthrough to a new moral vision differentiates her from the
Euripidean Iphigenia, who simply assents to Agamemnon's prior realization that she must die for Hellas since the gods demand her blood in exchange for a Greek victory (which may or may not be worth it); as Johann
Sturm observed in his 1567 edition of Buchanan's play, Jephthah's daughter "surpasses the Greek Iphigenia in greatness of soul."[104] She likewise
differs from Beza's portrayal of Isaac in *Abraham sacrifiant*. Beza's Isaac is
a good child who obeys his father, but that is all; the plot concerns Abraham's theological understanding. But Iphis's grasp of her death as an expiatory sacrifice transforms her into a type of Christ—the first female type,
strictly speaking, in Christian literature. The Christic resonances in her
final speech are unmistakable:

> Maker of all things, Father of mankind,
> Eternal God, at length thy love restore,
> Forgive thy people's errors, and accept
> This offering in thy great benignity,
> O, if to turn away thy enkindled wrath
> An expiating victim needs must die,
> Lo, here I stand! let the avenging stroke
> Fall on me, on me only, and the guilt
> Of proud and stubborn revolt from thee
> Be rased and quitted by the life I give.[105]

Medieval commentators regularly considered the *father* a typological
figure (while still condemning his rash vow) but never his daughter. However, in Cappel's commentary on Judges 11, which, as mentioned previously,
shows clear signs of Buchanan's intertextual presence, the identification of
the daughter with Christ is explicit:

> And perhaps God seems to have allowed Jephthah to conceive this rash
> vow . . . so that in this example might appear a notable type of Christ

consecrated by the Father as a *katharma*. . . . In the deed of Jephthah's daughter we find a type of Christ, who was consecrated to death (*devotus*) by his Father for our salvation and made a curse (*katharma*), and who, like her, willingly obeyed and at the same time [felt] a natural terror at that cursed death—and of the solemn annual commemoration of His death by participation in the holy Eucharist [which was prefigured by the annual celebration of her sacrifice].[106]

In casting the daughter as a type of Christ, Buchanan in one sense "solves" the theological crisis pervading the earlier part of the play by irradiating the scene of sacrifice with an ardent *caritas* that, as for Colet, transforms torture into theophany. The symbolic plenitude released here empties out moral objections; they seem largely beside the point. But this resolution still leaves untouched Buchanan's unprecedented typological cross-gendering. Cappel provides no help on this, since he passes over the peculiarity of *daughter* sacrifice in silence. But in *Jephthah*, Iphis's femaleness alters and complicates both the theological implications of the plot and its sexual politics (which, incidentally, turn out to be inseparable).

From the moment when Iphis accedes to her sacrifice, the narrative switches focus from Jephthah to his daughter. He offers to die in her place, and she cuts him off in a manner reminiscent of the way male heroes typically dismiss fearful women; that is, she tells him to be quiet: "Father, cease to contrive these delays, and to weaken my purpose with soft words."[107] And at this point, the father simply disappears for the rest of the play. Likewise, beginning with this scene, the play's attention shifts to the daughter's moral subjectivity, to her choice rather than her father's. Iphis thus stresses that she offers herself voluntarily (*sponte*), perhaps echoing Storge's earlier accusation that her husband intends voluntarily (*sponte*) to kill his daughter.[108] But Storge's accusation ironically calls attention to the terrible compulsion pinioning Jephthah; conversely, Iphis's surrender marks the first truly voluntary act in the tragedy and hence the restoration of heroic agency—for the decision to die for one's patria is not specifically female, all heroism entailing the preference for glorious death over ignoble survival.[109]

By giving her assent to the vow, one Renaissance exegete notes, Jephthah's daughter in effect declares "herself free from her father's authority (*a potestate patria emancipata*) and henceforth subject only to God."[110] That is, according to Grotius's commentary on the same passage, the text constitutes her as an *apheton*, since "among the Greeks, animals consecrated to the gods are called *apheta*, because they do not serve a master."[111] Paradoxically, by freely choosing to obey her father, Iphis slips out of his power. Yet (through a second paradox) she gains the autonomy of a subject only by renouncing her autonomy as a *suppositum*, for, like all ancient heroes, she achieves heroic selfhood by submerging her individuality in the communal identity of the group. Iphis thus imagines herself as embodying her father's "name and race," as becoming one with her "dead forefathers." This tension between autonomy and identification echoes the rhythms of Dionysian myth: on the one hand, the *sparagmos* of the infant Dionysius—the child's "dismemberment" from parental bonds—symbol of the individuation that is the source of all suffering; on the other, the self's ecstatic dissolution in the "mystical experience of the collective."[112] This Nietzschean distinction between *sparagmos* and *exstasis* enables one to resist collapsing these moments into equivalent assertions of patriarchal control over daughters; by herself entering this ancestral genealogy (as by entering its typological correlate), Iphis renders her father unnecessary. She no longer requires him to mediate her participation in either her spiritual or tribal lineage.

Hence, the gender of the Dionysian victim in Buchanan's play casts a further shading over this scene. The configuration of heroic moral choice as openness to the male hints at a homology between female sexual passivity and daughterly sacrifice, but this openness also entails appropriation of masculine strength, transfiguring Iphis, in the chorus's words, into the *virgo virilis* (the inverse equivalent to the ephebic *virginalis vir* of the Calvinist passion narratives).[113] This appropriation has a transgressive edge precisely insofar as it allows the daughter to displace her father as both tragic protagonist and Christic type, in turn "feminizing" the father as one who shrinks from the heroic choice with "soft words."[114] Iphis simultaneously images and replaces her father—a female text transcribed by a male pen, perhaps, but a New Critical text whose meaning is independent of authorial intention.[115]

Jephthah, as previously mentioned, disappears after Iphis proclaims her willingness to die; Storge, however, comes back on stage for the final scene of the play, where the messenger relates to her the circumstances of her daughter's death. As in *Paradise Regained*, the play ends with the return to the "Mother's house." The messenger concludes his report by describing how, after the fatal blow,

> a murmur of relief rose high;
> And many kindly voices spoke of thee
> As one . . .
> That justly might be named, in thy sole self,
> At once the happiest and most miserable

Of womankind. For be it that her wounds
Have cleft thee to the marrow, deep and sore,
Yet hast thou given thee solace with thy grief
Great as thy sorrow.[116]

Curiously, the messenger reports that the crowd praised Storge, not Jephthah, who seems to have been forgotten. Furthermore, the messenger's
words mark her as a type of the Blessed Virgin; *"feminam unam beatam
maxime"* echoes the Magnificat's "blessed art thou among women" (Luke
1:42), while *"plaga quamvis alte ad ossa sederit"* recalls Simeon's prophetic "a sword shall pierce through thy own soul also" (Luke 2:35). This
second allusion also resonates in Storge's last lines—the final lines of the
play—where she responds to the messenger's consolations by declaring
that "grief / Shall pierce my soul till this heart too is cold."[117] But if Storge
is a type of the Virgin, as Iphis is a type of Christ, then the final scene of
Jephthah becomes a pieta in which the daughter takes the place of the Son
in the domestic triad of mother, child, and the heavenly Father Iphis invokes in her dying prayer. This closing passage thus restructures the nuclear family central to the first half of the play into a type of the Holy
Family—a family *without* human fathers (and hence one that may also
distantly recall the lesbian lineage of the daughter's name).

Why is the father absent here? It seems possible to read the domestic
relations in the play as an allegory of nature, law, and grace, so that the
deadly transition from instinctive self-preservation to sacrifice would correspond to Iphis's progression from mother to father, while the second
shift from the bleak legalism of the vow to Iphis's intuition of redemptive
sacrifice signals the movement from law to grace. By returning to Storge
rather than Jephthah in the end, the play hints at a dialectic whereby grace
redeems nature but abolishes the law by fulfilling it.

Yet this allegorization seems more than a little mechanical. Whether
valid or not, such an interpretation fails to account for the triple displacement that concludes this play: of father by Father, of Son by daughter, and
of father by daughter.[118] Any satisfactory reading of these displacements,
furthermore, needs to take into account their gendering while keeping in
mind, first, that this play was written for boys, who in all likelihood would
not be very interested in daughters per se, and second that, in both antiquity and the Renaissance, the sacrificial child need not be female.[119]

The Absent Father

Medieval and Renaissance paintings of the infant Jesus often omit Joseph,
sometimes substituting Saint Anne as the third figure in the domestic

grouping; when he is present, he tends to be portrayed comically—frequently asleep. He never, of course, appears in representations of the Passion. By granting the father only a marginal status within its aphallically conceived Holy Family, Christianity seems to intensify anxieties already visible in the Old Testament concerning the father's procreative role.[120] It has thus historically given rise to a destabilizing tension between the claims of domestic (whether filial or marital) and spiritual kinship—of father and Father—to unconditional allegiance.[121] From the subapostolic period on, the virgin daughter who defies paternal and civic authorities comes to symbolize Christian liberation from the ancient constraints of the household and city. In early Christian narrative, the daughter who unescorted crosses the threshold of the paternal *oikos* is perceived as the radiant harbinger of a new, spiritual community. In the apocryphal Acts, Peter Brown notes, the apostles

> were regularly portrayed drawing unmarried girls out of staid seclusion and wives out of the beds of their husbands. . . . Thecla, the exposed, virgin traveler, did not merely resist the advances of the noble Alexander of Antioch; she boxed his ears with such force that the great golden crown of a priest of the Imperial cult, heavy with images of the Emperors themselves, toppled from his head. . . .
>
> The shimmering, ethereal figures of *daimones*, of heroes and of the souls of the wise, that had linked heaven to earth, towering above the human race in the middle regions of the late Platonic universe, were eclipsed, in the Christian imagination, by the bodies of the virgin young on earth.[122]

This symbolization survived through the seventeenth century. The religious drama of the Renaissance abounds with daughters who deliberately violate their fathers' commands and thereby attain sainthood.[123] As in the early church, these texts announce the breakthrough to a new order not based on human paternity.

John Christopherson's Greek *Jephthah* (c. 1544) eloquently marks the Christian displacement of father and husband with their heavenly rival in the daughter's affections. Before being led away to her death, the (unnamed) daughter implores God's help, reminding him that "husband art Thou / To me, Thou art my children and my father; / Thou art my light, my life; Thou art my all."[124] These lines, of course, come from the *Iliad*, from Andromache's final speech to Hector as he departs to encounter Achilles. In Christopherson's version, however, God takes the place of husband, father, and family as sole object of the daughter's love. Likewise, by aligning Jephthah's daughter with the *apheton*—the sacred animal that passes out of male control—Renaissance exegesis structures this story around a similar distinction between paternal and sacred space. As the loving, obedient daughter whose submission to her father's authority displaces him from the typological chain of sacred signifiers and annuls his paternal *potestas*, Iphis embodies all that gives value to the *oikos* and also represents the site of its rupture, where the heteronomous pieties of the family and the transcendent conflict, allowing the Beyond to shatter the domestic enclosure. As Boose notes, "The tangent at which the father and daughter meet is the line that potentially threatens almost every enclosing structure of the family unit."[125]

Buchanan's absent father thus belongs to a centuries-old narrative structure created by men to represent their own marginalization within the new social forms developed by Christianity. But the proliferation of Jephthah and virgin-martyr texts during the Renaissance suggests a more specific historical context for the competition between father and Father. Throughout Europe, but particularly in Buchanan's France, domestic and religious loyalties came into direct conflict. During the early years of the Reformation, as Donald Kelley observes, filial defiance suddenly erupted "on a grand scale. . . . The massive defection of sons and daughters was surely one of the fundamental elements of historical change in this period."[126] For many, conversion to Protestantism entailed repudiating paternal authority out of obedience to the Father's will. Thus, French archives record a massive surge "of family divisions, disinheritances and confiscations reflecting a fundamental social disruption a generation before the civil wars" (the same period, that is, during which Buchanan composed his tragedy). Exiled from the patriarchal *oikos*, young Protestants found substitute fathers in their ministers and, often, a heavenly Father in their martyrdoms. In its social praxis, as in its theology, early Protestantism thus moved from immanence to transcendence, from locating the sacred in social forms—whether ecclesiastical or domestic—to restoring the holy to its "metahistorical and immaterial" heteronomy, a heteronomy reproduced in the opposition between sect and family.[127] In *Jephthah*, this movement is played out in terms of the tragic tension between the biological continuity of the paternal domus and the sacrificial economy, precisely because sacrificial killing is "the basic experience of the sacred" and hence symbol of the rivalry between spiritual and familial ties.[128]

In sixteenth-century France, paternal authority also clashed with religious doctrine over the question of marriage. In 1556 Henri II declared marriages contracted without parental permission to be criminal offenses punishable by disinheritance of both parties. This legislation climaxed an increasingly bitter struggle between the Roman church, which since the twelfth century had held that mutual consent constituted a valid marriage, and parents who resented this infringement of their right to control such alliances for their own dynastic and political ends.[129] In the modern marriage ceremony of both the Anglican and Roman communions, the father must first "give away" his daughter to the priest, who then places the woman's hand in her husband's. This transfer captures the superimposition over the nuclear family

> of a more powerful geometry constructed around a rival father. . . .
> By standing directly above the bride, the representative of the divine
> Father creates the dominant triangle that visually defeats the earthly
> one. . . . Once a father has performed his prescribed role, it is he who
> becomes the displaced and dispossessed actor of the script. And—like
> every father of every bride—he must leave the sanctified space alone.[130]

The struggle between the clergy and laity over clandestine marriages configures the daughter—the child who is given away—as the contested center of the agon between the father and the Father.

The conflicts between paternal rights and sacred authority fissuring the social fabric of the sixteenth century provide the historical connection between Buchanan's theological grappling in *Jephthah* and his representation of the family. The alien God manifests himself when sacred obligations transgress a culture's ordinary sense of goodness and justice embodied in its basic social forms. Hence, the generational conflict attendant on the Reformation and (more tangentially perhaps) the debate over clandestine marriage seem implicated in Buchanan's Hegelian intimations of "*die in das Diesseits und Jenseits zerrissene Welt*" or, paraphrasing Herbert, of a culture "tortur'd in the space / Betwixt this world and that of grace."[131] But, unlike Hegel, Buchanan does not locate the major fault line between the claims of the private conscience and the state nor, as previously mentioned, between those of the "female" *oikos* and the "male" *polis*. This latter tension corresponds to the secondary conflict between Storge and Jephthah, but since both the priest and Jephthah himself acknowledge the *moral* primacy of the family—a primacy that only Iphis rejects—there exists no real opposition between domestic and social ideologies. Moreover, since Jephthah (who is the Israelite chieftain as well as Iphis's father) and his daughter both acknowledge the same sacred imperative, it seems awkward to describe the play's tragic agon in terms of conscience and the state. Rather, the play inscribes the specifically Renaissance clash between an ethical rationalism grounded in the duties and affections cementing the nuclear family and a sacrificial theology based on the alien economics of blood expiation. The Renaissance discovered its own theological aporia reflected in the parricidal sacrifice of *Iphigenia*—along with Euripides' *Hecuba* (another drama of child sacrifice), the most widely translated and imitated Greek tragedy during the sixteenth century. *Antigone* belongs to a later era.

A curious passage in the final chorus suggests a further relation between the play's daughter and the sons who performed and watched her tragedy. The chorus first praises Iphis's heroic death and then addresses an unspecified "*vos*":

> But ye, the opprobrium of your land,
> Craven in heart and slack of hand,
> Too craven and unnerved by fear
> To meet the thrust of hostile spear,
> And in your country's cause to yield
> Your life-blood on the battlefield—
> Your name and memory shall die
> And buried in oblivion lie.[132]

The implicit parallel here between sacrifice and death in battle seems to echo another Euripidean staging of daughter sacrifice; in *Erechtheus*, the victim's mother justifies herself by explaining, "If I had sons I would send them out to fight; my daughter equally can face death and be sacrificed."[133] Sacrifice, in other words, is the female equivalent of war. Jephthah's daughter thus provides an idealized mirror for Buchanan's pupils, who will perhaps be sent to their deaths by their own fathers or perhaps, given the religious persecutions of the 1540s, by their Father. The play projects the boys' anxieties about having to die for their country or their faith and, by ennobling the sacrificial daughter, consoles these fears—holding out the promise, as it were, of displacing their own fathers by risking death for the Father/fatherland.[134]

Yet sacrifice is not merely the female equivalent of war. The shadow of the cross, and hence the whole spiritual value of Christianity, marks the scene of the daughter's sacrifice, giving the story a theological weight generally absent from the father/son plots of Renaissance political narratives. *Jephthah* is not *Henry IV* in drag. Moreover, while the displacement of the father by his child seems gender-neutral, the Son's displacement by the daughter is not. If only because Iphis is (to the best of my knowledge) the *first* female type of Christ, her gender seems odd, or better, oddly significant. The usual explanation—the daughter is the sacrificial victim because daughters are always sacrificial victims—conveniently overlooks the fact that Christianity venerates *male* sacrifice; by ignoring the Son, this explanation makes his displacement invisible and hence cannot account for it.

Tragic *Katharsis*

Throughout most of *Jephthah*, one has the impression that Iphis is still quite young. Unlike Iphigenia, she evinces no interest in either men or marriage, her attachments remaining confined to her beloved parents. But the final scene portrays her differently. In the messenger's account of her death, for the first time Iphis is represented as a beautiful and self-consciously erotic young woman:

> When at the altar steps the maiden stood,
> As the appointed victim now displayed—
> Unwont to meet the gaze of men, who there
> Gazed on her crowding—maiden modesty
> O'er her wan cheeks . . .
> Suffused a glowing crimson; as if one
> Should stain the purest ivory of Ind
> With dye of Tyrian shell, or intermix
> With the red rose the lilies white as snow.[135]

In this passage, the crimson staining Iphis's ivory skin seems a proleptic allusion to the sacrificial spectacle, eliding the images of chaste feminine beauty and bloody death. The rose and lily associate her virgin blood with Christ's, a typological overtone strengthened in subsequent lines that liken her heightened beauty on the verge of death to "the descending glory of the sun, / When speeds his fiery orb to sink below / The western ocean."[136] But the description also closely resembles Vergil's portrait of Lavinia in the last book of the *Aeneid*.[137] Iphis's mortal loveliness thus simultaneously evokes the dying Christ and the Classical text, the latter configuring the sacrificial victim as the radiantly lovely woman of Greco-Roman poetry; the Scriptures know no such persona. The following lines, which combine allusions to Polyxena's sacrifice in Seneca's *Troades* with additional echoes of *Iphigenia*, further specify this woman as the sacrificial heroine of ancient tragedy—a figure found in virtually all the Greek tragedies translated before 1560. Interestingly, the one other Renaissance text that sees Jephthah's daughter as a type of Christ—Cappel's commentary—also identifies her with Iphigenia. The typological woman derives from the superimposition of the Greek sacrificial daughter onto the Gospel narrative.

Iphis's beauty transforms her death from a revolting crime into a scene suffused with majestic loveliness and solemn grandeur. As she approaches the altar, in her face

> there shone
> A fixed unfaltering purpose, and, alone
> Tearless amid the weeping, meek she stood.
> Serenely calm, and to her fate resigned.
>
> . . . And others wept
> To mark her bloom of youth, and eyes that shone
> Clear as twin stars behind a white-rimmed cloud,
> And the profusion of her golden hair
> Twined with the lingering sunbeam, and her firm
> Intrepid bearing, far beyond the strain
> Of woman's nature. And perchance on her
> Nature had breathed a beauty that excelled,
> To dignify with her supremest gifts
> The obsequies of the heroic maid.
> As the descending glory of the sun,
> When speeds his fiery orb to sink below
> The western ocean, all the waves ablaze
> Under his dipping rim, is beautiful
> More than the light of other sunlit hours;
> Or as the hue and fragrance of the rose
> That lingers latest of the blooming year
> Compels the sense and holds the eye enthralled
> With a peculiar power; even so this maid,
> Her foot upon the threshold of her doom,
> To death addressed, and resolute to die.[138]

The daughter's beauty transfigures the horror of this scene, disclosing the stately and mysterious splendor of the sacrificial rite. In the end it is her beauty, at once moral and physical (*kalokagathia* in Greek), that justifies the ways of God to men, that, in Nietzsche's words, "vanquishes the suffering that inheres in all existence"[139]—a beauty intensified in death, created by death, for such death is "the mother of beauty." The play reconciles us to the sacrificial law by the sheer aesthetics of it all. Iphis's radiant dignity is thus itself answer to the bitter theological doubts pervading the earlier scenes of the tragedy.

But since the beautiful victim derives from Classical tragedy—an ancestry underscored by the passage's thickly woven allusions to Euripides, Seneca, and Vergil—one may view the daughter's beauty as a synecdoche for the tragic poem itself. The persona seems so specifically linked to the genre that she may represent it.[140] Her beauty in particular marks her as a figure of the text, since, according to the discursive conventions of Renaissance aesthetics, "the portrayal of a beautiful woman . . . stands characteristically for the descriptive power of words."[141] Petrarch's puns on "Laura" and "laurel," for example, depend on this entanglement of erotic and aesthetic intentions. It is not, of course, finally the daughter's beauty but the beauty of Buchanan's neoclassical Latin that effects the reconciliation with the alien God; her beauty figures the formal consolations of the tragic text. The theophantic beauty of the poem, symbolized by the radiant loveliness of its heroine, takes over the offices of revelation, much as Iphis supplants her father in the typological genealogy.

Such recuperation has transgressive edges: the displacement of the Son by the feminized text, but also his resemblance to the pagan woman. Although Buchanan's classically beautiful daughter affirms the mysterious decorum of the sacrificial economy against rationalist cost-cutting, she also diminishes the uniqueness of Christ's atonement by assimilating it to tragedy's pagan self-oblations. The play itself registers this threat; thus, both Storge and the priest object that the human sacrifice Jephthah intends nullifies the distinction between Israel and the Ammonites. The same recognition that this sacrifice blurs cultural difference surfaces in Poole, who raises the possibility that the god to whom Jephthah offered his terrible vow was, under a different name, in fact "Moloch, the god of the Ammonites, against whom he was about to fight."[142] Iphis's sacrifice at once betrays the kinship between Christ and Iphigenia and compromises the opposition between Israel and idolatry; or rather—as in Grotius—precisely by disclosing this unsettling fraternal likeness, it deconstructs the ideological opposition. The sacrificial daughter of ancient tragedy turns out to be a suspect guest in the Father's house, a foreign presence who threatens the stable contours differentiating this enclosure from external profanations.[143] *Timeo Danaides et dona ferentes.*

Here, too, the daughter can be seen as standing for the literary text. The cultural syntax that Poole describes—a syntax in which ideological distinctions are erased in the process of being inscribed, so that the victorious antagonist ends up resembling his opponent—has an odd affinity to the strategies of Christian neoclassicism. The religious poet appropriates the pagan text for his own purposes, but the intertext (like the sheep that the boa constrictor swallows in *The Little Prince*) remolds the surfaces of the containing narrative. Buchanan's project, the Christian humanist project of giving aesthetic form to sacred subjects, itself seems to efface the boundaries dividing culture from holiness. It is this category confusion to which the Council of Trent objected in prohibiting all "seductive charm" in religious art and which likewise elicited Milton's scornful charge that Charles I had made "the living God" into "a buzzard Idol" by "borrowing to a Christian use Prayers offer'd to a Heathen God," offered, that is, by "*Pammela* in the Countesses *Arcadia*." For Milton, the presence of Sidney's lovely Greek—although not Attic—sacrificial daughter "hath as it were unhallow'd, and unchrist'nd the very duty of prayer it self."[144] The Reformation and Counter-Reformation both demanded "the depaganization of Renaissance literature and culture, the repression or removal from Christian culture of the large admixture of pagan theology or mythology that early humanists with their love of Greek and Latin letters had allowed to color their own religious attitudes."[145] The ancient texts, like Jephthah's Greekling daughter, seem to anticipate Christian revelation—vestiges of an ancient theology or distant recollections of biblical events—but their pagan beauty, Iphis's beauty that draws "the eyes of the whole multitude, who gazed / Awe-struck and wondering," upstages both father and Son. Religious reformers (whether Catholic or Protestant) preferred to exclude such distractions from sacred precincts. The result of walling off the holy in this way, however, was to secularize the arts, particularly the theater, where pagan associations clustered most thickly.

Hence, despite its popularity, *Jephthah* had few successors. Instead, throughout the sixteenth and seventeenth centuries a majority opinion expressed firm antagonism to dramatizing biblical narratives. On this matter, Jonas Barish notes, "Protestant and Catholic polemicists are in firm agreement."[146] Henry Crosse's 1603 *Vertues Commonwealth* thus attacks scriptural plays on the ground that they "intermixe the sacred worde of God, that never ought to be handled without feare and trembling, with their filthy and scurrillous Paganisme."[147] In England, the 1589 ban against playing "matters of divinitye," while partly motivated by political considerations, expressed the Protestant conviction that actors should keep their hands off holy things; Reformation scripturalism itself tended to make the Bible unavailable for theatrical exploitation.[148]

But these objections generally postdate Buchanan's play; prior to 1560, even militant Calvinists like Bale and Beza wrote biblical dramas without any apparent qualms. Furthermore, to claim that *Jephthah* is somehow transgressive implies that it is transgressive of *something*, that one can locate a relevant orthodoxy against which to measure deviations. But at least before the Council of Trent, the ideological landscape conspicuously lacked such clearly defined boundaries; what was permissible in Bordeaux might be dangerous in Paris and could (as Buchanan discovered) be considered heresy in Lisbon. Even after the hardening of confessional lines, transgression and orthodoxy remained slippery terms; clearly Ascham and Sidney did not find *Jephthah* offensive despite the general Protestant disapprobation of religious drama. Greenblatt's observation that we label subversive those ideas that no longer seem subversive to us suggests the need for caution in these matters.[149]

Literature and Dogma

If, however, we give "transgression" a more limited reference by contrasting Buchanan's play with works of unimpeachable Calvinist slant, the startling otherness of *Jephthah* becomes apparent. While the play may or may not engage Reformed theology directly (Buchanan claimed that it criticized Bucer's position on vows, but that was during his trial before the Portuguese Inquisition), there is a particular reason for specifying this contrast.[150] Beza's *Abraham sacrifiant* is crucial here. Although this play appeared in print four years before *Jephthah*, the latter had previously been circulating in manuscript and was almost certainly known to Beza, who had become friendly with Buchanan during their joint residence in Paris in the mid-1540s—the same time Buchanan was busy revising the original text of *Jephthah*.[151] Since *Abraham sacrifiant* also is a biblical play about child sacrifice modeled in part on Euripides' *Iphigenia*, it would seem to be a deliberate rewriting of Buchanan's tragedy, a Calvinist response, as it were, to the neoclassical daughter.

The differences between the two texts are instructive. Beza's play is far closer to the Mysteries than to Greek tragedy: the language in particular has none of Buchanan's poetic luxuriance, none of its richly metaphorical and allusive splendor; instead, it uses the homespun plain style characteristic of medieval biblical drama. Since one cannot paint without colors, the absence of verbal beauty entails the absence of the beautiful victim. The story obviously dictated the child's gender, but Beza could have, and did not, emphasize Isaac's youthful grace and majestic bearing. Beza also allows the mother—the only woman in the play—a far less significant role than Storge. Since Abraham never reveals God's dreadful command to his wife, she cannot respond to the theological issue at stake; she remains outside the spiritual arena where men struggle with God.

The issue at stake, however, closely resembles that in *Jephthah*: the moral perversity of a God who commands a father to murder his adored child. But Beza handles the matter differently. He replaces the aesthetic transfiguration of sacrifice that resolves the ethical crisis in Buchanan with a theology based on faithful obedience to the incomprehensible and terrible dictates of the divine will. Abraham points the moral with painful clarity. Golding's 1577 translation has him resolve:

> O my God, my God, sith thow
> Doost bid me, I will doe it. Is it right
> That I so sinfull and so wretched wight,
> Should fall to scanning of the judgements
> Of thy most perfect pure commaundments.
>
> For sith it is thy will, it is good right
> It should de [*sic*] doone. Wherefore I will obey.[152]

Interestingly, Beza gives Satan some of the arguments the priest had used against Jephthah. Rational considerations turn out to be the insidious whispers of the devil; whereas in Buchanan such considerations appear mistaken, in Beza they are evil. "Nothing," Abraham concludes, "is good or reasonable, / Which to Gods will is not agreeable."[153]

Abraham's faith—which in this play means a willingness to violate human reason and moral sense—takes the place of expiatory sacrifice. For Isaac of course does not die. The sudden entry of God's angel just as Abraham lifts the knife averts the tragedy, in contrast to *Jephthah*, where reconciliation, if achieved at all, is achieved by means of sacrifice, by its typological evocations as well as by the mortal beauty and courage of the victim. In Beza, God justifies his own ways to man by stopping the sacrifice, which thus turns out to have been a trial of obedience rather than a pagan *lustratio*, an ethical test rather than a ritual expiation. In Buchanan, however, the Classical beauty of the daughter and of the poetry jointly disclose the beauty of holiness "transfiguring all that dread."

But if Beza's play differs from Buchanan's, it has significant affinities with the Calvinist passion narratives. One notes in both the absence of the beautiful victim, the radical heteronomy of the divine will, the insistence on obeying God even when he seems to be an enemy, the marginalization of women. In these texts, men struggle to submit to an alien God: to be patient, self-controlled, dutiful, subservient. They (both the texts and the men) lack the daughter's joy and loveliness and exquisite poise. Moreover, since Beza's play rewrites Buchanan's, one may regard the Calvinist sacrificial plot as a counternarrative to sacred neoclassicism as well as medieval exegesis. The transgressiveness of *Jephthah* thus emerges retrospectively in its radical divergence from the narrative paradigms crystallizing within sixteenth-century Protestantism.

One can, I think, legitimately trace this divergent trajectory into the nineteenth century. As Grotius's *De satisfactione* oddly resembles Frazer's anthropological investigations, so the issues raised by *Jephthah* point toward the late nineteenth-century poetics of "spilt religion" and the transformation of the literary text into a secular sacrament. In these syncretic representations of biblical sacrifice, the Noah's Ark theory of cultural diffusion unexpectedly germinates comparative anthropology and Arnold's aesthetic soteriology. The origins of modern cultural analysis and the modern conceptualization of "literature" begin to present themselves to the imagination (Dryden's witty spaniel) in the shape of trilingual humanists brooding over the Cross.

Meyer Abrams's *Natural Supernaturalism* and the ensuing critical debate have already canvassed both the ramifications of and objections to similar generalizations. Such continuities derive from the uninterrupted centrality granted the classics and the Bible in the humanistic paideia through the first quarter of the present century and need not imply essentialist premises. In any case, the notion that literature appropriates the offices of religion is not a new one, although the precise moment of this transference of power has been variously assigned anywhere from the Homeric era to the Romantic—a confusion consequent upon the untenable premise that only beginnings possess historical importance, leading scholars (present company included) to confuse change with origin. But while the competition between literature and dogma seems to date from a very early period—it is explicit enough in Plato—it undergoes significant and culturally specific alterations. To suggest the import of this *paragone* in the sixteenth century, it will be useful to pursue the contrast between Buchanan's play and Beza's. We may begin with what should already be obvious, namely, that *Abraham sacrifiant* leaves out both the sacrifice and the aesthetic/erotic nuances that conclude *Jephthah*.

Clearly, the biblical story dictates the omission of sacrifice from Beza's text, but patristic and medieval exegetes tend to pass over the fact that Isaac was not sacrificed, instead viewing him as a type of Christ. Beza, however, mutes the typological overtones of the Old Testament narrative and hence largely divests the story of its sacrificial resonance. The play explores inner conflict and obedience to the divine will. This focus, coupled with the work's verbal plainness and voluntarist theology, points ahead to the narrative structures of Calvinist autobiography, practical theology, and passion sermons. Conversely, *Jephthah*, with its poetic richness, debt to pagan models, and pervasive evocations of Christ's sacrifice, seems to draw on the aesthetics and thematics of the Mass: its (in Protestant eyes) pagan ceremonial, its sacrificial mimesis, its ritual splendor. This is not an arbitrary comparison. It is well known that Protestant writers frequently conflate sacrifice, theater, and Catholic worship, objecting to eucharistic sacrifice because it resembled a stage play and to plays because they resembled papist ceremonies. Thus, John Rainolds denounces the priests who "have transformed the celebrating of the Sacrament of the *Lords supper* into a *Masse-game,* and all other partes of the *Ecclesiasticall service* into *theatricall sights*; so, in steede of *preaching the word,* they caused it to be played." "The Popish Masse," in Stubbes's words, "is now no other but a Tragicke Play."[154]

Protestants found the Mass offensive because it distracted the congregation with outward "shews." But the objection was not simply or even principally directed against the "theatricality" of the Roman liturgy. Reformed theology not only abolished the pageantry of the Roman rite but rejected the sacrificial character of the Eucharist altogether, instead reading it as a sign of grace or token of Christ's spiritual presence; it thus weakened the connection between sacrament and sacrifice. Even then, in most Reformed churches, the Lord's Supper became an occasional and fairly peripheral affair.[155] The moral inwardness of Protestantism—its ethical rationalism, which drives its antipathy to the spectacular "magic" of the Mass—also problematizes sacrifice. Radical Protestant sects like the Socinians, Zwinglians, and Anabaptists registered this discomfort most stridently, but even Calvinism, which did not overtly dissent from Anselm's theology of the Atonement, preferred to represent the Crucifixion as a trial of obedience rather than as an expiatory satisfaction.[156] This much seems evident from the Calvinist passion narratives. Reformed spirituality stressed inner regeneration and moral duty and therefore found both ritual magic and the sacrificial economy hollow, albeit dangerously seductive, consolations.

In an article on Herrick's "Tragicus Rex," Thomas Moisan offers the interesting observation that the poem portrays Christ under a "three-fold characterization . . . as God and actor and king."[157] Where the article has "actor," the customary description of Christ's threefold office would have put "priest." The actor, that is, displaces the priest.[158] Although Moisan does not say so, this displacement corresponds to the substitution of actor for exorcist that Greenblatt analyzes in his influential essay on *King Lear.*

And it also corresponds to *Jephthah*'s substitution of the Classical tragic daughter for the incarnate Son. In both plays, exorcism and priestly sacrifice—the spectacular rituals of medieval Christendom—migrate from the sanctuary to the stage. As Shakespeare's tragedy, according to Greenblatt, reconstitutes exorcism as theater by awaking our longing for its saving magic, so Buchanan's tragedy takes over the functions of eucharistic sacrifice: its transformation of a divinely orchestrated political murder into the longed-for drama of God's amazing grace.[159] One thinks again of Sidney's remark that *Jephthah* elicits "divine admiration," a tribute that seems to echo the Polybian concept of *tragodia* as that which turns religion into wonder. *Jephthah* narrates the aesthetic recuperation of the sacrificial.[160] Expiatory sacrifice, the narrative center of Christianity, moves from theology to art. Unintelligible to rational consciousness—to the priest and Jephthah and also, one suspects, to the Protestant exegetes who erased the offensive rite from Judges—sacrifice is recuperated as tragedy. "Only as an esthetic product," Nietzsche observes in his own study of Greek tragedy, "can the world be justified to all eternity."[161]

The absence of aesthetic/erotic shadings from Beza's play is not unrelated to its suppression of sacrifice, because sacrifice itself releases erotic energies. Christianity, like Greek tragedy, understands sacrifice as an act of love, one that elicits an erotic response. In the *Disputatiuncula*, Erasmus thus remarks that Colet's Christ, whose immense love disregards all suffering in its eagerness to serve the beloved, resembles the Ovidian lovers "who are not wearied by their nightly vigils nor feel hunger nor fear meeting ghosts and goblins. . . . [but] eagerly endure wounds, even death itself." This comparison is not wholly serious, but Erasmus never doubts the erotic character of sacrificial pain, for "under the weight of suffering, as from under a pile of kindling, the flame of love, since it cannot be extinguished, shines more brightly." Hence, Erasmus concludes, Christ's torment itself makes him lovable (*amabilis*), an object of desire.[162] In the Calvinist passion narratives, the ephebic Christ glimpsed amid the scenes of torture hints at the seductive afterimage produced by pain, but in general Protestant texts are wary of this transcendental eros. The frustrated, grotesque love that torments Nashe's Christ, a love that finally destroys its object, seems more characteristic of the Calvinist focus on structures of violence. The passion narratives produced by Reformed theology stress the patient obedience required in the face of suffering rather than the desire aroused by self-oblation. The erotic mysticism that suffuses medieval piety has little place in the worship of Milton's God, "whom to love is to obey." Sacrifice and erotic/aesthetic beauty disappear together in *Abra-*

ham sacrifiant, as in Calvinism as a whole, because they are themselves intrinsically connected.

Protestantism replaces the erotic and sacrificial spirituality of the medieval church with a practical theology based on the family, obedience, and, somewhat paradoxically, ethical rationalism—the apparently incompatible copresence of the latter two items a result of the Reformation's double inheritance from late medieval voluntarism and Erasmian moralism. But *storge*, obedience, and ethical rationalism are precisely the values interrogated and finally superseded in *Jephthah* by the daughter's beautiful and erotically charged sacrifice. Yet it seems misleading to view the play as an affirmation of Catholic piety against the new Protestant ethos. In Buchanan's play, as in ancient tragedy, earlier religious forms are transmuted into aesthetic pleasures, where "aesthetic" now needs to be understood as charged with numinous as well as erotic valences—the textual/ sexual transcendence proffered by Neoplatonism and the Longinian sublime as well as Romantic poetics.[163] Tragic sacrifice simultaneously elicits and hence fuses aesthetic, erotic, and transcendent desires, an interlacing disclosed in Shelley's remarkable confession that "some of us have in a prior existence been in love with an Antigone, and that makes us find no full content in any mortal tie."[164] The literary text—not the religious ritual—awakens and configures supernatural yearnings. In *Jephthah*, the restaging of sacrifice as tragedy becomes the overarching displacement that governs the multiple displacements structuring the play. Literature replaces religion as the space for the articulation of desires and needs unavailable or forbidden in ordinary social life—for the transcendent eroticism, sacrificial magic, theatrical wonder, and ecstatic beauty distrusted by Protestant sensibilities.[165]

At the same time, literature partly replaces and partly supplements religion as the discourse of moral conflict, subjectivity, and volition. What modern critical theory calls the subject does not first come into being during the Renaissance; the Psalms, Augustine's *Confessions*, *The Sayings of the Desert Fathers*, and Bernard's sermons on Canticles (no less than Hamlet's soliloquies) attempt to speak "that within which passes show"— what Saint Thomas calls the "hidden interior actions of the soul" as opposed to its "external activities."[166] The impression that subjectivity rather suddenly emerges during Shakespeare's lifetime results from the fact that *literary* characterization acquires a new interiority and self-consciousness.[167] The language of introspection, desire, and inner struggle migrates from devotional praxis, from the monasteries and the confessional, to literature—a process enabled (and perhaps partly caused) by the mimetic recovery of the ancient literary discourses of the self.[168] If Classical tragedy, in Eric Voegelin's words, "is the study of the human soul in the process of making decisions," then the form itself engenders the subject.[169] "Engenders" in a double sense, for, at least in *Jephthah*, the language of introspection, desire, and inner struggle constructs the tragic subject as an eroticized, neoclassical, female type of Christ.

Most Renaissance tragedies do not, however, concern erotic, typological women; *Jephthah* is not a direct "source" for later works but the seminal allegory of their means of production. It stages the displacements, exchanges, and appropriations involved in the transmutation of awe into wonder, of liturgy (the Greek term for "work") into play, of ritual into aesthetic *katharsis*. The beautiful, transgressive creature who displaces the Son is not the protagonist of Renaissance literature; it (or she) is Renaissance literature.

It would be nice to end on such a rhetorically satisfying note, but the claim made in the preceding paragraph, that some connection exists between the classical-typological woman and literary representations of subjectivity, seems more a flourish than an argument. *Jephthah* points to an unfamiliar linkage between gender, subjectivity, devotion, and desire. One's training suggests that the unfamiliar is the outward and visible sign of the significant, but to deduce cultural generalizations from a single play is not likely to be convincing—particularly given the generally held view that Renaissance texts by and large confine subjectivity to male figures, women serving mainly as props and scenery. The next and final chapter will therefore examine another group of Renaissance biblical narratives that, like *Jephthah*, depict the passion of a Classical and Christic *virgo virilis*.

5   Saints and Lovers
Mary Magdalene
and the Ovidian Evangel

And Courage Lovers: Jesus *will allow*
Your Noble Passion
Immoderation
Who was excessive in His Love to you.
Joseph Beaumont,
"S. Mary Magdalen's Ointment"

I was teaching at the University of Arkansas in 1988–89, the year the movie version of Nikos Kazantzakis's *The Last Temptation of Christ* came out. There were, as I recall, protests throughout the state against the movie's notorious dream sequence in which Christ and Mary Magdalene make love. At the university, the student governing body voted to ban the film from campus. It was one of the few times I felt that I would not last long in Fayetteville.

The sex scene between Christ and Mary Magdalene was not very explicit, nor was the underlying idea particularly novel. In *The Man Who Died*, D. H. Lawrence, rather predictably, also eroticizes their relationship. Rumors about this pair, in fact, go back a long time. One detects them three centuries earlier behind Donne's glancing allusion in "The Relique" and among the blasphemies attributed to Marlowe.[1] Over a millennium before this, Celsus's second-century anti-Christian polemic dismisses Mary's vision of the resurrected Christ as the hallucination of a sexually excited (*paroistros*) female.[2] The sexualization of the Magdalene's relationship to Christ seems to be a subversive topos of long standing—one congenial to persons repelled (and amused) by the traditional Christian ethics of purity.

Many orthodox versions of the Mary Magdalene story bear out this hypothesis, since they stress precisely the opposite implications, focusing on Mary's renunciation of her sinful sexuality and subsequent life of austere penitence. Donatello's statue of the ravaged penitent Magdalene (fig. 1) thus portrays a body wasted and drained by the rigors of ascetic discipline—the body bruised to pleasure soul. Most Protestant treatments of the Magdalene legend similarly center on her conversion from a life of sensual delight to one of chaste and contrite faith.[3]

But a little further investigation makes it clear that this schematic contrast between subversive eroticism and puritanical orthodoxy has limited applicability. Even unquestionably orthodox representations of Mary's conversion exude an erotic fragrance; a late twelfth-century life of Mary Magdalene, probably of Cistercian origin, renders her tearful penitence in a manner reminiscent of Kazantzakis:

> Having sprinkled the feet of the Saviour with the precious nard, she spread it over them and massaged them with her hands and fingers; then she wrapped them gently in her hair, which was of surpassing beauty. Drawing them to her breast and lips, she tenderly washed them. She held them and caressed them for a long time, then let them go.[4]

Likewise, Renaissance portraits of Mary as a penitent anchorite often have an unexpected sensual beauty (fig. 2) that occasionally descends into something that looks like hagioporn (fig. 3); one does not know what else to call Bellavia's sketches of the naked Mary lying above a crucifix's nearly naked corpus, her eyes gazing intently and passionately on Christ's face and thighs. Leo Steinberg classifies such works as "pure erotomania."[5]

But this seems premature. Bellavia's apparently blatant erotic fantasies belong to his series of otherwise unremarkable devotional engravings. Moreover, they are curiously akin to passages in Donne's sermons (including one preached shortly before his death) where he describes how Christ covers sin "by comming to me, by spreading himself upon me . . . Mouth to mouth, Hand to hand" and conversely how Donne, like Bellavia's Mary Magdalene, spreads himself atop Christ's crucified body: "I put my hands into his hands, and hang upon his nailes, I put mine eyes upon his. . . . I put my mouth upon his mouth. . . . to *hang* upon *him* that *hangs* upon the *Crosse*, there *bath* in his *teares*, there *suck* at his *woundes*."[6] Sexuality and piety seem surprisingly difficult to distinguish. Donne's ardent longings remain erotic, but one hesitates to label them symptoms of "erotomania," and they have nothing to do with *female* sexuality. It is, however, tempting to attach some significance to the fact that the only picture Donne had in his bedroom was of Mary Magdalene—unusual decor, perhaps, for a Protestant minister.[7]

Kazantzakis's sexualized reading of the relationship between Mary Magdalene and Christ challenges the orthodox insistence on *Christ's* sexual purity. Mary's passionate and erotic love for Christ, however, was an immensely popular topos of medieval and Renaissance devotional literature. But since contemporary scholarship affirms with a rare unanimity that Renaissance men found female sexuality simultaneously terrifying and disgusting, the eroticism of the Magdalene—the only remaining female saint in the 1549 Book of Common Prayer—seems unaccountable. To understand the implications of this anomaly, we need to examine a group of texts, dating from the twelfth to the seventeenth century, that focus on Mary's anguished longing for her divine (and dead) lover—a scriptural subgenre that bears significantly on questions of sexuality, gender, and subjectivity in medieval and early modern Christianity.

Although Magdalene narratives figure in patristic biography, the cycle plays, and saints' lives, only two pre-Reformation versions survived into the English Renaissance. Both are rewritings of the twentieth chapter from the Gospel according to John, which describes how Mary waited alone at the empty tomb of Christ weeping, until finally the risen Lord appeared to her disguised as a gardener.[8] We may label these versions the "Chaucerian" and the "Origenist," since the former appears as part of the Chaucerian canon in every Renaissance edition of his works and the second is a medieval Latin sermon generally attributed to Origen (although both Erasmus and Bellarmine questioned this ascription).[9] There may have been some contamination between the two versions, since Chaucer himself, in the *Legend of Good Women*, mentions that he translated "Orygenes upon the Maudeleyne,"[10] evidence that the sermon was available in England by the late fourteenth century.

The Origenist version starts out as a sermon but halfway through slips into a dialogue between Mary Magdalene, the angels, and Christ. The narrator, who initially functions simply as an exegete, also becomes a character, interrogating Mary, expostulating with Christ, asking questions, and offering (often useless) advice. The text employs a rhythmic and elaborately schematic Latin prose, although some late versions are written in doggerel. Recent scholarship has identified the pseudo-Origen's homily as a Benedictine or Cistercian work of the late twelfth or early thirteenth centuries. More than 130 manuscript versions from the thirteenth through the sixteenth century survive; at least twelve editions were printed between 1504 and 1604.[11] During the same period, the sermon was translated into French, Italian, Provençal, Castilian, Portuguese, Dutch, Czech, and English—the *Homilie of Marye Magdalene, declaring her fervent love and zele towards CHRIST* of 1565 and a fragmentary, probably earlier, English translation.[12] The pseudo-Origen, furthermore, supplied the principal source for Robert Southwell's *Marie Magdalens Funeral Tears*, which itself went through nine editions between 1591 and 1624, as well as

Lancelot Andrewes's fourteenth Easter sermon (1620) and, via Southwell, Gervase Markham's *Marie Magdalens Lamentations* (1601).[13]

The Chaucerian variant, *The Lamentatyon of Mary Magdaleyne*, probably dates from the late fifteenth century; it is composed in macaronic verse and has Mary herself speaking alone. Unlike the Origenist homily, it ends before Mary's encounter with the risen Christ. No versions survive prior to its anonymous publication, entitled the *Complaynte of the Lover of Cryst Mary Magdaleyn*, in 1520. But in 1532 William Thynne reprinted it as part of the Chaucerian canon in his editio princeps of Chaucer's works, and it was thereafter included in all subsequent sixteenth- and seventeenth-century editions.[14] It did not drop out of the Chaucer canon until Tyrwhitt's 1775 edition rejected its traditional authorship, at which point it plummeted into oblivion.

Love among the Ruins

Both the Origenist homily and the Chaucerian verse prosopopoeia are recastings of the biblical narrative on the model of Ovid's *Heroides*— probably the most popular Ovidian work in the late Middle Ages.[15] The *Heroides* constitute a female version of the rhetorical *suasoria*, an imaginary speech (or letter) urging someone to do something: in this case, epic and mythological forsaken women writing to their lovers—Achilles, Theseus, Aeneas, Jason—pleading with them to come back. Along with the *Aeneid* (to which it is closely related), the *Heroides* contain probably the most influential Classical representation of female voice: of female desire and subjectivity articulated in contrast to and competition with the male arena of heroic and tragic action. The Mary Magdalene narratives, in turn, fuse this highly eroticized Ovidian representation of abandoned females with the Song of Songs and the hagiographic tradition, producing a self-conscious amalgam of the ancient rhetoric of female desire and the biblical language of erotic spirituality.[16]

The influence of the *Heroides* drastically reshaped the medieval hagiographic accounts of the Magdalene. The miracles, ascetic penance, and evangelism, detailed in most medieval versions of her life, disappear in the Origenist and Chaucerian narratives. More important, her life of sin and subsequent repentance, which figure prominently in the cycle dramas and hagiographic legend, are barely mentioned; she is not, in these texts, a reformed prostitute. Instead, both the Chaucerian and Origenist versions deal exclusively with Mary's desolation at the tomb of Christ. In these texts, she exhibits the characteristic features of the abandoned women familiar from Vergil's Dido and Ovid's forsaken heroines. Unlike the masculine hero (Aeneas, Achilles, Jason) who acts, she can only weep: passive, frozen—in a word, maudlin. So Andrewes describes her: "Whose presence she wished for, *His* misse she wept for; whom she dearly loved, while she had *Him*, she bitterly bewailed, when she lost *Him. Amor amare flens,* Love running downe the cheekes."[17] In all the versions she simply stands at the tomb and decides to remain until she dies, when she hopes some by-stander will wrap her in Christ's now-empty winding sheet.

She is, in fact, almost hysterical with grief: "dread and amazement hath dulled her senses, distempered her thoughts, discouraged her hopes, awaked her passions, and left her no other liberty but onely to weepe."[18] She often exhibits a pathological obsessiveness, refusing to eat, sleep, move, talk. In Markham and Southwell she begins to hallucinate, imagining that Christ is before her, that she is embracing him and folding his feet in her arms.[19] She is frequently suicidal. This grief is not religious despair but manifestly erotic; she is miserable because the man she loves is dead and even his body has disappeared.

Her language thus borrows heavily from the vocabulary of romance heroines. In the *Lamentatyon,* for example, Mary refers to Christ as "my swete herte, my gostly paramour," "my turtel dove so fresshe of hue," and "dere herte";[20] the Latin version of the pseudo-Origen describes her as Christ's *amatrix* and *dilectrix.*[21] In Markham, she speaks of her "hearts hot desire," "deepest passion of true burning love," and "love-sicke heart."[22] The grief, passion, longing, and confusion all come out in the pseudo-Origen's reweaving of Canticles. This is Mary thinking:

> But what may I do to finde him? whither shall I turne me? to whom shall I go? . . . who shall shew me whom my soul loveth, where he is bestowed, where he lieth at noontide? where he resteth? I beseche you tel him how I pyne with love and consume with sorowe. . . . Turne againe my beloved, turn again my hartes desire and dearling.[23]

Repeatedly she pleads to touch him: to "amplect" his body, to die in the arms of his corpse, to wrap her body in his gravecloth.[24] Southwell's narrator thus imagines Mary carrying the body of Jesus "naked in [her] armes" and pictures the Resurrection as a sort of Venus and Adonis scene, telling Mary that "all hazards in taking . . . [Christ's body] should have beene with usury repaid, if lying in thy lap, thou mightest have seene him revived, and his disfigured and dead body beautified in thy armes with a divine majesty."[25]

Over and over Mary emphasizes her need for physical contact. In Markham she thus asserts:

> To see him therefore, doth not me suffice,
> To heare him doth not quiet whole my mind,
> To speake with him in so familiar wise,
> Is not ynough my loose-let soule to bind:
> No, nothing can my vehement love appease,
> Least by his touch my wo-worne heart I please.[26]

There is something macabre in the insistent physicality of her longing for this corpse. Again, the feelings expressed are not "religious": she has no notion of the Resurrection; what she wants is at least the dead body of the man she loves. In pseudo-Origen she thus decides to remain by Christ's grave until her (imminent) death so "that yet at leste wyse I may be buried nye the sepulchre of my Lorde . . . [and] my Soule . . . passing forth of thys bryckle vessel of my bodie, may by and by enter into my Lords glorious Sepulcher." She does not long for spiritual reunion with him after death, just an attenuated contact with a place his body had touched.[27]

Like all abandoned women, she refuses to resolve eroticism into some sort of transcendence, whether of duty (Vergil) or devotion (Dante). Thus, in Markham and Southwell, when Christ finally does come and tells her to announce the Resurrection to his disciples, this responsibility throws her into renewed hysterics. She is not particularly interested in being part of salvation history; she wants to stay with Jesus and touch him. Instead of moderating or sublimating either desire or grief, she insists on the rightness of both.

One begins to hear, at this point, the monitory whispers of learned medievalists pointing out that such narratives should be read allegorically, to do otherwise evincing either historical ignorance or spiritual vulgarity. There is no question but that the Mary Magdalene narratives draw on the traditional allegorization of the Song of Songs, but with a crucial difference. Allegories of Canticles resolve the surface eroticism into relationships between the soul (or the church) and the glorified Christ: that is, into relations between incorporeal or metaphorical persons. Hence, the locus classicus of sacred eroticism, Bernard of Clairvaux's commentary on the Song of Songs, explicates the love between the bridegroom (Christ) and bride (soul/church) in a way that radically differentiates spiritual union from ordinary erotic relationships.

> But the bride—in what form or exterior loveliness, in what guise did St John see her coming down? . . . It is more accurate to say that he saw the bride when he looked on the Word made flesh, and acknowledged two natures in the one flesh. For . . . when we came to know the visible image and radiant comeliness of that supernal Jerusalem, our mother,

revealed to us in Christ and by his means, what did we behold if not the bride in the Bridegroom?[28]

There is no possible literal/romantic reading of a relationship where the woman is the flesh of the man as well as, in some sense, a city and a mother. Bernard consistently spiritualizes his erotic terminology, carefully distancing supernatural from romantic desire. At one point he thus imagines Christ speaking to the Bride, who at this moment has coalesced with "the woman . . . forbidden to touch the risen flesh of the Word"—that is, Mary Magdalene: "Become beautiful and then touch me; live by faith and you are beautiful. In your beauty you will touch my beauty all the more worthily, with greater felicity. You will touch me with the hand of faith, the finger of desire, the embrace of love; you will touch me with the mind's eye."[29] This overt allegorization is not found in the exegeses of John 20 considered here. These depict a woman alone, waiting almost hopelessly for her dead and absent lover; their mode is not allegory but rhetorical romance, leaving them susceptible to literal/erotic interpretation. Hence, Calvin, who violently rejects the whole Ovidian exegesis of this passage, conflates it with the parallel scene in Luke, in which Mary comes to the tomb accompanied by two other women—apparently precisely to preclude any private encounter between this heterosexual couple in their early thirties.[30] The eroticism resists allegorization and can be removed only by erasure. In both the Chaucerian and Origenist texts, Mary is a real woman interested in a conspicuously physical man. This realism does not divest the scene of spiritual implications, but it does thwart efforts to efface the letter under the proprieties of allegory. Instead, the generic conventions adopted in both versions accentuate the literal sense. Unlike medieval commentaries on Canticles, which employ the conventional system of verse-by-verse explication, these rewritings of John 20 are either soliloquies or dialogues; that is, they use dramatic modes. For example, in a wonderful scene Southwell's narrator tries to convince Mary that she is behaving foolishly, and she devastates him in reply.[31] The exegete here becomes a character, the voice that traditionally discloses the allegory being subsumed into the letter of the fiction.

Moreover, the Origenist texts in particular make it quite clear that a purely spiritualized reading is impossible. These works explicate the epistemological basis of their eroticism, and this, put simply, is identical to the phantasmic psychology spelled out by Aristotle and thereafter characteristic of virtually all premodern epistemologies. According to this paradigm, desire and thought depend on a process of imaging, for "the words of the soul's language are phantasms," and thus *"the phantasm has absolute primacy over the word."*[32] But if love requires images, then the corporeal is a sine qua non of desire. As Mary says, Christ's image has been sculpted in her soul, and she needs his body to renew the image, enabling her love to endure; she is afraid of falling out of love if she cannot see and touch Jesus, worrying "if that she found not his body, the love of him her Mayster wold sone waxe colde within her breaste, by the syghte yet whereof shee hoped shee mighte waxe warme againe."[33]

Her grief is likewise a product of this phantasmic psychology: her soul/image has been literally sucked into Christ's body: "for the spirite of Mary was rather in thy body, then in her owne body, and when she eaftsones soughte for thy body, she did then also seeke for her own spirit: and when she lost thy body, she lost with it her own spirit."[34] She is in his corpse, not in herself, and thus experiences the obsessive suffering and anxiety, detailed by Ioan Culiano in his *Eros and Magic in the Renaissance*, in which one is deprived of one's state as a subject, tortured by the absence of the other who contains one's very self, desperately needing the other—the body—to keep from collapsing into nothingness.[35] Christ's body therefore is not simply a metaphor or allegorical sign; rather, its physical actuality is essential to the opposition of presence and absence that governs these texts. "Yea doubtlesse," in Southwell's remarkable phrase, "if shee had thee within her, she would not envye the fortune of the richest Empresse."[36]

One can see the link between eroticism and epistemology by contrasting the medieval Magdalene narratives with Calvin's commentary on John 20. The earlier works consistently valorize the tangible over the verbal, a preference sharply etched in pseudo-Origen (a passage later incorporated into Cornelius à Lapide's conservative Catholic commentary); when Mary hears Christ call her name, she interrupts him with "Rabboni," for, pseudo-Origen notes, "she thought she needed no word that had found the word, and thought it farre more profitable to handel the word then to hear any manner of wordes."[37] As More and Bellarmine subsequently argue against Protestant scripturalism, language is "an imperfect method of communicating what could in principle be more exactly conveyed in images."[38]

In Reformed theology, however, this preference for the body over the text is reversed. Knowledge in Calvin is based on reading rather than seeing. This "inner iconoclasm," which becomes explicit in Ramus, replaces the "phantasmic essence of intellect" with a verbal/textual account of cognition. Since, according to Calvin, Mary and the other disciples had "abundantly clear testimonies" from Scripture for the Resurrection, they have no excuse for their grief and confusion. He thus brushes away Mary's weeping as "idle and useless." In this juridic, textualized epistemology, Mary's desire "only to obtain the dead body of Christ" is folly; it "leaves out the most important matter, the elevation of her mind to the divine power of his resurrection." She has "grovelling views" and an "earthly," "carnal" mind.[39] The risen Christ forbids her to touch him precisely because the lesson of this verse is that "all who endeavour to go to [Christ] must rid themselves of the earthly affections of the flesh."[40] As the verbal sign displaces Christ's body, Mary's need for that body becomes evidence of her carnality. That is, the shift from a phantasmic to a text-based epistemology accompanies and authorizes the familiar dualist oppositions of earthliness and elevation, carnality and spirituality.

What is surprising is the absence of such dualism in the Mary Magdalene narratives. In these there is no movement toward rising above the body, no transcendence. Corporeal and spiritual longing instead merge into an undifferentiated urgency, the desire for Christ racking Mary's flesh with a pervasiveness that reminds one of Sappho: "For him onely thou tyrest thy feete, thou bendest thy knees, thou wringest thy handes. For him thy heart throbbeth, thy brest sigheth, thy tongue complaineth. For him thy eye weepeth, thy thought sorroweth, thy whole body fainteth."[41] She desires nothing except this man, this body. She rejects heaven—or is totally indifferent to it. So in the pseudo-Chaucer she confesses:

> The joye excellent of blyssed paradyse,
> Maye me, alas! in no wyse recomforte,
> Songe of angel nothyng may me suffyse
> As in myne herte nowe to make disporte.[42]

In all the versions, she refuses even to speak to the angels when they show up at the tomb, despite the horrified urgings of the narrator. Her love undergoes no Platonic ascent; there is no moment when she realizes that her desires are misdirected or guilty or sinful; the erotic impulse is never spiritualized. She wants only Christ; as Andrewes remarks, "she had rather finde his dead body, than [angels] in all their glory."[43] What Calvin terms her carnal feelings should be seen in contrast not only to Protestant logocentrism but also, more generally, to narratives of male desire, which, as mentioned above, almost always finally etherealize or abandon the object of erotic pursuit. In male narratives, one has the sense that the transformation or annihilation of eros is the terrible yet liberating price of the hero's *Bildung*. For this trajectory, female narratives (secular as well as Christian) substitute the stasis of passion—a *passio amoris* with strange affinities to the *passio crucis*.

Love's Body

To grasp these resemblances, we need to investigate the implications of erotic abandonment in these texts—trying to get at the significance of both the eroticism and the abandonment. The question of sacred eroticism is particularly important, since without an adequate understanding of such desires, it seems hard to avoid, in Peter Brown's trenchant phrase, scoring "cheap triumph[s] of modern clinical knowingness at the expense of the dead."[44] But to find a satisfactory alternative to our nearly automatic assumption that the language of religious desire articulates imperfectly sublimated sexual frustrations, we need to broaden our inquiry from the Magdalene narratives to the problem of sacred eroticism in general.

To ask why these texts represent spirituality in terms of sexual desire may be a misleading question. It seems, first of all, unlikely that the dominant metaphor for affective spirituality from Plato up to the early modern period would so overtly signal its libidinal origins; the unconscious usually disguises repressed material more effectively. Second, the question assumes that desire is prior to and largely untouched by cultural inflections, an assumption rendered dubious by much recent criticism.[45] As John Winkler puts it, "Sex is not, except in a trivial and uninteresting sense, a natural fact."[46] One can, in fact, reverse the terms of the question, since the representation of sexual desire in the Middle Ages borrows heavily from the affective spirituality of Augustine and the twelfth-century Cistercians. That is, medieval secular eroticism (courtly love) is itself modeled on the analysis of spiritual longing, so that the latter is theoretically anterior to the former, rather than the reverse. Thus, the medieval historian Nicholas Perella observes that

> the whole matter of yearning for the beloved, the restless longing for something superior to and beyond the immediate grasp of mortality, accompanied by the belief that it would, if possessed, bring an untold bliss and solace—this is at the very heart of troubadour love poetry; but all this was first at the very heart of Christian spirituality.[47]

To the extent that medieval sexuality is shaped by the language of spiritual desires, it need not be viewed as the repressed origin of sacred eros.

But this may not be an adequate answer. Even if Cistercian spirituality precedes troubadour poetry, its imagery still seems to bear the marks of only very partially repressed libidinal urges. To get at the significance of sacred eroticism, we should perhaps begin at the other end: that is, instead of focusing on the origin of the link between religious subjectivity and erotic desire, we should look at when and why this link snaps.

In England, the break had already occurred by the early eighteenth century, as Pope's attempt at Christian Ovidianism makes evident. "Eloisa to Abelard" (1717)—like the Mary Magdalene narratives, a Christian rewriting of the *Heroides*—is, unlike them, about the "pious fraud of am'rous charity,"[48] about the *contamination* of religious devotion by erotic longing, where "erotic" has now become identical to "sexual." Eloisa's love for Abelard manifests itself in sexual dreams where

> Provoking Daemons all restraint remove,
> And stir within me ev'ry source of love.
> I hear thee, view thee, gaze o'er all thy charms,
> And round thy phantom glue my clasping arms.[49]

Her attempts at pious devotion melt into orgasmic swooning:

> When from the Censer clouds of fragrance roll,
> And swelling organs lift the rising soul;
> One thought of thee puts all the pomp to flight,
> Priests, Tapers, Temples, swim before my sight:
> In seas of flame my plunging soul is drown'd,
> While Altars blaze, and Angels tremble round.[50]

Whereas in the Mary Magdalene narratives the saint's desire to see and touch her beloved remains undifferentiated from supernatural love, for Eloisa these have become essentially antithetic impulses: "all is not Heav'n's while *Abelard* has part."[51] Sexual needs, only half-concealed by her attempts at sublimation, muddy and corrupt the spiritual. Pope's heroic epistle differs from the Mary Magdalene narratives because, by disclosing the bodily desires that filter up through the "pious fraud" of religious sublimation, it uncovers the mechanisms of repression that structure and subvert sacred eroticism.

The difference between Pope's epistle and earlier accounts of the relation between the erotic and the religious points to a major shift in the cultural history of the body, occurring sometime during the later seventeenth century. Put very simply, what happened was the discovery of genital sexuality—not that people learned how to make babies sometime around 1660, but for the first time one finds the assertion that sexual drives constitute the authentic substance of the erotic, other manifestations of desire (including religious ones) being disguised symptoms of repressed genital urges. Before this, what Culiano observes of the Greeks seems generally applicable, namely, that "physical desire, aroused by the irrational soul and appeased by means of the body, only represents, in the phenomenology of love, an obscure and secondary aspect."[52] In the Middle Ages and Renaissance, sexuality usually seemed either funny or sinful—a subject for bawdy stories or a painful reminder of the Fall.[53] The identification of the erotic with sexuality, already apparent in Pope, emerged sometime after 1650.

The primary evidence for this shift is found in works on erotic and religious pathology but is supported by other cultural evidence as well. Before 1650, erotic desire was represented as a process originating in the desirable object (especially the eyes), whose simulachrum enters the erotic subject through his own eyes, traveling thence to the imagination or fantasy and finally dwelling in the heart. In descriptions of romantic love, which is (of course) generally sexual, the trajectory is the same: from object to eye to imagination to heart, but finally in this case to the bowels or liver.[54] For Plato, love is an ocular disorder (*ophthalmia*), or as Southwell puts it: "In true lovers every part is an eie, and every thought a looke."[55] For Robert Burton, whose *Anatomy of Melancholy* conveniently summarizes two millennia of erotic speculation, love melancholy "is a passion of the brain, as all other melancholy, by reason of corrupt imagination," most commonly originating in "sight, which conveys those admirable rays of beauty and pleasing graces to the heart."[56]

The same model of what we may call "ocular eroticism" informs Renaissance secular literature: one thinks of Wyatt's "Through mine eye the stroke from hers did slide, / Directly down unto my heart it ran," or perhaps an even more pointed privileging of ocular over genital eroticism: "And if an eye may save or slay, / And strike more deep than weapon long. . . ."[57] The same psychology occurs in both Neoplatonic and Petrarchan contexts: in the "eye-sonnets" of Spenser and Sidney, in Bembo's peroration in *The Courtier*, in Shakespeare's "Tell me where is fancy bred" from *The Merchant of Venice*. It is perhaps needless to multiply examples since the same ocular eroticism is presupposed by virtually every Renaissance writer. The movement of eros is always inward and down, so that sexual desire is an inflection of erotic longing, not its origin or essence; by contrast, in the model that privileges genital sexuality, movement takes place outward and up, via cathexis and sublimation. Nor is there any reason to claim that a model that locates eros in the head and chest is merely a disguise or periphrasis for a libidinal one, since the bodily experience of eros, especially unhappy eros, has (even now) more to do with a fluttering heart, constricted chest, and upset stomach than any form of genital arousal.[58]

The ocular model entails that spiritual desire has no inherent or necessary connection to genital excitement, nor does such a connection surface in Renaissance treatments of religious pathology, where, if the paradigm of libidinal repression were available, one would expect to find it. This is particularly noticeable in Burton, where the section on religious melancholy comes immediately after that on love melancholy, yet no relation (besides both being forms of melancholy) is established between the two. Burton discusses sacred eroticism only in the opening paragraphs prefacing his analysis of religious melancholy, where he lays out the nature of a *nonpathological* love of God. Here the language is suffused with erotic imagery drawn from Canticles and the Platonism of the Church Fathers: the "divine form" that is "the quintessence of all beauty . . . ravish[es] our souls"; Christ "woos us by His beauty, gifts, promises, to come unto Him; 'the whole Scripture is a message, an exhortation, a love-letter'"; his is "'a divine beauty, an immortal love, an indefatigable love and beauty,' with sight of which we shall never be tired nor wearied, but still the more we see the more we shall covet Him."[59] According to Burton, the *perversions* of religion emerge not from this psychological matrix but rather—and this is wholly traditional—from diabolic malice, priestly greed, ignorance, fear, pride, ambition, and the pope.[60] Interestingly, when Burton does turn to the physiological causes of spiritual pathologies, he never mentions celibacy but rather focuses on immoderate fasting and solitude.[61]

The shift from ocular to genital eroticism belongs not to the history of the secular/sexual body but rather to that of ecclesiastical politics. It originates as a form of ideological demystification (both demystifying sectarian ideologies and itself an ideology whose fundamental trope is demystification) in the Restoration critique of religious enthusiasm; it thus originates simultaneously with the disappearance of sacred eroticism from English religious discourse. The relocation of the erotic in the genitals and the consequent link between sexual desire and spiritual excitement emerge together in the Cambridge Platonist Henry More's *Enthusiasmus triumphatus*, first published in 1656 and frequently reprinted. Like Burton, More diagnoses religious enthusiasm as a form of melancholy but relocates its seat from the brain to regions below the waist. Bodily fluids (and gases) thus reverse the path of the ocular *species*, surging upward from the loins to the heart and finally the imagination, so that "the *Enthusiast* . . . [is] as it were drunk with new wine drawn from that Cellar of his own that lies in the lowest section of his Body, though he be not aware of it, but takes it to be pure *Nectar*, and those waters of life that spring from above."[62] Sacred eroticism is thus reconceived as a sexual pathology, for "*Religious heat* in men, as it arises merely from Nature, is like *Aurum fulminans*, which though it flie upward somewhat, the greatest force when it is fired is found to goe downward."[63] Hence, "*Enthusiastical Love*" arises from "venereous fumes and vapours," from the "hidden and lurking fumes of *Lust*."[64]

After the Restoration, the identification of eroticism with genital sexuality becomes standard. That is, I take it, the point of Rochester's salacious lyricism or Pope's Cave of Spleen, where "Maids turn'd Bottels, call aloud for Corks."[65] Of course, at least since *Astrophel and Stella*, the problematic relation of "Platonic" (or Petrarchan) eros to sexuality had been articulated, but within the framework of the older ocular eroticism; Astrophel's surprise that "desire . . . so clingst" to his "pure love" makes sense only in a context where the erotic and sexual remain, at least conceptually, distinct.[66] The reconfiguration of the body first becomes explicit in More's *Enthusiasmus triumphatus*, precisely as it impinges on and problematizes sacred eroticism.[67] Swift then appropriates this reconfiguration for his "Discourse Concerning the Mechanical Operation of the Spirit" and the sections on Aeolism in *A Tale of a Tub*, published together in 1704. These presuppose and extend More's thesis—that spiritual passions originate in scatosexual vapors—for, as Swift puts it, "Persons of a visionary Devotion, either Men or Women, are in their Complexion, of all others, the most amorous."[68]

Like More, Swift analyzes enthusiasm, both religious and political, as a sexual disorder caused by the reversion of sperm from the loins upward. When, in *A Tale of a Tub*, Henry IV finds his intended mistress out of reach, "the collected part of the *Semen*, raised and enflamed, became adust, converted to Choler, turned head upon the spinal Duct, and ascended to the Brain."[69] The discourse of sacred eroticism is likewise anatomized, privileging, as it were, the phallic signifier, as in the case of the "*Saint* [who] felt his *Vessel* full *extended* in every Part (a very natural Effect of strong *Inspiration*)."[70] Similarly, the "*Orgasmus* of their Spiritual exercise" culminates in its physical correlative.[71] For Swift, as for More, the critique of religious enthusiasm rests on exposing the libidinal origins of sacred eroticism, for "however Spiritual Intrigues begin, they generally conclude like all others; they may branch upward towards Heaven, but the Root is in the Earth."[72]

This mapping of the erotic body pathologized religious longing, since the incongruity between erotic desire and spirituality results from locating the former in the genitals. The discursive transformation of sexuality that

Foucault describes, in which the analysis of perversions and "unnatural" practices replaces juridic prohibition, corresponds to and converges with the reinterpretation of erotic desire as neurotic sublimation. Sexual behaviors and erotic desires become diagnostic categories, symptoms of one's mental/moral health or sickness. This construct has become so familiar that it takes an effort to remember that it was virtually unavailable before 1660, but that unavailability constitutes the precondition for sacred eroticism.

According to the ocular model, there exists no necessary physiological or affective difference between sacred and secular desire. One is not "spiritual," the other "bodily," but each engenders the same sense of lack, the same longing, constriction of the heart, excited apprehension of beauty, alternations of joy and desolation, desire for presence, and lachrymose pain. Hence, the language of romantic passion can articulate religious desires because the bodily/emotional experiences of such desires are *like* those felt by, as it were, women in love. Furthermore, and this is Perella's point, this likeness at least in part results from the fact that the medieval representation of romantic passion was patterned after the discourse of spiritual longing in much the same way that the romantic "Platonism" of the Renaissance evolved from Plato's analysis of eros as a metaphysical appetite for the permanent possession of the Good. It follows from this, it would seem, that identifying the eroticism of the Mary Magdalene narratives with some sort of displaced sexuality is as fallacious (from a historical point of view) as its allegorical erasure—and, furthermore, both strategies derive from the modern definition of the body as the sexual body.

However, the premodern distinction between eroticism and sex cannot fully account for the peculiar fusion of Ovidian and Canticles material characteristic of the Mary Magdalene narratives. In particular, it does not explain either the significance of *abandoned* women for sacred eroticism or what cultural work may have been carried out by these texts, for although they are not, strictly speaking, allegorical, they are (like most cultural artifacts) symbolic.

The Subject of the Passion

In *Abandoned Women and the Poetic Tradition*, Lawrence Lipking distinguishes two senses of abandonment; to be abandoned is to be forsaken by one's lover, but it is also to violate norms, conventions, respectability.[73] Curiously (since the texts under consideration are "orthodox" religious works), both senses of abandonment characterize the Chaucerian and Origenist Mary Magdalene. That is, although her grief is passive, a sort of paralyzed weeping that finds no vent in action—and is therefore typically feminine—it also has a subversive edge, especially but not exclusively in Southwell's version. In all the variants, the intensity of Mary's love and grief pushes her toward disregard of hierarchy and authority, especially in the scene where the angels address her and she refuses to answer them. In the pseudo-Origen, the narrator tells her to "heare my advice. Let the comfortinge of angels content and satisfye the," to which she replies, "Do they therefore question with mee, to let me from wepinge? I beseche them, not to swade me to that. . . . What needes mo wordes? I will not obey them."[74] The narrator is shocked by her defiance, by the fact that she is not honored or pleased by the angels' attention. Yet this paternalist preacher who tries to normalize her response fades and shrinks beside her passion.

The exchanges between the conservative male narrator and the transgressive female disciple are particularly vivid in Southwell, who, as a Jesuit in Elizabethan England, may have had more sympathy with transgression than most, but Southwell only expands on a disobedience already evident in his medieval source. Thus, Southwell's narrator tries to dissuade Mary from attempting to find the body by accusing her of stepping outside the norms of morality and decency; if she tries to reclaim Christ's remains, she will become a thief. She responds with indignation that she would be happy to be a thief or anything else for her lover's sake, and furthermore that her love justifies her transgression of moral rules:

> And if no other means would serve to recover him but force, I see no reason why it might not very well become me. . . . O Judith lend me thy prowesse for I am bound to regard it.
> But suppose that my force were unable to winne him by an open enterprise, what scruple should keepe me from seeking him by secret means: yea and by plain stealth[?] It wilbe thought a sinne, and condemned for a theft. O sweete sinne why was not I the first that did commit thee? . . . If this be so great a sinne, and so heinous a theft, let others make choice of what titles they will: but for my part, I would refuse to be an Angel, I would not wishe to be a Saint . . . if I might both live and die such a sinner, and be condemned for such a theft.[75]

She accepts abandonment—her own lawlessness and freedom. And her passion silences the narrator. The "male" voice of reason, hierarchy, decorum, and law is mocked and silenced by Mary Magdalene's anguish.

Besides Lipking's two senses of abandonment, there is also a third sense or connotation: the association of abandonment with Christ's lonely suffering on the cross. And to the extent that the Magdalene texts allow this meaning to emerge, they implicitly liken the abandoned woman to the dying savior, erotic passion to Christ's Passion. And this is in fact what happens. Both the Origenist and Chaucerian variants identify the sufferings of Mary and Jesus by the same typological maneuver, although the Chaucerian version develops the equation more fully. The connection is always made by putting in Mary's mouth biblical phrases traditionally associated with the Crucifixion. In all the versions, Mary thus claims that "there is no dolor as is my dolor," or in the Latin, "*nec est dolor sicut dolor meus*"[76]—a quotation of the christological passage in Lamentations 1:12. More strikingly, she turns back on Christ his own last words on the cross, crying out to him (in the pseudo-Origen), "Where is my sweete Lorde? why hast thou my health forsaken me?"[77] The allusion claims a parity of suffering. It seems to suggest that the sorrows of abandoned women are not of less weight than the adventures of the men who leave them.

The same allusion climaxes the Chaucerian *Lamentatyon*. The poem ends *before* Mary identifies the gardener; it concludes rather with a long, elegiac, and pathetic farewell song addressed to her absent lover, the final lines of which read:

> My soule for anguysshe is nowe ful thursty,
> I faynt right sore for hevynesse,
> My lorde, my spouse, Cur me dereliquisti,
> Sith I for the suffre al this distresse?
> What causeth the to seme this mercylesse?
> Sith it the pleseth of me to make an ende,
> (In manus tuas) my spirite I commende.[78]

Whereas in the pseudo-Origen the echo of Christ's desolate prayer occurs fairly early in the text, these are the last lines of the *Lamentatyon*. The identification they set up between Mary and Christ involves rather more than a postfigural comparison. By appropriating these words and gestures—this time a woman addressing her lover rather than the Son pleading with his Father—Mary makes her own desolation equal to Christ's, at the same time casting Christ in the role of the now distant and indifferent lover and herself as the voice of exiled and suffering humanity. Human pain not only parallels Christ's passion but seems to supplant it. In the *Lamentatyon*, it is Mary who (like Jephthah's daughter) offers a "devout sacrifyce."[79]

Even in the versions where Christ does come, and all Mary's pain is soothed, the suspicion always remains that the man is being thoughtless or insensitive by staying away for so long; it is the woman left behind who bears the helpless pain of longing and forsakenness. Both she and the

Origenist narrator thus come very close to blaming Christ for Mary's suffering. He, that is, assumes the lineaments of the faithless male—the necessary narrative counterpart to the abandoned woman—even though this is narratively incoherent since he is presumably dead and therefore not responsible for the disappearance of his body. But disregarding this technicality, pseudo-Chaucer's Mary cries: "Why suffrest thou me than to stande alone? / Thou hast, I trowe, my wepynge in disdayne"; so in Southwell, the narrator reproaches Christ: "Why art thou so hard a Judge to so soft a creature, requiting her love with thy losse?"; likewise in pseudo-Origen: "O moste gentle Master, what hath this disciple since offended the? and wherein hath this thy dere lover displeased the kyndenes of thy heart, in that thou goest so from her? . . . If truly thou lovedst her after thy wonted manner, what meanest thou to prolonge her desire?"[80] Both the narrator and Mary try to understand what she might have done wrong, how she might be responsible for her own abandonment, yet both tend to shift the blame from Mary to Christ: he seems indifferent to her pain for no reason.

In other words, the theological "solution" of the Augustinian-Calvinist tradition, which justifies God by blaming humankind, is here called into question.[81] This time, it is not the lady who is culpable but—at least hypothetically—her lord. The texts will not allow the metamorphosis of human pain into guilt and punishment. The narrator tries to blame Mary for her dereliction but fails; she likewise attempts to locate her pain in some fault of her own but finally denies her guilt. "I have," she insists, "endured without variaunce, / Right as thou knowest, thy lover just and trew."[82] She becomes, instead, simply an abandoned woman, or as the Origenist narrator tells her, "he whom thou sekest semeth to set nought by thy sorowinge, he semeth not to regarde thy teares. Thou calleste him, and he heareth not."[83] The same abyss opens up in Southwell:

> Thou hast hitherto sought in vaine, as one either unseene, or unknown, or at the least unregarded, sith the party thou seekest, neither tendereth thy teares, nor aunswereth thy cries, nor relenteth with thy lamentings. Either he doth not heare, or he will not helpe, he hath peradventure left to love thee, and is loath to yeelde thee reliefe.[84]

In the conclusion of the Origenist narratives the story deviates from Ovid: Christ comes and with him abundant recompense. In the Chaucerian versions, however, he does not come. Mary, not Christ, remains the one who has been forsaken—and so the narrative focus and authorial sympathy shift from the Lord to the lady. This is sentimental and subversive realism.

The term *subversive* implies some notion of the authorship, audience, and function of a text, and here we have to be careful. Since the primary texts are anonymous, one cannot absolutely rule out female authorship. Yet, since they are all addressed to men, female authorship seems unlikely, despite Walter Skeat's sneering description of the *Lamentatyon* as a "lugubrious piece [that] was probably the wail of a nun, who had no book but a Vulgate version of the Bible."[85] The pseudo-Origen concludes by remarking, "Let us therefore (bretherne) follow the good affection of thys woman, that we may come to the like effecte"; similarly Southwell: "Learne O sinfull man of this once a sinfull woman."[86] These stories about forsaken women are intended for male use. They exemplify the "deeply ingrained tendency of all men in the ancient [and Renaissance] world, to use women 'to think with.'"[87]

It is important to note, however, that the explicit "function" of Mary Magdalene in these texts is rather different from that of most female symbols, who are almost always objects, even if infinitely valuable objects—whether abstractions (Dame Nature, Lady Philosophy) or ideals (Beatrice, Stella, Laura). Mary Magdalene is an exemplary figure but in a curious way: she is not the goal of the quest but is lost in the forest along with everyone else. That is, she supplies a model of suffering, solitary, forsaken humanity. She is neither Madonna nor Whore but a figure for all that is marginalized, powerless, solitary, unhappy; as she says in Southwell, "Poore I [am] left alone to supplie the teares of all creatures."[88] This should not be surprising since most societies symbolize forsakenness and loss of love as female; to be abandoned means to be female, and therefore when a man wishes to write about his own abandonment, he writes as a woman or about a woman.[89] As Flaubert once confessed, "*Madame Bovary, c'est moi.*"

But what sort of abandonment? The Mary Magdalene texts are popular devotional works articulating the fundamental spiritual anxiety of the late medieval and early modern eras—anxieties centering on desolation and the absence of God.[90] Furthermore, although the Origenist version was probably written for a monastic community, after the Reformation it seems specifically connected to Catholic and Anglo-Catholic piety: Cornelius à Lapide, Southwell, Lancelot Andrewes. Protestant writers like Calvin, Lewis Wager, Thomas Robinson, and Henry Smith (the latter three of whom wrote, respectively, a play, poem, and sermon on the Magdalene) reject or ignore this material. This confessional difference points to the specific theological interest of the Magdalene texts considered here.

Mary does not believe in the Resurrection; she thinks Christ is dead. Nevertheless, because she loves him, she is made first witness to the risen

Christ and apostle to the apostles. She is justified despite her lack of faith.
That is, these texts critique the Protestant doctrine of justification by faith
and the concomitant fear that disbelief implies reprobation. They are pastoral works, designed to relieve such fears by affirming that love, even
without faith, is sufficient. This undercurrent is, not surprisingly, most explicit in the later versions. Andrewes's sermon thus begins, "She loved
much: we cannot say, Shee beleeved much. For . . . it seemes, shee beleeved
no more, than just as much as the High Priests would have had the world
beleeve, that *He was taken away by night.*" But he concludes by quoting
Saint Bernard: "*Domine, amor quem habebat in Te, et dolor quem habebat
de Te, excuset eam apud Te, si forte erravit circa Te*: That the love she bare
to Him, the sorrow shee had for Him, may excuse her with Him, if she
were in any error concerning Him."[91] Southwell makes this motif explicit
in his dedicatory epistle, commenting, "And if her weakenes of faith, (an
infirmity then common to all Christes disciples) did suffer her understanding to be deceived, yet was her will so setled in a most sincere and
perfect love, that it ledde all her passions with the same bias, recompensing
the want of beliefe, with the strange effectes of an excellent charity." Although Southwell's narrative persona repeatedly attempts to show Mary
that her desolation is her own fault, in the end even he admits to her that
"the Angels must still bathe themselves in the pure streams of thy eies."[92]

The claim made by these texts that love suffices even without faith is
inseparable from their epistemology. The Magdalene narratives presuppose an *erotics* of knowledge. The conjunction of this erotic epistemology
with the Mary Magdalene story is already visible in Gregory the Great's
sermon on John 20, the standard liturgical reading for the Feast of the
Magdalene in the Roman missal.

> But as she was weeping, Mary bent down and looked into the tomb.
> Certainly she had already seen that the tomb was empty since she an-
> nounced that the Lord had been taken away. Why then does she again
> bend down, again desire to see? But for a lover it is not enough to have
> looked once, for the power of love increases one's attempt to make in-
> quiry. Thus she first sought and found nothing; she persevered in her
> search and accordingly she found, for desires that have been deferred
> dilate and grow (*desideria dilata crescerent*) and, having expanded, can
> grasp what they have found.[93]

Inquiry advances by the *dilatio* of desire—simultaneously a deferment
and dilation, or rather a dilation effected by deferral. Eros, that is, governs
both spiritual and cognitive symbolization, subsuming faith (and the other
intellectual virtues) into the structures of desire.

This epistemology is not restricted to the Magdalene narratives; rather, it is quite ancient and traditional. It suffuses medieval commentaries on Canticles, of course, but also the secularized epistemology of early modern theorizing. Thus, in *De anima et vita* (1538), the Spanish humanist Juan Luis Vives offers this general account of the deep structure of knowledge:

> A thing must first be known in order to be loved; but it need only be known to the extent that it can elicit love. . . . Wherefore the fruit of love is enjoyment (*fruitio*), which is the act of pleasure (*delectationis actus*)—not only of the will but also of the intellect, as in God. Therefore love is the middle point between inchoate knowledge and the full knowledge of union in which desire always vanishes but love does not; it, rather, burns more fiercely.[94]

As Southwell's narrator explains to Mary, "the nature of love coveteth not onely to be united, but if it were possible wholly transfourmed out of it selfe into the thing it loveth."[95] The movement from desire to enjoyment, from deferred longing to loving union, configures knowledge as an erotic praxis—a subject/object passion, as it were. Hence, the deferred and dilating desires of abandoned women correspond not "merely" to the affective experience of the devout soul but also to the intellective movements of the inquiring mind. The Reformation debates over the respective operations of faith and love forced an absolute separation between epistemic and emotional structures previously only loosely and partially differentiated.

Foucault's remarks on pre-Cartesian epistemology have a bearing here. As he notes, even Greek philosophy

> always held that a subject could not have access to the truth if he did not first operate upon himself a certain work which would make him susceptible to knowing the truth—a work of purification, conversion of the soul by contemplation of the soul itself. . . . In Western culture up to the sixteenth century, asceticism and access to truth are always more or less obscurely linked.[96]

These "ascetic" practices, however, include not only the *removal* of desire by means of interior discipline and regulation but (except in Stoicism) also the enlargement of desires, enabling them, in Gregory's words, "to grasp that which they have found" ([*ut*] *caperent quod invenissent*). As in Colet, the martyr and the lover—asceticism and eroticism—mutually imply one another.

If Mary's passion figures the access to truth through love's dilating deferrals rather than (as in Calvin) through faith in the text, it also adumbrates a second Reformation controversy. The Magdalene narratives concern the *body* of Christ, that is, the real presence. Their emphasis on Christ's body is eucharistic as well as erotic—or, rather, both at once. The Origenist versions thus imply that Christ's self-revelation to Mary repeats itself in each sacramental encounter between the transsubstantiated flesh and a hungry soul; the texts promise the desolate communicant that a love which goes beyond faith shall be filled by the tangible gift of Christ's body and blood. This is particularly clear in Southwell, whose narrator thus addresses Christ:

> Doe not sweet Lord any longer delay her. Behold shee hath attended thee these three daies, and shee hath not what to eate, nor wherewith to foster her famished soule, unlesse thou by discovering thy selfe doest minister unto her the bread of thy body, & feede her with the foode, that hath in it all taste of sweetnesse.[97]

The analogy, one notes, works both ways: the longing for the real presence of Christ discovers itself as erotic desire, and simultaneously this desire for corporeal touch tropes sacramental theology. Thus, the corresponding passage in the pseudo-Origen reads, "Wherefore, if thou wilte that she faynte not by the way, refresshe and comforte the bowels (*viscera*) of her soule with the plesauntes of thy taste (*dulcedo saporis tui*)."[98] "Bowels" (or *viscera*) can mean the internal organs in general, but also, more specifically, the generative organs—the womb and testicles.[99] As in Herbert's "Love [III]," eroticism and eating constitute overlapping pleasures.[100]

Eros—the desire to touch and taste real bodies—became the master discourse of medieval culture, structuring such apparently nonerotic activities as thinking and eating and worshiping. In antiquity, such activities constituted the materials of what Foucault calls an aesthetic *pratique de soi*;[101] in the Middle Ages and at least the Catholic Renaissance, they were modes of desire reaching toward union. Premodern subjectivity in the Christian West is erotic: "*Pondus meum, amor meus*; my weight is my love," as Saint Augustine writes toward the end of his *Confessions*.[102] Following the efflorescence of Canticles mysticism in the twelfth century, this erotic subjectivity articulates itself in the language of female desire: the voice of the bride and Mary Magdalene—and of Ovid's forsaken heroines. But this conflation of the heroic epistle with the traditional bridal allegory crucially modifies the representational energies of erotic symbolization. As in *Jephthah*, the Classical intertext reshapes the biblical myths that appropriate it.

In Colet and the ancient martyrologies, sacrificial eros annihilates the self, radically subordinating the soul's "*rapport à soi*"—the relationship one has with oneself—to its relationship with the numinous object of desire.[103] Eros, that is, becomes *caritas*, a love wholly oriented toward the other; the martyr's ardent affection is like a light streaming out, away from himself, to illumine the divine beloved. The Ovidian intertext turns these beams on their source by opening up the possibility of inconsolable loss and the infinite deferral of union. In the Magdalene narratives, erotic spirituality thus folds back on itself and becomes a discourse of the soul's *own* desires and interiority. As I have elsewhere suggested, the personal soul is the creation of frustrated eros, subjectivity becoming conscious of itself as longing for the absent other.[104] The reflexive recoil of desire appears most clearly in the Chaucerian *Lamentatyon*, the most pervasively Ovidian of the Magdalene narratives, where Mary displaces Christ as the sacrificial victim. Theological romance here opens onto psychological tragedy, the abandoned soul crying out in solitude, "Why hast thou forsaken me?"

But even in the *Lamentatyon*, subjectivity remains unified by its own desire; the intensity and fixity of Mary's love, like that of Colet's martyrs, leaves no energy for any centrifugal complication of inner life. What the Calvinist passion narratives discussed in chapter 3 suggest is that in Renaissance Protestantism violence replaces desire as the fundamental operation of the soul's *pratique de soi*, and hence the decentering conflicts of the chimerical self replace the unified erotic subjectivity of medieval Christianity.[105] This conflictual selfhood, as Erasmus's *Disputatiuncula* indicates, depends less on the Pauline division between flesh and spirit than on the division between *nature* and spirit. But this latter opposition abrogates the metaphysical basis of erotic spirituality, which presupposes a continuity between natural and transcendent desire, between the bodily experiences of tasting or touching and the soul's experience of God. The humanist/Protestant division between nature and spirit thus tends to separate erotic (which then moves toward the sexual) from religious discourse and likewise to supplant image and sacrament with the less material mediations of the inspired text.

Hence, the polarization of nature and spirit approaches the Cartesian division between body and mind. In both, one's natural faculties—whether instinctual, affective, or cognitive—no longer possess an intrinsic relation to ethical/spiritual existence. Thus, for Descartes, as Foucault notes, "I can be immoral and know the truth."[106] One cannot quite apply the same formula to Calvinism; that is, the division between nature and spirit does not imply that I can be profligate and still love God. The spirit not only disentangles itself from bodily nature but also disciplines and torments it—the self-crucifixions of the introjected passion. In fact, Calvinist anthropology, which derives from Erasmus's tripartite division of the psyche into sinful flesh, self-protective maternal nature, and the spiritual law of the Father, seems less an early version of Cartesian dualism than a precursor of the Freudian allegory of id, ego, and superego. In the Calvinist passion narratives, the divided and discontented urban male who struggles to repress "nature" out of obedience to the interior sacrificial command is an early victim of the civilizing process.

But in English Protestantism, the protomodern chimerical self does not simply replace medieval erotic subjectivity; the popularity of the Magdalene narratives in England through the first quarter of the seventeenth century points to cultural continuity rather than disjunction. Nor does this residual narrative serve primarily as a discursive instrument for containing/mystifying doubt, transgressive excess, and female desire within a society that prohibits all three. Its function is not merely negative, for the symbols of erotic spirituality are themselves implicated in the early modern structuring of subjectivity—that is, in the discursive formation of inwardness as erotic, abandoned, and female: the inwardness of Donne's *Holy Sonnets* as well as *Clarissa*. To the extent that Renaissance Christianity installs transgressive and excessive desires in the center of religious subjectivity, the practices of piety are central—as central, let us say, as courtesy manuals or penal disciplines—to the economy and organization of Renaissance selfhood.

We can catch a glimpse of this by looking at two Renaissance title pages. The first comes from the Great Bible of 1541 and seems ideologically unambiguous: Henry VIII dominates the scene, distributing Bibles to his prelates, who then hand them to the parochial clergy, who in turn read them to a populace enthusiastically exclaiming, "God save the King" (fig. 4). The divine word circulates out from the royal head through the hierarchical body-ecclesiastic and returns to the throne as the language of political obedience.

One may usefully compare this piece of visual propaganda with the frontispiece from the 1612 edition of Hooker's *Of the Lawes of Ecclesiastical Politie* (fig. 5). In the top third of the picture, the beams issuing from the divine light fall separately on the king, the church, and a third figure who seems to emblematize the individual soul or inner faith.[107] If this reading is correct, then the picture offers an extraordinarily accurate visualization of Hooker's treatise. *The Laws* rests on a twofold distinction: on the one hand, the separation of the church as a "society supernatural" or "body mystical" from the ecclesiastical and secular institutions of "politic society";[108] on the other hand, the separation of the church as a "power external and visible" needed to carry out various administrative and disciplinary functions from the "spiritual power of Christ's own regiment" that acts "secretly, inwardly, and invisibly" on the soul of each individual Christian.[109] In the frontispiece, the king thus represents Hooker's "politic society"; the cathedral, the visible church; and the woman, the secret, inward, and invisible spaces of the soul. It thus symbolizes Hooker's disincorporation of the subject from the mediating hierarchies of both state and church.

But who is the subject? She holds a book, presumably a Bible—in fact, the light falls on the Bible, indicating a link between private reading and private selfhood; a skull lies under one knee and something that looks like a whip or bridle hangs over her left arm. But the skull, book, and whip are the conventional iconographic attributes of Mary Magdalene.[110] The exemplary figure of the Middle Ages's highly materialist erotic mysticism is thus also the decorous symbol for the Protestant (although not Calvinist) *individual* subject, the *suppositum* existing apart from the mystical conjunctions of both church and state, with room (and book) of her own.

The sacred eroticism of Mary Magdalene suggests that female sexuality, like female transgression, although proscribed as cultural praxis, inhabits a traditional construct of religious subjectivity, one that passes from the cloistral devotions of the Middle Ages into early modern representations of a privatized, autonomous inwardness. Lisa Jardine is therefore mistaken in her claim that "female sexuality (personified in Mary Magdalene, the anti-type of Mary, mother of Christ) negates all those attributes which bring women closer to the ideal model."[111] Rather, the premodern appropriations of the Magdalene hint at an inverse relation between the interior gendering of the subject and the gendering of social codes, rules specifying sex-typed behaviors being more rigid as subjectivity remains sexually ambiguous/androgynous. Female "sexuality" pervades an ancient ideal model—not, of course, a model of female behavior, but of male (and female) inwardness. "That women might not be objects but subjects, not the other but the self"—what Stephen Orgel has called the age's "greatest anxiety"—seems nevertheless implicit in a strain of late medieval piety that remained in circulation through the middle of the seventeenth century, for the specter of female desire is also the structure of religious (and male) subjectivity. Even up to the middle of the eighteenth century—and I am thinking of Bach's cantatas now—the voice of the soul is always soprano.

Conclusion

Madness, in which the values of another age, another art, another
morality are called into question. . . .

        Michel Foucault, *Madness and Civilization*

The preceding chapters follow a more or less reverse chronological order
from late Renaissance exegesis to the early thirteenth-century Magdalene
homily. This unusual, and quite accidental, *dispositio* makes it tempting to
conclude by simply rearranging the material sequentially as a historical
progression according to which spiritual eroticism gave way to the psychological violence of the Calvinist end myth and was then superseded by
a philological antiquarianism slouching toward the gray dawn of Higher
Criticism. But although this arrangement does correspond to pivotal
changes in the substance and mode of Renaissance biblical interpretation,
its simple linearity seems more convenient than historically defensible.
The chapters deal with incommensurate materials that do not share the
same discursive genealogy and hence should not be lined up as stages
along a single trajectory. As the previous chapter demonstrates, various
biblical discourses have their own histories; the pseudo-Origen evolves not
into Grotius but into Southwell.

Nor can the foregoing discussion ground generalizations about the nature of the Renaissance Bible. Too much has been omitted: prophecy,
psalm, apocalypse, epistle, to name only the most important biblical genres.
Yet even if these had been included, the *wunderkammerlich* diversity of
the relevant texts would still resist systematic articulation. In any case, I
have not attempted an encyclopedic rehearsal of biblical discourses but
rather a fragmentary investigation of the ways this heterogeneous material bears on the interpretation of Renaissance culture.

So what conclusions, however tentative, can be drawn? It may be helpful at this point to return to an issue previously dismissed—namely, exegesis as evidence of encroaching secularization. If by "secularization" one
means that European society slowly dechristianized between the sixteenth

and twentieth centuries—a sort of skimming the supernatural cream off the milkpail—then the claim is too obvious to warrant repetition. But secularization is not simply a quantitative change peculiar to religion—not simply, that is, a decline of religious belief—because religion does not float like a single, separable "layer" atop the surface of Renaissance culture but informs it, shapes its conceptual categories, social behavior, and moral codes. The erosion of biblical faith affects the basic organization of the Western episteme.

Affects it in what way? An unanticipated pattern connecting several of the previous chapters suggests a continuity between Renaissance biblical discourses and modern formulations. Thus, Grotius's analysis of the Atonement seems prophetic of nineteenth-century anthropology; the chimerical self resembles the painfully divided subject of Freud's *Civilization and Its Discontents*; the Magdalene narratives' account of spiritual eroticism might serve as a case study in sexual repression. But in each instance, the juxtaposition of Renaissance and modern versions discloses a consistent and crucial difference. What the earlier texts present as having ideal value is subsequently reclassified as primitive or pathological. Thus, for Calvin, self-tormenting violence characterizes the inner life of the elect; for Freud, it typifies neurosis. Likewise, the Magdalene texts understand eroticism as supernatural *caritas*, not libidinal frustration, and Grotius analyzes the sacrificial economy as the deep structure of the sacred rather than as evidence of the barbarous and primitive essence of Christian myth. Secularization, it would seem, involves the massive redefinition of ideal selfhood as psychosocial disorder. It is a redefinition explicit in Gibbon's biting descriptions of early Christian monasticism and, later, in Freud's account of religion as collective neurosis.

Modernity did not invariably reclassify traditional religious values as aberrations; post-Renaissance ethics retains, for instance, the previously Christian virtues of almsgiving and sexual fidelity. Nor, in fact, did secularization eradicate private religious belief. The condemnations fall instead on sacrifice—on the self-crucifixions of the Calvinist saint and the sacrificial eros of martyrdom as well as on the mystical mechanics of substitution within the *conjunctio*.[1] Secularization rewrites sacrifice as pathology.

The texts discussed in the preceding chapters suggest that, over the past three centuries, sacrifice—or, more specifically, the representation of ideal subjectivity by means of sacrificial symbols—became unacceptable for two interconnected reasons. First, in all its manifestations, sacrifice violates the contours demarcating the autonomous individual. The erotic longing for total union with the beloved, the collapse of the individual into the *conjunctio,* the violent inner divisions of the chimerical self either erode the boundary separating self and other or disintegrate the self into warring factions. The individual dissolves into the group, the desired object, or the personae of the *automachia.* Hence, to the extent that post-Renaissance ideologies privilege rational individualism, sacrificial inwardness is reinterpreted as psychological disorder. Second, sacrifice also involves excess: a frightening inner violence, consuming passion, and defiance of social norms—whether by stealing corpses, displacing fathers, or defying authorities. But these excessive and transgressive energies are precisely the impulses threatening individuation and hence subsequently classed as symptoms of neurosis. "The long road of the Passion," as Foucault remarks, "was also the road of the passions . . . and of madness."[2] To modern eyes, the Calvinist narratives of the Crucifixion display a pervasive sadomasochism; Mary Magdalene suffers from "erotomania"; the chimerical self is convulsed by unresolved oedipal conflicts; sacrificial substitution typifies the primitive, scapegoat mechanism. But in the Renaissance these constituted the *imitatio Christi,* supernatural *caritas,* Christian warfare, and the logic of the Atonement.

At times, the secularizing process makes itself felt as the *difference* between habits of thought implied in an earlier text and our own presuppositions. We are likely to consider the Calvinist passion narratives perverse, likely to be perplexed by Grotius's seeming blindness to the radical implications of his ethnographic comparisons. The works seem to stand on the far side of a cultural abyss, innocent alike of psychology and anthropology. Yet the landscape on the other side of this narrowing gulf has already become visible; Renaissance biblical discourses themselves register the confrontation between the traditional Christian categories for construing existence and an emergent ideology based on individualism, rationalism, and affective control. The debates in *Jephthah,* Socinus's objections summarized by Grotius, and the anxious disapproval of Southwell's narrator articulate counterdiscourses from whose perspectives sacrifice—its violence, transgressive eros, and disregard for individual and domestic boundaries—seems appalling.

The condemnation of sacrifice, moreover, affects not merely "religion" but the whole cultural field: restricting eros to sexuality; stipulating a necessary connection between punishment and personal guilt; replacing the binding sanctities of the vow, the *conjunctio,* and the inner law of the Father with the inalienable rights of the individual as fundamental postulates of both jurisprudence and ethics. The same secularizing process also alters the status of literature. On the one hand, the discourses of excess, transgressive desire, and psychic conflict move from religion to literature.

On the other, as Foucault has remarked, the object of literary representation shifts from ideal types to the soul's guilty sickness and secret passions.[3] That is, literary discourse incorporates the ideal selfhood of Christian devotion but at the same time tends to pathologize this selfhood—to secularize it. The guilt, conflict, depression, violence, infantile longings, and acute self-abasement, which in Donne, Herbert, and Bunyan characterize the inner lives of the saints, in Baudelaire, Berryman, and Plath seem rather evidence of deep psychological disturbances. Confessional lyric and autobiography no longer present the *iter mentis ad Deum* but the unhappy consciousness of the tormented artist.[4]

Secularization thus translates the discourses of the sacrificial subject into what Norbert Elias calls "a psychological view of man."[5] It is an aspect of the civilizing process in which the increasing regulation of bodily fluids in matters of social conduct described by Elias parallels an increasing regulation of sacrificial excess with respect to subjectivity. Operating along the fleshly borders dividing self from others, a "compulsion to self-control" establishes a protective shell of manners; within the subject, the same compulsion intensifies the inner fear "of one sector of the personality for another"—the fear of one's own unmannerly drives and desires.[6] Both the prophylactic disciplines exercised over the body and the repression of exorbitant psychospiritual drives attempt to demarcate the "I" from the "not-I." They police the fluid margins, whose excrescences and excesses threaten to compromise the integral solidity of the individual.

This close connection between manners and subjectivity entailed that civilizing (and secularizing) constraints fell first and most drastically on practices exhibiting *both* bodily and spiritual excess. From its inception, the Reformation thus rejects the heroic asceticism of medieval and Tridentine piety; in Protestant cultures, flagellation, stigmatic miracles, maceration of the flesh, sucking of ulcerated wounds, and all the old incarnate manifestations of spiritual extravagance evoke primarily a mixture of contempt and disgust. More subtly and slowly, the same constraints file away the exorbitances of both social behavior and inner life. Hence, if secularization liberated the individual from a coercive religious culture, it substituted a new repressive economy.[7] Like urinating in a stairwell or sneezing into one's hand, inner violence, self-consuming passion, and all the transcendent excesses released in the sacrificial *katharsis* retreat beyond the margins dividing modern from archaic culture and, more important, dividing healthy from neurotic personality.

This retreat belongs to a general shift from spiritual to psychological categories of interpretation that took place between the late seventeenth and late nineteenth centuries. Before that period, analysis of inner life—the modern fascination with conscious and unconscious motives—remained circumscribed within ethical and devotional domains.[8] These two domains, in turn, give modern psychological classifications their curious double lineage to earlier notions of both moral depravity and spiritual excess. The metamorphosis of sin into disease converged with the more radical transvaluation of premodern ideal subjectivity into pathological states. It is this second shift that marks psychotherapy as the characteristic modern discipline: the privileged *techne* of secular self-fashioning, designed to produce individuals no longer haunted by memories of a divine lover or shattered by transcendent law, but persons at home in the world.

Appendix

CATALOGUS
CRITICORUM SACRORUM,
QUORUM
ANNOTATA & TRACTATUS
in hoc opere continentur.

In VETUS TESTAMENTUM.

Sebastiani Munsteri *Annotationes in Vetus Testamentum.*
Pauli Fagii *in Paraphrasin Chaldaicam Pentateuchi succinctæ Annotationes.*
   Ejusdem fusior Expositio quatuor priorum capitum Geneseos.
   Ejusdem Translationum præcipuarum Veteris Testamenti inter se variantium Collatio.
Francisci Vatabli *Annotata in libros Canonicos Veteris Testamenti.*
Claudii Badvelli *Annotationes in libros Apocryphos.*
Sebastiani Castalionis *Annotata in Vetus Testamentum.*
Isidori Clarii *Annotationes in Vetus Testamentum.*
Lucæ Brugensis *in Variantia SS. Bibliorum loca Notationes.*
* Andreæ Masii *Annotationes in Deuteron. Cap. XVIII. & sequentia.*
* - - - *in aliquot loca Jeremiæ.*
  - - - *in Josuam Annotationes & Commentaria* , quibus accesserunt * *Additamenta Nova ex MS.*
Joannis Drusii *Annotationes in Pentateuchum.*
  - - - *Josuam.*
  - - - *Librum Judicum.*
  - - - *Ruth.*
  - - - *Libros Samuelis.*
  - - - *Estheram.*
  - - - *Jobum.*
  - - - *Coheleth , seu Ecclesiasten.*
  - - - *XII Prophetas minores.*
  - - - *Ecclesiasticum.*
  - - - *Tobit.*
  - - - *Lib. I. Machabæorum.*
  - - - *Veterum Veteris Testamenti Interpretationum Græcorum Fragmenta.*
* - - - *Notæ Majores in Genesin, Exodum, Leviticum & priora XVIII. Cap. Numerorum.*
* - - - *Scholia in Versionem Hieronymi Psalmorum priorum LIV.*
* - - - *Commentatio in Psalmos XIX. priores.*
* - - - *Salomonis Sententiæ juxta ordinem Alphabeti per Locos Communes digestæ cum explicatione ejusdem.*
* - - - *Annotationes in Versionem Vulgatam Hoseæ, Joëlis, Amosi , Michæe , Habacuc & Sophoniæ.*
* - - - *Lectiones ad Michæam , Habacuc , Zephaniam & Zachariam.*

* Sixtini

CATALOGUS ANNOTATORUM.

* Sixtini Amamæ *Cenſura Vulgatæ atque à Tridentinis Canonizatæ Verſionis Quinque Librorum Moſis.*
* - - - *Ejuſdem Notæ in Libros Hiſtoricos*, *Pſalmos*, *Proverbia & Eccleſiaſten.*

Simeonis de Muis *Varia Sacra in Pentateuchum & quædam loca Judicum*, *ut & 1 Samuelis.*

Philippi Codurci *Annotationes in Jobum.*

Rodolfus Baynus *in Proverbia Salomonis.*

Franciſci Forerii *Commentarius in Jeſaiam.*

Edovardi Livelæi *Annotationes in Oſeam.*
- - - *Joelem.*
- - - *Amoſum.*
- - - *Abdiam.*
- - - *Jonam.*

Davidis Hœſchelii *Notæ in Eccleſiaſticum.*

Hugonis Grotii *Annotationes in Vetus Teſtamentum.*

* Chriſtophori Cartwrighti *Electa Thargumico - Rabbinica ſive Annotationes in Geneſin & Exodum.*

Joannis Priczæi *Annotata ad Pſalmorum Librum.*

TRACTATUS INSERTI.

Joannes Druſius *de Mandragoris.*

Hugo Grotius *in Decalogum.*

Joſephus Scaliger *de Decimis.*

Sixtinus Amama *de Decimis.*

Ludovicus Cappellus *de Voto Jephtæ*
- - - *Ejuſdem Excerpta ex Villalpando.*

Martini Helvici *Diatribe de LXX Hebdomadis Danielis.*

Alberici Gentilis *ad 1 Machæorum Diſputatio.*
- - - *De Linguarum mixtura Diſputatio Parergica.*

Joannis Druſii *Tractatus de Haſidæis.*

TRACTATUS SUFFIXI.

Joannis Druſii *Elohim cum Notis ex MS.*
- - - *Tetragrammaton cum Notis ex MS.*
- - - *De Patriarcha Henoch.*

* Moſis Bar Cephæ *Syri Commentarius de Paradiſo ex Interpretatione* Andreæ Maſii.

Chriſtophori Helvici *Deſiderium Matris Evæ.*
- - - *Protevangelion Paradiſiacum.*

Johannis Buteonis *Libellus de Arca Noë.*

Matthæi Hoſti *Inquiſitio in Fabricam Arcæ Noah.*

Martini Helvici *Sceptrum Judæ.*

Franciſci Moncæji *Libri duo de Vitulo Aureo.*

Petri Pithœi *Moſaicarum & Romanarum Legum Collatio.*

Georgii Rittershuſii *Tractatus de Jure Aſylorum.*

Matthæus Hoſtus *in Monomachiam Davidis & Goliathi.*

Michaëlis Rothardi *Samuel redivivus & Saul* αὐτόχυς.

Leonis Allati *de Engaſtrimytho Syntagma.*

Gaſparis Varrerii *de Ophyra regione Diſputatio.*

Wilhelmus Schickardus *de Feſto Purim.*

* * 3

Au-

CATALOGUS

Auguſtini Juſtiniani *Epiſcopi Nebienſis Gloſſemata in Octaplum Pſalterii.*

Joannis Druſii *Additamenta ad Initium Jeſaiæ.*

Ludovici Cappelli *Templi Hieroſolymitani Delineatio triplex una cum * Iconographia,* quæ huic editioni acceſſit.

Benedicti Ariæ Montani *Antiquitates Judaicæ accuratis figuris æneis illuſtratæ.*

Bonaventura Cornelius Bertramus *de Republica Hebræorum.*

Petrus Cunæus *de Republica Hebræorum.*

Gaſparus Waſerus *de Antiquis Numis Hebræorum , &c. cum figuris.*

- - - *de Antiquis Menſuris Hebræorum.*

Edouardi Brerewood *de Ponderibus & Pretiis Veterum Numorum.*

CATALOGUS
CRITICORUM SACRORUM,
QUORUM
ANNOTATA & TRACTATUS
in hoc opere continentur.

In NOVUM TESTAMENTUM.

Sebaſtiani Munſteri *Annotationes in D. Matthæi Euangelium Hebraicum.*

Laurentii Vallæ *De Collationibus Novi Teſtamenti Libri II.*

Jacobi Revii *Notæ in* Vallam.

Eraſmi Roterodami *Annotationes in Novum Teſtamentum.*

Franciſci Vatabli *Annotationes in Novum Teſtamentum.*

Sebaſtiani Caſtalionis *Annotationes in Novum Teſtamentum.*

Iſidori Clarii *Annotationes in Novum Teſtamentum.*

Nicolai Zegeri *Annotationes in Novum Teſtamentum.*

* Andreæ Maſii *ad quædam Loca Euangeliſtarum Notæ.*

Lucæ Brugenſis *Notationes ad Novum Teſtamentum.*

Henrici Stephani Κεφάλαια *D. Matthæi & D. Marci.*

Ejuſdem Interpretatio Latina obſcuriorum vocum & Phraſium Novi Teſtamenti.

Joannis Druſii *Præteritorum lib. X.*

- - - *Ad voces Ebræas Novi Teſtamenti Commentarius Prior & Poſterior.*

- - - *Annotata in Novum Teſtamentum. Pars altera.*

Omnia in unum Corpus collecta, & ad Capita ac Verſus inſtar perpetui Commentarii redacta.

Joſephus Scaligeri *Notæ in Novum Teſtamentum.*

Iſaaci

ANNOTATORUM.

Ifaaci Cafauboni *Notæ in Novum Teſtamentum.*
Joannis Cameronis *Myrothecium.*
Jacobi Cappelli *Annotationes in Novum Teſtamentum.*
Ludovici Cappelli *Spicilegium.*
Othonis Gualtperii *Sylloge vocum exoticarum Novi Teſtamenti.*
Abrahami Sculteti *Annotata in Epiſtolas ad Timotheum.*
- - - *Titum.*
- - - *Philemonem.*
Hugonis Grotii *Annotationes in Novum Teſtamentum.*
Joannis Pricæi *Annotata ad Euangelium D. Matthæi.*
- - - *D. Lucæ.*
- - - *D. Johannis cap. X. & XI.*
- - - *Acta Apoſtolorum.*
- - - *Epiſtolas D. Pauli ad I Corinth. cap. XII.*
- - - *Timotheum.*
- - - *Titum.*
- - - *Philemonem.*
- - - *D. Jacobi.*
- - - *D. Johannis.*
- - - *D. Judæ.*
- - - *Apocalypſin.*

TRACTATUS INSERTI.

Ludovici Cappelli *Corban.*
Nicolaus Faber *de Myrrhata potione & peccato in Fratrem.*
Guilielmus Klebitius *de Buccella intincta, quam comedit Judas.*
Marquardus Freherus *de Numiſmate Cenſus.*
Jacobus Uſserius *de Cainane Arphaxadi Filio.*
Matthæus Hoſtus *de Sex Hydriarum capacitate.*
Johannis Antonii van der Linden *Exercitatio* Vini pleni.
Ludovici Cappelli *Hiſtoria Apoſtolica.*
Prologus in XIV. Epiſtolas Pauli.
* Claudii Salmaſii *ſub ficto nomine* Joannis Simplicii, *Notæ in* H. *Grotii Commentationem ad* 2 *Theſſal.* II.
Jacobi Gothofredi *Sacræ Exercitationes de Eccleſia & Incarnatione Chriſti* 1 *Timoth.* III. 14, 15, 16.
Philippus Codurcus *de Teſtamento ad Hebr. IX.*

TRACTATUS SUFFIXI.

Abrahami Sculteti *Exercitationes Euangelicæ.*
Guilielmus Ader *De Ægrotis & Morbis in Euangelio.*
Joannis Druſii *Parallela Sacra.*
Jacobi Lopidis Stunicæ *Annotationes contra Eraſmum Roterodamum, in Defenſionem Tralationis Novi Teſtamenti.*
Eraſmi Roterodami *Apologia,* ad *Jacobum Lopidem Stunicam.*
Angeli Caninii *Diſquiſitiones in Loca aliquot Novi Teſtamenti obſcuriora.*
Petrus Pithœus *de Latinis Bib. Interpretibus.*
Nicephori Patriarchæ *CP. Canon Scripturarum.*

Adriani

CATALOGUS ANNOTATORUM.

Adriani *Isagoge SS. Literarum & Antiquissimorum Græcorum in Prophetas Fragmenta cum Notis Davidis Hœschelii.*

Bon. Cornelii Bertrami *Lucubrationes Franktallenses , sive Specimen expositionum in difficillima Utriusque Testamenti Loca.*

Antonii Nebrissensis *Quinquagena , sive Quinquaginta S. Scripturæ locorum Explanatio.*

Joannis Drusii *Animadversorum Lib. II.*

- - - *Observationum Sacrarum Lib. XVI.*

- - - *Quæstionum Ebraicarum Lib. III.*

- - - *Proverbiorum Classes II.*

- - - *Scholia in Proverbia Ben-Syræ.*

- - - *Adagia Hebraica.*

- - - *Miscellanea Locutionum Sacrarum.*

- - - *De Quæsitis per Epistolam.*

Nicolai Fulleri *Miscellaneorum Sacrorum Lib. VI.*

Samuelis Petiti *Variæ Lectiones in S. Scripturam.*

Johannis Gregorii *Notæ & Observationes in aliquot SS. Scripturæ loca.*

Christophori Cartwright *Ebor. Mellificium Hebraicum , sive, Observationes ex Hebræorum antiquiorum monumentis desumptæ.*

Johannis Cloppenburgi *Collationes Criticæ Sacræ per Epistolas cum Ludovico de Dieu.*

* Petri Danielis Huetii *De Situ Paradisi Terrestris.*

* - - - *Commentarium de Navigationibus Salomonis.*

Notes

1. Richard Helgerson, *Forms of Nationhood: The Elizabethan Writing of England* (Chicago: University of Chicago Press, 1992), 251.

2. Mark Pattison, *Isaac Casaubon, 1559–1614* (London: Longmans, 1875), 414.

3. H. S. Bennett, *English Books and Readers, 1558–1603.* (Cambridge: At the University Press, 1965), 112; William T. Costello, *The Scholastic Curriculum at Early Seventeenth-Century Cambridge* (Cambridge: Harvard University Press, 1958), 107; Douglas Bush, *English Literature in the Earlier Seventeenth Century, 1600–1660*, Oxford History of English Literature (New York: Oxford University Press, 1945), 294.

4. Amos Funkenstein, *Theology and the Scientific Imagination from the Middle Ages to the Seventeenth Century* (Princeton: Princeton University Press, 1986), 3.

5. Before the late 1970s, of course, a vast amount of scholarship was devoted to the religious backgrounds of English Renaissance literature; the main reason religion has dropped out of Renaissance scholarship is that people got tired of articles on eucharistic imagery in *The Faerie Queene*, etc. Even this earlier research, however, usually conceived of religion as a circumscribed category unrelated to the constructions of gender, subjectivity, sexuality, power, nationalism, and so forth.

6. A. G. Dickens, *The English Reformation*, 2d ed. (University Park: Pennsylvania State University Press, 1989), 156.

7. Following the periodization customary among students of English literature, I use "Renaissance" and "early modern period" interchangeably to cover the mid-fifteenth through the mid-seventeenth centuries, although scholarship on the Continental Renaissance usually distinguishes the Renaissance (the fourteenth to mid-sixteenth centuries) from the early modern era (mid-sixteenth through the seventeenth centuries).

8. "Religion" is here a catchall term for belief, exegesis, systematic theology, devotional lyrics, biblical poetry, religious art, ascetic practices, ritual, inquisitions, canon law, etc.

9. Recent exceptions, however, include some of the most original and important studies of Renaissance culture: William Bouwsma, *John Calvin: A Sixteenth-Century Portrait* (New York: Oxford University Press, 1988); Stephen Greenblatt, *Marvelous Possessions: The Wonder of the New World* (Chicago: University of Chicago Press, 1991); and Helgerson, *Forms of Nationhood.*

10. The freeway should perhaps be imagined as dotted with helicopter pads, since these biblical discourses also pave a vertical trajectory connecting earth and heaven. For the purposes of this study, however, I am interested primarily in their horizontal axis.

11. Eric Voegelin, *Order and History*, 6 vols., vol. 2, *The World of the Polis* (Baton Rouge: Louisiana State University Press, 1957), 127; for this whole section, I draw heavily on Voegelin's discussion of the transition from myth to philosophy in pre-Hellenic Greece (2:127–37).

12. Ibid., 137.

13. Ibid.

14. According to Bennett, 20 percent of all books published under Elizabeth were translations (*English Books*, xvi). I have omitted discussing biblical texts written in the Continental vernaculars—much to my regret, since Vondel's biblical tragedies are considered among the masterpieces of Dutch literature. My only justification is that I suspect most Renaissance Englishmen could not read Dutch either.

15. This narrowly nationalist focus weakens J. W. Binns's *Intellectual Culture in Elizabethan and Jacobean England*, ARCA: Classical and Medieval Texts 24 (Leeds: Francis Cairns, 1990), the only extant survey of English Renaissance neo-Latin scholarship and literature.

16. There is a second reason for selecting these particular narratives: we have little more definitive evidence for or against their truth than did Renaissance scholars. For the study of pre-nineteenth-century exegesis, the contingent fact that modern science discredited the historicity of certain biblical episodes has proven a highly distracting irrelevancy. To frame a history of exegesis by focusing, as commonly done, on Noah's Ark or the Garden of Eden is to submit a priori to the formulaic plot of reason's slow conquest over error and credulity.

1. AFTER ALLEGORY

1. The classic works on this subject are volume 4 of Henri de Lubac's *Exégèse médiévale: Les quatre sens de l'écriture*, 4 vols. (Paris: Aubier, 1959–1964), and Beryl Smalley's *The Study of the Bible in the Middle Ages*, 2d ed. (1952; rpt. Notre Dame: University of Notre Dame Press, 1964). See also Smalley,

"The Bible in the Medieval Schools," in *The Cambridge History of the Bible: The West from the Fathers to the Reformation*, ed. G. W. Lampe, (Cambridge: At the University Press, 1969), 197–219; G. R. Evans, *The Language and Logic of the Bible: The Road to Reformation* (Cambridge: Cambridge University Press, 1985); Jerry H. Bentley, *Humanists and Holy Writ: New Testament Scholarship in the Renaissance* (Princeton: Princeton University Press, 1983); Erika Rummel, *Erasmus' Annotationes on the New Testament: From Philologist to Theologian*, Erasmus Studies 8 (Toronto: University of Toronto Press, 1986). For the fairly large bibliography on Erasmus's biblical scholarship, see Jean-Claude Margolin, "The Epistle to the Romans (Chapter 11) According to the Versions and/or Commentaries of Valla, Colet, Lefevre, and Erasmus," in *The Bible in the Sixteenth Century*, ed. David Steinmetz, Duke Monographs in Medieval and Renaissance Studies 11, (Durham: Duke University Press, 1990), 241–42.

2. By far the best survey of Renaissance biblical scholarship is François Laplanche's *L'écriture, le sacré et l'histoire: Érudits et politiques protestants devant la Bible en France au XVIIe siècle* (Amsterdam: Holland University Press, 1986), which focuses on Cappel and French Protestant exegesis but includes an intelligent discussion of the whole development of scholarly exegesis from Valla through late seventeenth-century Protestant scholarship in terms of its political, theological, and philological ramifications. See also the fourth volume of Stanislaus von Dunin-Borkowski's *Spinoza*, 4 vols. (Munster: Aschendorffschen Verlagsbuchhandlung, 1936), a bibliographic survey of sixteenth- and seventeenth-century historical and philological scholarship, both secular and sacred, with a fairly strong Roman Catholic bias; Ludwig Diestel's *Geschichte des Alten Testamentes in der christlichen Kirche* (Jena, 1869), which focuses on Protestant contributions to the development of modern biblical scholarship; Don Cameron Allen's *The Legend of Noah: Renaissance Rationalism in Art, Science, and Letters*, Illinois Studies in Language and Literature 33.3–4 (Urbana: University of Illinois Press, 1949), which treats the secularization of exegesis—the increasing skepticism about the literal truth of the Bible; S. L. Greenslade, ed., *The West from the Reformation to the Present Day*, vol. 3 of *The Cambridge History of the Bible* (Cambridge: At the University Press, 1963), fairly superficial but good for an overview; and Richard Simon's *Histoire critique des principaux commentateurs du Noveau Testament* (Rotterdam, 1693), an exhaustive survey but vitiated by the pervasive confessional polemic and irritating omission of dates/chronology.

3. *Critici sacri, sive annotata doctissimorum virorum in Vetus ac Novum Testamentum*, ed. John Pearson, A. Scattergood, F. Gouldman, and R. Pearson, 9 vols., 2d ed. (Amsterdam, 1698). Diestel comments, "So entstand das Werk *Critici sacri* . . . das des Guten wenig auslässt, doc auch vom Mittelmässigen viel bietet, im Ganzen einer wissenschaftlichen Richtung im Sinne von Drusius huldigend. Sie geben ein ziemlich getreues Bild der Exegese von

1550–1660" (*Geschichte*, 439). The Appendix gives its (unpaginated) table of contents.

4. Hugh Trevor-Roper, *Catholics, Anglicans, and Puritans: Seventeenth-Century Essays* (London: Secker and Warburg, 1987), 192.

5. Except, of course, in relation to Milton and a few other canonical authors. See, for example, Arnold Williams, *The Common Expositor: An Account of the Commentaries on Genesis, 1527–1633* (Chapel Hill: University of North Carolina Press, 1948); J. Martin Evans, *Paradise Lost and the Genesis Tradition* (Oxford: Clarendon, 1968); Michael Lieb, *Poetics of the Holy: A Reading of Paradise Lost* (Chapel Hill: University of North Carolina Press, 1981); Chana Bloch, *Spelling the Word: George Herbert and the Bible* (Berkeley: University of California Press, 1985); James G. Turner, *One Flesh: Paradisal Marriage and Sexual Relations in the Age of Milton* (Oxford: Oxford University Press, 1987); Mary Ann Radzinowicz, *Milton's Epics and the Book of Psalms* (Princeton: Princeton University Press, 1989); and Regina Schwartz, *Remembering and Repeating: Biblical Creation in Paradise Lost* (Cambridge: Cambridge University Press, 1988).

6. Brian Stock, *Listening for the Text: On the Uses of the Past* (Baltimore: Johns Hopkins University Press, 1990).

7. Turner's discussion of patristic and Renaissance Genesis commentaries in *One Flesh* gives an immensely learned overview of these disparate exegetic traditions.

8. The sources for this section include the *Dictionary of National Biography*; B. Rekers, *Benito Arias Montano (1527–1598)* (London: Warburg Institute, 1972); H. J. de Jonge, "The Study of the New Testament," trans. J. C. Grayson, in *Leiden University in the Seventeenth Century: An Exchange of Learning*, ed. Th. H. Lunsingh Scheurleer and G. H. M. Posthumus Meyjes (Leiden: Brill, 1975), 65–110; Paul Sellin, *Daniel Heinsius and Stuart England*, Publications of the Sir Thomas Browne Institute 3 (Leiden: At the University Press, 1968); G. Lloyd Jones, *The Discovery of Hebrew in Tudor England: A Third Language* (Manchester: Manchester University Press, 1983); J. Brugman, "Arabic Scholarship," in *Leiden University in the Seventeenth Century*, ed. Lunsingh Scheurleer and Posthumus Meyjes, 203–15; W. S. M. Knight, *The Life and Works of Hugo Grotius*, Grotius Society Publications 4 (1925; rpt. London: Wildy, 1965); Peter T. van Rooden, *Theology, Biblical Scholarship, and Rabbinical Studies in the Seventeenth Century: Constantijn L'Empereur (1591–1648), Professor of Hebrew and Theology at Leiden*, trans. J. C. Grayson, Studies in the History of Leiden University 6 (Leiden: Brill, 1989); Pattison, *Isaac Casaubon*; Laplanche, *L'écriture*; and the biography of Johannes Drusius given in the prefatory material to volume 6 of the *Critici sacri* (xxxiii–xli).

9. De Jonge, "Study," 83, 87, 100.

10. Sellin, *Heinsius*, 79.

11. Ibid., 103–5.

12. Andrewes was master of Pembroke from 1589–1605, but from 1589 on he was also the rector of St. Giles, Cripplegate, and prebend at St. Paul's and Southwell; thus, after 1589 he may not have spent much time at the university.

13. Lloyd Jones, *Hebrew in Tudor England*, 146–47.

14. Florence Higham, *Lancelot Andrewes* (London: SCM Press, 1952), 40.

15. Laplanche, *L'écriture*, 27; Diestel, *Geschichte*, 420.

16. Knight, *Grotius*, 98–103.

17. Anthony Grafton, *Joseph Scaliger: A Study in the History of Classical Scholarship*, vol. 1, *Textual Criticism and Exegesis* (Oxford: Clarendon, 1983), 1.

18. Smalley, *Study of the Bible*.

19. *Biblia Sacra cum glossa ordinaria . . . et postilla Nicholai Lirani . . . necnon additionibus Pauli Burgensis . . . & Matthiae Thoringi replicis*, 6 vols. (Antwerp, 1617), 5:421. The King James Bible translates the passage as "Verily I say unto you, Wheresoever this gospel shall be preached in the whole world, *there* shall also be this, that this woman hath done, be told for a memorial of her."

20. *Collatio Novi Testamenti* was Valla's own title; Erasmus published it in 1505, however, as *Adnotationes in Novum Testamentum*.

21. *Critici sacri* 6:862; further references to the *Critici sacri* will appear in the text. The pagination of the volumes is a little complicated since each volume often has several sections each paginated separately, and the volumes have no table of contents to clarify matters. (There are also two volume 1s, which doesn't help matters, especially since the index seems keyed to the 1660 edition, which was bound differently.) For example, there are three sections in volume 6, each with its own pagination: one covers Matthew, the second Mark and Luke, and the third John. As long as the reader knows the biblical verse under discussion, however, it is not difficult to find the relevant page.

22. Jacques Chomarat, "Les *Annotations* de Valla, celles d'Erasme et la grammaire," in *Histoire de l'exégèse au XVIe siècle*, ed. Olivier Fatio and Pierre Fraenkel, (Geneva: Librairie Droz, 1978), 204, 211–12.

23. Lorenzo Valla, *Elegantiarum libri sex*, in *Opera omnia*, intro. Eugenio Garin, 2 vols. (Turin: Bottega d'Erasmo, 1962), 1:143, 215.

24. Donald Kelley, *Foundations of Modern Historical Scholarship: Language, Law, and History in the French Renaissance* (New York: Columbia University Press, 1970), 32–33.

25. In the dedicatory epistle to Sir Philip Sidney prefacing his edition of the New Testament, Stephanus (Henri Estienne) observes concerning Castellio's translation: "Sed quantum illorum hominum qui nec *everrit* pro *evertit*, nec *sporta* pro *porta* reponi sinebant plenam ignorantia superstitiosa timiditatem deploraret, tantum profecto eam quae in hoc nostrum seculum erupit non irreligiosam tantum sed religionis profanatricem audaciam detestaretur, quae in

interpretando hoc sacrosancto opere . . . non solum pro *idolis Deastros*, & pro *idololatris Deastricolas*, aliaque id genus multa, sed *Genios* etiam pro *Angelis*, pro *Baptismo lotionem* (sicut *lavare* pro *baptizare*) & *fiduciam* pro *fide* passim dixit . . . tam multa denique novavit ut Testamentum hoc sic interpretatum alio etiam sensu *novum* appellari possit" (6:xvii).

26. De Jonge, "Study," 67.

27. Cf. Bentley, *Humanists and Holy Writ*, 180; Chomarat, "Les *Annotations*," 222–23.

28. Chomarat, "Les *Annotations*," 220–21.

29. Rummel, *Erasmus' Annotationes*, 74.

30. For this whole paragraph, I am indebted to Kathy Eden's "Hermeneutics and the Ancient Rhetorical Tradition," *Rhetorica* 5 (1987): 59–86; "The Rhetorical Tradition and Augustinian Hermeneutics in *De doctrina Christiana*," *Rhetorica* 8 (1990): 45–63; "Equity and the Origins of Renaissance Historicism: The Case for Erasmus," *Yale Journal of Law and the Humanities* 5 (1993): 137–45; "Strategies of Accommodation in Erasmus' Later Works," paper given at the conference of the International Society for the History of Rhetoric, September 1991.

31. Bentley, *Humanists and Holy Writ*, 212.

32. Theodore Beza, *Jesu Christi Domini Nostri Novum Testamentum, sive Novum Foedus, cujus Graeco contextui respondent interpretationes duae: una, vetus; altera, Theodori Bezae . . . Accessit etiam Joachimi Camerarii in Novum Foedus Commentarius* (Cambridge, 1642), 89; Caesar Baronius, *Annales Ecclesiastici*, ed. Augustinus Theiner, 37 vols. (Paris, 1864–1883), 1:144.

33. One finds the same ahistorical approach in the *loci communes* of Melanchthon, Bucer, and other Protestant scholastics but based on Aristotelian/rhetorical method rather than typological ecclesiology; see, for example, Bucer's comment that "in the observations I have aimed at providing a *sylvulam* for the unlearned, so that, from Paul's limited dogmas and precepts (limited on account of the complex of things, persons and times and other *peristaseon* [circumstances], and which are called *hypotheses*) we may ascend more easily and surely *anagoge* to *theses*, that is, the universal [infiniti] dogmas and precepts, which are not bound to persons, places, and times" (quoted in T. H. L. Parker, *Calvin's New Testament Commentaries* [Grand Rapids, Mich.: Eerdmans, 1971], 46; I have put Greek in Roman letters). As in Erasmus, the exegete divests historical narratives of local specificity in order to separate out general truths.

34. Parker, *Calvin's Commentaries*, 91.

35. Richard Muller, "The Hermeneutic of Promise and Fulfillment in Calvin's Exegesis of the Old Testament Prophecies of the Kingdom," in *The Bible in the Sixteenth Century*, ed. David Steinmetz, Duke Monographs in Medieval and Renaissance Studies 11 (Durham: Duke University Press), 73, 81.

36. Laplanche, *L'écriture*, 32.

37. Kelley, *Foundations*. Cf. Dunin-Borkowski: "Man kann in einem gewissen Sinn sogar sagen, dass die Kunst, die wir mittlere und höhere Kritik nennen, in einem iherer vorzüglichsten Ansätze, hier bei den juristischen 'Philologen' geboren wurde; was man bisher kaum jemals erkannt hat. Und eben deshalb war es noch um die Mitte des 17. Jahrhunderts Pflicht jedes Kritikers, dieses Schifttum genau zu kennen" (*Spinoza* 4:207).

38. Anthony Grafton, *Defenders of the Text: The Traditions of Scholarship in an Age of Science, 1450–1800* (Cambridge: Harvard University Press, 1991), 142–44.

39. De Jonge, "Study," 86.

40. Casaubon, *De rebus sacris et ecclesiasticis exercitationes XVI ad Cardinalis Baronii* (London, 1614), 603–4.

41. Marjorie O'Rourke Boyle, *Erasmus on Language and Method in Theology* (Toronto: University of Toronto Press, 1977), 13–31.

42. Casaubon, *Exercitationes*, 476 (misprinted as 464).

43. Ibid., 610–17.

44. Daniel Heinsius, *D. Heinsii sacrarum exercitationum ad Novum Testamentum libri XX*, 2d ed. (Cambridge, 1640), 85.

45. Joachim Camerarius, *Commentarius in Novum Foedus* (1572; Cambridge, 1642), 17 (bound with Beza's *Novum Testamentum*).

46. The latter possibility was particularly controversial, since it weakens the authority of the biblical witness and seems incompatible with belief in literal inspiration. Such criticism implicitly desacralizes the text, forcing one to treat it *like other texts*, as subject to the same authorial vicissitudes (Laplanche, *L'écriture*, 368–69). Hence, in order to place Spinoza's biblical scholarship in its disciplinary and historical context, Dunin-Borkowski gives a fairly lengthy monograph on the development of Classical philology and historiography during the Renaissance; Spinoza's radicalism, Dunin-Borkowski argues, consists mainly of applying to the Bible the methods that had been used in secular philology for close to two centuries (*Spinoza* 4:160, 194–95).

47. Drusius was one of the earliest Protestant scholars to argue that some books of the Old Testament had disappeared—a position he connected to the further claim that the earliest canon of the Old Testament contained only the Pentateuch, the inclusion of the Prophets as part of the liturgy having begun only after Antiochus Epiphanes prohibited the reading of the Law (1.2.384–86).

48. Modern scholarship has thought this point worth making again; cf. Stock, *Listening for the Text*, 7–8.

49. "Archeology" (ἀρχαιολόγος) is, significantly, the ancient term for what we would call antiquarian studies; see Arnaldo Momigliano, *The Classical Foundations of Modern Historiography* (Berkeley: University of California Press, 1990), 60.

50. Frank Kermode, *The Genesis of Secrecy: On the Interpretation of Narrative* (Cambridge: Harvard University Press, 1979), 55–60.

51. *Biblia Sacra* 5:636.

52. Beza, *Novum Testamentum,* 143.

53. Baronius, *Annales* 1:128.

54. Casaubon, *Exercitationes,* 593.

55. Grotius, *Critici sacri* 6:176; Henry Hammond, *A Paraphrase and Annotations upon all the Books of the New Testament,* 5th ed. (London, 1681), 175.

56. John Lightfoot, *A Commentary on the New Testament from the Talmud and Hebraica, Matthew–I Corinthians,* 4 vols. (1859; rpt. Grand Rapids, Mich.: Baker Book House, 1979), 2:354.

57. For other Renaissance studies of ancient Jewish polity, see Laplanche, *L'écriture,* 30; Rooden, *Theology,* 219; and William McCuaig, *Carlo Sigonio: The Changing World of the Late Renaissance* (Princeton: Princeton University Press, 1989), which unfortunately deals only with Sigonius's secular scholarship. Volume 5 of the *Critici sacri* reprints Cornelius Bertramus's *De republica & politia Judaica* (1574) and Petrus Cunaeus's *De republica Hebraeorum libri III* (1617).

58. Erich Auerbach, *Mimesis: The Representation of Reality in Western Literature,* trans. Willard Trask (Princeton: Princeton University Press, 1953), 44.

59. Ibid., 22–23.

60. Although at least some of this material was known to medieval exegetes, they rarely applied it to the interpretation of the New Testament; furthermore, the decline of humanistic studies after the mid-fourteenth century meant that Renaissance Hebrew scholarship did not build on a continuous tradition but at the time seemed "unprecedented" (Smalley, "The Bible in the Medieval Schools," 219). For Hebrew and Oriental philology in the Renaissance, see Allen, *Noah;* Brugman, "Arabic Scholarship"; Basil Hall, "Biblical Scholarship: Editions and Commentaries," in *The Cambridge History of the Bible: The West from the Reformation to the Present Day,* ed. S. L. Greenslade, (Cambridge: At the University Press, 1963), 38–93; De Jonge, "Study"; Aaron L. Katchen, *Christian Hebraists and Dutch Rabbis: Seventeenth Century Apologetics and the Study of Maimonides' Mishneh Torah,* Harvard Judaic Texts and Studies 3 (Cambridge: Harvard University Press, 1984); Laplanche, *L'écriture;* Lloyd Jones, *Hebrew in Tudor England;* Rooden, *Theology;* Jerome Friedman, *The Most Ancient Testimony: Sixteenth-Century Christian-Hebraica in the Age of Renaissance Nostalgia* (Athens: Ohio University Press, 1983).

61. Conrad Pellican had published an elementary Hebrew grammar three years earlier, but this rather mediocre work was swiftly superseded by Reuchlin's text; see Friedman, *The Most Ancient Testimony,* 24, 31.

62. This, however, was largely filched from Raymundus Martini's *Pugio Fidei,* published 250 years earlier in 1278—a debt Galatinus did not acknowledge.

63. Hall, "Biblical Scholarship," 40.

64. See Katchen, *Christian Hebraists*.

65. Rekers, *Montano*, 53.

66. Hammond, *A Paraphrase*, 275.

67. For example, Camerarius, *Novum Foedus*, 16.

68. Joseph Justus Scaliger, *Opus de emendatione temporum* (Leiden, 1598), 534–36.

69. Beza, *Novum Testamentum*, 87.

70. Hammond, *A Paraphrase*, 131.

71. Baronius, *Annales*, 116–18; Cornelius à Lapide, *The Great Commentary*, ed. and trans. Thomas Mossman, 6 vols. (London, 1876–1887), 3:161–64.

72. Casaubon, *Exercitationes*, 474–78, 481; see also Laplanche, *L'écriture*, 286–88. "That day," of course, refers to the Hebrew day, which goes from sunset to sunset.

73. As did several important Roman Catholic exegetes—for example, Maldonatus and Cornelius Jansenius. Casaubon lists the advocates on either side in *Exercitationes*, 468.

74. Cloppenburg's argument and Cappel's replies are summarized in the other great Restoration compendium of biblical scholarship: Matthew Poole's *Synopsis criticorum aliorumque S. Scripturae interpretum*, 5 vols. (London, 1669), 4:607–10; see also Laplanche, *L'écriture*, 286–87.

75. Hence, Erasmus remarks, "Nam fieri potest ut de die Paschae statuendo labatur numero Ecclesia, cum is error ad pietatis aut fidei negotium proprie non pertineat" (7:1026).

76. Casaubon, *Exercitationes*, 482; see also the comments of the early sixteenth-century Hebraicist Sebastian Munster, in *Critici sacri* (6:859). Grafton discusses these calendrical matters in *Defenders*, 127.

77. Scaliger, *De emendatione*, 532.

78. Diestel, *Geschichte*, 280.

79. John Selden, *De jure naturali & gentium juxta disciplinam Ebraeorum* (London, 1640), 487–88.

80. Ibid., 490–91, 498.

81. Ibid., 490.

82. Mieke Bal, *Death and Dissymmetry: The Politics of Coherence in the Book of Judges* (Chicago: University of Chicago Press, 1988).

83. *Biblia sacra cum glossa interlineari, ordinaria, et Nicolai Lyrani postilla, eiusdemque moralitatibus, Burgensis additionibus, & Thoringi replicis*, 7 vols. (Venice, 1588), 5:7–10.

84. See Josephus, *Against Apion*, in *Jospehus*, trans. H. St. J. Thackeray, 8 vols., Loeb Classical Library (London: William Heinemann, 1926), 1:30–36.

85. Daniel P. Walker, *The Ancient Theology: Studies in Christian Platonism from the Fifteenth to the Eighteenth Century* (Ithaca: Cornell University Press, 1972), 18–19; Grafton, *Defenders*, 145–77.

86. Grafton, *Scaliger*, 116.

87. Rooden, *Theology*, 59n.

88. Quoted in De Jonge, "Study," 84.

89. Diestel considers this "Fülle von Anmerkungen und Parallelen aus den Klassikern" the distinctive feature of Grotian exegesis (*Geschichte*, 432).

90. Mark Pattison, *Essays by the Late Mark Pattison*, ed. Henry Nettleship, 2 vols. (Oxford: Clarendon, 1889), 1:163; cf. Laplanche, *L'écriture*, 94–95.

91. *Biblia Sacra* (1617) 5:453; Erasmus, *Critici sacri* 6:932.

92. Justus Lipsius, *De cruce libri tres* (Antwerp, 1594).

93. Casaubon, *Exercitationes*, 601.

94. See chapter 3 for the Calvinist reading of this episode.

95. Hammond, *A Paraphrase*, 103.

96. Pierre Pithou, *Mosaicarum et Romanarum legum collatio* (1572), reprinted in *Critici sacri* 1.2.193–248.

97. Grotius, *Critici sacri* 6:891–92, 896–97; Scaliger, *De emendatione*, 534; Baronius, *Annales*, 120–21; Casaubon, *Exercitationes*, 488–89, 525, 608–9, 672; Hammond, *A Paraphrase*, 129–30.

98. Scaliger, *De emendatione*, 530.

99. Walker, *Ancient Theology*, 65.

100. Alan Richardson, "The Rise of Modern Biblical Scholarship and Recent Discussion of the Authority of the Bible," in *The Cambridge History of the Bible: The West from the Reformation to the Present Day*, ed. S. L. Greenslade (Cambridge: At the University Press, 1963), 300.

101. Zachary Sayre Schiffman observes a similar shift from "the lives of kings, captains, and saints" to "the institutional structure of ancient Gaul, Roman Gaul, and the kingdom of the Franks" in late sixteenth-century French historiography in his *On the Threshold of Modernity: Relativism in the French Renaissance*, Johns Hopkins University Studies in Historical and Political Science (Baltimore: Johns Hopkins University Press, 1991), 33–34, 38.

102. See the notes to Matthew 27:46–47 in the *Critici sacri* by Munsterus, Erasmus, Clarius, Zegerus, Drusius, and Grotius.

103. À Lapide, *The Great Commentary* (1876–1887) 3:151–2.

104. Diestel's comments on Grotius register his nineteenth-century perplexity at this combination: "so eigenthümlich verschlingt sich hier der strenge Supernaturalismus mit naturalistischen Ahnungen!" (*Geschichte*, 433).

105. The fusion of historical/antiquarian research and traditional hermeneutic pieties comes through clearly in the summary of the contents prefacing the original edition of the *Critici sacri* (reprinted at the beginning of volume 8 in the 1698 edition): "Whatever seems worth of mention in the sacred volumes—things, persons, actions, places, times, regions, cities, temples, tools, vessels, weights, measures, coins, attire, gesture, duties, rituals, laws, customs—all here are learnedly and clearly described. Not only are the mysteries of types, enigmas of prophecies and parables, and all the more difficult places of the sacred text here elucidated, but also the etymologies of the words them-

selves, their meanings, even the dots and dashes are minutely examined. Here is shown whatever the Rabbis of the Synagogue or the Doctors of the Church subtly observe concerning the sacred writings. Here the holy oracles of God are compared with the monuments of other peoples; the laws of the Hebrews with the ordinances of the gentiles; the odes of David, the proverbs of Solomon, and inspired maxims of other writers with the parallel passages from the ethnic poets, rhetoricians, and philosophers. Here finally one can see the wonderful harmony and accord of the sacred books, where one text asks help from another and calls upon it as a friend—the best kind of interpretation."

106. For a (rather predictable) analysis of Renaissance exegesis in terms of the secularization of the West, see Klaus Scholder, *The Birth of Modern Critical Theology: Origins and Problems of Biblical Criticism in the Seventeenth Century*, trans. John Bowden (London, SCM Press, 1990).

107. Lorenzo Valla, *The Treatise of Lorenzo Valla on the Donation of Constantine*, trans. Christopher Coleman (New York: Russell and Russell, 1922), 105–7, 115–17.

108. See Anthony Kemp, *The Estrangement of the Past: A Study in the Origins of Modern Historical Consciousness* (New York: Oxford University Press, 1991), 62–63, 79.

109. Aristotle, *History of Animals*, trans. d'A. W. Thompson, in *The Complete Works of Aristotle*, ed. Jonathan Barnes, 2 vols., Bollingen Series 71 (Princeton: Princeton University Press, 1984), 1.1.487b–488a, 5.7–8.541b–542a, 6.8.564a (1:776–77, 855–56, 887). ("Treads," for those who have forgotten their Chaucer, means "copulates with.")

110. Pseudo-Aristotle, *On Marvellous Things Heard*, trans. L. D. Dowdall, in *The Complete Works of Aristotle* 2:1280.

111. Francis Bacon, *The Proficience and Advancement of Learning, Divine and Human*, in *Francis Bacon: A Selection of His Works*, ed. Sidney Warhaft (New York: Odyssey Press, 1965), 204; Richard Hooker, *Of the Laws of Ecclesiastical Polity*, intro. Christopher Morris, 2 vols. (London: Dent, 1907), 1.8.5.

112. On the *Wunderkammer*, see Steven Mullaney, "Strange Things, Gross Terms, Curious Customs: The Rehearsal of Cultures in the Late Renaissance," in *Representing the English Renaissance*, ed. Stephen Greenblatt (Berkeley: University of California Press, 1988), 65–92; Schiffman, *On the Threshold*, 3–4, 10–11.

113. Erasmus, *De duplici copia verborum ac rerum commentarii duo*, ed. Craig Thompson, trans. Betty Knott, in *The Collected Works of Erasmus* (Toronto: University of Toronto Press, 1974–), 24:637.

114. Once again, Scaliger is a seminal figure here. Discussion of the Hasids begins with the opening section of book 6 of *De emendatione*, which argues, contra Eusebius, that the monastic "Therapeutae" mentioned by Philo were not Christians but rather Essenes; furthermore, the name does not mean "healers" but "holy ones." He then goes on to note in passing the similarity

between Philo's Essenes and "Asidaioi" mentioned in 1 and 2 Maccabees (502–3). Drusius continued this line of inquiry in a brief passage in *Quaestionum Ebraicarum libri tres* (1599), where he argues that the Hasids mentioned in Maccabees were forerunners of Pharisees; hence, there were two main Jewish sects in Israel during the Hellenistic period—Hasids and Saducees. The Jesuit Nicholas Serarius rejected this interpretation, instead claiming that the Hasids were Essenes, and hence three groups existed within intertestamental Judaism. Drusius's *De Hasidaeis* (1603) then responded to Serarius, who replied in the *Trihaeresium*, defending his original opinion. In 1605 Drusius wrote an extended essay on the religious beliefs and politics of intertestamental Judaism, the *De sectis Judaicis*, dedicated to James I (to which was appended Scaliger's critique of Serarius, the *Elenchus Trihaeresii*). The contributions of Scaliger and Drusius were republished together by Amama in 1619 as *De sectis Judaicis commentarii trihaeresio . . . accessit denuo Iosephi Scaligeri I.C.F. Elenchus Trihaeresii* (Arnheim, 1619). See also Abraham Scultetus, *Exercitationes Evangelicae* 1.20–33, in *Critici sacri* 6:367–79; Bonaventura Bertramus, *De republica Ebraeorum*, in *Critici sacri* 5:367; and Petrus Cunaeus, *De republica Hebraeorum libri III*, in *Critici sacri* 5:420. This debate is also discussed by Grafton in *Defenders*, 137f.

115. Katchen, *Christian Hebraists*, 68; cf. Grafton, *Defenders*, 79.

116. For the relation between Renaissance legal historiography and the managment of diversity in the Renaissance, see also Schiffman, *On the Threshold*, 1–39.

117. Donald Kelley, "Louis le Caron *Philosophe*," in *Philosophy and Humanism: Renaissance Essays in Honor of Paul Oskar Kristeller*, ed. Edward Mahoney (Leiden: Brill, 1976), 30.

118. John Barton, "The Faculty of Law," in *The Collegiate University*, ed. James McConica, vol. 3 of *The History of the University of Oxford*, gen. ed. T. H. Aston (Oxford: Oxford University Press, 1984–), 279.

119. See Thomas Greene, *Light in Troy* (New Haven: Yale University Press, 1982).

120. James A. Boon, "Comparative De-enlightenment: Paradox and Limits in the History of Ethnology," *Daedalus* 109 (1980): 79; Schiffman, *On the Threshold*, 7.

121. Mullaney, "Strange Things," 65–66.

122. The contrast between tribal peoples and ancestors should, however, not be drawn too rigidly, since the Renaissance tended to regard Amerindians and other "primitive" societies as fundamentally similar to earlier phases of their own cultures, i.e., as resembling ancestors. Chapter 2 deals in greater depth with the Renaissance tendency to identify archaic and exotic cultures.

123. Grafton, *Defenders*, 172.

124. Erasmus, *Ciceronianus; or, A Dialogue on the Best Style of Speaking* (1517), trans. Izora Scott (1908; rpt. New York: AMS, 1972), 61–62, 121–22.

2. THE KEY TO ALL MYTHOLOGIES

1. Hugo Grotius, *Defensio fidei catholicae de satisfactione Christi adversus Faustum Socinum,* in *Opera omnia theologica in tres tomos divisa,* 4 vols. (Amsterdam, 1679), 4:335–36. References to this work will hereafter appear in the text.

2. James G. Frazer, *The New Golden Bough,* ed. Theodor Gaster, abridged ed. (New York: Criterion, 1959), 534–41.

3. Jaroslav Pelikan, *The Christian Tradition: A History of the Development of Doctrine,* 5 vols., vol. 4, *Reformation of Church and Dogma, 1300–1700* (Chicago: University of Chicago Press), 1984), 360.

4. Knight, *Grotius,* 270. Christian Gellinek notes that the work went through fifteen editions (four in Grotius's lifetime) and was translated into three languages (*Hugo Grotius,* Twayne's World Authors Series [Boston: Twayne, 1983], 148).

5. Saint Anselm, *Cur Deus Homo,* in *St. Anselm: Basic Writings,* trans. S. N. Deane, 2d ed. (La Salle, Ill.: Open Court, 1962), 202.

6. Ibid., 280, 257.

7. Robert S. Franks, *The Work of Christ: A Historical Study of Christian Doctrine* (London: Thomas Nelson, n.d.), 371.

8. Myron Piper Gilmore, *Argument from Roman Law in Political Thought, 1200–1600,* Harvard Historical Monographs 15 (Cambridge: Harvard University Press, 1941), 49.

9. Grotius seems here to be using Bodin's analysis of *imperium,* which rests on the distinction between the *actio legis* possessed by ordinary magistrates, who are authorized only to carry out the sentence mandated by the law, and the *merum imperium* or "the power of life and death, when the law itself leaves no room for extenuation or grace," which is the highest mark of sovereignty. See Jean Bodin, *Method for the Easy Comprehension of History,* trans. Beatrice Reynolds (New York: Columbia University Press, 1945), 173–75; cf. Gilmore, *Roman Law,* 105.

10. Franks, *The Work of Christ,* 405.

11. Grotius apparently knew and admired this work, probably at second hand since he could not read English; see Gellinek, *Grotius,* 90.

12. Here payment (*solutio*) should, as Grotius makes clear, be understood to include both monetary payment and "paying the penalty"; that is, it can apply to either civil or criminal obligation.

13. Kelley, *Foundations,* 38–58, 67–68, 102–3; see also Julian H. Franklin, *Jean Bodin and the Sixteenth-Century Revolution in the Methodology of Law and History* (New York: Columbia University Press, 1963); George Huppert, *The Idea of Perfect History: Historical Erudition and Historical Philosophy in Renaissance France* (Urbana: University of Illinois Press, 1970). Kelley has more recently, however, begun to emphasize the lasting significance of Roman

law not only in jurisprudence but also in the development of social and political thought through and after the Renaissance; see especially his *"Gaius Noster*: Substructures of Western Social Thought," *American Historical Review* 84 (1979): 619–48.

14. Paul Koschaker, *Europa und das römische Recht* (Munich: Biederstein, 1947), 116, 119–20, 124; R. Stintzing, *Geschichte der Deutschen Rechtswissenschaft*, Geschichte der Wissenschaft in Deutschland 18 (Munich, 1880–1884), 121–22, 139.

15. Stintzing, *Deutschen Rechtswissenschaft*, 121, 391.

16. Ibid., 385–86; H. D. Hazeltine, "The Renaissance and the Laws of Europe," in *Cambridge Legal Essays* (Cambridge: W. Heffer, 1926), 152, 157.

17. Hazeltine, "The Renaissance," 148–49.

18. Josef Bohatec, *Calvin und das Recht* (1934; rpt. Darmstadt: Scientia Verlag Aalen, 1971), 119 (my translation).

19. Bohatec, *Calvin*, 117; Stintzing, *Deutschen Rechtswissenschaft*, 284–86.

20. James Q. Whitman, *The Legacy of Roman Law in the German Romantic Era: Historical Vision and Legal Change* (Princeton: Princeton University Press, 1990), 4, 27.

21. Bohatec, *Calvin*, 27, 121; Alberico Gentili, *De jure belli libri tres*, trans. John Rolfe, intro. Coleman Phillipson, 2 vols., Classics of International Law (Oxford: Clarendon, 1933), 2:21a.

22. Kelley, *Foundations*, 204; Koschaker, *Europa*, 118, 249; cf. Donne, *Biathanatos*, ed. Ernest Sullivan (Newark: University of Delaware Press, 1984), 65–66: "that Law hath most force and valew, which is most generall. . . . to my understanding, the Civill or Imperiall Law, having had once the largest extent, and being not abandon'd now, in the reason, and essence, and nature thereof, but only least the accepting of it should testify some dependency upon the Impire, we ow the first place in this Consideration to that Law."

23. However, he left Leiden (or rather was forced out) before Grotius arrived.

24. Quoted in Franklin, *Bodin*, 34.

25. Stintzing, *Deutschen Rechtswissenschaft*, 123, 377–79; A. P. Th. Eyssell, *Doneau: Sa vie et ses ouvrages* (1860; rpt. Geneva: Slatkine Reprints, 1970), 204, 209, 215.

26. Franklin, *Bodin*, 34–35.

27. Jonathan Culler, *Framing the Sign: Criticism and Its Institutions*, Oklahoma Project for Discourse and Theory 3 (Norman: University of Oklahoma Press, 1988), 15. On the theoretical uses of Roman law in the Renaissance, see Kelley, "Vera Philosophia: The Philosophical Significance of Renaissance Jurisprudence," *Journal of the History of Philosophy* 14 (1976): 267–79.

28. Gilmore, *Roman Law*, 70; Koschaker, *Europa*, 122; Quentin Skinner, *The Foundations of Modern Political Thought*, 2 vols. (Cambridge: Cambridge University Press, 1978), 2:263.

29. Koschaker, *Europa*, 249–52. This transposition is evident in Grotius's earliest contribution to international law, the *Mare librum* of 1609, which cites extensively from the *Corpus juris* as well as numerous medieval and Renaissance commentators, including Donellus, Papinian, Duaren, and Bartolus. Even though in Grotius's magisterial *De jure belli ac pacis* (1625) the hand of Roman law appears less visibly, much of what professes to be a strict deduction from natural law and the *jus gentium* is, on inspection, an elegant and erudite commentary on Roman municipal law, a debt that subsequent editors have betrayed by cramming Grotius's margins with Justinian (Knight, *Grotius*, 219).

30. Gentili, *De jure belli* 1.1.17.

31. Hugo Grotius, *The Jurisprudence of Holland*, trans. R. W. Lee (Oxford: Clarendon, 1936), 11.

32. Knight, *Grotius*, 195.

33. Its conception of the prince as *legibus solutus* often and explicitly supplied ideological legitimation for absolutism, but, as Skinner has shown, principles taken from Roman civil law could, when transferred to public law, underwrite resistence theory as well (*Foundations* 2:124).

34. See J. G. A. Pocock, *The Ancient Constitution and the Feudal Law: A Study of English Historical Thought in the Seventeenth Century*, rev. ed. (Cambridge: Cambridge University Press, 1987), 23; Skinner, *Foundations* 2:263; Gilmore, *Roman Law*, 3–4, 70.

35. Gilmore, *Roman Law*, 95.

36. Kelley, *Foundations*, 138.

37. Grafton, *Defenders of the Text*, 23–46.

38. Harold J. Berman, *Law and Revolution: The Formation of the Western Legal Tradition* (Cambridge: Harvard University Press, 1983), 44, 151.

39. Franks, *The Work of Christ*, 77, 85, 135–36, 140, 221.

40. Funkenstein, *Theology and the Scientific Imagination*, 6.

41. Lancelot Andrewes, *Sermons*, ed. G. M. Story (Oxford: Clarendon, 1967), 159.

42. John Calvin, *Commentary on a Harmony of the Evangelists, Matthew, Mark, and Luke*, ed. William Pringle, 3 vols. (Edinburgh: Calvin Translation Society, 1846), 3:316–17; see likewise his explanation in *The Adultero-German Interim* (1547) that, following the Crucifixion, "the Father, softened by the odour of this most precious victim, laid aside his anger" (in *Tracts and Treatises in Defense of the Reformed Faith*, trans. Henry Beveridge, ed. Thomas Torrance, 3 vols. [Grand Rapids, Mich.: Eerdmans, 1958], 3:221).

43. John Calvin, *Institutes of the Christian Religion*, trans. Ford Lewis Battles, ed. John T. McNeill, 2 vols., Library of Christian Classics (London: SCM Press, 1960), 2.16.2.

44. To untangle the apparent contradiction between this claim and the examples given in the previous paragraph, one needs to distinguish martial law (which allowed substitution of physical penalties) from civil law (which did

not) and likewise to distinguish the early laws of pre-Christian Rome from those preserved in Justinian's redaction.

45. The Greeks apparently required even animal victims to signify consent before being sacrificed; see Marcel Detienne, "Culinary Practices and the Spirit of Sacrifice," in *The Cuisine of Sacrifice among the Greeks*, ed. Marcel Detienne and Jean-Pierre Vernant, trans. Paula Wissing (Chicago: University of Chicago Press, 1989), 9.

46. Cf. Grotius's *De jure belli ac pacis libri tres*, ed. and abridged trans. William Whewell, 3 vols. (Cambridge: At the University Press, 1853), 2.21.13: "'Neque virtutes, neque vitia parentum,' inquit Hieronymus, 'liberis imputantur. . . . Et huc illud vulgatum pertinet: 'noxa caput sequitur.' 'Sancimus,' aiunt Imperatores Christiani, 'ibi esse poenam, ubi et noxa est.' Diende: 'peccata igitur suos teneant auctores: nec ulterius progrediatur metus, quam reperiatur delictum.'"

47. Gentili, *De jure belli* 1.24; see also his *De jure belli commentatio tertia* (London, 1589), F(r).

48. Gentili, *De jure belli* 2.19.

49. Alberico Gentili, *In titulos codicis si quis Imperatori maledixerit, ad legem Juliam majestatis disputationes decem*, 2d ed. (Hanover, 1607), 181–82. See also Gesina H. J. van der Molen, *Alberico Gentili and the Development of International Law: His Life and Times*, 2d ed. (Leiden: A. W. Sijthoff, 1968), 95–97.

50. Gentili, *Si quis Imperatori*, 186.

51. Bernice Hamilton, *Political Thought in Sixteenth-Century Spain: A Study of the Political Ideas of Vitoria, De Soto, Suarez, and Molina* (Oxford: Clarendon, 1963), 155–56; Domingo de Soto, *De justitia et jure libri decem*, 5 vols. (1556; rpt. Madrid: Instituto de Estudios Politicos, 1967–1968), 5.1.7; James Brown Scott, *The Spanish Origin of International Law: Francisco de Vitoria and His Law of Nations* (Oxford: Clarendon, 1934), appendix B, p. lxv; appendix F, p. cxxv. For Salamanca and sixteenth-century Spanish Thomism, see Anthony Pagden, *The Fall of Natural Man: The American Indian and the Origins of Comparative Ethnology* (Cambridge: Cambridge University Press, 1982), 60–61.

52. Gentili, *De jure belli commentatio tertia*, E3(v)–E4(v).

53. Grotius, *De jure belli ac pacis* 2.21.12.

54. Ibid. 2.21.14.1–3; cf. 2.21.8.3.

55. See, for example, the distinction in *De jure belli ac pacis* between the primitive law (*priscum jus*) of the Hebrews and Greeks, which permits putting a citizen to death without trial, and the *lex evangelica* (2.20.9–10).

56. Cf. ibid. 2.21.11.

57. Thus, Grotius comments that only as God did Christ have the right to lay down his life (315).

58. Edmund Law, *A Defence of Mr. Locke's Opinion Concerning Personal Identity* (Cambridge, 1769), 10–11; quoted in R. C. Tennant, "The Anglican Response to Locke's Theory of Personal Identity," in *Philosophy, Religion and Science in the Seventeenth and Eighteenth Centuries*, ed. John W. Yolton (Rochester: University of Rochester Press, 1990), 190.

59. John Locke, *An Essay Concerning Human Understanding*, ed. Alexander C. Fraser, 2 vols. (New York: Dover, 1959), 2.27.7.

60. De Soto, *De justitia* 5.1.7. "Subject" (*suppositum*) here does not pick out the political relation of subjection but rather the ontological category of substance, i.e., that which *underlies* the accidental characteristics of appearance, occupation, class, age, etc. See Rodolphus Goclenius, *Lexicon philosophicum quo tanquam clave philosophiae fores aperiuntur* (Frankfurt, 1613; rpt. Hildesheim: Georg Olms, 1964), 1107.

61. Hamilton, *Political Thought*, 129; Pagden, *The Fall of Natural Man*, 90.

62. This right *does* presuppose self-ownership, a notion that considerably predates Locke; thus Marsilius of Padua (c. 1280–1343) comments in passing that the "term 'ownership' [*dominium*] is used to refer to the human will or freedom in itself. . . . Man alone among the animals is said to have ownership or control of his acts" (*The Defender of Peace*, trans. Alan Gewirth, 2 vols. [New York: Columbia University Press, 1956], 2.13.16).

63. Richard Tuck, "The 'Modern' Theory of Natural Law," in *The Languages of Political Theory in Early-Modern Europe*, ed. Anthony Pagden (Cambridge: Cambridge University Press, 1987), 105–19.

64. The King James Bible translates *redemptionis pretium* as "as a ransom."

65. It is instructive to contrast Grotius's analysis with Socinus's "modern" argument that the "*dignitas*" of Christ—the fact that he is the Son of God—is irrelevant to the efficacy or value of his death; for Socinus, bodies resemble cash—fungible units of identical value (330).

66. The intimate relation between slaughtering and sacrifice occurs also in the Hebrew, where *zebah*, the Old Testament word for "sacrifice," comes from the verb "to kill."

67. Walker, *The Ancient Theology*, 75. F. Saxl's "Pagan Sacrifice in the Italian Renaissance," *Journal of the Warburg Insititute* 2 (1939): 346–67, mentions several paintings of the Crucifixion where the background includes scenes of ritual sacrifice, but he locates only one late (1667) text where the Crucifixion is compared to pagan sacrifice, and even this text is, in fact, anti-Romanist propaganda: i.e., it claims that the Mass is a sacrifice in order to show that Roman Catholics are pagans. One occasionally does, however, find brief comparisons between gentile blood sacrifice and the Crucifixion; see, for example, Donne, *Bianthanatos*, 53, and Melanchthon's comment on Isaiah 53 (quoted in chapter 4 at note 16).

68. Sir John Suckling, *An Account of Religion by Reason* (1646), in *The*

Works of Sir John Suckling, ed. Thomas Clayton, 2 vols. (Oxford: Clarendon, 1971), 2:173; Hooker, *Ecclesiastical Polity* 5.78.3. See also the notes to Hebrews 13:14 in the Geneva and Bishops' Bibles.

69. Saxl, "Pagan Sacrifice"; Margaret T. Hodgen, *Early Anthropology in the Sixteenth and Seventeenth Centuries* (Philadelphia: University of Pennsylvania Press), 309.

70. Hodgen, *Early Anthropology*, 238, 302–3, 339; Bohatec, *Calvin*, 18; Pagden, *The Fall of Natural Man*, 174–75.

71. Cicero, *Tusculan Disputations*, trans. J. E. King, Loeb Classical Library (London: W. Heinemann, 1927), 1.13; Hooker, *Laws* 1.8.3.

72. *Digest* 1.1.9, in the *Corpus juris civilis*, ed. Paul Krueger and Theodor Mommsen, 3 vols. (Berlin: Weidmann, 1954).

73. For example, the *jus naturale* sometimes means instinctual behaviors common to men and animals (Ulpian); sometimes, as in Gaius, the dictates of natural reason; sometimes the laws of unfallen nature (as in the claim that natural law disallows slavery and private property), in which case the *jus gentium* is used to designate the fundamental laws of fallen existence, although elsewhere the distinction between the *jus naturale* and *jus gentium* does not distinguish pristine from fallen nature.

74. On natural law, see Charles S. Edwards, *Hugo Grotius, the Miracle of Holland: A Study in Political and Legal Thought*, intro. Richard A. Falk (Chicago: Nelson Hall, 1981), 27–113; Frederick Pollock, "The History of the Law of Nature: A Preliminary Study," *Columbia Law Review* 1 (1901): 11–32, and "The Sources of International Law," *Columbia Law Review* 2 (1902): 518–24.

75. The last two fields are interrelated, since in the hands of the Spanish theological jurists the study of international law, especially the *jus belli*, frequently centered on the legitimacy of the colonization of the Indies; see Pagden, *The Fall of Natural Man*, 107.

76. Bodin, *Method*, 8.

77. Hodgen, *Early Anthropology*, 277; Franklin, *Bodin*, 68–74.

78. Bodin, *Method*, 35.

79. Ibid., 298–99.

80. However, some Protestants—for example, Oldendorp and Selden—rejected the notion that natural laws, which are based on reason and divine authority, can be derived from the shared customs of fallen humanity; see Selden, *De jure naturali*, 73–98; Carl von Kallenborn, *Die Vorlaufer des Hugo Grotius auf dem Gebiete des jus naturae et gentium* (1848; rpt. Frankfurt: Antiquariat Sauer & Auvermann, 1965), 2.12–13.

81. Gentili, *De jure belli* 1.1. Cf. van der Molen, *Gentili*, 199–205.

82. Nevertheless, this empirically derived natural law has, as in Hooker, a transcendent ontological foundation, since the practices and beliefs common to

all cultures manifest the innate principles inscribed by God in the human heart (*De jure belli* 1.1).

83. This is basically Grotius's position in *The Jurisprudence of Holland*, begun only two years after *De satisfactione*.

84. De Soto, *De justitia* 3.1.3. The work was first published in 1553/54; De Soto brought out a revised edition in 1556/57—the text cited here; there were twenty-seven further editions before 1600.

85. Hooker, *Laws* 1.7.4.

86. De Soto, *De justitia* 9.1.1. De Soto is echoing Aquinas's discussion in *Summa Theologiae* 2.2.85.

87. Pagden, *The Fall of Natural Man*, 122.

88. On the relation between the *jus gentium, jus naturale*, and Thomist discussions of Spanish colonial policy, see Pagden, *The Fall of Natural Man*, 62–65. See also his discussion of Las Casas, 119–45.

89. Manuel Gimenez Fernandez, "Fray Bartolome de Las Casas: A Biographical Sketch," in *Bartolome de Las Casas in History: Toward an Understanding of the Man and His Work*, ed. Juan Friede and Benjamin Keen (De Kalb: Northern Illinois University Press, 1971), 109; and, in the same volume, Angel Losada, "The Controversy Between Sepulveda and Las Casas in the Junta of Valladolid, 279–308.

90. Bartolome de Las Casas, *In Defense of the Indians*, trans. Stafford Poole (De Kalb: Northern Illinois University Press, 1974), 228–29, 226, 234, 221.

91. Las Casas, *Defense*, 230, 222.

92. Cf. Donne, *Biathanatos*: "Immolation of Men was so ordinary that *allmost every Nation, though not barbarous, had receiv'd it*. The *Druides* of *France* made theyr Devinuations from Sacrifices of Men. And, in theyr warres, they presaged allso after the same fashion. And, for our tymes, it appears by the *Spanish* relations, That in onely *Hespaniola* they Sacrificed yearely 20000 children" (43).

93. Las Casas, *Defense*, 238.

94. Hamilton, *Political Thought*, 30, 128–29, 155–56.

95. Greenblatt, *Marvelous Possessions*, 131–32.

96. Cf. Michel Foucault, *The Order of Things: An Archaeology of the Human Sciences* (New York: Random House, 1970), 54.

97. John Bossy, *Christianity in the West: 1400–1700* (Oxford: Oxford University Press, 1985), 169.

98. See Pagden, *The Fall of Natural Man*, 78–79; Michel de Montaigne, *The Complete Essays of Montaigne*, trans. Donald Frame (Stanford: Stanford University Press, 1958), 2.12, pp. 432–33.

99. The English edition of 1974 seems to have been the first published version; a facsimile edition of the Latin manuscript, the *Argumentum apologiae adversus Genesium Sepulvedam*, ed. Angel Losada, came out the next year in

Madrid. Las Casas's *Apologetica historia,* which also treats Amerindian sacrifices, likewise remained in manuscript until this century.

100. Las Casas does, at one point, suggest that the sacrifice of Isaac may have been the origin of all human sacrifice, for when other nations heard that the "all-powerful God of the Jews" had commanded Abraham to offer his son, they concluded such gifts would be acceptable to God (*Defense,* 239–41).

101. Compare Grotius's conclusion "verus tamen Sacerdos fuit & vera victima. . . . non figurate dictam, sed maxime veram, quippe cum sacerdotium ipsius Levitico sacerdotio, quod verum fuit sacerdotium, opponantur, ut ejusdem generis species perfectior, alteri speciei minus perfectae" (338) with Calvin: "The sacrificial victims which were offered under the law to atone for sins . . . were so called, not because they were capable of recovering God's favor or wiping out iniquity but because they prefigured a true sacrifice such as was finally accomplished in reality by Christ alone" (*Institutes* 4.18.13).

102. Thus, the more theologically conservative late seventeenth-century exegete Abraham Calov complained (in Ludwig Diestel's words) that Grotius "citire uberreich Klassiker, als ob Heidenthum und Gottesoffenbarung dasselbe seien" (*Geschichte,* 404).

103. The Socinian implications of Grotius's posthumous Pauline commentaries were the subject of a pamphlet debate between Henry Hammond and the rigidly orthodox Calvinist John Owen; see Hammond's *A second defense of the learned Hugo Grotius* (London, 1655), to which Owen responded with *A review of the Annotations of Hugo Grotius, in reference unto the doctrine of the deity and satisfaction of Christ* (Oxford, 1656), which in turn occasioned Hammond's *A continuation of the defense of Hugo Grotius in an answer to the review of his Annotations* (London, 1657).

104. Hodgen, *Early Anthropology,* 349; Allen, *Noah,* 117–19; Grafton, *Scaliger* 1:176.

105. "Necessarium ergo fuit sacrificium institui, quod religio Christiana quotidie Deo suo offerret. . . . Alioqui ut dicebamus, inferior obscuriorque hac parte esset lex nostra, non modo quam vetus, verum & quam lex naturae" (*De justitia* 9.2.1). There is a remarkable passage in the *Discorsi sopra Deche di Tito Livio* where Machiavelli laments the passing of blood sacrifice: "When I meditated on the reason why people were more in love with freedom in those ancient times than they are now, I saw it was because they have grown weaker now than formerly, which is a result of the difference in education, this again being based on the difference of their religion from ours. . . . This may be seen from . . . the magnificence of their sacrifices as compared with ours. There is more delicacy than splendor in our display, and no ferocious or jubilant action whatsoever. There was no lack of display then, nor lack of magnificence in their ceremonies, but added to it was the action of the sacrifice full of blood and ferocity, where a multitude of animals were slaughtered; which sight, being so terrible, made man behave likewise" (2.2; quoted in Saxl, "Pagan Sacrifice,"

367). See also Greenblatt, *Marvelous Possessions*, 47–48. A similar flickering modernist nostalgia for the unembarrassed and unambiguous blood rituals of pre-Christian religion can be glimpsed in Grotius; the perception of the distance between modern and archaic cultures engendered ambivalent emotions from very early on.

106. Quoted in Las Casas, *Defense*, 223, from Lactantius's *Divinarum institutionum*, 1.21, and *Problemata*, 465.

107. Stephen D. Benin, "Sacrifice as Education in Augustine and Chrysostom," *Church History* 52 (1983): 10, 16; Frances M. Young, *The Use of Sacrificial Ideas in Greek Christian Writers from the New Testament to John Chrysostom*, Patristic Monograph Series 5 (Cambridge, Mass.: Philadelphia Patristic Foundation, 1979), 87. Funkenstein offers the fascinating suggestion that this patristic/medieval explanation of Israelite sacrifice led, during the Renaissance, to a "search for correspondences and concordances of legal, religious, and political institutions that express the *qualitas temporum*" and hence that sixteenth-century legal historicism may itself have been inspired by the traditional Christian explanation of sacrifice (*Theology and the Scientific Imagination*, 241).

108. Greenblatt, *Marvelous Possessions*, 134, 136.

109. Ibid., 138; for the crucial, although concealed, presence of the Christian understanding of the Atonement in anthropological theory up through the twentieth century, see Detienne, "Culinary Practices," 13–20.

110. Foucault, *The Order of Things*, 32.

111. "O Nimium facilis . . .," in *De Dichtwerken van Hugo Grotius*, ed. B. L. Meulenbroek (Assen: Van Gorcum, 1977), I:2a:2, p. 129, ll. 75–82; the translation is from Gellenik, *Grotius*, 32.

112. Simon Schama, *The Embarrassment of Riches: An Interpretation of Dutch Culture in the Golden Age* (Berkeley: University of California Press, 1988), 29–33. Schama also records the interesting fact that "in Leiden, bread and herrings—the food that had been distributed immediately after the siege was lifted—was symbolically shared around the citizenry every October third, in a kind of historical eucharist" (93), replacing the rejected supper of van der Werff's body and blood.

3. THE DEATH OF CHRIST

1. Helen C. White, *The Tudor Books of Private Devotion* (Madison: University of Wisconsin Press, 1951), 246–47; cf. Sacvan Bercovitch, *The Puritan Origins of the American Self* (New Haven: Yale University Press, 1975), 25; Bossy, *Christianity in the West*, 94.

2. For example, the passion sermons of Thomas Adams and Lancelot Andrewes. The only Lutheran exemplar I have come across is Foxe's passion sermon: *A Sermon of Christ crucified, preached at Paules Crosse* (1570), in *The*

English Sermons of John Foxe, intro. Warren Wooden (Delmar, N.Y.: Scholars' Facsimiles, 1978). Sibbes's passion sermons are anomalous; they seem influenced by the Calvinist paradigm, but all the hard edges have been softened, and I am primarily interested in hard edges.

3. Rather than confuse the reader with a lot of inessential information about these minor figures, I have generally chosen to cite in the text the works of Heinsius, Calvin, Hall, and (later) Nashe, mentioning the more obscure works in the footnotes. But a brief comment on these authors (based on the *DNB, STC,* and title pages of individual works) is not out of place.

Thomas Wilson (1563–1622): From 1586 to his death, Wilson was the rector of St. George the Martyr at Canterbury, although more than once he was accused of nonconformity. *Christs Farewell to Jerusalem and last Prophesie* was preached at the funeral of Doctor Colfe, vice dean of Canterbury Cathedral, on October 12, 1613, and published in London the next year. Wilson describes himself on the title page as "Minister of Gods word," suggesting Puritan sympathies.

Samuel Walsall (d. 1626): At the time of his death, Walsall was master of Corpus Christi, Cambridge; *The Life and Death of Jesus Christ* (Cambridge, 1607) was originally preached before James at Royston and printed five times between 1607 and 1622. The sermon is not exclusively "Calvinist," since it quotes extensively from Saint Bernard (who was, however, the one medieval theologian frequently cited by Calvinists).

Thomas Ailesbury [Aylesbury] (fl. 1622–59): The *DNB* describes Ailesbury as a Calvinist theologian. *The Passion Sermon at Pauls-Crosse, upon Good-Friday last* was published in London in 1626.

Bartholomew Chamberlaine, D.D.: *The Passion of Christ, and the Benefits thereby* (London, 1613) was first printed in 1584 and again, with variants, in 1613, 1615, and 1623.

Henry Jacob (1563–1624): Jacob was a Brownist and founder of first congregational church in England. *A Treatise of the Sufferings and Victory of Christ, in the work of our redemption* (London, 1597) was composed during one of Jacob's returns from exile, in response to Bishop Bilson's 1597 Paul's Cross sermon on Christ's descent into hell.

The only poem I have used is Nicholas Breton's "The Countesse of Penbrook's Passion," in vol. 1 of *The Works in Verse and Prose,* 2 vols., ed. Alexander Grosart, Chertsey Worthies' Library (1879; rpt. New York: AMS Press, 1966). This poem begins like the Calvinist passions, although it ends rather differently.

4. On the role of myth in relieving anxiety, see William J. Bouwsma, "Anxiety and the Formation of Early Modern Culture," in his *A Usable Past: Essays in European Cultural History* (Berkeley: University of California Press,1990), 157–89; Paul Ricoeur, *The Symbolism of Evil,* trans. Emerson Buchanan, Religious Perspectives 17 (New York: Harper and Row, 1967), 5, 167–68.

5. Charles and Elaine Hallet, *The Revenger's Madness: A Study of Revenge Tragedy Motifs* (Lincoln: University of Nebraska Press, 1980), 111; cf. Martin Mueller, *Children of Oedipus and Other Essays on the Imitation of Greek Tragedy, 1550–1800* (Toronto: University of Toronto Press, 1980), 25; Michael Shaw, "The Female Intruder: Women in Fifth-Century Drama," *Classical Philology* 70 (1975): 258n.

6. One might also add here the Renaissance transformation of Terentian comedy into the tragic prodigal son plays discussed by Richard Helgerson in *The Elizabethan Prodigals* (Berkeley: University of California Press, 1976), 3, 35.

7. This resemblance suggests that although Grotius's treatment of the Atonement is unprecedented, it is not merely anomalous; its disturbing acknowledgment of the violence lurking within Christian formularies does not distinguish *De satisfactione* from Calvinist orthodoxy but rather locates it within the discourses of the Protestant end myth.

8. William Empson, *Seven Types of Ambiguity*, 2d ed. (1947; rpt. New York: New Directions, 1966), 226–33; see also Louis Martz, *The Poetry of Meditation: A Study in English Religious Literature of the Seventeenth Century*, rev. ed. (New Haven: Yale University Press, 1962), 90–96. In fact, the Calvinist passion narratives evince much of the sadistic perversity that Empson attributes to Christianity as a whole in the final chapter of *Milton's God* (London: Chatto and Windus, 1961); unlike Professor Empson, however, I do not find this perversity typical of or intrinsic to Christianity.

9. Jean Delumeau, *Sin and Fear: The Emergence of a Western Guilt Culture, Thirteenth–Eighteenth Centuries*, trans. Eric Nicholson (New York: St. Martin's, 1990), 242–43.

10. Huldrich Zwingli, *A briefe rehersal of the death resurrection, & ascention of Christ* (London, c. 1561), 122.

11. Calvin, *Harmony* 3:240–41, 253, 256, 278, 281, 317.

12. Daniel Heinsius, *The Mirrour of Humilitie: or two eloquent and acute Discourses upon the Nativitie and Passion of Christ*, trans. I. H. (London, 1618), 63–64; Joseph Hall, *The Works*, ed. Philip Wynter, 10 vols. (Oxford: At the University Press, 1863), 2:647; Chamberlaine, *The Passion of Christ*, A5(v).

13. Heinsius, *The Mirrour*, 77.

14. Hall, *Works* 2:662.

15. Heinsius, *The Mirrour*, 70; cf. Hall, *Works* 2:641; Calvin, *Harmony* 3:248. The claim that the Jews killed Christ out of malice rather than ignorance is traditional; see Gavin Langmuir, *History, Religion, and Antisemitism* (Berkeley: University of California Press, 1990), 288.

16. This representation of agency in terms of inner moral or spiritual states—i.e., the soul or conscience—disappears from the scholarly commentaries discussed in chapter 1, which interpret the biblical narratives in terms of public, cultural logics rather than the orientation of the soul toward Good or

Evil. The point of this shift seems to be, at least in part, to remove the symbolic underpinnings of post-Reformation religious violence: the identification of one's opponent as the local incarnation of Evil. The scholarly exegetes depict Christ's persecutors as bureaucratic functionaries, not deicidal fiends. In this sense, their erasure of the soul performs an Erasmian exorcism; it is an attempt to banish demons from historical interpretation.

17. Elaine Scarry, *The Body in Pain: The Making and Unmaking of the World* (New York: Oxford University Press, 1985), 58.

18. This identification of Christ's torturers with the cultural other is powerfully inverted in Bartolome de Las Casas's *Brevisima relacion de la Destruycion de las Indias occidentales* (1539), twice translated into English during the Renaissance: once as *The Spanish Colonie* (trans. M. M. S. [London, 1583]) and then as *The Tears of the Indians* (trans. John Phillips [London, 1656; rpt. Stanford, Calif.: Academic Reprints, 1953]). In the opening chapter of the earlier edition, Las Casas describes the Indians as "very humble, very patient, very desirous of peace making, and peacefull. . . . very gentle, and very tender. . . . very poore folke, which possesse litle, neither yet do so much as desire to have much worldly goodes. . . . lambes so meeke" (A[r]–A2[v]). In my UCLA library copy, someone has written next to this description, "noble savage." This marginalium, however, is incorrect; Las Casas's adjectives cast the Indians as types of Christ, not savages, whether noble or otherwise. Conversely, Las Casas depicts the Spaniards in the same language used for Christ's torturers in the passion narratives; they are "as wolves, as lions, & and as tigres most cruel" (A2[v]). One's impressions that Las Casas is describing the Spanish conquest as a version of the Crucifixion—and that the Catholic Spaniards intended that *imitatio*—are confirmed by the dreadful story of how the soldiers "made certayne Gibbets long and low, in such sort, that the feete of the hanged on, touched in a maner the ground, every one enough for thirteeve [*sic*], in the honour and worship of our Saviour and his twelve Apostles (as they used to speake) and setting to fire, burned them all quick that were fastened" (A4[v]). A similar irony occurs in Montaigne's essay on cannibals, but Las Casas's evocation of the Passion makes the inversion of the conventional contrast between barbarian and Christian more bitterly tragic.

19. Heinsius, *The Mirrour*, 55–57; cf. Hall, *Works* 2:646; Calvin, *Harmony* 3:263, 329.

20. Since most of these printed texts were originally preached, "hearer/reader" might be the more accurate term for their audience, but to avoid such unidiomatic awkwardness, "reader" will have to stand for both.

21. This is the principal point of the two Elizabethan homilies for Good Friday, especially the first, which explains at the outset that if we consider "that for our sins this most innocent Lamb was driven to death, we shall have much more cause to bewail ourselves, that we were the cause of his death, than to cry out of the malice and cruelty of the Jews, which pursued him to his death"

(*The Two Books of Homilies Appointed to be Read in Churches,* ed. John Griffiths [Oxford: Oxford University Press, 1859], 412).

22. Hall, *Works* 5:41.

23. Heinsius, *The Mirrour*, 65.

24. Chamberlaine, *The Passion of Christ*, C3(v).

25. Ibid., B8(r). In Calvin, however, the emphasis does not fall on tenderness but self-control (see below).

26. Heinsius, *The Mirrour*, 76–77.

27. Hall, *Works* 2:655. These outbursts of hatred are not a standard feature of Renaissance passion sermons; they do not occur in either Andrewes or Adams and are explicitly rejected in the first Homily. Since there were only a handful of Jews in pre–Civil War England, I doubt that they are literally anti-Semitic (i.e., intended to arouse hatred towards real Jews); on the uses and dangers of this sort of figurative anti-Semitism, see Stephen Greenblatt, "Marlowe, Marx, and Anti-Semitism," in his *Learning to Curse: Essays in Early Modern Culture* (New York: Routledge, 1990), 40–41.

28. Hall, *Works* 5:45.

29. Calvin, *Harmony* 3:295.

30. Hall, *Works* 2:654.

31. Calvin, *Harmony* 3:257.

32. Calvin, *Harmony* 3:289.

33. Hall, *Works* 2:655.

34. Emile Mâle, *Religious Art from the Twelfth to the Eighteenth Century,* Bollingen 90 (Princeton: Princeton University Press, 1982), 101–13.

35. Terence Cave, *Devotional Poetry in France, c. 1570–1613* (Cambridge: At the University Press, 1969), 55.

36. Richard Strier, "Changing the Object: George Herbert and Excess," *George Herbert Journal* 2 (1978): 26.

37. Hall, *Works* 2:654, 661.

38. Heinsius, *The Mirrour*, 63.

39. Ibid., 59.

40. Walsall, *The Life and Death*, D2(v).

41. Ibid., D2(r); Hall, *Works* 2:662. See also Samuel Clark, *The Blessed Life and Meritorious Death of our Lord & Saviour Jesus Christ* (London, 1664), 51; Ailesbury, *The Passion Sermon*, 18–19; Hall, *Works* 5:37; Heinsius, *The Mirrour*, 59, 63.

42. Scarry, *The Body in Pain*, 53.

43. E.g., Calvin, *Harmony* 3:223, 288, 299; Hall, *Works* 5:34–35.

44. Clark, *The Blessed Life*, 54.

45. Calvin, *Harmony* 3:290; see also 3:259, 275, 282, 298; Jacob, *A Treatise*, 27; Hall, *Works* 5:47.

46. Heinsius, *The Mirrour*, 89.

47. Calvin, *Harmony* 3:304; also 3:276, 279, 291; cf. Bouwsma, *Calvin*, 184.

48. Ailesbury, *The Passion Sermon*, 29; Heinsius, *The Mirrour*, 62; see also Hall, *Works* 2:662, 5:35.

49. Erasmus, *Disputatiuncula de taedio, pavore, tristitia Jesu, instante supplicio crucis* (1503), in *Opera omnia*, ed. Joannes Clericus, 11 vols. (1703–1706; rpt. Hildesheim: Georg Olms, 1962), 5:1289–90.

50. On the tortured Christ as a beautiful youth, see John Heigham, *The Life of our Blessed Lord and Saviour Jesus, Gathered out of . . . Saint Bonaventure*, 2d ed. (Douai, 1622), 572.

51. Jon. Augustinus Dietelmaier, *Historia dogmatis de descensu Christi ad Inferos litteraria* (Nürnberg, 1741), 160–91; Jacob, *A Treatise*.

52. Hall, *Works* 5:47; Heinsius, *The Mirrour*, 74–75. See also Calvin, *Harmony* 3:285; *Institutes* 2.16.6, 2.16.11.

53. Since the reader (or auditor) and author generally share the same textualized subject position—usually as members of a comprehensive "we"—I will henceforth refer to the implicit reader/author/auditor simply as "the reader."

54. So too in Greville's *Caelica* 99, it is syntactically unclear whether the refrain's "deprived of human graces and divine" refers back to an implicit "I" or to the "saving Lord" of the subsequent line (in *Five Courtier Poets of the English Renaissance*, ed. Robert Bender [New York: Washington Square Press, 1967], 552–53); see also Bouwsma, *Calvin*, 92.

55. A similar rhetoric is at work in Shakespeare's *Lucrece*, where the delicately erotic portrayal of the heroine seems designed to titillate the (male) reader into a guilty half identification with the rapist, a complicity that does not cancel out ethical judgment but complicates it.

56. George K. Hunter makes a similar point about *The Spanish Tragedy*: "Kyd establishes a new relationship between tyrant and victim, presenting them as quasi-psychological polarities set up by a single mind rather than social polarities or religious opposites" ("Tyrant and Martyr: Religious Heroisms in Elizabethan Tragedy," in *Poetic Traditions of the English Renaissance*, ed. Maynard Mack and George deForest Lord [New Haven: Yale University Press, 1982], 94).

57. On the pieta at the end of *Lear*, see C. L. Barber, "The Family in Shakespeare's Development: Tragedy and Sacredness," in *Representing Shakespeare: New Psychoanalytic Essays*, ed. Murray Schwartz and Coppélia Kahn (Baltimore: Johns Hopkins University Press, 1980), 200.

58. On the loss of the "benign Holy Mother" in Protestantism, see Barber, "The Family," 196.

59. *Stabat Mater*, in *The Oxford Book of Medieval Latin Verse*, ed. F. J. E. Raby (Oxford: Clarendon, 1959), 436.

60. Calvin, *Harmony* 3:293.

61. Ailesbury, *The Passion Sermon*, 25.

62. Leo the Great, *The Letters and Sermons*, trans. Charles L. Feltoe,

Nicene and Post-Nicene Fathers, 2d ser., 12 (Grand Rapids, Mich.: Eerdmans, 1979), 179.

63. Or, more correctly, the incarnate Christ is a divine *person* with both a divine and a human *nature*. In terms of orthodox Christology, then, Christ's human nature is *not* personal; he assumes our humanity, not his own. The last third of the *Summa Theologica* spells out the psychological implications of this unique compound with vermiculate precision.

64. Franks, *The Work of Christ*, 244.

65. Caroline Bynum, "The Body of Christ in the Later Middle Ages: A Reply to Leo Steinberg," *Renaissance Quarterly* 39 (1986): 399–439.

66. The essay would have been widely known, since later it was often published together with the *Enchiridion*. The best modern study of the *Disputatiuncula* can be found in John B. Gleason's *John Colet* (Berkeley: University of California Press, 1989), 94–125; see also J. H. Lupton's *A Life of John Colet, D.D.*, 2d ed. (London: George Bell, 1909), 100–109. All references to the *Disputatiuncula* will appear in the text.

67. "At tu [Colet] mihi in Christo Chimaeram quandam fabricaris, absolutissimam caritatem, cum acerbissima reformidatione, velut aquam igni commiscens" (1279). For the Thomist elements in Erasmus's argument, see Franks, *The Work of Christ*, 216, 222.

68. Fulke Greville, *Mustapha*, in *Poems and Dramas of Fulke Greville, First Lord Brooke*, ed. Geoffrey Bullough, 2 vols. (Edinburgh: Oliver and Boyd, 1939), 2:136.

69. Henry Vaughan's "Jesus weeping [II]" seems to allude to Erasmus's argument here, first disagreeing with it, then assenting: "Should not thy sighs refrain thy store / Of tears, and not provoke to more? / Since two afflictions may not raign / In one at one time, as some feign / . . . Dear Lord! thou art all grief and love, / But which thou are most, none can prove" (ll. 14–17, 22–23; in *Major Poets of the Earlier Seventeenth Century*, ed. Barbara Lewalski and Andrew Sabol [Indianapolis: Odyssey, 1973], 555).

70. Calvin, *Harmony* 3:230.

71. Ibid. 3:226; cf. 3:232–33; *Institutes* 2.16.11–12; Hall, *Works* 2:633–34; Jacob, *A Treatise*, 56.

72. Calvin, *Harmony* 3:318–19.

73. Calvin, *Institutes* 3.2.15–17; cf. Bouwsma, *Calvin*, 184–85.

74. Calvin, *Institutes* 3.2.18.

75. Ibid. 3.2.18

76. Calvin, *Commentary upon the Epistle of Saint Paul to the Romans*, trans. Christopher Rosdell (1583), ed. Henry Beveridge (Edinburgh: Calvin Translation Society, 1844), 181–90.

77. Montaigne, *The Complete Essays*, 2.1, p. 239. The Calvinist interpretation of Romans 7 sparked intense controversy during this period. Arminians (and anti-Calvinists generally) denied that the Pauline agon between flesh and

spirit applied to the regenerate precisely because they wished to affirm, contra Calvin, that grace does allow the elect to achieve a stable and unified selfhood.

78. Calvin, *Harmony* 3:233.

79. Heinsius, *The Mirrour*, 84. The same division of the self into flesh (Turk) and priest (Venetian) lurks behind Othello's presentation of his own suicide/sacrifice: "in Aleppo once, / Where a malignant and a turban'd Turk / Beat a Venetian and traduc'd the state, / I took by the throat the circumcised dog, / And smote him thus" (*Othello*, ed. Tucker Brooke and Lawrence Mason, The Yale Shakespeare [New Haven: Yale University Press, 1947], 5.2.352–56).

80. Hall, *Works* 5:384–85.

81. Calvin, *Harmony* 3:202; Chamberlaine, *The Passion of Christ*, A6(r), B8(r), C2(r); see also Ailesbury, *The Passion Sermon*, 32; Heinsius, *The Mirrour*, 95.

82. John Owen, *The Duty of Pastors and People Distinguished* (London, 1644), 24. See also Donne's "The Crosse": "Then are you your own physicke, or need none, / When Still'd, or purg'd by tribulation. / For when that Crosse ungrudg'd, unto you stickes, / Then are you to your selfe, a Crucifixe" (in *The Complete English Poems of John Donne*, ed. by C. A. Patrides [London: Dent, 1985], ll. 29–32).

83. Michael Schoenfeldt, *Prayer and Power: George Herbert and Renaissance Courtship* (Chicago: University of Chicago Press, 1991), 130.

84. Chamberlaine, *The Passion of Christ*, C2(r).

85. Quoted in Bouwsma, *Calvin*, 183. It is helpful to compare these evocations of self-crucifixion to the more traditional imagery of contemporary Roman Catholic devotion; Lorenzo Scupoli's *Spiritual Combat* (1589) thus recommends that the reader "consider yourself as on the field of battle, facing the enemy and bound by the iron-clad law—ether fight or die. Imagine the enemy before you, that particular vice or disorderly passion that you are trying to conquer. . . . At the same time, picture at your right Jesus Christ, your Invincible Leader, accompanied by the Blessed Virgin, St. Joseph, whole companies of angels and saints. . . . At your left is Lucifer and his troops, ready to support the passion or vice you are fighting" (quoted in Martz, *The Poetry of Meditation*, 126). In such combat, aggression is directed against an alien intruder (vice, passion, Lucifer) rather than the self; the symbols represent the scene as a heroic combat rather than a form of torture; the conflict takes place in an "impersonal" arena, populated by objective, supernatural presences, rather than in the private, interior solitude of the chimerical self.

86. Michael Walzer, *The Revolution of the Saints: A Study in the Origins of Radical Politics* (New York: Atheneum, 1974), 24–25. See also W. Haller's remark that "the Puritan saga did not cherish the memory of Christ . . . on the cross. . . . The mystic passion was the crucifixion of the new man by the old and the true propitiation the sacrifice of the old to the new" (*The Rise of Puritanism* [New York: Columbia University Press, 1938], 151).

87. Hall, *Works* 5:36.

88. Calvin, *Harmony* 3:234, 319; cf. Hall, *Works* 2:634, 660; 5:36–38; Ailesbury, *The Passion Sermon*, 15–16; Heinsius, *The Mirrour*, 54.

89. See Lynda Boose's observation that "the father-son relationship is repeatedly mythologized as a potentially patricidal struggle for authority. . . . If the narrative includes a third person, it is a woman (usually the mother), who objectifies this mutual desire. Her presence, however, essentially only intensifies, and does not prevent or redraw, the collision-course formula" ("The Father's House and the Daughter in It: The Structures of Western Culture's Daughter-Father Relationship," in *Daughters and Fathers*, ed. Lynda Boose and Betty Flowers [Baltimore: Johns Hopkins University Press, 1989], 32). On the father-son agon in Shakespeare, see Barber, "The Family," 189.

90. Heigham, *The Life of our Blessed Lord . . . Gathered out of . . . Saint Bonaventure*, 600–601.

91. Jacob, *A Treatise*, 80, 33; Calvin, *Institutes* 2.16.8–12, and *Psychopannychia; Or, a Refutation of the Error that the Soul Sleeps in the Interval Between Death and the Judgment*, in *Tracts and Treatises in Defense of the Reformed Faith*, trans. Henry Beveridge, ed. Thomas Torrance 3 vols. (Grand Rapids, Mich.: Eerdmans, 1958), 3:480–81; Hall, *Works* 2:635.

92. Hall, *Works* 2:664.

93. Chamberlaine, *The Passion of Christ*, B3(v).

94. Hall, *Works* 5:39; cf. Calvin, *Harmony* 3:225–26.

95. Calvin, *Harmony* 3:304.

96. Ibid. 3:242, 269, 295, 307–8, 310, 321; Wilson, *Christs Farewell*, D5(r)-D6(v).

97. Hall, *Works* 5:42.

98. Heinsius, *The Mirrour*, 74.

99. Hall, *Works* 5:39–40, 2:664; Calvin, *Harmony* 3:318.

100. Jacob, *A Treatise*, 42.

101. Heinsius, *The Mirrour*, 75; Ailesbury, *The Passion Sermon*, 18.

102. Hall, *Works* 5:47; cf. Calvin, *Harmony* 3:296.

103. Heinsius, *The Mirrour*, 73, 75.

104. Hall, *Works* 5:25, 38; cf. Jacob, *A Treatise*, 45; Chamberlaine, *The Passion of Christ*, A4(v).

105. Heinsius, *The Mirrour*, 65.

106. See Gustav Aulén, *Christus Victor: An Historical Study of the Three Main Types of the Idea of the Atonement*, trans. A. G. Herbert, intro. J. Pelikan (London: SPCK, 1970), 101–22.

107. Hall, *Works* 2:653.

108. George Sandys, *The Poetical Works of George Sandys*, 2 vols., ed. Richard Hooper (London, 1872), 2:409.

109. Hall, *Works* 5:42.

110. Wilson, *Christs Farewell*, C3(v)–C3(r). See also the comment by the

Puritan Christopher Love: "If preaching of Terrour be legal preaching, then the Law was more preacht in the new Testament that ever it was under the old. . . . the Gospell is more backt with terrour, and with the doctrines of hell and damnation, than ever the law was" (quoted in Delumeau, *Sin and Fear*, 502).

111. Calvin, *Harmony* 3:289; cf. Hall, *Works* 2:655; Heinsius, *The Mirrour*, 79.

112. Calvin, *Harmony* 3:293; cf. Wilson, *Christs Farewell*, B3(v), E5.

113. So, he continues, Christians should pray for their persecutors in the cheerful confidence that God will destroy them anyway (*Harmony* 3:300–1).

114. Hall, *Works* 5:37; cf. Calvin, *Harmony* 3:328; Ailesbury, *The Passion Sermon*, 21.

115. Calvin, *Harmony* 3:288. Richard Helgerson's discussion of Foxe presents interesting parallels: "Misled by its reputation . . . we expect the violence in Foxe's *Book of Martyrs* to go all one way. And certainly there is much to support that expectation. The persecutions and martyrdoms of those whom Foxe considers members of the true church of Christ are the book's most persistent subject. But God's punishment of persecutors makes a strong countertheme. Not every persecutor suffers, at least not in this world, but a great many do"—often in particularly grisly ways (*Forms of Nationhood*, 255).

116. Peter Brown thus describes the ideal monk of fourth-century Egyptian asceticism as "a man who had gained a heart that was all of one piece, a heart as unriven by the knotted grain of private, unshared meanings and of private, covert intentions as was the solid, milk-white heart of the date-palm" (*The Body and Society: Men, Women, and Sexual Renunciation in Early Christianity* [New York: Columbia University Press, 1988], 227).

117. Bouwsma, *Calvin*, 179–80; cf. Bercovitch, *Puritan Origins*, 18–21.

118. Breton, "The Countesse of Penbrook's Passion," stanza 54; Thomas Nashe, *Christs Teares over Jerusalem*, in *The Works of Thomas Nashe*, ed. Ronald B. McKerrow and F. P. Wilson, 5 vols. (Oxford: Basil Blackwell, 1958), 2:58; Shakespeare, *King Lear*, ed. Tucker Brooke and William Phelps, The Yale Shakespeare (New Haven: Yale University Press, 1917), 3.4.73. By contrast, Crashaw's "soft self-wounding Pelican! / Whose brest weepes Balm for wounded man" (ll. 45–46) emblematizes Christ's compassion and human suffering ("The Hymn of Sainte Thomas in Adoration of the Blessed Sacrament," in *Major Poets of the Earlier Seventeenth Century*, ed. Barbara Lewalski and Andrew Sabol [Indianapolis: Odyssey, 1973], 689).

119. Thomas Wilson, *Arte of Rhetorique* (1553), ed. Thomas J. Derrick, Renaissance Imagination 1 (New York: Garland, 1982), 87.

120. Walsall, *The Life and Death*, D2(r).

121. Calvin, *Harmony* 3:234; *Institutes* 2.16.12.

122. Shakespeare, *Lear* 5.3.40.

123. See Barber, "The Family," 191.

124. Sir Philip Sidney, *Astrophel and Stella* 106, in *Silver Poets of the Sixteenth Century*, ed. Gerald Bullett (London: Dent, 1947).

125. Charles Nicholl, *A Cup of News: The Life of Thomas Nashe* (London: Routledge and Kegan Paul, 1984), 166–67; Jonathan Crewe, *Unredeemed Rhetoric: Thomas Nashe and the Scandal of Authorship* (Baltimore: Johns Hopkins University Press, 1982), 59, 62.

126. Nashe, *Christs Teares*, 52. Further references to this work will be given in the text.

127. Shakespeare, *Othello* 5.2.5.

128. See Spenser's description of Lecherie in *The Faerie Queene* 1.4.24 (*The Complete Poetical Works of Edmund Spenser*, ed. R. E. Neil Dodge [Boston: Houghton Mifflin, 1908]).

129. Cf. Crewe, *Unredeemed Rhetoric*, 56–57.

130. Shakespeare, *Othello* 5.2.21–22. The parallels between *Christs Teares* and *Othello*, which Crewe also remarks (*Unredeemed Rhetoric*, 56), may not be fortuitous. J. J. M. Tobin has shown that Shakespeare's major tragedies repeatedly echo *Christs Teares*; see his "Nashe and *Othello*," *Notes and Queries* 31 (1984): 202–3; "*Macbeth* and *Christs Teares over Jerusalem*," *Aligarh Journal of English Studies* 7 (1982): 72–78; and "*Hamlet* and *Christ's Tears over Jerusalem*," *Aligarh Journal of English Studies* 6 (1981): 158–67. Addition evidence for this parallel appears in Ailesbury's *The Passion Sermon*, which quotes Bernard of Clairvaux to the effect that the crucified Christ, "like his Spouse the Church, is blacke" (29).

131. Delumeau, *Sin and Fear*, 96.

132. Norbert Elias, *Power and Civility*, vol. 2 of *The Civilizing Process*, trans. Edmund Jephcott, 2 vols. (New York: Pantheon Books, Random House, 1982), 230.

133. Delumeau, *Sin and Fear*, 298.

134. Richard C. McCoy, *Sir Philip Sidney: Rebellion in Arcadia* (New Brunswick: Rutgers University Press, 1979), 161.

135. Ibid., 207.

136. Similarly, in *The Rites of Knighthood: The Literature and Politics of Elizabethan Chivalry*, The New Historicism: Studies in Cultural Poetics (Berkeley: University of California Press, 1989), Richard McCoy notes that Daniel's *The Civil Wars* "is supposed to be a simple tale of crime and punishment and redemption, but redemption is indefinitely deferred, and crime and punishment 'as in a circle' are endlessly repeated" (108).

137. Bouwsma, "Anxiety," 167–73. Cf. Hugh Trevor-Roper, *Religion, the Reformation, and Social Change* (London: Macmillan, 1967), 58–61.

138. I am looking only at English texts, but I suspect similar claims could be made about Continental Calvinist literature, for example, D'Aubigne's *Tragiques* and Vondel's *Fall of Jerusalem*.

139. *A Larum for London* (1602), ed. W. W. Gregg, Malone Society Reprints (Oxford: Oxford University Press, 1913), ll. 74–84.

140. Thomas Deloney, *Canaans Calamitie, Jerusalems Misery* (1618), in *The Works of Thomas Deloney*, ed. Francis Oscar Mann (Oxford: Clarendon, 1912), 419–23.

141. *A Larum*, l. 90; Deloney, *Canaans Calamitie*, 419.

142. *A Larum*, ll. 8–10.

143. Ibid., ll. 86–88.

144. Ibid., ll. 833–34. The representation is strongly politically inflected; the good men in the play—Egmont and the English—are republican heroes, set in opposition to the barbaric, aristocratic men raping the civic lady; one is reminded of Shakespeare's *Lucrece*. The Protestant patriotism of the English and Dutch characters, like Brutus's Stoic republicanism, point toward a new civilizational order and new ideal of male responsibility.

145. Deloney, *Canaans Calamitie*, ll. 241, 247, 374, 377.

4. IPHIGENIA IN ISRAEL

1. Donne, "Holy Sonnet 4," in *The Complete English Poems*, 436.

2. In both New Testament and Classical Greek, *katharsis* (including the whole family of *katha-* terms) has a broad semantic range, covering medical purging (enemas, bloodletting, etc.), ablution, bathing, moral purity, stylistic correctness, and (in general) freedom from defilement, as well as sacrificial purification; the first and last senses, however, seem primary.

3. On the Aristotelian *katharsis*, see Gerald F. Else, *Aristotle's Poetics: The Argument* (Cambridge: Harvard University Press, 1967), 225–27; "Catharsis," in *Dictionary of the History of Ideas: Studies of Selected Pivotal Ideas*, ed. Philip Wiener, 5 vols. (New York: Scribner's, 1973), 1:264–70. Else's definition of *katharsis* as ritual purification from blood guilt (424) preserves the sense of expiation but at the same time obscures the fact that such purifications generally involved the shedding of blood: one expiates the pollution attendant on homicide by making sacrifice.

4. Grotius, *De satisfactione* 4:326–38.

5. In chapter 17—the only other reference to *katharsis* in the *Poetics*—Aristotle does use the term to mean ritual purification, but he is speaking specifically about Euripides' *Electra*, not tragedy in general.

6. Although Else argues that Aristotle never claimed that the *katharsis* of pity and fear was the tragic telos, he also notes that virtually all prior commentators on the *Poetics* (including all Renaissance commentators) understood it in this sense (*The Argument*, 439).

7. Walter Burkert, "Greek Tragedy and Sacrificial Ritual," *Greek, Roman, and Byzantine Studies* 7 (1966): 87–121; Robert N. Watson, "Tragedy," in

The Cambridge Companion to English Renaissance Drama, ed. A. R. Braunmuller and Michael Hattaway (Cambridge: Cambridge University Press, 1990), 307, 310.

8. "Postclassical" since *Christus patiens,* a cento of Euripides, has often been ascribed to Saint Gregory Nazianzen, although the attribution now seems doubtful.

9. The dates represent the *first* translation into either Latin or a modern language. While Helene P. Foley lists *Medea* and *Electra* among Euripides' sacrificial tragedies, at least according to modern classifications they seem closer to revenge tragedies, although the distinction may be anachronistic (e.g., Orestes' killing of Aegistus and Clytemnestra both avenges their murder of his father and purifies the state) (*Ritual Irony: Poetry and Sacrifice in Euripides* [Ithaca: Cornell University Press, 1985], 21).

10. Quoted in George Steiner, *Antigones* (New York: Oxford University Press, 1984), 45.

11. Guillaume Bude, I. Tusanus, and R. Constantinus, *Lexicon sive dictionarium Graecolatinum,* 2 vols. (n.p., 1562), 2:904.

12. Stephanus [Henry Estienne], *Thesaurus Graecae linguae,* rev. ed., 10 vols. (London, 1816–1828), 5:4671–72.

13. Poole, *Synopsis criticorum* 5:1324.

14. Calvin, *Commentaries on the Epistle of Paul the Apostle to the Hebrews,* trans. John Owen (Edinburgh: Calvin Translation Society, 1853), 213.

15. Stephanus, *Thesaurus* 5:4671; cf. Bude, *Lexicon* 2:903.

16. Quoted in Stanislas Lyonnet, *Sin, Redemption, and Sacrifice: A Biblical and Patristic Study,* ed. Leopold Sabourin, trans. Fidelis Buck, Analecta Biblica (Rome: Biblical Institute Press, 1970), 234–35. Calvin likewise describes Christ as an *'asham/katharma* (*Institutes* 2.16.6; *Commentary upon the Epistle of Saint Paul to the Romans,* 199).

17. Stephanus, *Thesaurus* 8:9932; cf. Bude, *Lexicon* 2:1890.

18. Poole, *Synopsis criticorum* 1:568–70; cf. *Biblia Sacra* (1617) 2:1045–50; Lyonnet, *Sin,* 241–42.

19. Poole, *Synopsis criticorum* 1:568; see Burkert, *Homo Necans: The Anthropology of Ancient Greek Sacrificial Ritual and Myth,* trans. Peter Bing (Berkeley: University of California Press, 1983), 16.

20. Stephanus, *Thesaurus* 5:4674; Bude, *Lexicon* 2:904.

21. Similarly, *purgatio* in Latin can mean both menstruation and expiatory sacrifice.

22. Bude, *Lexicon* 2:904; Stephanus, *Thesaurus* 5:4672.

23. At least on one occasion, an actual killing took place on stage. In his *Poeticarum institutionum libri tres* (in *Opera in sex tomos divisa* [Amsterdam, 1701] 3:91), Vossius recounts how Domitian ordered a criminal crucified and dismembered by a bear as part of a tragedy—not precisely a sacrifice, but for

Renaissance readers (I think) crucifixion would invariably carry sacrificial overtones.

24. Burkert, "Greek Tragedy," 88, 93. For the sacrificial origins of tragedy, see also Bennett Simon, *Tragic Drama and the Family: Psychoanalytic Studies from Aeschylus to Beckett* (New Haven: Yale University Press, 1988), 22–24; Foley, *Ritual Irony*, 52–54. For the Renaissance etymologies of tragedy, see Julius Caesar Scaliger, *Poetices libri septem* (1561), intro. August Buck (Stuttgart: Friedrich Frommann Verlag, 1964), 11; Stephanus, *Thesaurus* 7:9197; Vossius, *Poeticarum institutionum*, 71, 83, and *Etymologicon linguae Latinae*, in *Opera* 1:609–10.

25. Stephanus, *Thesaurus* 7:9197.

26. Vossius, *Poeticarum institutionum*, 71, 83, 157.

27. For the importance of Polybius in seventeenth-century English political thought, see Trevor-Roper, *Catholics, Anglicans, and Puritans*, 210–11.

28. Modern dictionaries of Classical Greek do not give these as possible meanings for *ektragodeo/tragodia*. These are the definitions in the Renaissance Greek lexica. Stephanus thus has "rursum ἐκτραγῳδεῖν Bud. poni ait et pro Admirationem ciere, Ita narrare ut in admirationem evadere rem velimus: velut ap. Polyb. (6, 56, 8) loquentem de religionibus Romanorum quam δεισιδαιμονίαν vocat. . . . inquit, In admirationem et terrorem vertitur, et mirifice commemoratur ab iis, qui ea tractarunt, quae ad cultum et cerimonias deorum attenent. Quomodo Idem τραγῳδιαν vocat Admirationem ac terrorem religionis injectae populo ab auguribus et pontificibus" (7:9201). Cf. Bude, *Lexicon* 2:1803.

Edward Grimeston's *The History of Polybius* (London, 1633) mistranslates the passage, perhaps in order to conceal its Machiavellian intimations. Neither Grimeston's English version nor Casaubon's Latin trot to his *Polybii . . . historiarum libri qui supersunt* (Paris 1609) preserves any trace of Polybius's "tragic" terminology, but Wolfgang Musculus's *Polybii Megalopolitani historiarum libri* (Lyon, 1554) gives the following translation: "Et arbitror apud universos mortales esse probrosum, quod hoc in factis Romanorum continetur. Loquor autem de superstitione. Usque adeo nanque haec pars tragice apud eos depraedicatur . . . ut augeri nequeat. . . . Quoniam autem plebs universa huius & illegitimis desideriis admodum obnoxia, irae inconsideratae, furori ac violentiae, reliquum est, metu incerto et huiusmodi tragoedia retinendam esse multitudinem" (529).

29. Polybius, *The Histories*, trans. W. R. Paton, Loeb Classical Library (Cambridge: Harvard University Press, 1979), 6.56.6–13, 6.58.1–13.

30. See Greenblatt, *Marvelous Possessions*, 79–82, and J. V. Cunningham, "Wonder," in *The Collected Essays of J. V. Cunningham* (Chicago: Swallow Press, 1976), 53–96. Most of Cunningham's examples treat wonder either as an effect of poetry in general or, with respect to tragic wonder, as closer to surprise rather than awe. Bude's and Stephanus's interpretation of the Polybian

ektragodein/tragodein is thus particularly important for establishing the philological connection between tragedy and *religious* wonder.

31. Robert Herrick, "*Good Friday*: Rex Tragicus, or Christ going to His Crosse," in *Major Poets of the Earlier Seventeenth Century*, ed. Barbara Lewalski and Andrew Sabol (Indianapolis: Odyssey, 1973), 1048–49; Don Cameron Allen, "Herrick's 'Rex Tragicus,'" in *Studies in Honor of Dewitt T. Starnes* (Austin: University of Texas Press, 1967), 215–26; Thomas Moisan, "Robert Herrick's 'Rex Tragicus' and the 'Troublesome Times,'" *Viator* 21 (1990): 349–84. None of Allen's examples, however, calls the Passion a tragedy; Moisan does little better with one reference from a 1621 sermon by Barton Holyday (355).

32. For the dating of the play, see I. D. McFarlane, *Buchanan* (London: Duckworth, 1981), 93–94.

33. Montaigne, *The Complete Essays*, 1.26, p. 131.

34. Philip Ford, *George Buchanan: Prince of Poets* (Aberdeen: Aberdeen University Press, 1982), vii; P. G. Walsh, "Buchanan and Classical Drama," in *Acta Conventus Neo-Latini Sanctandraeni*, ed. I. D. McFarlane, (Binghamton: Medieval and Renaissance Texts and Studies, 1986), 99.

35. On Buchanan's acquaintance with the *Poetics*, see Walsh, "Classical Drama," 103; by 1536 three Greek editions and one Latin translation were in print. On Scaliger and Buchanan, see McFarlane, *Buchanan*, 89.

36. McFarlane, *Buchanan*, 499–510; Wilbur Sypherd, *Jephthah and His Daughter: A Study in Comparative Literature* (Newark: University of Deleware Press, 1948), 131–39.

37. Quoted in Walsh, "Classical Drama," 103. Francis Meres praises the play in similar terms (McFarlane, *Buchanan*, 201).

38. Sir Philip Sidney, *An Apology for Poetry*, ed. Forrest Robinson (New York: Macmillan, 1970), 80.

39. Mueller, *Children of Oedipus*, 154, 193–96; Murry Rosten suggests that Milton translated Buchanan's *Baptistes*, published in 1642 by order of Parliament as *Tyrannical-Government Anatomized or a Discourse concerning Evil-Councillors* (*Biblical Drama in England: From the Middle Ages to the Present Day* [London: Faber and Faber, 1968], 81).

40. The libretto was by Thomas Morell, but Morell, in turn, based his version on Buchanan. Buchanan's tragedy may also lie behind the lost Jephthah play of Dekker and Munday (Louise George Clubb, "*The Virgin Martyr* and the *Tragedia Sacra*," *Renaissance Drama* 7 [1964]: 117) and another lost play on the same subject by Duplessis-Mornay (Sypherd, *Jephthah*, 26–27). Chronology will not allow it to have influenced the almost exactly contemporary *Jephthah* by John Christopherson; this play, which dates from around 1544 and which, like Buchanan's tragedy, was based on Euripides' *Iphegenia*, is the earliest English tragedy, as well as probably the only English tragedy written in Greek (ed. and trans. Francis Howard Forges, intro. Wilbur Sypherd

[Newark: University of Delaware Press, 1928]). It was not, however, published until 1928, and while it has some striking passages, it generally seems less coherent and focused than Buchanan's play.

41. Boose, "The Father's House," 20.

42. Debora K. Shuger, *Habits of Thought in the English Renaissance: Religion, Politics, and the Dominant Culture*, The New Historicism: Studies in Cultural Poetics (Berkeley: University of California Press, 1990), 224–27.

43. Daniel Heinsius, *On Plot in Tragedy* (1611), trans. Paul Sellin and John McManmon, ed. Paul Sellin (Northridge, Calif.: San Fernando Valley State College Foundation, 1971), 134. Several Renaissance scholars argued that Euripides' Iphegenia was actually Jephthah's daughter, that the Greek myth narrates the distorted echo of biblical history; see Louis Cappel's commentary in *Critici sacri* 2:660; Vossius, *De theologia gentili* (1641), 3 vols., The Renaissance and the Gods 28 (New York: Garland, 1976), 1:xii–xiii.

44. Compare Burkert's observation that ritual forms (and their dramatization) are not necessarily *about* their origins; e.g., ritual sacrifices may have originated as part of a hunting ceremony but by the Hellenic era need no longer have had anything to do with hunting per se (*Homo Necans*, 23). Many recent studies of sacrifice exhibit a questionable tendency to assume that origin fixes signification once and for all; Freud and Girard come to mind at once.

45. *Biblia Sacra* (1617) 2:231.

46. Ibid. 2:230. Augustine, Justin Martyr, Chrysostom, and (later) Peter Martyr held both that Jephthah is a type of Christ and that he was morally wrong to sacrifice his daughter. Tertullian, Ambrose, Gregory of Nazianzen, Theodoret, Procopius, and Peter Comestor mentioned only Jephthah's culpability. Among the Fathers, only Ambrose defended Jephthah's action, arguing that, like Abraham, he was inspired by the Holy Spirit; see ibid. 2:224–30; Poole, *Synopsis criticorum* 1:1154–55.

47. Most of the leading humanist exegetes denied that Jephthah in fact killed his daughter; see *Critici sacri* 2:644–66; Selden, *De jure naturali*, 530–36; and Thomas Hayne, *The general view of the Holy Scriptures*, 2d ed. (London, 1640), 213.

48. George Buchanan, *Jephthah*, in *The Sacred Dramas of George Buchanan*, trans. Archibald Brown (Edinburgh: James Thin, 1906), 5–6. I will quote from Brown's beautiful free translation rather than P. G. Walsh's flatter but more literal version in *George Buchanan: Tragedies*, ed. P. Sharrat and P. G. Walsh, trans. P. G. Walsh (Edinburgh: Scottish Academic Press, 1983); I give the Latin in the notes. In the original, this passage reads: "Porro ne Iephthes quoque / se metiatur exitu huius proelii / et intumescat insolens rebus bonis, / damno obruetur protinus domestico, / cedentque fracti contumaces spiritus. / . . . . heu, quanta moles imminet tibi mali, / miserande! quantis obruere luctibus!" (ll. 51–55, 60–61).

49. Buchanan, *Jephthah*, 28: "Regnator orbis, unus et verus deus, / solumque numen propitium pollens potens, / idem severus ultor et clemens pater, / tuis tremendus et severus hostibus, / tuis amicis lenis et salutifer, / irae timendae sed tamen placabilis, / amore fervens idem et inritabilis" (ll. 431–36).

50. Cf. Mueller, *Children of Oedipus*, 159.

51. Buchanan, *Jephthah*, 31: "foederis memor tui, / placidus propitiusque accipe haec servi tui / exigua quamvis vota, grato pectore / tamen profecta" (ll. 480–83).

52. The passage, however, implies (although only implies) that Jephthah here reiterates a vow he made earlier.

53. Buchanan, *Jephthah*, 31: "Quod primum ad aedes sospiti occurret meas, / tuas id aras imbuet grata hostia / suo cruore" (ll. 484–86).

54. Donald Stone, Jr., *French Humanist Tragedy: A Reassessment* (Manchester: Manchester University Press, 1974), 111.

55. Stone, *French Humanist Tragedy*, 110; Paul Riceour, *The Symbolism of Evil*, trans. Emerson Buchanan, Religious Perspectives 17 (New York: Harper and Row, 1967), 212.

56. Cf. Walsh, "Classical Drama," 101, for the Senecan echoes in these passages on mutability of fortune.

57. Buchanan, *Jephthah*, 52–54: "Haec nimirum est addita nostrae / vitae sors, ut tristia laetis / vicibus subeant / . . . . si quid laeti inluxit, / velut arentes inter stipulas / flammae evanida lux fugitivae / celeri velox avolat aura, / dein perpetuis nexa catenis / longi subeunt agmina luctus" (ll. 818–20, 836–41).

58. On *Mustapha*, see Shuger, *Habits of Thought*, 210–17, 247–48.

59. Thomas Dekker, *The Virgin Martyr*, in *The Dramatic Works of Thomas Dekker*, ed. Fredson Bowers, 4 vols. (Cambridge: At the University Press, 1958), 3.1.80–82.

60. Ibid. 3.1.94–7.

61. Buchanan, *Jephthah*, 70: "Nunc me, insolenti saeviens ludibrio, / sortis furentis impotens immanitas / felicitatis de supremo culmine / deiecit, uno cuncta vertens impetu" (ll. 1133–36).

62. Mueller, *Children of Oedipus*, 156, paraphrasing Walter Benjamin, *Ursprung des deutschen Trauerspiels* (Frankfurt, 1969), 75.

63. Buchanan, *Jephthah*, 67–68: "Sed veluti sub luce maligna / per secretos nemorum anfractus / lubricus error mille viarum / dubio occursu ludit euntes, / inter varios semita flexus / nulla placet neque displicet ulla; / sic iter homines praeterpropter / dubia incerti mente vagamur" (ll. 1082–89).

64. There is an earlier debate between Jephthah and Symmachus, an old family friend, but since Symmachus does not yet know about Jephthah's vow, their discussion only obliquely touches on the theological crux of the play.

65. Buchanan, *Jephthah*, 54–55: "Aut tu, cruorem virginalem innoxium / potura tellus, hisce patulos in specus / sinuque vasto me vora; dum non nocens /

perire possim, quolibet me obrue loco. / vel ipsum adire non recuso Tartarum, / modo parricida Tartarum non incolam" (ll. 845–50). Buchanan's curious use of *"parricida"* for a father who kills his child probably derives from Livy's parallel usage in telling the story of Virginius (3.50.5).

66. Ibid., 55: "Tu miser sis an secus, / tua repostum est in manu" (ll. 859–60).

67. Ibid., 59: "Proinde voti quicquid illud est / . . . . divina vox est una simplex veritas / sibique constans" (ll. 933, 938–39).

68. Ibid., 57: "Nostro non litatur victimis / deo cruentis bubulove sanguine, / polluta nullo corda sed contagio / et mens recocta veritate simplice / illi offerenda et casta conscientia" (ll. 895–99).

69. Sharratt and Walsh, eds., *George Buchanan*, 47.

70. Lucretius, *Of the Nature of Things*, trans. William Ellery Leonard (New York: Dutton, 1957), 1.99–100: "But sinless woman, sinfully foredone, / A parent felled her on her bridal day, / Making his child a sacrificial beast / To give the ships auspicious winds for Troy: / Such are the crimes to which religion leads." For a different reading of this allusion, see Peter Sharratt, "Euripides latinus: Buchanan's Use of His Sources," in *Acta Conventus Neo-Latini Bononiensis*, ed. R. J. Schoeck (Binghamton: Medieval and Renaissance Texts and Studies, 1985), 617.

71. Buchanan, *Jephthah*, 56: "Nec scelere nostras inquinare dexteras / sat est; nefandum facinus adscribere iuvat / caelo. cruentis victimis confingimus / gaudere numen" (ll. 886–89).

72. Ibid., 61: "Nemo neglegentius / retus vetustos servat, et mysteria / facit minoris" (ll. 965–66).

73. Ibid., 76: "Ingrata nunc me vita mihi superstitem / luctus reservat semper ut videam novos" (1238–39).

74. Ibid., 73: "Plus iure matri parte cederet sua, / matri, salutis quae sit auctor, quae patri / iam sponte natam perdituro subtrahit" (ll. 1172–74).

75. Ibid., 74: "et / compensat aura sanctimoniae scelus" (ll. 1189–90).

76. Ibid., 15: "tua qui nefando / polluit ritu sacra" (ll. 197–98); 71: "liberorum carnifex / parens, scelesta sacra ritu barbaro, / arae cruentae victimis nefariis" (ll. 1143–44).

77. Unlike Euripides and Christopherson, Buchanan does not make the husband brutally contemptuous of his pleading wife; he is rather anguished at the prospect of hurting her.

78. Buchanan, *Jephthah*, 55–56: "Primum amare liberos / natura nostris inseruit affectibus / . . . nam patris hanc aeterna providentia / caelestis animis indidit mortalium / . . . . quoque nomen artius / imprimeret istud mentibus, dici pater / et esse voluit; nec modo exemplo sui, / sed et ferarum et alitum atque piscium / patriae probavit caritatis vinculum" (ll. 866–67, 873–74, 878–82).

79. For Freud's influential contrast between female/private and male/public, see *Civilization and Its Discontents*, in *Standard Edition of the Complete Psychological Works of Sigmund Freud*, trans. and ed. James Strachey, 24 vols. (London: Hogarth, 1964), 21:103–4.

80. Quoted in Steiner, *Antigones*, 24.

81. Isidore of Seville, *Quaestiones in Vetus Testamentum*, in *Patrologia Latina* ed. J. P. Migne, 221 vols. (Paris, 1844–1900), 83:388–89; cited in J. H. McGregor, "The Sense of Tragedy in George Buchanan's *Jephthes*," *Humanistica Lovaniensia: Journal of Neo-Latin Studies* 31 (1982): 134 (my translation).

82. Buchanan, *Jephthah*, 72: "[Storge] Quid? polliceri quod tuum non est potes? / [Jephthah] Mea nata not est? [Storge] Est, sed etiam ut sit mea" (ll. 1165–66).

83. Ibid., 73: "plus iure matri parte cederet sua, / matri, salutis quae sit auctor" (ll. 1172–73).

84. Ibid., 8: "Tum pavidi ovilis fida custodia canis / lupos abegit, atque ad infirmum pecus, / trepidi timoris exanime adhuc memoria, / denuo reversus e sinu timidam meo / agnam revulsam dente laniavit truci" (ll. 98–102).

85. On paternal infanticide in the Bible, see David Barkan's rather speculative *The Duality of Human Existence: An Essay on Psychology and Religion* (Chicago: Rand McNally, 1966), 205–6, and *Disease, Pain, and Sacrifice: Toward a Psychology of Suffering* (Boston: Beacon, 1968), 104–24.

86. Buchanan, *Jephthah*, 36: "heu misera, quidnam patri / mutavit animum pristinum erga liberos? / hoc nemo nuper fuerat indulgentior / nec liberorum quisquam amantior parens" (ll. 550–53).

87. Ibid., 32: "O mihi secundum deum / genitor verende, sine frui amplexu tuo" (496–97); 75: "Miserere, genitor / . . . [te rogo] per si quid unquam merita sum de te bene, si quando parvis comprimens te brachiis / onus pependi dulce de collo tuo" (ll. 1215–19).

88. Ibid., 79–80.

89. Heinsius, *On Plot*, 132.

90. Bal, *Death and Dissymmetry*, 63.

91. Boose, "The Father's House," 36, 46–47.

92. *Biblia Sacra* (1617) 2:232; Donne, *Bianthanatos*, 97.

93. Boose, "The Father's House," 62.

94. Curiously, Renaissance biblical plays about chastity tend to be about *male* chastity (e.g., the Joseph dramas), while plays with female protagonists celebrate their martial, political, and/or sacrificial heroism rather than their sexual purity; one thus notes the popularity of plays about Deborah, Judith, Esther, and virgin martyrs (Rosten, *Biblical Drama*, 55–57). To read Buchanan's theological tragedy as a story of incest and exogamy demeans Iphis in the same way that recent critics claim the Renaissance patriarchy demeaned women in general: namely, such a reading "contains" female subjectivity

"through sexualizing women's language" (Mary Ellen Lamb, *Gender and Authorship in the Sidney Circle* [Madison: University of Wisconsin Press, 1990], 5.

95. Mueller, *Children of Oedipus*, 196, 211.

96. Buchanan, *Jephthah*, 77: "quod non volentem dura te necessitas / istuc coegit" (ll. 1261–62). Were this all, one would have to agree with Boose that Iphis, like Antigone, exemplifies the "daughter's self-sacrificing complicity with the father's needs" ("The Father's House," 41) or with Bal's remark that "in later rewritings" of the Jepthah story the daughter becomes "qualified only as a virgin, a victim, obedient and submissive" (*Death and Dissymmetry*, 43). But the play does not end here, and the remainder presents a much more complex portrait of the daughter. One needs only to contrast this play with Christopherson's *Jephthah* to see how little Buchanan is concerned with filial obedience.

97. Buchanan, *Jephthah*, 79: "Quin potius illi iusta supplicia luant. / nos, si necesse est, immerentes sanguine / aras piemus, totque caedes hostium / pensemus una sponte gratique hostia" (ll. 1293–96).

98. On the association of the sacred and the household (*oikos*) with women in Greek drama, see Foley, *Ritual Irony*, 91; S. C. Humphreys, *The Family, Women, and Death: Comparative Studies* (London: Routledge and Kegan Paul, 1983), 20.

99. Buchanan, *Jephthah*, 81–82: "quod tibi vitae fors detraxit / fama adiciet postuma laudi. . . . te posteritas sera loquetur. / te qui primi flumina Nili / bibit, et curru qui Sarmatico / solidum non timet ire per Istrum, / concinet olim / non formidine mortis inerti / pavidam, patriae donasse alacrem / natura tibi quos dedit annos" (ll. 1338–49).

100. Ibid., 85–86: "Sic virgo / . . . commorat omnes, versaque in se lumina / vulgi stupentis traxerat miraculo, / et triste cunctis attulit silentium" (ll. 1400–5).

101. Ibid., 80–81: "Nec ulla Iephthae me redarguet dies / non stirpe dignam" (ll. 1319–20).

102. Ibid., 86 (l. 1413); this invocation echoes the opening of the great Ambrosian hymn *"Aeterne rerum conditor."*

103. Quoted in Steiner, *Antigones*, 57.

104. Quoted in Mueller, *Children of Oedipus*, 162 (my translation).

105. Buchanan, *Jephthah*, 86: "'Aeterne rerum genitor atque hominum parens, / tandem propitius gentis errori tuae / ignosce, et istam victimam lenis cape. / quod si furoris exigis piaculum, / quaecumque nostra contumax superbia / supplicia meruit, te parentem deserens, / utinam luatur hoc cruore'" (ll. 1413–19). For corroborating my impression that medieval exegesis does not cite Old Testament women as types of Christ, I am indebted to H. A. Kelly, Del Kolve, and Retha Warnicke.

106. *Critici sacri* 2:659, 664.

107. This is Walsh's translation (*George Buchanan*, 91); Brown's version—"O my father / Break not my heart with words of tenderness, / Nor meditate delay" (*Jephthah*, 80)—misses the peremptory tone of the Latin "omitte, genitor, has moras innectere, / meumque dictis mollibus frangere animum" (ll. 1314–15).

108. Buchanan, *Jephthah*, 72, 79.

109. For example, Achilles, Sarpedon, Christ, Sidney, and so on. See John Wilkins, "The State and the Individual: Euripides' Plays of Voluntary Self-Sacrifice," in *Euripides, Women, and Sexuality*, ed. Anton Powell (London: Routledge, 1990), 179. For the opposing view that Renaissance representations of female heroism simply reinforce the patriarchal ideal of the silent, obedient woman, see Lamb, *Gender and Authorship*, 12, 119–20.

110. Poole, *Synopsis criticorum* 1:1154.

111. *Critici sacri* 2:665.

112. Friedrich Nietzsche, *The Birth of Tragedy and The Genealogy of Morals*, trans. Francis Golffing (Garden City, N.Y.: Doubleday, 1956), 24, 66–67.

113. Thus, both Iphis and Christ are at once obedient children and yet potentially transgressive, both submitting to their fathers and displacing them. Yet the representations of "daddy's boy" in the Calvinist passions seem more ambivalent and troubling than Buchanan's female version.

114. Cf. Burkert's discussion of the hunting scenes on archaic vases, where the victim is always depicted as male while the predator seems sexless; Burkert goes on to suggest that, in antiquity, sacrificial killing was seen as a sort of parricide (the same word Buchanan uses for killing one's daughter), so that the victim, rather than being feminized, becomes a father symbol, while the killer is portrayed as emasculated (*Homo Necans*, 75).

115. Other Renaissance commentaries on this episode seem anxious to downplay the religious content of the daughter's choice, praising rather her obedience to her father, so that the daughter's submission to paternal authority corresponds to the father's to divine—or in Milton's words, "he for God only, she for God in him." See, for example, Christopherson, *Jephthah*, 157; Hall, *Works* 1:256. On transgressive women in Renaissance drama, see Peter Stallybrass, "Patriarchal Territories: The Body Enclosed," in *Rewriting the Renaissance: The Discourses of Sexual Difference in Early Modern Europe*, ed. Margaret Ferguson, Maureen Quilligan, and Nancy Vickers (Chicago: University of Chicago Press, 1986), 142. While Stallybrass refers specifically to "grotesque," "unruly" women, their obedient, self-sacrificing counterparts (e.g., Iphis, Lucrece, Desdemona, Alcestis, Cordelia) also seem, in Greenblatt's words, to enact "a peculiarly intense *submission* whose downright violence undermines everything it was meant to shore up" (*Renaissance Self-Fashioning from More to Shakespeare* [Chicago: University of Chicago Press, 1980], 254).

116. Buchanan, *Jephthah*, 87–88: "Ut vocis autem pervium patuit iter, / non ille gemitus, esse nec qualis solet / fremitus doloris atque lamentatio, / sed contionis gratulantis murmure / confusa turba, teque praedicantium, / adversa sortis inter asprae vulnera / et blandientis laeta dona, feminam / unam beatam maxime et miserrimam. / nam plaga quamvis alte ad ossa sederit, / magni doloris magnum habes solacium" (ll. 1435–44).

117. Ibid., 88: "Quo fortiore nata tulit animo necem, / hoc angit animum tristior meum dolor" (ll. 1449–50). The Blessed Virgin displays the same unmitigated sorrow in several earlier passion tragedies; cf. Raymond Lebègue, *La tragédie religieuse en France: Les débuts (1514–1573)*, Bibliothèque littéraire de la Renaissance (Paris: Librairie Ancienne Honoré Champion, 1929), 131–32, 137; Gregory of Nazianzen, *Christus patiens, tragoedia*, ed. J. P. Migne, in *Patrologia graeca*, 161 vols. (Paris: 1857–1912), 38:207–210, 237–38.

118. This last displacement runs counter to Boose's claim that in Western texts daughters separate from their fathers but never (unlike sons) displace them ("The Father's House," 33).

119. Although sacrificial women predominate in Greek tragedy, this gendering is not invariable. Thus, Euripides' *Bacchae* has a mother sacrificing her son; in the *Phoenissae* a son kills himself to deliver his city. The New Testament, Beza's *Abraham sacrifiant*, and Greville's *Mustapha* center on the father's sacrifice of his male child.

120. On male "womb envy" and paternal appropriation of female generativity, see Christine Froula, "When Eve Reads Milton: Undoing the Canonical Economy," *Critical Inquiry* 10 (1983): 330–33.

121. Barber, "The Family," 197ff.

122. Brown, *The Body and Society*, 155–57, 187–88.

123. Clubb, "The Virgin Martyr," 106–10.

124. Christopherson, *Jephthah*, 133. Cf. the competition between human and divine lover in Donne's Holy Sonnet, "Since she whome I lovd." One thinks also of the stories of Saint Francis fleeing naked from his paternal house and Saint Thomas ambushed and dragged home on his father's orders as he attempted to enter a monastery.

125. Boose, "The Father's House," 46.

126. Donald Kelley, *The Beginning of Ideology: Consciousness and Society in the French Reformation* (Cambridge: Cambridge University Press, 1981), 77–78.

127. Ibid., 80–81. Conversely, absolutist thinkers like Bodin, Hobbes, and Filmer tend, in rather different ways, to grant the father sacerdotal functions and thus to deprive religious institutions of any independent authority; see Bossy, *Christianity in the West*, 156.

128. Burkert, *Homo Necans*, 3.

129. Bossy, *Christianity in the West*, 23–24.

130. Boose, "The Father's House," 68–69.

131. Quoted in Steiner, *Antigones,* 31; George Herbert, "Affliction [IV]," in *Major Poets of the Earlier Seventeenth Century,* ed. Barbara Lewalski and Andrew Sabol (Indianapolis: Odyssey, 1973), 271.

132. Buchanan, *Jephthah,* 83: "At vos, vestri dedecus aevi, / animam patriae reddere segnes, / vos aeternis tenebrarum umbris / teget oblivio longa sepultos, / et generis pudor et telluris / pondus inutile, quos et praesens / spernit et altera nesciet aetas" (1354–60).

133. Quoted in Wilkins, "The State," 180. Cf. Burkert, *Homo Necans,* 47–48, 64–67, on virgin sacrifices before and after battle.

134. See John Winkler, *The Constraints of Desire: The Anthropology of Sex and Gender in Ancient Greece* (New York: Routledge, 1990), 90, and Froma Zeitlin, "Playing the Other: Theater, Theatricality, and the Feminine in Greek Drama," *Representations* 11 (1985): 80, on the theater's tendency to use "the feminine for the purposes of imagining a fuller model for the masculine self."

135. Buchanan, *Jephthah,* 84: "Cum staret aras ante tristes victima / iam destinata virgo, purpureum decus / per alba fudit ora virgineus pudor, / coetus viriles intuerier insolens, / ut si quis Indum purpura violet ebur, / rosave niveis misceat cum liliis" (ll. 1372–77).

136. Ibid., 85: "Ut iam ruentis aequor in Tartessium / Phoebi recedens esse gratior solet / splendor" (ll. 1396–98).

137. "Indum sanguineo veluti violaverit ostro / si quis ebur, aut mixta rubent ubi lilia multa / alba rosa; tales virgo dabat ore colores" (*Aeneid* 12.67–69).

138. Buchanan, *Jephthah,* 84–85: "Sed se per ora cum pudore fuerat / perspicua certae iuncta vis fiduciae, / interque flentes sola fletibus carens / vultu remisso constitit firma ac sui / secura fati. quas tenebat lacrimas propinqua morti virgo, populus non tenet. / . . . florem juventae deflet ille, et siderum / similes ocellos, aemulamque auro comam, / supraque sexum pectoris constantiam. / et forte solito gratiorem afflaverat / natura honorem, ceu supremo munere / dignata funus nobilis viraginis. / ut iam ruentis aequor in Tartessium / Phoebi recedens esse gratior solet / splendor, rosaeque vere supremo halitus / colorque cupidos detinet oculos magis, / sic virgo fati stans supremo in limine, / parata morti, nec recusans molliter / turpive torpens exitus formidine" (ll. 1378–83, 1390–1402).

139. Nietzsche, *The Birth of Tragedy,* 102.

140. See Zeitlin, "Playing the Other," for female characters in Greek drama as figures of drama itself.

141. Elizabeth Cropper, "The Beauty of Woman: Problems in the Rhetoric of Renaissance Portraiture," in *Rewriting the Renaissance: The Discourses of Sexual Difference in Early Modern Europe,* ed. Margaret Ferguson, Maureen Quilligan, and Nancy Vickers (Chicago: University of Chicago Press, 1986), 175–76. As Cropper notes, the primary source for this identification was

Lucian's dialogue *Essays in Portraiture*. The identification of Iphis with the beautiful text raises a methodological issue. The claim entails that her representation does not function primarily either to control or to enable female political and sexual energies and hence is not amenable to the sociological literalism informing much recent work on Renaissance literature, where textual gendering is assumed to comment on sexual politics. One needs to distinguish gender as a cultural semiotic from gender as a social ideology—a distinction obscured by the fact that feminist criticism originated in Victorian studies, where the "woman question" profoundly affects literary representation. In Renaissance scholarship, however, the conflation of symbolic with social forms has less historical warrant, since Renaissance texts—unlike Victorian novels—do not exclusively treat social experience. The distinction between the two is never absolute, since symbols occur within a social field and social behaviors are informed by cultural symbols; nevertheless, Donne's "Spit in my face ye Jews" is not about real Jews any more than "Goldilocks" is about real bears. Cf. Leah Marcus, *Childhood and Cultural Despair: A Theme and Variations in Seventeenth-Century Literature* (Pittsburgh: University of Pittsburgh Press, 1978), on the child in seventeenth-century poetry as a symbol of royalist nostalgia; and Greenblatt's "Marlowe, Marx, and Anti-Semitism," in his *Learning to Curse*, 40–58, on the Jew as a figure of Christian hypocrisy. For criticism of readings that treat women as symbols of something else (and presumably more important), see Dympna Callaghan, *Woman and Gender in Renaissance Tragedy* (New York: Harvester Wheatsheaf, 1989), 34.

142. Poole, *Synopsis criticorum* 1:1150.

143. Such ambiguities are part of a larger cultural tension between Neoplatonism and puritanism, between viewing pagan myths as "mystic symbols for sacred experience" and as the "filthy relics of a discredited creed, to be vituperated, ostracized, and wiped from the imaginations of men" (Jonas Barish, *The Antitheatrical Prejudice* [Berkeley: University of California Press, 1981], 108).

144. See Baxter Hathaway, *Marvels and Commonplaces: Renaissance Literary Criticism* (New York: Random House, 1968), 133–35; John Milton, *Eikonoklastes*, in *Complete Prose Works of John Milton*, ed. Merritt Hughes, 8 vols. (New Haven: Yale University Press, 1962), 3:362–66. The relevant excerpts from the *Canons and Decrees of the Council of Trent* can be found in Elizabeth Holt, ed., *A Documentary History of Art*, 2 vols. (Garden City, N.Y.: Doubleday, 1958), 2:64–65.

145. Hathaway, *Marvels*, 133–34.

146. Barish, *Antitheatrical Prejudice*, 199.

147. Quoted in Lily Bess Campbell, *Divine Poetry and Drama in Sixteenth-Century England* (Cambridge: At the University Press, 1961), 246; Campbell cites similar sentiments from Gosson and Stubbes, although the former specifically excludes Buchanan from this indictment, since (according to Gosson) his

plays were meant to be read, not acted (244–45). See also Vossius, *Poeticarum institutionum* 3:72; Baxter Hathaway, *The Age of Criticism: The Late Renaissance in Italy* (Ithaca: Cornell University Press, 1962), 153.

148. Campbell's *Divine Poetry* can come up with only a dozen or so English biblical plays between 1576 and 1603 that were intended for public performance (240–42); see also Rosten, *Biblical Drama*, 115–20.

149. Greenblatt, "Invisible Bullets: Renaissance Authority and Its Subversions, *Henry IV* and *Henry V*," in *Political Shakespeare: New Essays in Cultural Materialism*, ed. Jonathan Dollimore and Alan Sinfield (Ithaca: Cornell University Press, 1985), 29.

150. During his trial before the Portuguese Inquisition, Buchanan claimed that the play treated the Latomus/Bucer debate over vows. Modern critics, however, have been fairly unanimous in regarding this explanation with suspicion; cf. Sharratt and Walsh, eds., *George Buchanan*, 618; McFarlane, *Buchanan*, 197–99. Mueller concludes that "if we thus try to line up the opposition between Jephtha and the priest with that of Catholics and Protestants, we are left with Jephtha arguing a Catholic position in the manner of a Protestant against a fat prelate who takes his cues from Calvin's *Institutes*. This is not very promising" (*Children of Oedipus*, 166).

151. McFarlane, *Buchanan*, 94, 100.

152. Theodore Beza, *A Tragedie of Abrahams Sacrifice [Abraham sacrifiant]*, trans. Arthur Golding, ed. Malcolm Wallace (Toronto: University of Toronto Library, 1906), ll. 675–78, 695–96.

153. Ibid., ll. 780–81.

154. Barish, *Antitheatrical Prejudice*, 162–63; Moisan, "Herrick's 'Rex Tragicus,'" 362.

155. Socinianism, one recalls, is preeminently an ethical religion and nowhere more so than in its aversion to sacrifice.

156. Bossy, *Christianity in the West*, 113.

157. Moisan, "Herrick's 'Rex Tragicus,'" 350.

158. A priest, of course, differs from a minister because priests perform sacrifices.

159. Stephen Greenblatt, "Shakespeare and the Exorcists," in his *Shakespearean Negotiations: The Circulation of Social Energy in Renaissance England*, The New Historicism: Studies in Cultural Poetics (Berkeley: University of California Press, 1988), 125–27. Cappel, one recalls, treats the annual lament over Jephthah's daughter as a type of the Eucharist.

160. The function of this aesthetic recuperation, however, does not seem to be the concealment of cultural violence (i.e., violence against women), if only because Renaissance fathers were not prone to murder their daughters. The play grapples with the violence of the sacred, not with child abuse. To privilege a priori social meaning over theological exhibits the ethnocentric condescension one often notes among anthropologists: namely, that the "myths" of unfamiliar

cultures must, however seemingly metaphysical, "really" encode the mundane structures of tribal or domestic experience, as though such peoples were incapable of less prosaic concerns.

161. Nietzsche, *The Birth of Tragedy*, 42.

162. Erasmus, *Disputatiuncula* 5:1279, 1285, 1289–90. On the erotic content of Michaelangelo's *Pieta* and its theological context, see Leo Steinberg, "The Metaphors of Love and Birth in Michelangelo's *Pietas*," in *Studies in Erotic Art*, ed. Theodore Bowie and Cornelia Christenson (New York: Basic Books, 1970), 231–85. See also Crashaw's "The Flaming Heart": "For in love's feild was never found / A nobler weapon then a WOUND. / Love's passives are his activ'st part. / The wounded is the wounding heart" (ll. 71–74). See also his song beginning "Lord, when the sense of thy sweet grace" (in *Major Poets of the Earlier Seventeenth Century*, ed. Barbara Lewalski and Andrew Sabol [Indianapolis: Odyssey, 1973], 719–20).

163. I have discussed the Renaissance recovery of Longinus's fusion of religious and aesthetic/rhetorical emotion in *Sacred Rhetoric: The Christian Grand Style in the English Renaissance* (Princeton: Princeton University Press, 1988), 38–41, 155–92, 254–56.

164. Quoted in Steiner, *Antigones*, 4.

165. Robin Horton, "African Traditional Thought and Western Science," in *Rationality*, ed. Bryan R. Wilson (Evanston: Harper and Row, 1970), 161.

166. Aquinas, *Summa Theologica*, in *Aquinas: Selected Political Writings*, ed. A. P. D'Entrèves (Oxford: Basil Blackwell, 1954), 2.1.91.4, p. 117. See also Gregory the Great's further distinction between "the motive suppressed in the depths of the heart" and "what the surface of thought presents to the muser's mind" (*The Book of Pastoral Rule and Selected Epistles*, trans. James Barmby, Nicene and Post-Nicene Fathers, 2d ser., 12 [Grand Rapids, Mich.: Eerdmans, 1979], 6).

167. See David Aers, "Reflections on Current Histories of the Subject," *Literature and History* 2 (1991): 20–34; Watson, "Tragedy," 303. As a rule of thumb, one can assume that any culture that has private confession and/or confessional literature (as opposed to liturgy and/or saga) also acknowledges a distinction between subjectivity and public role. I am not, however, convinced by Lee Patterson's claim that Chaucer's characters—particularly the Wife of Bath and the Pardoner—evince subversive, oedipal subjectivities (*Chaucer and the Subject of History* [Madison: University of Wisconsin Press, 1991], 314–15, 411).

168. One sees this movement thematized in works where religious and literary motives brush up against one another. Thus, *Jephthah*'s self-consciousness about its own transgressive appropriations of the sacred recurs in seventeenth-century religious verse, particularly in Herbert's anxiety that his "lovely enchanting language," borrowed from the *Greek Anthology* and secular love poetry in order to create the introspective and passionate self of his devotional

poetry—the language that recuperates confession as lyric—tends to turn that self into a literary performance ("weav[ing] my self into the sense," in Herbert's words); as in Buchanan's play, the act of making literature out of ritual purgations threatens to dissolve the spiritual into the aesthetic (see Herbert's "Jordon [II]," "The Forerunners" in *Major Poets*, 284, 365–66).

169. Voegelin, *The World of the Polis*, 247.

5. SAINTS AND LOVERS

1. Donne, "The Relique," in *The Complete English Poems*, 112. According to the informer Richard Baines, Marlowe had asserted that "the woman of Samaria & her sister were whores & that Christ knew them dishonestly"; this allegation seems to conflate two New Testament figures: the woman of Samaria (John 4), whose sister is never mentioned, and Mary of Magdala, a prostitute and the sister of Martha. For Baines's testimony, see Millar Maclure, ed., *Marlowe: The Critical Heritage 1588–1896* (London: Routledge and Kegan Paul, 1979), 37.

2. Quoted in Winkler, *Constraints*, 93; fragments of Celsus's treatise survive as quotations in Origen's reply, the *Contra Celsum*, trans. Henry Chadwick (Cambridge: Cambridge University Press, 1953).

3. For example, Lewis Wager's *The Life and Repentaunce of Marie Magdalene* (London, 1567); Thomas Robinson, *The Life and Death of Mary Magdalene*, ed. H. Oskar Sommer, Early English Text Society 78 (London: Kegan Paul, 1899); and Herbert's "Marie Magdalene." Many Roman Catholic texts as well focus on Mary's conversion and penitence; see, e.g., Pierre Janelle, *Robert Southwell: The Writer* (New York: Sheed and Ward, 1935), 189–90.

4. *The Life of Saint Mary Magdalene and of Her Sister Saint Martha* [formerly attributed to Rabanus Maurus], trans. and ed. David Mycoff, Cistercian Studies 108 (Kalamazoo: Cistercian Publications, 1989), 55.

5. Steinberg, "Love and Birth," 277; see also Margaret R. Miles, *Carnal Knowing: Female Nakedness and Religious Meaning in the Christian West* (Boston: Beacon, 1989), 124–25.

6. John Donne, *The Sermons of John Donne*, ed. George Potter and Evelyn Simpson, 10 vols. (Berkeley: University of California Press, 1953–1962), 9:11.417–18; 2:14.480–85; 10:11.668–70.

7. Edmund Gosse, *The Life and Letters of John Donne, Dean of St. Paul's*, 2 vols. (1899; rpt. Gloucester, Mass.: Peter Smith, 1959), 2:360.

8. This account of Christ's appearance to Mary differs from the synoptic Gospels, where Mary Magdalene visits the tomb accompanied by one or more other women; cf. Matthew 28:1–10; Luke 24:1–11. The sequence of events recorded in Mark 16:1–11 is confusing, but it seems closer to John's version, where Christ first appears to Mary Magdalene separately.

9. Other manuscripts ascribe the sermon to Saint Bonaventure, Saint

Anselm, Geoffroy of Vendome, and Saint Bernard (Janelle, *Southwell*, 184; Victor Saxer, *Le culte de Marie Madeleine en Occident, des origines à la fin du moyen âge*, pref. Henri Marrou, 2 vols., Cahiers d'archeologie et d'historie [Paris: Librairie Clavreuil, 1959], 2:347n). It is also included in the 1508 Venice edition of the sermons of Zeno of Verona.

10. Geoffrey Chaucer, *The Legend of Good Women*, Text G, l. 418, in *The Works of Geoffrey Chaucer*, ed. F. N. Robinson, 2d ed. (Boston: Houghton Mifflin, 1957), 493.

11. Ten of these appear in editions of Origen and one in the sermons of Zeno of Verona; the one or perhaps two London versions include just the Magdalene sermon. It is also quoted extensively in Cornelius à Lapide's *The Great Commentary*—the standard Tridentine compendium of biblical exegesis.

12. Complete bibliographic information can be found in John P. McCall, "Chaucer and the Pseudo Origen *De Maria Magdalena*: A Preliminary Study," *Speculum* 46 (1971): 491–97.

13. General surveys of Magdalene material can be found in Saxer, *Le culte*; Marjorie M. Malvern, *Venus in Sackcloth: The Magdalen's Origins and Metamorphosis* (Carbondale: Southern Illinois University Press, 1975); Helen Meredith Garth, *Saint Mary Magdalene in Medieval Literature*, Johns Hopkins University Studies in Historical and Political Science (Baltimore: Johns Hopkins University Press, 1950); and John James McDermott,"Mary Magdalene in English Literature from 1500 to 1650," Ph.D. diss., University of California, Los Angeles, 1964.

14. See Bertha Skeat's preface to Chaucer [pseudonym], *The Lamentatyon of Mary Magdaleyne* (Cambridge: Fabb and Tyler, 1897), 7.

15. Lawrence Lipking, *Abandoned Women and Poetic Tradition* (Chicago, 1988), 35; Heinrich Dorrie, "L'épître héroïque dans les littératures modernes," *Revue de littérature comparée* 40 (1966): 48–64.

16. On the fusion of Ovid and Canticles in the Middle Ages, see Nicholas James Perella, *The Kiss Sacred and Profane: An Interpretative History of Kiss Symbolism and Related Religio-Erotic Themes* (Berkeley: University of California Press, 1969), 115.

17. Andrewes, *Sermons*, 198.

18. Robert Southwell, *Mary Magdalens Funeral Teares* (1591) (Delmar, N.Y.: Scholars' Facsimiles, 1975), 8; cf. Gervase Markham, *Marie Magdalens Lamentations* (London, 1601), C4(r). Compare with Ovid's "I have stretched myself prostrate on my sorrowful bed, then springing tears, not slumber, is the service of mine eyes. . . . Oft I am distraught with woe; I lose sense of where I am and what my fate" (*Heroides and Amores*, trans. Grant Showerman, 2d ed., Loeb Classical Library [Cambridge: Harvard University Press, 1986], 8.109–12).

19. Markham, *Lamentations*, G3(r); Southwell, *Funeral Teares*, 64.

20. Pseudo-Chaucer, *Lamentatyon*, ll. 216, 674, 693; cf. *The Complaynte of the Louer of Cryst Mary Magdaleyn* (London, c. 1620), 8, 18–19.

21. Origen [pseudonym], *Omelia origenis de beata Maria Magdalena* (London, c. 1504), n.p.

22. Markham, *Lamentations*, B2(v), C3(r).

23. Origen [pseudonym], *An Homilie of Marye Magdalene, declaring her fervent loue and zele towards CHRIST: written by that famous clerke ORIGENE* (London, 1565), B6(r). Compare with Ovid's "What am I to do? Whither shall I take myself. . . . where am I to go? . . . By these tears I pray you—tears moved by what you have done—turn about your ship, reverse your sail, glide swiftly back to me!" (*Heroides* 10.59, 64, 147–51).

24. Markham, *Lamentations*, B2(r); Southwell, *Funeral Teares*, 17–18; pseudo-Chaucer, *Lamentatyon*, ll. 622–37.

25. Southwell, *Funeral Teares*, 54. This startling image of Christ lying in a lady's lap recurs in Southwell's "At Home in Heaven," which explains how the "ghostly beautie" of the soul "lull'd our heavenly Sampson fast asleepe, / And laid him in our feeble natures lap" (in *Saint Peters Complaint, newly augmented with other Poems* [London, 1605], 61). Southwell's metaphor seems to envision the hypostatic union as sexual intercourse, the same phrase having an overtly bawdy sense in *Hamlet* 3.2.111–17.

26. Markham, *Lamentations* G(v); cf. Southwell, *Funeral Teares*, 61.

27. Pseudo-Origen, *An Homilie*, B4(r)-B5(v).

28. Bernard of Clairvaux, *On the Song of Songs II*, trans. Kilian Walsh, intro. Jean Leclercq, 4 vols., Cistercian Fathers Series 7 (Kalamazoo, Mich.: Cistercian Publications, 1976), 3:80, sermon 27.7.

29. Bernard, *Song of Songs*, 3:95–96, sermon 28.9–10. For Mary Magdalene as a type of the church, see Steinberg, "Love and Birth," 247; Malvern, *Venus in Sackcloth*, 58.

30. John Calvin, *Commentary on the Gospel According to John*, trans. William Pringle, 2 vols. (Grand Rapids, Mich.: Eerdmans, 1956), 2:254.

31. Suspecting her plan forcibly to recover Christ's body, the narrator warns her, "O Mary unlesse thy love have better warrant then common sence, I can hardly see how such designementes can be approved." She replies, "Approoved (saith shee) I would to God the execution were as easie as the proofe, and I should not so long bewaile my unfortunate losse" (Southwell, *Funeral Teares*, 39). Since Christ comes to Mary and not to the narrator, the latter's position is rendered ipso facto wrong.

32. Ioan P. Culiano, *Eros and Magic in the Renaissance*, trans. Margaret Cook (Chicago: University of Chicago Press, 1987), 4–5, 39–40; Shuger, *Sacred Rhetoric*, 202–7. Cartesian epistemology differs from the Aristotelian/scholastic tradition precisely because it breaks the ancient connection between knowledge and imaging.

33. Pseudo-Origen, *An Homilie*, A4(r); cf. Southwell, *Funeral Teares*, 3; Markham, *Lamentations*, C3(v), C4(v); pseudo-Chaucer, *Lamentatyon*, ll. 428–29. See also Augustine, *Lectures or Tractates on the Gospel According to St. John*, 2 vols., in *The Works of Aurelius Augustine, Bishop of Hippo*, ed. Marcus Dods, (Edinburgh: T. and T. Clark, 1874): "seeing that in the case even of such a Master, when His living presence was withdrawn from their eyes, His remembrance also had ceased to remain" (2:522).

34. Pseudo-Origen, *An Homilie*, C2(v); Markham, *Lamentations*, C4(r); Southwell, *Funeral Teares*, 6; Cornelius à Lapide, *The Great Commentary*, trans. Thomas Mossman, 3d ed., 6 vols. (London, 1889–1896), 6:261.

35. Culiano, *Eros and Magic*, 31–32.

36. Southwell, *Funeral Teares*, 13.

37. Pseudo-Origen, *An Homilie*, C5(r)-C6(v); cf. à Lapide, *The Great Commentary* (1889–1896) 6:262.

38. Bossy, *Christianity in the West*, 99–101.

39. Calvin, *Commentary on John* 2:252–60. But Calvin's criticism of Mary's disbelief closely resembles Bernard, *Song of Songs* 3:95, sermon 28.8.

40. Calvin, *Commentary on John* 2:259.

41. Southwell, *Funeral Teares*, 43.

42. Pseudo-Chaucer, *Lamentatyon*, ll. 295–98.

43. Andrewes, *Sermons*, 205.

44. Peter Brown, *The Making of Late Antiquity* (Cambridge: Harvard University Press, 1978), 45.

45. For two examples among many, see Thomas Laqueur, "Orgasm, Generation, and the Politics of Reproductive Biology," *Representations* 14 (1986): 1–41; Bynum, "The Body of Christ."

46. Winkler, *Constraints*, 17.

47. Perella, *The Kiss*, 85. For the purposes of this argument, it does not much matter whether the theological origins of courtly love be traced to Christian, gnostic, or Arabic mysticism, the latter two positions being held by Denis de Rougement (*Love in the Western World*, trans. Montgomery Belgion, rev. ed. [New York: Harper, 1974], 44–52) and Culiano (*Eros and Magic*, 16–18) respectively. According to all three analyses, the representation of spiritual experience structures secular eroticism.

48. "Eloisa to Abelard," in *The Poems of Alexander Pope*, ed. John Butt (New Haven: Yale University Press, 1963), l. 150.

49. Ibid., ll. 231–34.

50. Ibid., ll. 271–76.

51. Ibid., l. 25.

52. Culiano, *Eros and Magic*, 4; cf. Michel Foucault, *The Foucault Reader*, ed. Paul Rabinow (New York: Pantheon Books, Random House, 1984), 340.

53. Shakespeare's sonnets to the young man are thus, by and large, about

eros/love/longing; his dark lady sonnets, in contrast, concern sexuality, guilt, and carnality.

54. Robert Burton, *The Anatomy of Melancholy*, ed. Holbrook Jackson (New York: Vintage Books, Random House, 1977), 2.86.

55. Culiano, *Eros and Magic*, 30; Southwell, *Funeral Teares*, 12.

56. Burton, *Anatomy* 2.58, 65.

57. Sir Thomas Wyatt, in *Silver Poets of the Sixteenth Century*, ed. Gerald Bullett (London: Dent, 1947), 25, 37.

58. Cf. Spenser's *Faerie Queene*, 3.2.39, in *The Complete Poetical Works*. The identification of the bodily *tout court* with a person's sexual organs seems problematically implicit in some feminist attempts to link gender and writing, which assume that gendered selfhood originates in and is modeled on the secretions and tumescences of the genitals.

59. Burton, *Anatomy* 2.314–15.

60. Ibid. 2.325–40.

61. Ibid. 2.343, 397. The same basic analysis reappears in Meric Casaubon's digressive hodgepodge, *A Treatise Concerning Enthusiasme* of 1655, which diagnoses its subject as a form of melancholy or "depravation of the Understanding, as well as of the Imagination," caused perhaps by the devil or ambition ([Gainesville, Fla.: Scholars' Facsimiles, 1970], 52, 114–17, 130).

62. Henry More, *Enthusiasmus triumphatus*, intro. M. V. DePorte, Augustan Reprint Society 118 (Los Angeles: University of California Press, 1966), 12. Note that the path of this "new wine" traces that of semen (thought to originate in the brain and descend down the spinal column) in reverse.

63. Ibid., 17.

64. Ibid., 28, 37. The discovery of genital eroticism seems related to the simultaneous substitution of sexual wrongdoing for ambition and pride as the paradigmatic sin; as desire is traced to its sexual origin, Lovelace replaces Faustus and Iago.

65. Pope, *The Rape of the Lock*, in *The Poems of Alexander Pope*, 4.54.

66. Sidney, *Astrophel and Stella* 72, 199.

67. Already in the more liberal strains of sixteenth- and seventeenth-century theology one notes a discomfort with erotic spirituality; thus, Castellio and Grotius, who both develop the Erasmian/humanist stress on ethical responsibility, interpret Canticles as a poem about human, sexual love, Grotius providing copious analogies with the Classical erotic elegy (see *Critici sacri* 3:252–53; John Calvin, *Letters of John Calvin*, ed. Jules Bonnet, 4 vols. [Philadelphia: Presbyterian Board of Publication, 1858], 1:408–9). Stanley Stewart has, however, shown the continued vitality of medieval bridal mysticism among English Protestants through the mid-seventeenth century in his *The Enclosed Garden: The Tradition and the Image in Seventeenth-Century Poetry* (Madison: University of Wisconsin Press, 1966).

68. Jonathan Swift, *A Tale of a Tub to Which Is Added The Battle of the Books and The Mechanical Operation of the Spirit*, ed. A. C. Guthkelch and D. Nichol Smith, 2d ed. (Oxford: Clarendon, 1958), 287.

69. Ibid., 164–65.

70. Ibid., 281.

71. Ibid., 288.

72. Ibid., 288. Gavin Langmuir reports that, in a library copy of *The Idea of the Holy*, a student has scribbled next to Rudolph Otto's description of the *mysterium tremendum*: "Sounds like intercourse" (*History, Religion, and Antisemitism*, 78).

73. Lipking, *Abandoned Women*, xvii.

74. Pseudo-Origen, *An Homilie*, B2(r), B6; cf. Andrewes, *Sermons*, 205.

75. Southwell, *Funeral Teares*, 41–42.

76. Pseudo-Origen, *An Homilie*, B6(r); pseudo-Origen, *Omelia*, n.p.; pseudo-Chaucer, *Lamentatyon*, ll. 608–9.

77. Pseudo-Origen, *An Homilie*, B4(v); in the Latin, "cur derelinquisti me salus mea" (*Omelia*, n.p.)—an obvious echo of Matthew 27:46.

78. Pseudo-Chaucer, *Lamentatyon*, ll. 708–14; cf. *Complaynte*, 24.

79. Pseudo-Chaucer, *Lamentatyon*, l. 521.

80. Ibid., ll. 531–32; Southwell, *Funeral Teares*, 11; pseudo-Origen *An Homilie*, A8(r)–B(r).

81. Hans Blumenberg, *The Legitimacy of the Modern Age*, trans. Robert M. Wallace, Studies in Contemporary German Social Thought (Cambridge: MIT Press, 1983), 133–35. Note the curious similarity to Chaucer's treatment of the Griselda story, where the original allegory—in which Walter figures God and Griselda stands for humankind (or Christian obedience)—is suddenly rejected because by justifying Griselda *at the expense of* Walter it implicitly contrasts the humble, virtuous soul to a cruel and tormenting (male) deity.

82. Pseudo-Chaucer, *Lamentatyon*, ll. 561–62.

83. Pseudo-Origen, *An Homilie*, A7(r).

84. Southwell, *Funeral Teares*, 8–9.

85. Walter W. Skeat, ed., *Chaucerian and Other Pieces* (Oxford: Clarendon, 1897), xi. Bertha Skeat comes to the same conclusion, noting that the poem's "strong personal feeling, restricted within a narrow range" indicates female authorship, since "it is a characteristic of women to give general statements a personal application" (*Lamentatyon*, 32–33).

86. Pseudo-Origen, *An Homilie*, C6(r); Southwell, *Funeral Teares*, 67; cf. Markham, *Lamentations*, H2(v). Conversely, Nicholas Breton's *The Blessed Weeper* both muffles the erotic resonances of the medieval Magdalene narratives and explicitly addresses itself to a female audience, concluding, "Yet by her speech it seemèd it was she, / That wisht all women might such weepers be" (in *The Works in Verse and Prose*, vol. 1); similarly, Vaughan's "St. Mary

Magdalen" adjures: "Learn, *Ladies*, here the faithful cure / Makes beauty lasting, fresh and pure" (in *Major Poets of the Earlier Seventeenth Century*, ed. Barbara Lewalski and Andrew Sabol [Indianapolis: Odyssey, 1973], ll. 45–46, p. 561). Premodern texts by or for women usually make their gendering explicit.

87. Brown, *The Body and Society*, 153.

88. Southwell, *Funeral Teares*, 22.

89. See Lipking, *Abandoned Women*, xviii–xix.

90. This sense of desolation is movingly articulated by Southwell's Mary: "Alas O my onely desire, why hast thou left me wavering in these uncertainties, and in how wilde a maze wander my doubtfull and perplexed thoughts?" (*Funeral Teares*, 16).

91. Andrewes, *Sermons*, 196, 211; cf. à Lapide, *The Great Commentary* 6:259.

92. Southwell, *Funeral Teares*, 57.

93. Gregory the Great, *XL homiliarum in Evangelia libri duo*, ed. J. P. Migne, in *Patrologia latina*, 221 vols. (Paris, 1844–1900), 76:1189–90. In his sermon on Mary Magdalene, Andrewes thus remarks: "It is not enough for love, to *looke* in once. Thus we use, this is our manner when we seeke a thing seriously, where we have sought already, there to seeke againe, thinking wee did it not well, but, if we now looke againe, better, we shall surely find it, then. *Amor quaerens ubi quaesivit.* Love, that never thinkes, it hath looked enough" (*Sermons*, 198); see also à Lapide, *The Great Commentary* (1889–96), 6:257.

94. Juan Luis Vives, *De anima et vita* (1538; rpt. Turin: Bottega d'Erasmo, 1959), 178.

95. Southwell, *Funeral Teares*, 61.

96. *Foucault Reader*, 371.

97. Southwell, *Funeral Teares*, 55–56.

98. Pseudo-Origen, *An Homilie*, C5(v); *Omelia*, n.p.

99. See Gregory the Great: "humor viscerum ad virilia labitur, quae profecto cum molestia dedecoris intumescunt" (*The Book of Pastoral Rule*, 9). In explaining the phrase "*viscera miseracordiae*," Andrewes additionally notes that these are "the bowels or vessels near the womb, near the loins . . . the bowels of a father or mother" (*The Works of Lancelot Andrewes*, 11 vols., Library of Anglo-Catholic Theology [Oxford, 1841–1872], 4:272); the passage suggests that, for Andrewes, the adult sexual organs—the "vessels" near the womb and loins—are the organs of a nurturing instinct; they are associated with the care of children rather than sexual drive. Here again, Renaissance usage seems to dissolve the modern category of "sex" into something else—exactly the opposite of the modern tendency to view everything else as somehow sexual.

100. Perella thus cites a striking passage from a seventeenth-century French theologian: "In the ecstasy of human love, who is unaware that we eat

and devour each other, that we long to become part of each other in every way, and, as the poet said, to carry off even with our teeth the thing we love in order to possess it, feed upon it, become one with it, live on it? That which is frenzy, that which is impotence in corporeal love is truth, is wisdom in the love of Jesus: 'Take, eat, this is my body': devour, swallow up not a part, not a piece but the whole" (*The Kiss*, 3).

101. *Foucault Reader*, 355–62.

102. Saint Augustine, *The Confessions of Saint Augustine*, trans. Rex Warner (New York: New American Library, 1963), 13.9.

103. *Foucault Reader*, 352.

104. Shuger, *Habits of Thought*, 89.

105. Beginning with Gabriel Harvey, critics of Nashe's *Christs Teares* have argued for its debt to Southwell's *Marie Magdalens Funeral Teares* (McDermott, "Mary Magdalene," 144). If this is so, then Nashe's homily exemplifies the Calvinist transformation of female erotic spirituality into the mythos of male violence.

106. *Foucault Reader*, 372.

107. The lower figures represent two of the theological virtues—hope and charity—but the figure on the right symbolizes justice—a moral virtue— rather than the third theological virtue, faith. It is therefore tempting to identify the unnamed female in the upper left corner with the missing theological virtue, as though, by a sort of iconographic slippage, faith moves from the allegorical space of the lower portion of the façade into a historical arena comprising state, church, and soul.

108. *The Works of that Learned and Judicious Divine, Mr. Richard Hooker*, ed. John Keble, 7th ed., 3 vols. (1888; rpt. New York: Burt Franklin, 1970), 1:275–76, 338–39; cf. Shuger, *Habits of Thought*, 139–41.

109. Hooker, *Works* 3:341, 390; cf. Shuger, *Habits of Thought*, 39–40, 257, 262.

110. Malvern, *Venus in Sackcloth*, 160.

111. Lisa Jardine, *Still Harping on Daughters: Women and Drama in the Age of Shakespeare* (Sussex: Harvester, 1983), 77. For medieval parallels between the Virgin Mary and Mary Magdalene, see Saxer, *Le culte* 2:343.

CONCLUSION

1. After World War I, this condemnation also covers the patriotic sacrifices idealized by Classical authors.

2. Michel Foucault, *Madness and Civilization: A History of Insanity in the Age of Reason*, trans. Richard Howard (New York: Vintage Books, Random House, 1988), 81. See also his analysis of the late Gothic *Speculum humanae salvationis*, in which "the Passion of Christ . . . is surrounded by all the glories of torture and its innumerable dreams; Tubal the blacksmith and Isaiah's

wheel take their places around the Cross, forming beyond all the lessons of the sacrifice the fantastic tableau of savagery, of tormented bodies, and of suffering." The symbols of Christ's sacrifice twisted into nightmare images of madness and unreason register, for Foucault, the first glimmerings of "the dawn of madness" (18–19).

3. Michel Foucault, *Discipline and Punish: The Birth of the Prison*, trans. Alan Sheridan (New York: Vintage Books, Random House, 1979), 191–94.

4. Recent debates over NEA funding and the Mapplethorpe exhibit suggest the extent to which elite culture views perversity, alienation, and abnormality as touchstones of authentic art. Cf. Foucault, *Madness*, 285–89.

5. Elias, *Power and Civility*, 274.

6. Ibid., 294–98.

7. In *The Interpretation of Dreams*, Freud similarly comments on "the secular advance of repression in the emotional life of mankind" (in *Complete Psychological Works* 4:264).

8. Foucault, *Madness*, 197.

Bibliography

Aers, David. "Reflections on Current Histories of the Subject." *Literature and History* 2 (1991): 20–34.

Ailesbury, Thomas. *The Passion Sermon at Pauls-Crosse, upon Good-Friday last*. London, 1626.

A Larum for London (1602). Edited by W. W. Gregg. Malone Society Reprints. Oxford: Oxford University Press, 1913.

Allen, Don Cameron. "Herrick's 'Rex Tragicus.'" In *Studies in Honor of Dewitt T. Starnes*, 215–26. Austin: University of Texas Press, 1967.

———. *The Legend of Noah: Renaissance Rationalism in Art, Science, and Letters*. Illinois Studies in Language and Literature 33.3–4. Urbana: University of Illinois Press, 1949.

Andrewes, Lancelot. *Sermons*. Edited by G. M. Story. Oxford: Clarendon, 1967.

———. *The Works of Lancelot Andrewes*. 11 vols. Library of Anglo-Catholic Theology. Oxford, 1841–1872.

Anselm, Saint. *Cur Deus Homo*. In *St. Anselm: Basic Writings*, 177–288. Translated by S. N. Deane. 2d ed. La Salle, Ill.: Open Court, 1962.

Aquinas, Saint Thomas. *Aquinas: Selected Political Writings*. Edited by A. P. D'Entrèves. Oxford: Basil Blackwell, 1954.

Aristotle. *The Complete Works of Aristotle*. Edited by Jonathan Barnes. 2 vols. Bollingen Series 71. Princeton: Princeton University Press, 1984.

Auerbach, Erich. *Mimesis: The Representation of Reality in Western Literature*. Translated by Willard Trask. Princeton: Princeton University Press, 1953.

Augustine, Saint. *The Confessions of Saint Augustine*. Translated by Rex Warner. New York: New American Library, 1963.

———. *Lectures or Tractates on the Gospel According to St. John*. 2 vols. In *The Works of Aurelius Augustine, Bishop of Hippo*. Edited by Marcus Dods. Edinburgh: T. and T. Clark, 1874.

Aulén, Gustav. *Christus Victor: An Historical Study of the Three Main Types of the Idea of the Atonement.* Translated by A. G. Herbert. Introduction by Jaroslav Pelikan. London: SPCK, 1970.

Bacon, Francis. *Francis Bacon: A Selection of His Works.* Edited by Sidney Warhaft. New York: Odyssey, 1965.

Bal, Mieke. *Death and Dissymmetry: The Politics of Coherence in the Book of Judges.* Chicago: University of Chicago Press, 1988.

Barber, C. L. "The Family in Shakespeare's Development: Tragedy and Sacredness." In *Representing Shakespeare: New Psychoanalytic Essays,* edited by Murray Schwartz and Coppélia Kahn, 188–202. Baltimore: Johns Hopkins University Press, 1980.

Barish, Jonas. *The Antitheatrical Prejudice.* Berkeley: University of California Press, 1981.

Barkan, David. *Disease, Pain, and Sacrifice: Toward a Psychology of Suffering.* Boston: Beacon, 1968.

———. *The Duality of Human Existence: An Essay on Psychology and Religion.* Chicago: Rand McNally, 1966.

Baronius, Caesar. *Annales Ecclesiastici.* Edited by Augustinus Theiner. 37 vols. Paris, 1864–1883.

Barton, John. "The Faculty of Law." In *The Collegiate University,* edited by James McConica, 257–83. Vol. 3 of *The History of the University of Oxford,* gen. ed. T. H. Aston. 3 vols. Oxford: Oxford University Press, 1984–.

Benin, Stephen D. "Sacrifice as Education in Augustine and Chrysostom." *Church History* 52 (1983): 7–20.

Bennett, H. S. *English Books and Readers, 1558–1603.* Cambridge: At the University Press, 1965.

Bentley, Jerry H. *Humanists and Holy Writ: New Testament Scholarship in the Renaissance.* Princeton: Princeton University Press, 1983.

Bercovitch, Sacvan. *The Puritan Origins of the American Self.* New Haven: Yale, 1975.

Berman, Harold J. *Law and Revolution: The Formation of the Western Legal Tradition.* Cambridge: Harvard University Press, 1983.

Bernard of Clairvaux. *On the Song of Songs II.* Translated by Kilian Walsh. 4 vols. Kalamazoo, Mich.: Cistercian Publications, 1976.

Beza, Theodore. *Jesu Christi Domini Nostri Novum Testamentum, sive Novum Foedus, cujus Graeco contextui respondent interpretationes duae: una, vetus; altera, Theodori Bezae . . . Accessit etiam Joachimi Camerarii in Novum Foedus Commentarius.* Cambridge, 1642.

———. *A Tragedie of Abrahams Sacrifice [Abraham sacrifiant].* Translated by Arthur Golding. Edited by Malcolm Wallace. Toronto: University of Toronto Library, 1906.

Biblia Sacra cum glossa interlineari, ordinaria, et Nicolai Lyrani postilla, eiusdemque moralitatibus, Burgensis additionibus, & Thoringi replicis. 7 vols. Venice, 1588.

Biblia Sacra, cum glossa ordinaria . . . et postilla Nicolai Lirani . . . necnon additionibus Pauli Burgensis . . . & Matthiae Thoringi replicis. 6 vols. Antwerp, 1617.

Binns, J. W. *Intellectual Culture in Elizabethan and Jacobean England: The Latin Writings of the Age.* ARCA: Classical and Medieval Texts 24. Leeds: Francis Cairns, 1990.

Blumenberg, Hans. *The Legitimacy of the Modern Age.* Translated by Robert Wallace. Studies in Contemporary German Social Thought. Cambridge: MIT Press, 1983.

Bodin, Jean. *Method for the Easy Comprehension of History.* Translated by Beatrice Reynolds. New York: Columbia University Press, 1945.

Bohatec, Josef. *Calvin und das Recht.* 1934; rpt. Darmstadt: Scientia Verlag Aalen, 1971.

Boon, James A. "Comparative De-enlightenment: Paradox and Limits in the History of Ethnology." *Daedalus* 109 (1980): 73–92.

Boose, Lynda. "The Father's House and the Daughter in It: The Structures of Western Culture's Daughter-Father Relationship." In *Daughters and Fathers,* edited by Lynda Boose and Betty Flowers, 19–74. Baltimore: Johns Hopkins University Press, 1989.

Bossy, John. *Christianity in the West: 1400–1700.* Oxford: Oxford University Press, 1985.

Bouwsma, William J. "Anxiety and the Formation of Early Modern Culture." In his *A Usable Past: Essays in European Cultural History,* 157–89. Berkeley: University of California Press, 1990.

————. *John Calvin: A Sixteenth-Century Portrait.* New York: Oxford University Press, 1988.

Boyle, Marjorie O'Rourke. *Erasmus on Language and Method in Theology.* Toronto: University of Toronto Press, 1977.

Breton, Nicholas. *The Works in Verse and Prose.* Edited by Alexander Grosart. 2 vols. Chertsey Worthies' Library. 1879; rpt. New York: AMS Press, 1966.

Brown, Peter. *The Body and Society: Men, Women, and Sexual Renunciation in Early Christianity.* New York: Columbia University Press, 1988.

————. *The Making of Late Antiquity.* Cambridge: Harvard University Press, 1978.

Brugman, J. "Arabic Scholarship." In *Leiden University in the Seventeenth Century: An Exchange of Learning,* edited by Th. H. Lunsingh Scheurleer and G. H. M. Posthumus Meyjes, 203–15. Leiden: Brill, 1975.

Buchanan, George. *George Buchanan: Tragedies.* Edited by P. Sharrat and P. G. Walsh. Translated by P. G. Walsh. Edinburgh: Scottish Academic Press, 1983.

————. *The Sacred Dramas of George Buchanan*. Translated by Archibald Brown. Edinburgh: James Thin, 1906.

Bude, Guillaume, I. Tusanus, and R. Constantinus. *Lexicon sive dictionarium Graecolatinum*. n.p., 1562.

Burkert, Walter. "Greek Tragedy and Sacrificial Ritual." *Greek, Roman, and Byzantine Studies* 7 (1966): 87–121.

————. *Homo Necans: The Anthropology of Ancient Greek Sacrificial Ritual and Myth*. Translated by Peter Bing. Berkeley: University of California Press, 1983.

Burton, Robert. *The Anatomy of Melancholy*. Edited by Holbrook Jackson. New York: Vintage Books, Random House, 1977.

Bush, Douglas. *English Literature in the Earlier Seventeenth Century, 1600–1660*. Oxford History of English Literature. New York: Oxford University Press, 1945.

Bynum, Caroline. "The Body of Christ in the Later Middle Ages: A Reply to Leo Steinberg." *Renaissance Quarterly* 39 (1986): 399–439.

Callaghan, Dympna. *Woman and Gender in Renaissance Tragedy*. New York: Harvester Wheatsheaf, 1989.

Calvin, John. *The Adultero-German Interim Declaration of Religion, with Calvin's Refutation* (1547). In *Tracts and Treatises in Defense of the Reformed Faith*. Translated by Henry Beveridge. Edited by Thomas Torrance. 3 vols. 3:189–343. Grand Rapids, Mich.: Eerdmans, 1958.

————. *Commentaries on the Epistle of Paul the Apostle to the Hebrews*. Translated by John Owen. Edinburgh: Calvin Translation Society, 1853.

————. *Commentary on a Harmony of the Evangelists: Matthew, Mark, and Luke*. Edited by William Pringle. 3 vols. Edinburgh: Calvin Translation Society, 1846.

————. *Commentary on the Gospel According to John*. Translated by William Pringle. 2 vols. Grand Rapids, Mich.: Eerdmans, 1956.

————. *Commentary upon the Epistle of Saint Paul to the Romans*. Translated by Christopher Rosdell (1583). Edited by Henry Beveridge. Edinburgh: Calvin Translation Society, 1844.

————. *Institutes of the Christian Religion*. Translated by Ford Lewis Battles. Edited by John T. McNeill. 2 vols. Library of Christian Classics. London: SCM Press, 1960.

————. *Letters of John Calvin*. Edited by Jules Bonnet. 4 vols. Philadelphia: Presbyterian Board of Publication, 1858.

————. *Psychopannychia; Or, a Refutation of the Error that the Soul Sleeps in the Interval between Death and the Judgment* (1542). In *Tracts and Treatises in Defense of the Reformed Faith*. Translated by Henry Beveridge. Edited by Thomas Torrance. 3 vols. 3:413–90. Grand Rapids, Mich.: Eerdmans, 1958.

Camerarius, Joachim. *Commentarius in Novum Foedus* (1572). Cambridge,

1642. [Bound with Theodore Beza, *Jesu Christi Domini nostri Novum Testamentum.*]

Campbell, Lily Bess. *Divine Poetry and Drama in Sixteenth-Century England.* Cambridge: At the University Press, 1961.

Casaubon, Isaac. *De rebus sacris et ecclesiasticis exercitationes XVI ad Cardinalis Baronii.* London, 1614.

Casaubon, Meric. *A Treatise Concerning Enthusiasme.* 1655; rpt. Gainesville, Fla.: Scholars' Facsimiles, 1970.

Cave, Terence. *Devotional Poetry in France, c. 1570–1613.* Cambridge: At the University Press, 1969.

Chamberlaine, Bartholomew, D.D. *The Passion of Christ, and the Benefits thereby.* London, 1613.

Chaucer, Geoffrey. *The Legend of Good Women.* In *The Works of Geoffrey Chaucer,* edited by F. N. Robinson, 480–518. 2d ed. Boston: Houghton Mifflin, 1957.

Chaucer [pseudonym]. *The Lamentatyon of Mary Magdaleyne.* Edited by Bertha M. Skeat. Cambridge: Fabb and Tyler, 1897.

Chomarat, Jacques. "Les *Annotations* de Valla, celles d'Erasme et la grammaire." In *Histoire de l'exégèse au XVIe siecle,* edited by Olivier Fatio and Pierre Fraenkel, 202–28. Geneva: Librairie Droz, 1978.

Christopherson, John. *Jephthah.* Edited and translated by Francis Howard Forbes. Introduction by Wilbur Sypherd. Newark: University of Delaware Press, 1928.

Cicero. *Tusculan Disputations.* Translated by J. E. King. Loeb Classical Library. London: W. Heinemann, 1927.

Clark, Samuel. *The Blessed Life and Meritorious Death of our Lord & Saviour Jesus Christ.* London, 1664.

Clubb, Louise George. "*The Virgin Martyr* and the *Tragedia Sacra.*" *Renaissance Drama* 7 (1964): 103–26.

The Complaynte of the Lover of Chryst Mary Magdaleyn. London, c. 1620.

Corpus juris civilis. Edited by Paul Krueger and Theodor Mommsen. 3 vols. Berlin: Weidmann, 1954.

Costello, William T. *The Scholastic Curriculum at Early Seventeenth-Century Cambridge.* Cambridge: Harvard University Press, 1958.

Crashaw, Richard. Selections in *Major Poets of the Earlier Seventeenth Century,* edited by Barbara Lewalski and Andrew Sabol, 611–739. Indianapolis: Odyssey, 1973.

Crewe, Jonathan V. *Unredeemed Rhetoric: Thomas Nashe and the Scandal of Authorship.* Baltimore: Johns Hopkins University Press, 1982.

Critici sacri, sive annotata doctissimorum virorum in Vetus ac Novum Testamentum. Edited by John Pearson, A. Scattergood, F. Gouldman, and R. Pearson. 8 vols in 9. 2d. ed. Amsterdam, 1698.

Cropper, Elizabeth. "The Beauty of Woman: Problems in the Rhetoric of

Renaissance Portraiture." In *Rewriting the Renaissance: The Discourses of Sexual Difference in Early Modern Europe*, edited by Margaret Ferguson, Maureen Quilligan, and Nancy Vickers, 175–90. Chicago: University of Chicago Press, 1986.

Culiano, Ioan P. *Eros and Magic in the Renaissance.* Translated by Margaret Cook. Chicago: University of Chicago Press, 1987.

Culler, Jonathan. *Framing the Sign: Criticism and Its Institutions.* Oklahoma Project for Discourse and Theory 3. Norman: University of Oklahoma Press, 1988.

Cunningham, J. V. "Wonder." In *The Collected Essays of J. V. Cunningham*, 53–96. Chicago: Swallow Press, 1976.

Dekker, Thomas. *The Virgin Martyr.* In vol. 3 of *The Dramatic Works of Thomas Dekker.* Edited by Fredson Bowers. 4 vols. Cambridge: At the University Press, 1958.

Deloney, Thomas. *Canaans Calamitie, Jerusalems Misery* (1618). In *The Works of Thomas Deloney*, edited by Francis Oscar Mann. Oxford: Clarendon, 1912.

Delumeau, Jean. *Sin and Fear: The Emergence of a Western Guilt Culture, Thirteenth–Eighteenth Centuries.* Translated by Eric Nicholson. New York: St. Martin's, 1990.

Detienne, Marcel. "Culinary Practices and the Spirit of Sacrifice." In *The Cuisine of Sacrifice among the Greeks*, edited by Marcel Detienne and Jean-Pierre Vernant, translated by Paula Wissing, 1–20. Chicago: University of Chicago Press, 1989.

Dickens, A. G. *The English Reformation.* 2d. ed. University Park: Pennsylvania State University Press, 1989.

Dictionary of the History of Ideas: Studies of Selected Pivotal Ideas. Edited by Philip Wiener. 5 vols. New York: Scribner's, 1973.

Diestel, Ludwig. *Geschichte des Alten Testamentes in der christlichen Kirche.* Jena, 1869.

Dietelmaier, Jon. Augustinus. *Historia Dogmatis de descensu Christi ad Inferos litteraria.* Nürnberg, 1741.

Donne, John. *Biathanatos.* Edited by Ernest Sullivan. Newark: University of Delaware Press, 1984.

———. *The Complete English Poems of John Donne.* Edited by C. A. Patrides. London: Dent, 1985.

———. *The Sermons of John Donne.* Edited by George Potter and Evelyn Simpson. 10 vols. Berkeley: University of California Press, 1953–1962.

Dorrie, Heinrich. "L'épître héroïque dans les littératures modernes." *Revue de littérature comparée* 40 (1966): 48–64.

Drusius, Johannes. *De sectis Judaicis commentarii trihaeresio . . . accessit denuo Josephi Scaligeri I.C.F. Elenchus Trihaeresii.* Edited by Sixtinus Amama. Arnheim, 1619.

Dunin-Borkowski, Stanislaus von. *Spinoza*. 4 vols. Munster: Aschendorff-schen Verlagsbuchhandlung, 1936.

Eden, Kathy. "Equity and the Origins of Renaissance Historicism: The Case for Erasmus." *Yale Journal of Law and the Humanities* 5 (1993): 137–45.

———. "Hermeneutics and the Ancient Rhetorical Tradition." *Rhetorica* 5 (1987): 59–86.

———. "The Rhetorical Tradition and Augustinian Hermeneutics in *De doctrina Christiana*." *Rhetorica* 8 (1990): 45–63.

Edwards, Charles S. *Hugo Grotius, the Miracle of Holland: A Study in Political and Legal Thought*. Introduction by Richard A. Falk. Chicago: Nelson Hall, 1981.

Elias, Norbert. *Power and Civility*. Vol. 2 of *The Civilizing Process*. Translated by Edmund Jephcott. 2 vols. New York: Pantheon Books, Random House, 1982.

Else, Gerald F. *Aristotle's Poetics: The Argument*. Cambridge: Harvard University Press, 1967.

Empson, William. *Milton's God*. London: Chatto and Windus, 1961.

———. *Seven Types of Ambiguity*. 1947; rpt. New York: New Directions, 1966.

Erasmus, Desiderius. *Ciceronianus; or, A Dialogue on the Best Style of Speaking* (1517). Translated by Izora Scott. 1908; rpt. New York: AMS, 1972.

———. *De duplici copia verborum ac rerum commentarii duo*. Edited by Craig Thompson. Translated by Betty Knott. In *The Collected Works of Erasmus* 24:280–659. Toronto: University of Toronto Press, 1974–.

———. *Disputatiuncula de taedio, pavore, tristitia Jesu, instante supplicio crucis* (1503). In *Opera omnia*. Edited by Joannes Clericus (Le Clerc). 11 vols. 5:1263–94. 1703–1706; rpt. Hildesheim: Georg Olms, 1962.

Evans, G. R. *The Language and Logic of the Bible: The Road to Reformation* Cambridge: Cambridge University Press, 1985.

Eyssell, A. P. Th. *Doneau: Sa vie et ses ouvrages*. 1860; rpt. Geneva: Slatkine Reprints, 1970.

Fernandez, Manuel Gimenez. "Fray Bartolome de Las Casas: A Biographical Sketch." In *Bartolome de Las Casas in History: Toward an Understanding of the Man and His Work*, edited by Juan Friede and Benjamin Keen, 67–125. De Kalb: Northern Illinois University Press, 1971.

Foley, Helene P. *Ritual Irony: Poetry and Sacrifice in Euripides*. Ithaca: Cornell University Press, 1985.

Ford, Philip J. *George Buchanan: Prince of Poets*. Aberdeen: Aberdeen University Press, 1982.

Foucault, Michel. *Discipline and Punish: The Birth of the Prison*. Translated by Alan Sheridan. New York: Vintage Books, Random House, 1979.

———. *The Foucault Reader*. Edited by Paul Rabinow. New York: Pantheon Books, Random House, 1984.

———. *Madness and Civilization: A History of Insanity in the Age of Reason*. Translated by Richard Howard. New York: Vintage Books, Random House, 1988.

———. *The Order of Things: An Archaeology of the Human Sciences*. New York: Random House, 1970.

Foxe, John. *A Sermon of Christ crucified, preached at Paules Crosse* (1570). In *The English Sermons of John Foxe*. Introduction by Warren Wooden. Delmar, N.Y.: Scholars' Facsimiles, 1978.

Franklin, Julian H. *Jean Bodin and the Sixteenth-Century Revolution in the Methodology of Law and History*. New York: Columbia University Press, 1963.

Franks, Robert S. *The Work of Christ: A Historical Study of Christian Doctrine*. London: Thomas Nelson, n.d.

Frazer, James George. *The New Golden Bough*. Edited by Theodor Gaster. Abridged ed. New York: Criterion, 1959.

Freud, Sigmund. *Standard Edition of the Complete Psychological Works of Sigmund Freud*. Translated and edited by James Strachey. 24 vols. London: Hogarth, 1964.

Friedman, Jerome. *The Most Ancient Testimony: Sixteenth-Century Christian-Hebraica in the Age of Renaissance Nostalgia*. Athens: Ohio University Press, 1983.

Froula, Christine. "When Eve Reads Milton: Undoing the Canonical Economy." *Critical Inquiry* 10 (1983): 321–47.

Funkenstein, Amos. *Theology and the Scientific Imagination from the Middle Ages to the Seventeenth Century*. Princeton: Princeton University Press, 1986.

Garth, Helen Meredith. *Saint Mary Magdalene in Medieval Literature*. Johns Hopkins University Studies in Historical and Political Science. Baltimore: Johns Hopkins University Press, 1950.

Gellinek, Christian. *Hugo Grotius*. Twayne's World Authors Series. Boston: Twayne Publishers, 1983.

Gentili, Alberico. *De jure belli commentatio tertia*. London, 1589.

———. *De jure belli libri tres*. Translated by John Rolfe. Introduction by Coleman Phillipson. 2 vols. Classics of International Law. Oxford: Clarendon, 1933.

———. *In titulos codicis si quis Imperatori maledixerit, ad legem Juliam majestatis disputationes decem*. 2d ed. Hanover, 1607.

Gilmore, Myron Piper. *Argument from Roman Law in Political Thought, 1200–1600*. Harvard Historical Monographs 15. Cambridge: Harvard University Press, 1941.

Gleason, John B. *John Colet*. Berkeley: University of California Press, 1989.

Goclenius, Rodolphus. *Lexicon philosophicum quo tanquam clave philosophiae fores aperiuntur.* Frankfurt, 1613; rpt. Hildesheim: Georg Olms, 1964.

Gosse, Edmund. *The Life and Letters of John Donne, Dean of St. Pauls.* 2 vols. 1899; rpt. Gloucester, Mass.: Peter Smith, 1959.

Grafton, Anthony. *Defenders of the Text: The Traditions of Scholarship in an Age of Science, 1450–1800.* Cambridge: Harvard University Press, 1991.

———. *Joseph Scaliger: A Study in the History of Classical Scholarship.* Vol. 1, *Textual Criticism and Exegesis.* Oxford: Clarendon, 1983.

Greenblatt, Stephen. "Invisible Bullets: Renaissance Authority and Its Sub-versions, *Henry IV* and *Henry V.*" In *Political Shakespeare: New Essays in Cultural Materialism,* edited by Jonathan Dollimore and Alan Sinfield, 18–47. Ithaca: Cornell University Press, 1985.

———. *Learning to Curse: Essays in Early Modern Culture.* New York: Rout-ledge, 1990.

———. *Marvelous Possessions: The Wonder of the New World.* Chicago: Uni-versity of Chicago Press, 1991.

———. *Renaissance Self-Fashioning from More to Shakespeare.* Chicago: University of Chicago Press, 1980.

———. *Shakespearean Negotiations: The Circulation of Social Energy in Re-naissance England.* The New Historicism: Studies in Cultural Poetics. Ber-keley: University of California Press, 1988.

Greene, Thomas. *Light in Troy.* New Haven: Yale University Press, 1982.

Greenslade, S. L., editor. *The West from the Reformation to the Present Day.* Vol. 3 of *The Cambridge History of the Bible.* Cambridge: At the Univer-sity Press, 1963.

Gregory of Nazianzen. *Christus Patiens, tragoedia.* Edited by J. P. Migne. In *Patrologia Graeca.* 161 vols. 38:153–338. Paris, 1857–1912.

Gregory the Great. *The Book of Pastoral Rule and Selected Epistles.* Trans-lated by James Barmby. Nicene and Post-Nicene Fathers, 2d ser., 12. Grand Rapids, Mich.: Eerdmans, 1979.

———. *XL homiliarum in Evangelia libri duo.* Edited by J. P. Migne. In *Pa-trologia Latina.* 221 vols. 76:1075–1314. Paris, 1844–1900.

Greville, Fulke. *Caelica.* In *Five Courtier Poets of the English Renaissance,* edited by Robert Bender, 484–561. New York: Washington Square Press, 1967.

———. *Poems and Dramas of Fulke Greville, First Lord Brooke.* Edited by Geoffrey Bullough. 2 vols. Edinburgh: Oliver and Boyd, 1939.

Grotius, Hugo. *Defensio fidei catholicae de satisfactione Christi adversus Faus-tum Socinum* (1617). Edited by Theodore Hillensberg. In *Opera omnia theologica in tres tomos divisa.* 4 vols. 4:293–348. Amsterdam, 1679.

———. *De jure belli ac pacis libri tres* (1625). Edited and abridged translation by William Whewell. 3 vols. Cambridge: At the University Press, 1853.

———. *De veritate religionis Christianae* (1627). In *Opera omnia theologica in tres tomos divisa.* 4 vols. 4:3–96. Amsterdam, 1679.

————. *De Dichtwerken van Hugo Grotius*. Edited by B. L. Meulenbroek. Assen: Van Gorcum, 1977.

————. *The Freedom of the Seas* (1609). Translated by Ralph van Deman Magoffin. Edited by John Brown Scott. Carnegie Endowment for International Peace. New York: Oxford University Press, 1916.

————. *The Jurisprudence of Holland* (1631, but written 1619–1621). Translated by R. W. Lee. Oxford: Clarendon, 1936.

Hall, Basil. "Biblical Scholarship: Editions and Commentaries." In *Cambridge History of the Bible: The West from the Reformation to the Present Day*, edited by S. L. Greenslade, 38–93. Cambridge: At the University Press, 1963.

Hall, Joseph. *The Works*. Edited by Philip Wynter. 10 vols. Oxford: At the University Press, 1863.

Haller, William. *The Rise of Puritanism*. New York: Columbia University Press, 1938.

Hallet, Charles, and Elaine Hallet. *The Revenger's Madness: A Study of Revenge Tragedy Motifs*. Lincoln: University of Nebraska Press, 1980.

Hamilton, Bernice. *Political Thought in Sixteenth-Century Spain: A Study of the Political Ideas of Vitoria, De Soto, Suarez, and Molina*. Oxford: Clarendon, 1963.

Hammond, Henry. *A continuation of the defense of Hugo Grotius in an answer to the review of his Annotations*. London, 1657.

————. *A Paraphrase and Annotations upon all the Books of the New Testament*. 5th ed. London, 1681.

————. *A second defense of the learned Hugo Grotius*. London, 1655.

Hathaway, Baxter. *The Age of Criticism: The Late Renaissance in Italy*. Ithaca: Cornell University Press, 1962.

————. *Marvels and Commonplaces: Renaissance Literary Criticism*. New York: Random House, 1968.

Hayne, Thomas. *The general view of the Holy Scriptures*. 2d ed. London, 1640.

Hazeltine, H. D. "The Renaissance and the Laws of Europe." In *Cambridge Legal Essays*, 139–71. Cambridge: W. Heffer, 1926.

Heigham, John. *The Life of our Blessed Lord and Saviour Jesus, Gathered out of . . . Saint Bonaventure*. 2d ed. Douai, 1622.

Heinsius, Daniel. *D. Heinsii sacrarum exercitationum ad novum testamentum libri XX*. 2d ed. Cambridge, 1640.

————. *The Mirrour of Humilitie: or two eloquent and acute Discourses upon the Nativitie and Passion of Christ*. Translated by I. H. London, 1618.

————. *On Plot in Tragedy* (1611). Translated by Paul Sellin and John McManmon. Edited by Paul Sellin. Northridge, Calif.: San Fernando Valley State College Foundation, 1971.

Helgerson, Richard. *The Elizabethan Prodigals*. Berkeley: University of California Press, 1976.

———. *Forms of Nationhood: The Elizabethan Writing of England*. Chicago: University of Chicago Press, 1992.

Herbert, George. *The Temple*. In *Major Poets of the Earlier Seventeenth Century*, edited by Barbara Lewalski and Andrew Sabol, 173–389. Indianapolis: Odyssey, 1973.

Herrick, Robert. *Hesperides*. In *Major Poets of the Earlier Seventeenth Century*. Edited by Barbara Lewalski and Andrew Sabol. Indianapolis: Odyssey, 1973.

Higham, Florence. *Lancelot Andrewes*. London: SCM Press, 1952.

Hodgen, Margaret T. *Early Anthropology in the Sixteenth and Seventeenth Centuries*. Philadelphia: University of Pennsylvania Press, 1964.

Holt, Elizabeth, ed. *A Documentary History of Art*. 2 vols. Garden City, N.Y.: Doubleday, 1958.

Hooker, Richard. *Of the Laws of Ecclesiastical Polity*. Introduction by Christopher Morris. 2 vols. London: Dent, 1907.

———. *The Works of that Learned and Judicious Divine, Mr. Richard Hooker* Edited by John Keble. 3 vols. 7th ed. 1888; rpt. New York: Burt Franklin, 1970.

Horton, Robin. "African Traditional Thought and Western Science." In *Rationality*, edited by Bryan R. Wilson, 131–71. Evanston: Harper and Row, 1970.

Humphreys, S. C. *The Family, Women, and Death: Comparative Studies*. London: Routledge and Kegan Paul, 1983.

Hunter, George K. "Tyrant and Martyr: Religious Heroisms in Elizabethan Tragedy." In *Poetic Traditions of the English Renaissance*, edited by Maynard Mack and George deForest Lord, 85–102. New Haven: Yale University Press, 1982.

Huppert, George. *The Idea of Perfect History: Historical Erudition and Historical Philosophy in Renaissance France*. Urbana: University of Illinois Press, 1970.

[Jacob, Henry]. *A Treatise of the Sufferings and Victory of Christ, in the work of our redemption*. London, 1597.

Janelle, Pierre. *Robert Southwell: The Writer*. New York: Sheed and Ward, 1935.

Jardine, Lisa. *Still Harping on Daughters: Women and Drama in the Age of Shakespeare*. Sussex: Harvester Press, 1983.

Jonge, H. J. de. "The Study of the New Testament." Translated by J. C. Grayson. In *Leiden University in the Seventeenth Century: An Exchange of Learning*, edited by Th. H. Lunsingh Scheurleer and G. H. M. Posthumus Meyjes, 65–110. Leiden: Brill, 1975.

Josephus. *Against Apion*. In *Josephus*. Translated by H. St. J. Thackeray. 8 vols. 1:161–41. Loeb Classical Library. London: William Heinemann, 1926.

Kallenborn, Carl von. *Die Vorläufer des Hugo Grotius auf dem Gebiete des jus naturae et gentium*. 1848; rpt. Frankfurt: Antiquariat Sauer & Auvermann, 1965.

Katchen, Aaron L. *Christian Hebraists and Dutch Rabbis: Seventeenth Century Apologetics and the Study of Maimonides' Mishneh Torah*. Harvard Judaic Texts and Studies 3. Cambridge: Harvard University Press, 1984.

Kelley, Donald R. *The Beginning of Ideology: Consciousness and Society in the French Reformation*. Cambridge: Cambridge University Press, 1981.

————. *Foundations of Modern Historical Scholarship: Language, Law, and History in the French Renaissance*. New York: Columbia University Press, 1970.

————. "*Gaius Noster*: Substructures of Western Social Thought." *American Historical Review* 84 (1979): 619–48.

————. "Louis le Caron *Philosophe*." In *Philosophy and Humanism: Essays in Honor of Paul Oskar Kristeller*, edited by Edward Mahoney, 30–49. Leiden: Brill, 1976.

————. "Vera Philosophia: The Philosophical Significance of Renaissance Jurisprudence." *Journal of the History of Philosophy* 14 (1976): 267–79.

Kemp, Anthony. *The Estrangement of the Past: A Study in the Origins of Modern Historical Consciousness*. New York: Oxford University Press, 1991.

Kermode, Frank. *The Genesis of Secrecy: On the Interpretation of Narrative*. Cambridge: Harvard University Press, 1979.

Knight, W. S. M. *The Life and Works of Hugo Grotius*. Grotius Society Publications 4. 1925; rpt. London: Wildy, 1962.

Koschaker, Paul. *Europa und das römische Recht*. Munich: Biederstein, 1947.

Lamb, Mary Ellen. *Gender and Authorship in the Sidney Circle*. Madison: University of Wisconsin Press, 1990.

Langmuir, Gavin. *History, Religion, and Antisemitism*. Berkeley: University of California Press, 1990.

Lapide, Cornelius à. *The Great Commentary*. Edited and translated by Thomas Mossman. 6 vols. London, 1876–1887.

————. *The Great Commentary*. Edited and translated by Thomas Mossman. 3d ed. 6 vols. London, 1889–1896.

Laplanche, François. *L'écriture, le sacré et l'histoire: Érudits et politiques protestants devant la Bible en France au XVIIe siècle*. Amsterdam: Holland University Press, 1986.

Laqueur, Thomas. "Orgasm, Generation, and the Politics of Reproductive Biology." *Representations* 14 (1986): 1–41.

Las Casas, Bartolome de. *In Defense of the Indians*. Translated by Stafford Poole. De Kalb: Northern Illinois University Press, 1974.

———. *The Spanish Colonie, or Briefe Chronicle of the Acts and gestes of the Spaniardes in the West Indies, called the New World.* [Translation of *Brevisima relacion de la Destruycion de las Indias occidentales.*] Translated by M. M. S. London, 1583.

———. *The Tears of the Indians: Being an Historical and true Account of the Massacres and Slaughters of above Twenty Millions of innocent People; Committed by the Spaniards.* [Translation of *Brevisima relacion de la Destruycion de las Indias occidentales.*] Translated by John Phillips. London, 1656; rpt. Stanford, Calif.: Academic Reprints, 1953.

Lebègue, Raymond. *La tragédie religieuse en France: Les débuts (1514–1573).* Bibliothèque littéraire de la Renaissance. Paris: Librairie Ancienne Honoré Champion, 1929.

Leo the Great. *The Letters and Sermons.* Translated by Charles L. Feltoe. Nicene and Post-Nicene Fathers, 2d ser., 12. Grand Rapids, Mich.: Eerdmans, 1979.

The Life of Saint Mary Magdalene and of Her Sister Martha. Edited and translated by David Mycoff. Cistercian Studies 108. Kalamazoo: Cistercian Publications, 1989.

Lightfoot, John. *A Commentary on the New Testament from the Talmud and Hebraica, Matthew–I Corinthians.* 4 vols. 1859; rpt. Grand Rapids, Mich.: Baker Book House, 1979.

Lipking, Lawrence. *Abandoned Women and Poetic Tradition.* Chicago: University of Chicago Press, 1988.

Lipsius, Justus. *De cruce libri tres.* Antwerp, 1594.

Lloyd Jones, G. *The Discovery of Hebrew in Tudor England: A Third Language.* Manchester: Manchester University Press, 1983.

Locke, John. *An Essay Concerning Human Understanding.* Edited by Alexander C. Fraser. 2 vols. New York: Dover, 1959.

Losada, Angel. "The Controversy Between Sepulveda and Las Casas in the Junta of Valladolid." In *Bartolome de Las Casas in History: Toward an Understanding of the Man and His Work,* edited by Juan Friede and Benjamin Keen, 279–308. De Kalb: Northern Illinois University Press, 1971.

Lubac, Henri de. *Exégèse médiévale: Les quatre sens de l'écriture.* 4 vols. Paris: Aubier, 1959–1964.

Lucretius. *Of the Nature of Things.* Translated by William Ellery Leonard. New York: Dutton, 1957.

Lupton, J. H. *A Life of John Colet, D.D.* 2d ed. London: George Bell, 1909.

Lyonnet, Stanislas. *Sin, Redemption, and Sacrifice: A Biblical and Patristic Study.* Edited by Leopold Sabourin. Translated by Fidelis Buck. Analecta Biblica. Rome: Biblical Institute Press, 1970.

McCall, John P. "Chaucer and the Pseudo Origen *De Maria Magdalena*: A Preliminary Study." *Speculum* 46 (1971): 491–509.

McCoy, Richard C. *The Rites of Knighthood: The Literature and Politics of*

Elizabethan Chivalry. The New Historicism: Studies in Cultural Poetics. Berkeley: University of California Press, 1989.

————. *Sir Philip Sidney: Rebellion in Arcadia.* New Brunswick: Rutgers University Press, 1979.

McCuaig, William. *Carlo Sigonio: The Changing World of the Late Renaissance.* Princeton: Princeton University Press, 1989.

McDermott, John James. "Mary Magdalene in English Literature from 1500 to 1650." Ph.D. diss. University of California, Los Angeles, 1964.

McFarlane, I. D. *Buchanan.* London: Duckworth, 1981.

McGregor, J. H. "The Sense of Tragedy in George Buchanan's *Jephthes.*" *Humanistica Lovaniensia: Journal of Neo-Latin Studies* 31 (1982): 120–40.

Maclure, Millar, ed. *Marlowe: The Critical Heritage 1588–1896.* London: Routledge and Kegan Paul, 1979.

Mâle, Emile. *Religious Art from the Twelfth to the Eighteenth Century.* Bollingen 90. Princeton: Princeton University Press, 1982.

Malvern, Marjorie M. *Venus in Sackcloth: The Magdalen's Origins and Metamorphosis.* Carbondale: Southern Illinois University Press, 1975.

Marcus, Leah. *Childhood and Cultural Despair: A Theme and Variations in Seventeenth-Century Literature.* Pittsburgh: University of Pittsburgh Press, 1978.

Margolin, Jean-Claude. "The Epistle to the Romans (Chapter 11) According to the Versions and/or Commentaries of Valla, Colet, Lefevre, and Erasmus." In *The Bible in the Sixteenth Century*, edited by David Steinmetz, 136–66, 241–48. Duke Monographs in Medieval and Renaissance Studies 11. Durham: Duke University Press, 1990.

Markham, Gervase. *Marie Magdalens Lamentations.* London, 1601.

Marsilius of Padua. *The Defender of Peace.* Translated by Alan Gewirth. 2 vols. New York: Columbia University Press, 1956.

Martz, Louis. *The Poetry of Meditation: A Study in English Religious Literature of the Seventeenth Century.* Rev. ed. New Haven: Yale University Press, 1962.

Miles, Margaret R. *Carnal Knowing: Female Nakedness and Religious Meaning in the Christian West.* Boston: Beacon, 1989.

Milton, John. *Eikonoklastes.* In *Complete Prose Works of John Milton*, edited by Merritt Hughes. 8 vols. 3:355–601. New Haven: Yale University Press, 1962.

Moisan, Thomas. "Robert Herrick's 'Rex Tragicus' and the 'Troublesome Times.'" *Viator* 21 (1990): 349–84.

Molen, Gesina H. J. van der. *Alberico Gentili and the Development of International Law.* 2d ed. Leiden: A. W. Sijthoff, 1968.

Momigliano, Arnaldo. *The Classical Foundations of Modern Historiography.* Berkeley: University of California Press, 1990.

Montaigne, Michel de. *The Complete Essays of Montaigne.* Translated by

Donald Frame. Stanford: Stanford University Press, 1958.

More, Henry. *Enthusiasmus triumphatus*. Introduction by M. V. DePorte. Augustan Reprint Society 118. Los Angeles: University of California Press, 1966.

Mueller, Martin. *Children of Oedipus and Other Essays on the Imitation of Greek Tragedy, 1550–1800*. Toronto: University of Toronto Press, 1980.

Mullaney, Steven. "Strange Things, Gross Terms, Curious Customs: The Rehearsal of Cultures in the Late Renaissance." In *Representing the English Renaissance*, edited by Stephen Greenblatt, 65–92. Berkeley: University of California Press, 1988.

Muller, Richard A. "The Hermeneutic of Promise and Fulfillment in Calvin's Exegesis of the Old Testament Prophecies of the Kingdom." In *The Bible in the Sixteenth Century*, edited by David Steinmetz, 68–82. Duke Monographs in Medieval and Renaissance Studies 11. Durham: Duke University Press, 1990.

Nashe, Thomas. *Christs Teares over Jerusalem*. In *The Works of Thomas Nashe*, edited by Ronald B. McKerrow and F. P. Wilson. 5 vols. 2:1–175. Oxford: Basil Blackwell, 1958.

Nicholl, Charles. *A Cup of News: The Life of Thomas Nashe*. London: Routledge and Kegan Paul, 1984.

Nietzsche, Friedrich. *The Birth of Tragedy and The Genealogy of Morals*. Translated by Francis Golffing. Garden City, N.Y.: Doubleday, 1956.

Origen. *Contra Celsum*. Translated by Henry Chadwick. Cambridge: Cambridge University Press, 1953.

Origen [pseudonym]. *An Homilie of Marye Magdalene, declaring her fervent love and zele towards CHRIST: written by that famous clerke ORIGENE*. London, 1565.

———. *Omelia origenis de beata Maria Magdalena*. London, 1504.

Ovid. *Heroides and Amores*. Translated by Grant Showerman. 2d ed. Loeb Classical Library. Cambridge: Harvard University Press, 1986.

Owen, John. *The Duty of Pastors and People Distinguished*. London, 1644.

———. *A review of the Annotations of Hugo Grotius, in reference unto the doctrine of the deity and satisfaction of Christ*. Oxford, 1656.

Pagden, Anthony. *The Fall of Natural Man: The American Indian and the Origins of Comparative Ethnology*. Cambridge: Cambridge University Press, 1982.

Parker, T. H. L. *Calvin's New Testament Commentaries*. Grand Rapids, Mich.: Eerdmans, 1971.

Patterson, Lee. *Chaucer and the Subject of History*. Madison: University of Wisconsin Press, 1991.

Pattison, Mark. *Essays by the Late Mark Pattison*. Edited by Henry Nettleship. 2 vols. Oxford: Clarendon, 1889.

———. *Isaac Casaubon, 1559–1614*. London: Longmans, 1875.

Pelikan, Jaroslav. *The Christian Tradition: A History of the Development of Doctrine.* 5 vols. Vol. 4, *Reformation of Church and Dogma, 1300–1700.* Chicago: University of Chicago Press, 1984.

Perella, Nicholas James. *The Kiss Sacred and Profane: An Interpretative History of Kiss Symbolism and Related Religio-Erotic Themes.* Berkeley: University of California Press, 1969.

Pithou, Pierre. *Mosaicarum et Romanarum legum collatio* (1572). In *Critici sacri,* edited by John Pearson et al., 1:2:193–248. Amsterdam, 1698.

Pocock, J. G. A. *The Ancient Constitution and the Feudal Law: A Study of English Historical Thought in the Seventeenth Century.* Rev. ed. Cambridge: Cambridge University Press, 1987.

Pollock, Frederick. "The History of the Law of Nature: A Preliminary Study." *Columbia Law Review* 1 (1901): 11–32.

———. "The Sources of International Law." *Columbia Law Review* 2 (1902): 518–24.

Polybius. *The Histories.* Translated by W. R. Paton. Loeb Classical Library. Cambridge: Harvard University Press, 1979.

———. *The History of Polybius.* Translated by Edward Grimeston. London, 1633.

———. *Polybii . . . historiarum libri qui supersunt.* Translated and edited by Isaac Casaubon. Paris, 1609.

———. *Polybii Megalopolitani historiarum libri.* Translated by Nicolao Perotti (books 1–5) and Wolfgang Musculus (books 6–17). Lyon, 1554.

Poole, Matthew. *Synopsis criticorum aliorumque S. Scripturae interpretum.* 5 vols. London, 1669.

Pope, Alexander. *The Poems of Alexander Pope.* Edited by John Butt. London: Methuen, 1963.

Pseudo-Chaucer. *See* Chaucer [pseudonym].

Pseudo-Origen. *See* Origen [pseudonym].

Rekers, B. *Benito Arias Montano (1527–1598).* London: Warburg Institute. 1972.

Richardson, Alan. "The Rise of Modern Biblical Scholarship and Recent Discussion of the Authority of the Bible." In *The Cambridge History of the Bible: The West from the Reformation to the Present Day,* edited by S. L. Greenslade, 294–338. Cambridge: At the University Press, 1963.

Ricoeur, Paul. *The Symbolism of Evil.* Translated by Emerson Buchanan. Religious Perspectives 17. New York: Harper and Row, 1967.

Rooden, Peter T. van. *Theology, Biblical Scholarship, and Rabbinical Studies in the Seventeenth Century: Constantijn L'Empereur (1591–1648), Professor of Hebrew and Theology at Leiden.* Translated by J. C. Grayson. Studies in the History of Leiden University 6. Leiden: Brill, 1989.

Rosten, Murray. *Biblical Drama in England: From the Middle Ages to the Present Day.* London: Faber and Faber, 1968.

Rougement, Denis de. *Love in the Western World.* Translated by Montgomery Belgion. New York: Doubleday, 1956.

Rummel, Erika. *Erasmus' Annotationes on the New Testament: From Philologist to Theologian.* Erasmus Studies 8. Toronto: University of Toronto Press, 1986.

Sandys, George. *The Poetical Works of George Sandys.* Edited by Richard Hooper. 2 vols. London, 1872.

Saxer, Victor. *Le culte de Marie Madeleine en Occident, des origines à la fin du moyen âge.* Preface by Henri Marrou. 2 vols. Cahiers d'archeologie et d'histoire 3. Paris: Librairie Clavreuil, 1959.

Saxl, F. "Pagan Sacrifice in the Italian Renaissance." *Journal of the Warburg Institute* 2 (1939): 346–67.

Scaliger, Joseph Justus. *Opus de emendatione temporum.* Lugduni Batavorum [Leiden], 1598.

Scaliger, Julius Caesar. *Poetices libri septem* (1561). Introduction by August Buck. Stuttgart: Friedrich Frommann Verlag, 1964.

Scarry, Elaine. *The Body in Pain: The Making and Unmaking of the World.* New York: Oxford University Press, 1985.

Schama, Simon. *The Embarrassment of Riches: An Interpretation of Dutch Culture in the Golden Age.* Berkeley: University of California Press, 1988.

Schiffman, Zachary Sayre. *On the Threshold of Modernity: Relativism in the French Renaissance.* Johns Hopkins University Studies in Historical and Political Science. Baltimore: Johns Hopkins University Press, 1991.

Schoenfeldt, Michael C. *Prayer and Power: George Herbert and Renaissance Courtship.* Chicago: University of Chicago Press, 1991.

Scholder, Klaus. *The Birth of Modern Critical Theology: Origins and Problems of Biblical Criticism in the Seventeenth Century.* Trans. John Bowden. London: SCM Press, 1990.

Scott, James Brown. *The Spanish Origin of International Law: Francisco de Vitoria and His Law of Nations.* Oxford: Clarendon, 1934.

Selden, John. *De jure naturali & gentium juxta disciplinam Ebraeorum.* London, 1640.

Sellin, Paul R. *Daniel Heinsius and Stuart England.* Publications of the Sir Thomas Browne Institute 3. Leiden: At the University Press, 1968.

Sharratt, Peter. "Euripides latinus: Buchanan's Use of his Sources." In *Acta Conventus Neo-Latini Bononiensis,* edited by R. J. Schoeck, 613–20. Binghamton: Medieval and Renaissance Texts and Studies, 1985.

Shaw, Michael. "The Female Intruder: Women in Fifth-Century Drama." *Classical Philology* 70 (1975): 255–66.

Shuger, Debora K. *Habits of Thought in the English Renaissance: Religion, Politics, and the Dominant Culture.* The New Historicism: Studies in Cultural Poetics. Berkeley: University of California Press, 1990.

———. *Sacred Rhetoric: The Christian Grand Style in the English Renaissance.*

Princeton: Princeton University Press, 1988.

Sidney, Sir Philip. *An Apology for Poetry*. Edited by Forrest Robinson. New York: Macmillan, 1970.

————. *Astrophel and Stella*. In *Silver Poets of the Sixteenth Century*, edited by Gerald Bullett, 173–225. London: Dent, 1947.

Simon, Bennett. *Tragic Drama and the Family: Psychoanalytic Studies from Aeschylus to Beckett*. New Haven: Yale University Press, 1988.

Simon, Richard. *Histoire critique des principaux commentateurs du Nouveau Testament*. Rotterdam, 1693.

Skeat, Walter W., ed. *Chaucerian and Other Pieces*. Oxford: Clarendon, 1897.

Skinner, Quentin. *The Foundations of Modern Political Thought*. 2 vols. Cambridge: Cambridge University Press, 1978.

Smalley, Beryl. "The Bible in the Medieval Schools." In *The Cambridge History of the Bible: The West from the Fathers to the Reformation*, edited by G. W. Lampe, 197–219. Cambridge: At the University Press, 1969.

————. *The Study of the Bible in the Middle Ages*. 2d ed. 1952; rpt. Notre Dame: University of Notre Dame Press, 1964.

Soto, Domingo de. *De justitia et jure libri decem*. 5 vols. Facsimile reprint of 1556 edition. Madrid: Instituto de Estudios Politicos, 1967–1968.

Southwell, Robert. *Mary Magdalens Funeral Teares* (1591). Delmar, N.Y.: Scholars' Facsimiles, 1975.

————. *Saint Peters Complaint, Newly augmented with other Poems*. London, 1605.

Spenser, Edmund. *The Complete Poetical Works of Edmund Spenser*. Edited by R. E. Neil Dodge. Boston: Houghton Mifflin, 1908.

Stabat Mater. In *The Oxford Book of Medieval Latin Verse*, edited by F. J. E. Raby, 435–37. Oxford: Clarendon, 1959.

Stallybrass, Peter. "Patriarchal Territories: The Body Enclosed." In *Rewriting the Renaissance: The Discourses of Sexual Difference in Early Modern Europe*, edited by Margaret Ferguson, Maureen Quilligan, and Nancy Vickers, 123–44. Chicago: University of Chicago Press, 1986.

Steinberg, Leo. "The Metaphors of Love and Birth in Michelangelo's *Pietas*." In *Studies in Erotic Art*, edited by Theodore Bowie and Cornelia Christenson, 231–85. New York: Basic Books, 1970.

Steiner, George. *Antigones*. New York: Oxford University Press, 1984.

Stephanus, H. [Henri Estienne]. *Thesaurus Graecae linguae*. Rev. ed. 10 vols. London, 1816–1828.

Stewart, Stanley. *The Enclosed Garden: The Tradition and the Image in Seventeenth-Century Poetry*. Madison: University of Wisconsin Press, 1966.

Stintzing, R. *Geschichte der Deutschen Rechtswissenschaft*. Geschichte der Wissenschaft in Deutschland 18. Munich, 1880–1884.

Stock, Brian. *Listening for the Text: On the Uses of the Past*. Baltimore: Johns Hopkins University Press, 1990.

Stockwood, John. *A very fruitful and necessary sermon of the destruction of Jerusalem.* London, 1584

Stone, Donald, Jr. *French Humanist Tragedy: A Reassessment.* Manchester: Manchester University Press, 1974.

Strier, Richard. "Changing the Object: George Herbert and Excess." *George Herbert Journal* 2 (1978): 24–37.

Suckling, Sir John. *An Account of Religion by Reason* (1646). In *The Works of Sir John Suckling,* edited by Thomas Clayton. 2 vols. 2:169–80. Oxford: Clarendon, 1971.

Swift, Jonathan. *A Tale of a Tub to Which Is Added The Battle of the Books and The Mechanical Operation of the Spirit.* Edited by A. C. Guthkelch and D. Nichol Smith. 2d ed. Oxford: Clarendon, 1958.

Sypherd, Wilbur Owen. *Jephthah and His Daughter: A Study in Comparative Literature.* Newark: University of Delaware Press, 1948.

Tennant, R. C. "The Anglican Response to Locke's Theory of Personal Identity." In *Philosophy, Religion and Science in the Seventeenth and Eighteenth Centuries,* edited by John W. Yolton, 188–205. Rochester: University of Rochester Press, 1990.

Tobin, J. J. M. "*Hamlet* and *Christ's Tears over Jerusalem.*" *Aligarh Journal of English Studies* 6 (1981): 158–67.

———. "*Macbeth* and *Christs Teares over Jerusalem.*" *Aligarh Journal of English Studies* 7 (1982): 72–78.

———. "Nashe and *Othello.*" *Notes and Queries* 31 (1984): 202–3.

Trevor-Roper, Hugh. *Catholics, Anglicans, and Puritans: Seventeenth-Century Essays.* London: Secker and Warburg, 1987.

———. *Religion, the Reformation, and Social Change.* London: Macmillan, 1967.

Tuck, Richard. "The 'Modern' Theory of Natural Law." In *The Languages of Political Theory in Early-Modern Europe,* edited by Anthony Pagden, 99–119. Cambridge: Cambridge University Press, 1987.

Turner, James G. *One Flesh: Paradisal Marriage and Sexual Relations in the Age of Milton.* Oxford: Oxford University Press, 1987.

The Two Books of Homilies Appointed to Be Read in Churches. Edited by John Griffiths. Oxford: Oxford University Press, 1859.

Valla, Lorenzo. *Elegantiarum libri sex.* In *Opera omnia.* Introduction by Eugenio Garin. 2 vols. 1:1–235. Turin: Bottega d'Erasmo, 1962.

———. *The Treatise of Lorenzo Valla on the Donation of Constantine.* Translated by Christopher Coleman. New York: Russell and Russell, 1922.

Vaughan, Henry. *Silex Scintillans.* In *Major Poets of the Earlier Seventeenth Century,* edited by Barbara Lewalski and Andrew Sabol, 407–607. Indianapolis: Odyssey, 1973.

Vives, Juan Luis. *De anima et vita.* 1538; rpt. Turin: Bottega d'Erasmo, 1959.

Voegelin, Eric. *Order and History.* 6 vols. Vol. 2, *The World of the Polis.* Baton

Rouge: Louisiana State University Press, 1957.

Vossius, Gerhard. *De theologia gentili* (1641). 3 vols. The Renaissance and the Gods 28. New York: Garland, 1976.

——. *Etymologicon linguae Latinae* (1662). In *Opera in sex tomos divisa*, vol. 1. Amsterdam, 1701.

——. *Poeticarum institutionum libri tres* (1647). In *Opera in sex tomos divisa*, vol. 3. Amsterdam, 1701.

Walker, Daniel P. *The Ancient Theology: Studies in Christian Platonism from the Fifteenth to the Eighteenth Century*. Ithaca: Cornell University Press, 1972.

Walsall, Samuel. *The Life and Death of Jesus Christ . . . In a Sermon preached before the Kings Majesty at Royston*. Cambridge, 1607.

Walsh, P. G. "Buchanan and Classical Drama." In *Acta Conventus Neo-Latini Sanctandraeni*, edited by I. D. McFarlane, 99–112. Binghamton: Medieval and Renaissance Texts and Studies, 1986.

Walzer, Michael. *The Revolution of the Saints: A Study in the Origins of Radical Politics*. New York: Atheneum, 1974.

Watson, Robert N. "Tragedy." In *The Cambridge Companion to English Renaissance Drama*, edited by A. R. Braunmuller and Michael Hattaway, 301–51. Cambridge: Cambridge University Press, 1990.

White, Helen C. *The Tudor Books of Private Devotion*. Madison: University of Wisconsin Press, 1951.

Whitman, James Q. *The Legacy of Roman Law in the German Romantic Era: Historical Vision and Legal Change*. Princeton: Princeton University Press, 1990.

Wilkins, John. "The State and the Individual: Euripides' Plays of Voluntary Self-Sacrifice." In *Euripides, Women, and Sexuality*, edited by Anton Powell, 177–94. London: Routledge, 1990.

Wilson, Thomas. *Arte of Rhetorique* (1553). Edited by Thomas J. Derrick. Renaissance Imagination 1. New York: Garland, 1982.

Wilson, Thomas. *Christs Farewell to Jerusalem and last Prophesie. A Sermon*. London, 1613.

Winkler, John J. *The Constraints of Desire: The Anthropology of Sex and Gender in Ancient Greece*. New York: Routledge, 1990.

Wyatt, Thomas. Selections in *Silver Poets of the Sixteenth Century*, edited by Gerald Bullett, 3–109. London: Dent, 1947.

Young, Frances M. *The Use of Sacrificial Ideas in Greek Christian Writers from the New Testament to John Chrysostom*. Patristic Monograph Series 5. Cambridge, Mass.: Philadelphia Patristic Foundation, 1979.

Zeitlin, Froma I. "Playing the Other: Theater, Theatricality, and the Feminine in Greek Drama." *Representations* 11 (1985): 63–94.

Zwingli, Huldrich. *A briefe rehersal of the death resurrection, & ascension of Christ*. London, c. 1561.

Figures

Figure 1.   Donatello, Penitent Magdalene *(Alinari/Art Resource, New York)*

Figure 2.   Correggio, **The Magdalen** *(National Gallery, London)*

*Figures 3a, 3b.
Marcantonio Bella-
via, Mary Magdalene
contemplating a cru-
cifix, from* Pensieri
diversi lineati et in-
tagliati d'Annibale
Carracci *(New York
Public Library)*

Figure 4. Title page of the Great Bible of 1541 (The Huntington Library, San Marino, California)

OF THE
LAWES
of
ECCLESIASTICAL
Politie,

Eight Bookes

By RICHARD HOOKER.

Imprinted at Lond: by Will: Stansby.
Will: Hole fecit

Figure 5. *Title page to the 1611 edition of Richard Hooker,* Of the Lawes of Ecclesiastical Politie *(The Huntington Library, San Marino, California)*

Index

WIDENER UNIVERSITY
WOLFGRAM
LIBRARY
CHESTER, PA.

Compositor:	G & S Typesetters, Inc.
Text:	10/13 Aldus
Display:	Aldus
Printer:	Bookcrafters
Binder:	Bookcrafters